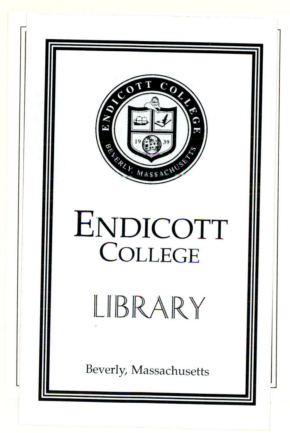

My
Fellow
Americans

MY FELLOW AMERICANS

Presidential Addresses That Shaped History

JAMES C. HUMES

Foreword by Senator Sam Nunn

PRAEGER

New York
Westport, Connecticut
London

Library of Congress Cataloging-in-Publication Data

Humes, James C.
    My fellow Americans : presidential addresses that shaped history /
James C. Humes ; foreword by Sam Nunn.
      p. cm.
    Includes bibliographical references and index.
    ISBN 0–275–93507–8 (alk. paper)
    1. Presidents—United States—Messages—History. 2. Presidents—
United States—Inaugural addresses—History. 3. United States—
Politics and government. I. Title.
J81.C92 1992
353.03′5—dc20   91–27248

British Library Cataloguing in Publication Data is available.

Library of Congress Catalog Card Number: 91–27248
ISBN: 0–275–93507–8

First published in 1992

Praeger Publishers, One Madison Avenue, New York, NY 10010
An imprint of Greenwood Publishing Group, Inc.

Printed in the United States of America

The paper used in this book complies with the
Permanent Paper Standard issued by the National
Information Standards Organization (Z39.48–1984).

10 9 8 7 6 5 4 3 2 1

To Phil Gramm, Fritz Hollings, and Warren Rudman

Three masters of Senate debate albeit with different styles: the first a classical rhetorician whose weapons are the eloquent phrase and historical anecdote; the second a rapier logician who thrusts with statistics and apt analogies; and the third a trenchant advocate who demolishes the opposition's case.

Contents

Foreword

In America, every bright young man—and today, every bright young woman as well—dreams of becoming president. But few young Americans dream of becoming a politician.

Respect for the Office of the Chief Executive and a healthy if sometimes excessive disrespect for the profession of politics have colored the popular history of the American presidency to a remarkable extent.

We tend to revere those presidents whom we remember as visionaries and prophets, men whose charismatic gifts allowed them to personify an age, a historic breakthrough, a cherished ideal, or even a temporary but vivid "mood."

But with rare exceptions, those presidents we deem "great" also have exhibited exceptional political skills—the ability to make our dreams come true, quite literally, in concrete legislation or executive action.

With the possible exceptions of George Washington and Abraham Lincoln, no president has inspired more genuine reverence among the American people than Franklin Delano Roosevelt. In the Georgia of my early childhood, I can remember seeing tattered magazine photographs of FDR hung in an honored spot in the backwoods tarpaper shacks of the poorest dirt farmers. Georgians considered themselves especially blessed that the president chose our own Warm Springs as his holiday retreat, and thousands lined the railroad tracks and roads each time he made the trek south.

But it is equally clear that Roosevelt was an immensely shrewd and resourceful politician who never issued a ringing challenge to the American spirit without a clear and practical objective in mind.

FDR's biographer James MacGregor Burns agreed with that assessment when he titled his book *Roosevelt, the Lion and the Fox*. Burns was alluding to the famous passage in Machiavelli's *The Prince* that said that every great leader has to play the lion as well as the fox.

The lion has always been the king of the beasts—the royal symbol of majesty. The fox, whose sly and crafty ways are embedded in folklore, represents the politician.

The President of the United States plays the lion as Chief of State. He embodies and should articulate the ideals and aspirations of Americans, something we call "vision," which cannot be paraphrased as an agenda for yesterday's headlines.

Yet the president also must play the fox as "head of government." He must be a politician—a strategist and tactician who crafts legislative majorities for his initiatives.

James Humes's book is a timely reminder that every president has sought to combine the inspirational role of the chief executive with the practical role of the effective politician. By examining the full historical context of sixteen great presidential addresses, Humes casts light on the complex motives that often lie just beneath the surface in the most familiar and accessible of executive communications. In so doing, Humes has provided a striking reinterpretation of the elements of presidential leadership and of the role of the presidency in American history and life.

As a speechwriter for four presidents (Eisenhower, Nixon, Ford, and Reagan), James Humes is exceptionally well qualified to explain the "hidden history" of presidential addresses—the surrounding circumstances, now forgotten, and the immediate objectives, now obscured by subsequent events.

As a learned and even worshipful scholar of the life and words of Winston Churchill, Humes is equally qualified to give us insight into the capacity of the rare leader to transcend the immediate circumstances of a given address and speak for his generation, his nation, or even his civilization.

It is the author's special perspective—equally appreciative of the lion and the fox in each president—that makes this book more than a familiar evocation of past rhetoric and much, much more than an extended series of "behind the scenes" anecdotes about presidential addresses.

Thomas Jefferson's first inaugural address is set out by Humes as a magnificent statement of the basic consensus underlying the federalist and democratic traditions in American politics. But we are also reminded that Jefferson, who had just been elected president by the House of Representatives in a controversial vote, was fighting to give his tenure the basic legitimacy necessary to govern.

The Monroe Doctrine address is still cited today as supplying a fundamental tenet of American foreign policy. But this ringing chorus of American principle also reflected Monroe's very practical need to appease hawkish sentiment in Congress without unduly provoking the European powers.

Even Lincoln's Gettysburg Address, the most frequently cited—and recited—political address in history, rightly called "the great American poem" by Carl Sandburg, was the work of a man whose sole preoccupation was maintenance of the Union at all cost. Just months before, this prophet of freedom had limited the emancipation of slaves to the rebellious states. Just months ahead, this herald of pure principle would offer the vice presidency to a Democrat, Andrew Johnson. Suffice it to say that Abraham Lincoln was very much a lion and very much a fox.

Each president examined by Humes possessed these characteristics in varying degrees. Some failed by lacking the proper balance. For example, few if any American leaders could match Woodrow Wilson's eloquence in offering this nation's values and institutions as a universal remedy for war and tyranny. But Wilson's disdain for Congress and his insistence on speaking directly to the people of the world fatally undermined his cherished goal of American participation in a League of Nations.

Conversely, Martin Van Buren was rivaled only by James Polk and Lyndon Johnson as a supremely talented practical politician, but "the little fox" could never inspire in the American people the confidence and energy he instilled in his political peers. He is now remembered mainly as an unsuccessful custodian of Andrew Jackson's legacy.

In suggesting that Humes's book revolves around these twin characteristics of the American presidency, I do not mean to imply that he reduces presidential leadership—or presidential addresses—to any pat formula. Indeed, a valuable feature of the book is its sophisticated analysis of the changing nature of both presidential characteristics. To cite just one example, the growing complexity of both domestic government and international affairs has made subtle but distinct changes in the qualities that make for a successful presidency. Today's lion may be characterized less by an eloquent evocation of American ideals than by an ability to explain issues in a manner that strikes the right chord of public understanding and response, as exemplified by many of President Reagan's remarkable speeches. But an increasingly critical "foxlike" quality was notably lacking in the Reagan administration's hands-off management style. Today's chief executive need not be an expert on every issue, but he must know enough to cross examine the experts.

It is especially appropriate that this book appears at a turning point of history—a time in which American ideals seem vindicated by the demise of totalitarian Marxism—and a time when American leadership is being challenged by the emergence of a truly global economy and society.

By brilliantly analyzing the presidency through the conflicting wants and needs that we ask our chief executive to address and fulfill, James Humes has given us an excellent starting point toward defining the kind of leadership we want—and need—in the even more challenging years ahead.

Senator Sam Nunn

Preface

The U.S. presidency is a hybrid institution. George Washington thought of himself as an "elected King." If it is an oxymoronic description, the presidency did fuse together two disparate forms of government: the old tradition of monarchy and the new idea of democracy. Our Founding Fathers designed an office that had the sanction of the people yet the majesty of a king. Their model was General Washington, who as the first president, gave form and substance to the abstract conception that has been the prototype for his successors.

A president, like a monarch, must embody his country, symbolizing its history, traditions and ideals. He is looked upon to express that nation's heritage and aspirations.

The constitutional beginning of the United States made it different from any other country. Former Prime Minister Margaret Thatcher of Great Britain said it when she declared: "America is the only country established on an idea." She was not the first to observe that the United States is the only nation that does not derive its identity from race, religion, language, or even a dynasty.

Some people say that the idea that anyone regardless of class, creed, color, or economic background can find opportunity and fulfillment is a dream. They are right. It is the American dream. It was a new idea in a New World—a land across the seas whose government charter guaranteed rights and afforded opportunity to the oppressed of other countries.

The paramount podium for expressing this promise of America is the presidency. The president, by his speeches, declarations, and pronouncements, is the chief interpreter of national purpose and destiny.

So this singular institution—the presidency—has come to be the chief articulator of a unique idea. All presidents, as they assume office, are suddenly conscious of the almost mystic mantle that has fallen upon them. Former President Ford told me as I was assisting him with his memoirs: "When I took the oath of office, it was different from when I was sworn in as Congressman or Vice President, it was as if all my predecessors were looking down at me and saying 'Godspeed, Gerry.' "

The president is both "king" and the servant of the people who elected him. He is "king" in the sense that he must transcend the passions and loyalties of party; yet at the same time he must also continue to operate as a politician, recruiting majorities and mobilizing public opinion to effect his will. He is then both chief of state like a king and chief politician like a prime minister.

This dual nature of the presidential office can call on different talents. Few of our presidents—Andrew Jackson and the two Roosevelts are three who come to mind—excelled in both roles. Some like George Washington, John Kennedy, and Ronald Reagan were blessed with regal presence and charisma. (Only in martyrdom did Lincoln attain such mythic proportions.) Others, like James Polk, Richard Nixon, and possibly Harry Truman, had the skills that would have enabled them to advance to prime minister in any parliamentary system.

Yet although a president may, as chief of state, outrank a prime minister, curiously he lacks the political power of a parliamentary premier. The U.S. president, under the constitutional separation of powers, does not automatically command a loyal legislative majority. To compensate, the president has to rally the nation behind him—to use his "bully pulpit" as chief of state—going over the heads of the politicians to the country. Thus his ability to state his agenda and to communicate his purpose are all the more important. Some presidents are more successful than others in manifesting their goals and framing their policies, but each president, to some degree, has shaped the American idea not only by his actions but also by his words.

When they delivered inaugurals, framed presidential messages, issued declarations of war and foreign policy pronouncements, or just expressed our American purpose and ideals from "the bully pulpit" of the White House, presidents shaped the principles upon which decisions are made and support for those decisions mustered. Sometimes it was a policy that served as a polar star for guidance or a phrase that captured the imagination of America and the world. Perhaps it was a statement that framed a national debate or a sentence like Lincoln's at Gettysburg that defined our ideals.

Two hundred years ago, President Washington, anxious to safeguard the new and fragile representative republic, warned against ensnaring European alliances. Then, in the next century, President Lincoln fought a war to preserve the Union and to prove that democracy was not a failed experiment.

The idea of democracy, which might have once perished, is now a doctrine of government amid collapsing one-party dictatorships. In the centuries since Washington's Farewell Address, America, like the idea of freedom itself, has grown to be a mighty force and its president, by virtue of his office, the leader of the free world.

Acknowledgments

I owe a special debt of thanks to James Ring, my friend and associate who helped me research and select the speeches for study. His advice and historical insight was invaluable.

I also want to thank the Woodrow Wilson School for International Scholars at the Smithsonian Institution, where I was a Fellow in 1982. Their award made this book possible.

I also want to thank John Gable, Director of the Theodore Roosevelt Library at Sagamore Hill, New York; the Eisenhower Library at Abilene, Texas; the Franklin Delano Roosevelt Library at Hyde Park, New York; the Harry Truman Library at Independence, Missouri; and the Calvin Coolidge Memorial Foundation at Plymouth Notch, Vermont.

Some old friends who offered counsel and made suggestions were J. D. Williams, an expert on the Washington political scene, Don Whitehead, a veteran of political wars, Elliot Curson, a media wizard, and former Congressman John LeBoutillier.

Other political friends who deserve thanks include William Schulz, National Editor of *Readers' Digest*; Democratic National Chairman, Charles Manatt; Richard Viguerie; former Chief Counsel of the Senate Government Operations Committee, Bob Smith; Jim Pinkerton at the White House; and two knowledgeable writers on recent Presidential history, Trevor Armbrister and John Taylor.

Former White House speechwriters who helped include Ray Price, Tony Dolan, and Joshua Gilder.

I also have had encouragement as well as occasional suggestions from various senators. Sam Nunn of Georgia read my draft and wrote a splendid foreword. Pete Domenici of New Mexico, the financial conscience of the

Senate, has been a real friend and advisor. Arlen Specter of Pennsylvania is an old friend from Philadelphia whose brilliant legal mind is always a delight. Jesse Helms of North Carolina is another staunch friend who has been a student of senatorial rhetoric.

I also am grateful to Connie Price of Williams & Jensen, who has put up with most of my idiosyncrasies with the exception of my cigar smoking.

I would also like to thank my old friend, Jamie Crathorne. As a member of the House of Lords in Great Britain, Lord Crathorne provided me with insights on Reagan's speech in London.

Clerical help was rendered by Phyllis Sparks, Mary Duffey, and Elizabeth Stone.

One who assisted me in assembling the bibliography is rhetorician and poet Howard Shaffer.

Finally, I must mention my wife, Dianne, and daughter, Mary, who proofread and edited various drafts.

My
Fellow
Americans

1 _____

The Farewell Address: Washington's Declaration of Independence in Foreign Policy

Tis our true policy to steer clear of any permanent alliance.

George Washington was the first and greatest president of the United States. Abraham Lincoln may have saved the nation, but George Washington established it.

If Washington had not accepted its command, it is unlikely that a Continental Army could have been fielded. If Washington had resigned from that command to return to Mount Vernon before 1781, there would have been no victory at Yorktown, and the struggle for independence would have collapsed.

If Washington had not agreed to preside over the rump convention of delegates in Philadelphia, there would not have been a Constitution. If he had not accepted the presidency, the states would not have been forged into a union.

Washington had not sought the office; the office had sought him. He had earlier spurned the crown offered by his troops. His acceptance of the election as president by the Electoral College did not bring him prestige. His world-wide fame brought prestige to the office. Those who succeeded him would find their stature enhanced by occupying the office General Washington first held.

After his first term ended in 1792, Washington had wanted to return to Mount Vernon. His sense of duty, however, overcame that of heart. The republic, still in its infancy, was too young, its place in the world too uncertain, for him to remove his steady hand. By 1796, however, he could convince himself that twelve years of George Washington as president could, in itself, be destabilizing. The nation had to prove it had a government of laws, not of men.

Although some of his countrymen might not have accepted it, George Washington was a man, not a god. He was a shy and proud man whose sense of duty had propelled him to a succession of high offices and increased responsibilities. But even the discipline of a lifetime was no defense against personal attacks. What Washington found hard to forget or forgive was the one person he deemed to be the instigator of those slurs: Thomas Jefferson.

Washington had chosen his fellow Virginian to be the secretary of state in his first term. That post in the early days of the Republic had assumed the aura and prestige of the prime minister in Britain; at the least, it was considered a stepping stone to the presidency. Yet to Washington, his one-time protegé was now orchestrating the chorus of attacks.

John Beckley, a minion of Jefferson, had charged that, among other heinous offenses, Washington should be impeached for having stolen public funds. Since Beckley's appointment as Clerk of the House had been arranged by Jefferson, Washington knew his accusation must have been approved by Jefferson.

Washington felt betrayed by Jefferson—the anguished betrayal a father suffers when a son turns against him. Jefferson, writing to his Italian friend Felipe Mazzei, had accused Washington "of being a Samson shorn by the harlot England." Although Jefferson did not directly accuse Washington of wanting to make himself king, he had sanctioned the attacks on Washington by his silence.

William Duane, the radical editor of the *Aurora*, published in Philadelphia, was a Jefferson confidant. Duane charged in an open letter to the president that Washington was seeking "monarchial privilege" and was guilty of "tyrannical acts." In a letter laden with guilt, Jefferson composed an artful letter to his old mentor and commander-in-chief denying his complicity. Jefferson pointed out that there existed no public record of his ever criticizing Washington and that he disdained partisan disputes and "political discussions." In his disassociation from his political editor friends, however, Jefferson did not disassociate himself from their sentiments. Washington must have had a sardonic laugh at Jefferson's claim to abhor political intrigues. Jefferson, for all his multi-faceted genius, was first and foremost a professional politician. It was Washington and not Jefferson who detested the machinations of politics. Washington's cool reply snapped the long bond of correspondence between the two Virginians.

What galled President Washington was that it was Jefferson who had pleaded with him to serve a second term. Jefferson rightly saw that if Washington did not stay on as president his rival John Adams would be elected president in 1792. Yet here Jefferson was silent while letting his supporters fan nasty rumors about Washington's monarchial designs.

Indeed, in 1792 Washington had sought out Jefferson's chief lieutenant,

James Madison, for help in fashioning a closing message to his American countrymen. Madison had suggested a "valedictory address" to be issued in September 1792, time enough for would-be candidates to present themselves for the consideration of the Electoral College. The college at the outset, unlike today's formalistic procedural ritual, assembled and voted like an expanded board of directors would choose a chief executive officer.

By 1796 the sixty-four-year-old Washington could not be dissuaded from returning to his beloved Mount Vernon. He believed the greatest service he could render to his nation and to the Constitution that upheld that nation's government was by leaving the presidency by choice and not by death. His decision to return to Virginia was one of the head as well as the heart. He was happy to leave Philadelphia.

Philadelphia at the close of the eighteenth century was the second largest city in the English-speaking world. The city of Benjamin Franklin, which boasted architect Benjamin Latrobe, physician Benjamin Rush, naturalist John Bartram, and artist Charles Wilson Peale, may have been one of the more exciting intellectual centers in the Age of Enlightenment, but George Washington was no intellectual. If a congenial companion had to be found for George Washington at a dinner party today, a possible choice would be someone like Queen Elizabeth. Like Washington, the present Queen is no scholar, but she is familiar with statesmen and problems of state. Like Washington, she is most at home walking through the meadows, talking with farmers about crops, and riding horseback through the fields. She also would share with her distant kinsman a passion about breeding and betting on horses. Washington was, in short, an English country squire. Though he enjoyed the company of some of the wealthy Philadelphia financiers and merchants like Robert Morris (in that sense he was somewhat like an Eisenhower), he much preferred plantation life. He had discharged his obligations to his country, and he wanted to go home.

So Washington found in his files, kept in the Philadelphia house that was the official presidential residence, the four-year-old draft of "the valedictory" Madison had once penned. Madison had spliced together a lofty justification of Washington's decision to retire, with praise for the federal constitutional system.

In the four years since Madison had written that draft, however, much had happened to make additional comments necessary. If the problems in Washington's first term—that of consolidating the new government—were mostly domestic, the crises in the second term were foreign. The war between Britain and France threatened to embroil the young nation.

When he sat down to add additional thoughts in 1796, Washington wrote that he had done his best and hoped he would be forgiven any involuntary errors. He noted that he had arrived at an age when retirement was necessary and that, in any case, a rotation of office helps sustain liberty. He penned a few sentences endorsing the amendment process to the Constitution. He then came to his central concern—the future foreign policy of the young nation—writing that the country should avoid unnecessary alliances and that twenty years of peace and national unity would make the country so strong it could defy all outside influence.

What followed was a bitter outburst from the usually stoic Washington. He spat out a spate of words that only proved what they pretended to deny:

> As this address, fellow citizens, will be the last I shall ever make to you, and as some of the gazettes of the United States have teemed with all the invective that disappointment, ignorance of facts and malicious falsehoods could invent, to represent my politics and affections—to wound my reputation and feelings—and to weaken, if not entirely destroy, the confidence you have been pleased to repose in me: it might be expected at the parting scene of my public life that I shall take some notice of such virulent abuse. But, as heretofore, I shall pass over them in utter silence.

He then added angrily:

> I did not seek the office with which you have honored me, that charity may throw her mantle over my want of my abilities to do better; that the gray hairs of a man who has, excepting the interval between the close of the Revolutionary War and of the new government, either in a civil or military character, spent five and forty years—*all the prime of his life*—in serving his country, be suffered to pass guilty to the grave, and that his efforts, however numerous, if they are not criminal, may be consigned to the tomb of oblivion as he himself soon will be to the mansions of retirement.

Washington closed by saying he had not served his country "from ambitious views." His finances had received "no additions from his services but the reverse." Then, upon second thought, he crossed out "but the reverse." "I leave you," he wrote, "with undefiled hands, an uncorrupted heart, and ardent vows to heaven for the welfare and happiness of that country in which I and my forefathers to the third or fourth progenitor drew our first breath."

If this angry and defensive message, albeit in the formalistic language of the eighteenth century, is not quite the equivalent of Nixon saying in 1974, "I'm not a crook," it is reminiscent of the 1962 Nixon press conference, after his gubernatorial defeat, when a tired and exhausted Nixon blurted, "You won't have Dick Nixon to kick around any more."

In his New York law office, the forty-year-old Alexander Hamilton must have winced as he read the letter packet from President Washington. For the disciplined general to give vent to such an emotional tirade was most untypical. Throughout most of his adult life Hamilton had enjoyed the rare opportunity of observing America's greatest hero at close range.

As his youthful military aide-de-camp in the Revolutionary War, Hamilton had marvelled at the general's serenity in battle. As a delegate to the Constitutional Convention, he had admired the cool and detached presence Chairman Washington had exercised to give force to his presiding chairman's role. As a secretary of the Treasury in Washington's cabinet, he had witnessed the quiet, commanding way the chief executive listened to contending viewpoints before making a decision.

The essence of Washington was his presence—the looming height, the erect military bearing, the fixed blue eyes that instilled in his associates or any audience a sense of awe. At six feet, three-and-a-half inches, Washington had a heightened stature comparable to that of DeGaulle in this century, and he commanded even more adoration and reverence. Washington was not unaware of his leadership looks and had sensed early in his career that any lapse of demeanor would detract from his aura of authority. He reined in emotions as he would a spirited steed. A soldier by profession, he would let himself be dictated only by duty. Control was the root of his character, and he wielded that character as Churchill would words to inspire soldiers and lead citizens. The effect of such character is called charisma, and George Washington was more charismatic than any of the presidents who would follow him.

If Washington's austere public presence veiled the earthier tastes of an eighteenth-century country squire, it also masked some of his early insecurities. Washington, the unlettered surveyor-soldier, was inarticulate in both tongue and pen. But in his youth he learned to turn his awkwardness of speech into an asset.

At age twelve—with his full height of seventy five and a half inches—the boy Washington had all the appearance of a man. And as the eldest of the widow Washington's children, he had been thrust into the man-of-the-house role. The less he said, the less he betrayed his youthful age and boyish awkwardness. Reticence for Washington was not only part of his character—it was a deliberate choice. Over the years the habitual silence gradually became interpreted as strength. Though patrician in background, he still was the early prototype of Owen Wister's *Virginian*—the tall man of few words who let the force of his appearance and the worth of his actions do his talking for him.

So for Washington to leave exposed his anguish and vulnerability in his Farewell Address was disturbing to Hamilton. The defensive outburst may make Washington all the more human to contemporary eyes, but to Hamilton it would make him less heroic. The general should not descend from his Olympian heights to the level of mere mortals.

But what upset Hamilton even more than the inclusion in the packet of Madison's 1792 draft were the instructions to fuse that draft with Hamilton's revision of his additional updated comments. It was so typical of Washington to pretend that his leadership bridged both factions in the government. Washington liked to think he was a carriage driver trying to rein in

two horses of widely different temperaments—Jefferson and Hamilton pulling in different directions,. But Hamilton believed that he alone was proceeding on Washington's course.

Hamilton usually enjoyed assisting President Washington in the composition of state documents, but he chafed at the idea that his work would
be presented as a joint Madison-Hamilton effort. Washington even wanted
a public acknowledgement to Madison included in the address!

To Hamilton, Madison was the opposition—the deputy leader of a radical
faction trying to undermine the constitutional government. Hamilton and
Madison once had been friends. Indeed, both (with John Jay) had written
the *Federalist Papers* urging the ratification of the Constitution. Madison,
however, was now Jefferson's man and the leader in the House of Representatives of the anti-administration forces. In fact, Madison had just led
the effort to block the Jay Treaty with Britain—the Washington and Hamilton diplomatic initiative to balance the long-standing treaty with France.
To Hamilton, the obstruction of the treaty by the House, which unlike the
Senate has no constitutional authority to ratify treaties, was almost trea-
sonous.

From Madison's vantage, Hamilton was the arch-manipulator who had
made Washington the unwitting prisoner of extreme pro-England and even
pro-monarchial sentiments. Hamilton, however, saw Madison as a radical
consorting with pro-French and Jacobin elements that would overthrow
the consolidating achievements of the Washington administration and the
hope for a lasting permanent union. Why should Hamilton help promote
Madison's career and prestige by making him the co-drafter of Washington's
"Valedictory"?

Hamilton, like his chief, once detested the idea of political parties, but it
was he, along with Jefferson, who caused their formation. By the end of
Washington's second term, "the Federalists," as they came to be known,
were those who supported the objectives of Washington's "Federal" administration. Hamilton, as Washington's secretary of the Treasury, had organized a bloc of supporters in Congress—those who could be counted on to
vote for the funding of the national debt, the imposition of an excise tax,
and the establishment of the national bank.

Jefferson in a stroke of genius chose for his followers (who opposed
Hamilton's cadre) the name "Republicans," or "Democrat Republicans."
(The Democrat-Republican party is the ancestor of today's Democratic
party, although they were called "Republicans" for short. The present-day
Republican party was established in 1855 in opposition to the Democratic
party.) While "Federalist" connoted the support of some abstract central
structure of government, "Republican" meant "no King." The choice of
name was not the least of the factors that would doom the Federalists to
extinction in the early part of the nineteenth century. Few Americans wanted

to describe themselves as "not Republican," which implied that they wanted a king.

But even more than a Federalist, Alexander Hamilton was an imperialist, the first in America. Born on the island of Nevis, in the Virgin Islands, as the illegitimate son of a Scottish merchant and his Creole mistress, Hamilton had no roots in the colonies. He was not a Virginian like Washington or a "Massachusetts man" like John Adams—he was an American. His was not a parochial but a national vision, and it was fueled by his own ambition.

Hamilton alone saw America as a future mercantile power. In a sense Hamilton was a would-be Napoleon. Like the Corsican, Hamilton's remote island birth seemed to focus his perspective as a nationalist. Although Hamilton was not a professional soldier, he did thirst for military glory. Upon leaving King's College in New York City (now Columbia University) he attached himself to Washington's command as his aide-de-camp.

At the close of the war Hamilton bristled under the restraint of his secretarial duties and sought a command of his own, so he engineered a minor quarrel with Washington to effect his departure. At the battle of Yorktown Hamilton did distinguish himself with his assault on an English battery. Some political scientists, Garry Wills for one, have wondered aloud whether Hamilton would have taken control of the army and the country if Washington had been killed in action. He had not only the organizational ability of a Napoleon but the latter's overweening ambition as well.

Plato may have idealized the "philosopher-king," but Hamilton's ideal would have been the "philosopher-general." The figure who came closest to that in the eighteenth century was Frederick the Great of Prussia. In an age when some rulers valued erudition as only second to empire, Frederick could lay claim to being the Age of Enlightenment's most enlightened king. The soldier's writings that lay on Hamilton's shelf in New York City seemed an apt guide to the tenor of his own general's farewell remarks. To the people of Prussia, Frederick had penned not a valedictory but a testament. Though based on rational principles and couched in the lofty philosophical language of the Age of Enlightenment, it was actually an attempt to control the course of Prussian foreign policy from the grave.

In Washington's request to fashion a draft of a Farewell Address, therefore, Hamilton saw the opportunity of writing the political equivalent of a last will and testament. For the Father of his Country, the lawyer Hamilton would execute a document that would stipulate the principles for protecting the constitutional framework of the governmental house and preserving the political estate of the nation.

With such a grand manifesto, Hamilton saw a way out of his problems of trying to tack on Washington's updated comments to Madison's old draft. By making the Farewell Address a set of foreign policy principles, he could downplay Washington's defensive outburst, which was not worthy of the general. He also could ignore altogether Madison's earlier draft. To Hamilton, by orchestrating the Republican attacks on Washington, Madison had forfeited any claim to having his earlier draft linked to the general's Farewell Address.

Hamilton's real rival, however, was not Madison but Jefferson. It was Jefferson he feared, and the feeling was reciprocated. Each had tried to steer the new government toward his own ideal. Jefferson saw a nation of planters, farmers, and artisans. Hamilton envisioned a community of merchants, manufacturers, and shopkeepers.

For both men, who grew up more or less without a father, Washington was the paternal figure, and each bitterly resented the other's claim upon that paternal affection. The personality, temperament, and style of each grated on the other.

To Jefferson, the bastard from the West Indies was a vulgar upstart. To Hamilton, the squire of Monticello was a hypocritical snob who ranted about equality and consorted with slaves.

Both men were given to hyperbole. Hamilton would sneer at the rabble. Jefferson would praise the effects of the French guillotine. To Jefferson, Hamilton was a social climber, the worst kind of royalist. To Hamilton, Jefferson was someone who, while being a member of high society, professed sympathy with trendy revolutionary causes. Hamilton knew that aristocrats like Jefferson in France were among the first to receive the edge of the Jacobin blade.

Like a Jacob, Hamilton now saw his chance to permanently disinherit the Esau Jefferson from the Isaac who was Washington. In the Bible Isaac felt closer in spirit to Esau. They were both men of the fields. Jacob was more of a trader, like Hamilton. Hamilton's personal relationship with Washington was not unlike that of Nixon to Eisenhower. Washington, as Eisenhower would later treat Nixon, never invited Hamilton for a weekend at Mount Vernon. Hamilton must have brooded over the intimate social familiarity between General Washington and his fellow Virginian, Thomas Jefferson. Yet Washington, just as the patriarch Isaac chose the slick and smooth Jacob, made Hamilton his political beneficiary.

If Jefferson had the fame of writing the Declaration of Independence, Hamilton could now pen his own historic masterpiece. His effort would not be a patchwork but a splendid garment that would clothe Hamilton as Washington's successor. Hamilton's solution was to write a whole new draft—a document that would live for the ages. With Frederick the Great's Testament as a model for inspiration and Addison and Steele's English *Spectator* as a guide to style, Hamilton sat down to fashion a political masterpiece.

Hamilton chose the theme of foreign policy because it would most easily lend itself to incorporating most of Washington's reflections. Aside from the personal defense, six of the Chief Executive's nine "wishes" dealt with

foreign policy. And even in the other three, the first—to avoid party fac-
tionalism—and the last—to maintain the separation of powers—were triggered by the recent furor over the ratification of the Jay Treaty.

The first problem was how to begin, or rather how to turn farewell
sentiments into foreign policy principles. Hamilton accomplished this in
the first eight paragraphs by having Washington announce his intention
to retire from political life and then express his hopes for America's future
under its new Constitution. Then Hamilton let Washington say, "Here I
should perhaps stop." But he did not do so because concern for the welfare
of the American people prompted him "to offer some sentiments the result
of mature reflection confirmed by observation and experience which appear
to be essential to the permanency of your felicity as a people." These views,
he wrote, should be regarded as "the disinterested advice of a parting
friend."

As a practicing trial lawyer, Hamilton knew how to establish the authority
of a star witness. Here Hamilton was raising Washington above the political
controversies of the day and imputing to him the lofty objective that only
disinterest in office and foreswearing of ambition can impart.

Hamilton then smoothly moved the discourse from domestic to foreign
policy by warning that party spirit opens the doors to intrigues by foreigners
and may lead to an attachment in which the small nation revolves around
the larger one "as its satellite."

At this point Hamilton repeated Washington's advice to "avoid con-
necting ourselves with the politics of any Nation." Hamilton, however,
modified it by writing "as little political connection as possible."

At this point the practical advice of Washington became the geopolitical
principles of Hamilton. Hamilton was a Kissinger working with more of
an Eisenhower than a Nixon. A disciple of what would later be called
realpolitik, he had deduced that all countries have certain national interests
and that power was sought to pursue and defend those interests.

Hamilton was no reformer eager to purify the practices of old-world
diplomacy. He did not see, as Jefferson did, that America was to be a pure
country undefiled by Old World ideas and considerations. He wanted to
keep America out of Europe's orbit not because Europe practiced the old
power politics but because it was the only way America would be able to
exercise any power at all.

For America to take sides in European quarrels was, to Washington, who
had seen the meddling in American politics by the Frenchman Citizen Genet,
a threat to the unity of the young nation. To Hamilton, involvement in the
affairs of the Old World would sap her hegemony in the affairs of the New.
If Washington was more the pragmatist, Hamilton was the imperialist. No
wonder Theodore Roosevelt preferred Hamilton to Jefferson.

It is interesting to note that a year before Hamilton went to work on the
Farewell Address, he had written a defense of the Jay Treaty under the

name of "Horatius." Because that treaty with England was meant to roughly balance the alliance with France forged during the War of Independence, the effect was to promote neutrality. Hamilton as Horatius warned against entanglement "in all the contests, broils and wars of Europe."

But if he was an imperialist, Hamilton was not a jingoist. Indeed, he felt that many needless wars are stirred up by popular opinion. Hamilton, unlike Jefferson, had no blind faith in the wisdom of the people. He had written in Federalist Paper #6 that "there have been . . . almost as many popular as royal wars."

The writing of the Federalist papers almost a decade before had crystallized in Hamilton's mind the belief that America should carve out its own place in world affairs. In Federalist Paper #11 he said that the United States should "aim at an ascendant in the system of American affairs." In the Farewell Address he muted this naked imperialism for Washington's sake by emphasizing the corollary that Europe had a special and different political system.

Washington advised neutrality on the basis of his experience; Hamilton would lift it to the philosophical realm of political science. What seemed practical to Washington was treated by Hamilton as an immutable principle. In revising Washington's first draft for a valedictory, Hamilton transformed it into a political testament.

When Washington received Hamilton's draft for the Farewell Address, he immediately sat down to copy it out in his own hand. Ever since his surveying days, he found that penning a map or paper in his own hand helped him see mistakes as well as absorb the material.

For the most part, Washington was pleased with his former aide's draft of the Farewell Address. After all, he had picked out the nineteen-year-old Hamilton to write his military papers and letters in the Revolution, and the years following the war had only vindicated his judgment. Contrary to the Jeffersonian propaganda, Washington was never anyone's tool. Hamilton, if anything, was the instrument Washington wielded to organize and promulgate his thoughts and ideas.

The wording of the address was more ornate than Washington's and employed a more muscular style, but of course the president expected a literary man to produce a document more fashionably in tune with the language of the current English essayists.

On reflection, Washington saw that Hamilton was right in scrapping the emotional defense. Indeed, he even scratched out Hamilton's abbreviated restatement of the Washington apology: "the involuntary errors I have probably committed have been the source of no serious or lasting mischief to our country." Writing in the margin, Washington stated that he wanted to "avoid the imputation of affected modesty."

Washington left in Hamilton's statement that the central government must be strong enough "to withstand the enterprises of faction," but he deleted what he considered a Hamiltonian exaggeration:

> I shall not conceal from you the belief I entertain that your government as at present is far more likely to prove too feeble than too powerful.

He also eliminated Hamilton's sentiment that "the extraordinary influence . . . of birth, riches and other sources of distinction" was particularly dangerous in small countries that were susceptible to a coup d'état, but that in larger countries like the United States mass popular factions were more to be feared.

Washington, however, left untouched Hamilton's unsolicited assertion on the importance of establishing public credit. After all, Squire Washington's limited experience in fiscal affairs had already made him adopt his finance minister's sweeping proposals for monetary stability, and he saw no reason to discontinue taking his advice.

The section Washington spent most time studying was the foreign policy section—the heart of the address. In rewriting those paragraphs, Washington did little more than minor pruning of sentence length. He left intact the key phrases of Hamilton's enumerated principles for foreign policy.

> Excessive partiality for one foreign nation and excessive delight of another, cause those whom they actuate to see danger only on one side, and serve to veil and even second the arts of influence on the other.
>
> The great rule of conduct for us, in regard to foreign Nations is, in extending our commercial relations, to have with them as little political conversation as possible.

Then Washington put his imprimatur on Hamilton's geopolitical insight.

> Europe has a set of primary interests, which to us have none, or a very remote relation. Hence, she must be engaged in frequent controversies, the causes of which are essentially foreign to our concerns.
>
> Our detached and distant solution invites and enables us to pursue a different course. If we remain one people under an efficient government, the period is not far off, when we may defy material injury from external annoyance; when we may take such an attitude as will cause the neutrality we have at any time resolve upon to be scrupulously respected—when belligerent nations under the impossibility of making acquisitions upon us, will not lightly regard the giving as provocation when we may choose peace or war, or our interest guided by justice shall counsel.
>
> Why forego the advantages of so peculiar a situation? Why quit our own to stand upon foreign ground? Why, by intertwining our destiny with that of any part of Europe, entangle our peace and prosperity in the tools of European Ambition, Rivalship, Interest, Humor or Caprice?

If George Washington was not an imperialist, he was a nationalist, and he must have noted with approval the rationale Hamilton had developed to undergird the principle of neutrality.

But Washington did not sense from the documents that he was the patriarch passing down the tablet for the ages. Rather, he saw himself as an elder statesman defending what he saw as the most important accomplishment of his second administration: the Act of Neutrality of 1793. Hamilton had helped with that document, too, as he had with the Jay Treaty, which helped secure neutrality with England. Like Woodrow Wilson with Colonel House, Franklin Roosevelt with Harry Hopkins, or Richard Nixon with Henry Kissinger, Washington and Hamilton had been a close-knit team when working out foreign policy breakthroughs.

Washington, of course, did not deliver the Farewell Address from any balcony or to any public chamber. It was not even printed by the government as a public document. Instead, it came to print almost the way an op-ed article would today—through the hands of a friendly newspaper editor. He decided to give it to David Claypoole, owner of the *American Daily Advertiser* and "suffer it to work its way afterward."

Washington's understatement rivals Lincoln's line at Gettysburg: "the world will little note . . . what we say here." The Farewell Address, though neither a speech nor even a state document, became in terms of policy impact the most powerful and influential statement ever delivered by a U.S. president. For over a century it was the cornerstone of our foreign policy. It is the only speech that an act of Congress requires to be read annually.

Jefferson would paraphrase it in his first inaugural, saying "no entangling alliances," which curiously became identified as the Washington pronouncement. (Few can quote by memory the actual line "to steer clear of any permanent alliance.") Monroe and Adams then codified it in the Monroe Doctrine. Later foreign policy statements of both Polk and Cleveland would be rooted in the Farewell Address. Woodrow Wilson would interpret "no entangling alliances" as no covert alliances in his call for a League of Nations. Franklin Roosevelt would take "no entangling alliances" to mean no alliances with the Axis as a justification for the Lend–Lease Act of 1941. Each president felt obliged to follow the holy words of the "Gospel of Saint George," although Hamilton was the apostle writing the epistle.

When the address first appeared in the *American Daily Advertiser* on the street corners of Philadelphia on September 17, 1796, George Washington was in his carriage rolling toward Mount Vernon. Filled as usual with advertising notices, the front page yielded no indication of the sensational scoop it carried on its second page. It was entitled:

> To the People of the United States
> Friends and Fellow Citizens

At the end were the words, "G. Washington, United States, September 17, 1796."

It is interesting to mark that the only word Washington double-underlined in the first page of the final manuscript from his pen was "American." "The name of *American* which belongs to you, in your national capacity, must always exalt that just pride of patriotism."

The world regarded George Washington as the first American, and at home he was recognized as "father of the country." Even if he was too practical to be a visionary, he did have a vision for the country.

George Washington may not have been a mercantilist like Alexander Hamilton, but neither did he believe as Jefferson did, that Virginia plantation life was Eden. Unlike any of the Virginia dynasty of presidents that followed, he freed his slaves and even purchased some labor-saving machinery for Mount Vernon. An economic nationalist, he tried to encourage New England manufacturers by wearing a suit of American-spun cloth at his inauguration.

He had the surveyor's dream of America. He advocated a wide system of canals and national roads to unite the country and further its commercial power. He even supported a national university, the subject of which he tacked on—against Hamilton's advice—to the Farewell Address.

George Washington *was* the first American, and he saw in his mind an American nation. To preserve that nation, he bequeathed to his countrymen a Declaration of Independence in foreign policy.

2 _____

Jefferson's First Inaugural: The Revolutionary as Reconciler

We are all republicans, we are all federalists.

The first presidential inaugural of the nineteenth century was also the first ever held in Washington, It was staged in the undomed and uncompleted capitol. Perhaps never in our history would a presidential inauguration be witnessed with such fear and foreboding. Chaos seemed imminent and civil war a distinct possibility. Indeed, many people laid bets that Thomas Jefferson would never actually be sworn in as the nation's third president. Rumors circulated that the new chief justice, John Marshall, would assume the presidency in an interim government. Militias under governors' orders in nearby Maryland, Virginia, and Pennsylvania stood poised—ready to intervene if Jefferson were not installed. Although the incumbent, President John Adams, had lost the election, it was not at all certain that his Federalist administration would relinquish power.

The Federalists—two terms under George Washington and one term under John Adams—had reigned for twelve years. The Federalists were the Founding Fathers, or at least they purported to represent the Founding Fathers. The legitimate heirs to the late great and sainted George Washington, the Federalists constituted "the better sort of people." They were the substantial people—the merchants, the lawyers, the bankers—those whose decisions shaped and determined the growth of the young republic.

To turn the government over to a bunch of ragtail trappers and pioneer farmers in the hinterlands who had no breeding, no education, no knowledge of finance, and, in many cases, scant respect for the teachings of church and creed was an unthinkable prospect. Many pious women in Boston and Hartford, recoiling at the idea of Jefferson's French-loving "atheistic" friends in power, were hiding their bibles in their wells in fear the new edicts of his administration would confiscate them.

Although the Electoral College, meeting in December following the November election, had given only a minority of their votes to President John Adams, who was running for a second term, it did not mean that they had elected Thomas Jefferson. Today the Electoral College is merely a procedural rubber stamp for transmitting the votes of the assembled states. But in the early days of the nineteenth century, these electors, chosen in congressional districts across the country, had the responsibility of selecting the President of the United States.

During the campaign of 1800, the electors had openly identified themselves as either pro-Adams or pro-Jefferson in their local districts. In that sense it was not unlike some of our Presidential primary voting, in which delegates run as either pro-Nixon or pro-Kennedy but are not legally bound to vote for Nixon or Kennedy at the party convention. Thus, the Electoral College members were much like the delegates to a national party convention, except that the meeting of the Electoral College, instead of operating in the circus atmosphere of today's convention, more closely resembled the arcane selection process of the College of Cardinals in the Vatican when choosing a new pope.

Most Americans awaiting the newspaper reports expected the re-election of John Adams. To be sure, Adams did not have the legendary stature of George Washington. In fact, the pompous personality of our second president, notwithstanding his preeminent intellectual ability, made him a rather sorry figure in contrast to the august Washington.

As Washington's vice president, Adams was nicknamed by scoffing critics "His rotund superfluity." But at the beginning of the nineteenth century, there was neither television to reveal his uncongenial public image nor public opinion polls to record any public dissatisfaction.

If there had been no television and no Gallup or Harris polls in 1960, many people might have been surprised by the defeat of Richard Nixon, Eisenhower's vice president. The defeat of Adams, who had already been elected in his own right as president came as a political earthquake.

Yet when the dust cleared following the Electoral College's vote in December 1800, Jefferson's partisans found that in dislodging Adams they had not necessarily installed Jefferson.

Jefferson had joined forces with New York's Aaron Burr to defeat Adams. The forging of that axis—the Southern states allied with New York City's Tammany Hall—would shape the Democratic Party for many years to come. The electors favorable to the Jefferson–Burr team had cast their votes for both men. But when Jefferson and Burr received the same number of votes, the proceedings foundered, and the election was thrown into the House of Representatives. Of course, the plan had been to elect Jefferson as president and Burr as vice-president, but it did not work out that way.

Under the Constitution, the candidate receiving the second highest number of votes would be vice president. But both Jefferson and Burr received the same amount of votes for president, so now the House of Representatives by stipulation of the Constitution had to choose the president when one candidate did not receive a majority of the electoral vote. The Federalist congressmen in the House of Representatives might decide to strike a deal with the wily Burr and make him president.

Such an outcome would have dashed the plans of Thomas Jefferson to remold the government.

To Jefferson, the Federalist administration of Washington and Adams was turning the young republic into Britain's little brother. The presidency, like the monarchy, was an aloof and exalted station. In no way was the president a tribune of the people, one who championed their dreams and embodied their sentiments. In other words, Jefferson was the first politician to fight the notion of an imperial presidency.

What triggered Jefferson's anger was Adams's imposition of the controversial Alien and Sedition Act. The law had jailed his friend and supporter Thomas Cooper for his newspaper attacks on the president's foreign policy vis-à-vis revolutionary France. To Jefferson, the clamp-down on free speech was tearing up the Declaration of Independence, which he had drafted twenty-five years before. Jefferson saw the very soul of the nation at stake. Working behind the scenes, he orchestrated the Virginia and Kentucky State Resolutions, which raised the threat of rebellion. In a sense it was the forerunner of John C. Calhoun's nullification doctrine. (Interestingly, John Calhoun appropriated the doctrine of nullification from Cooper, who, at the end of his life, was president of the University of South Carolina. Calhoun, like Cooper, maintained that a state could veto the act of the federal government.)

The issue was not John Adams but the kind of presidency and government his followers were putting into place for future generations. Jefferson held no personal vendetta against Adams, although he thought that Adams's attempt to make himself a regal figure was less comical than tragic. Adams had described himself as "the first prince of the country and the heir apparent to sovereign authority." It was one thing for George Washington to see himself in a monarchial cast, but for John Adams to do so invited only Jefferson's scorn.

Jefferson had revered the late General Washington, who had died in December 1799, but in Jefferson's mind the old man had become in his later years almost a puppet manipulated by Alexander Hamilton. The establishment of the national bank, which served to promote the speculative financial deals of Hamilton's merchant and banker friends, only proved Washington's pliability.

Although some of Jefferson's more radical followers might have thought that Washington yearned for a monarchy in the dynastic sense, Jefferson knew that such a belief was absurd even if for the only reason that the general had no children. Indeed, Washington had turned down a suggestion to become king in the years after the Revolutionary War and before the Constitutional Convention. But Washington had patterned his presidency after the British monarchy. In a real way, Washington had become an elective "king," with Hamilton's position in his second term approaching that of prime minister.

Washington had even donned some of the trappings of royalty. He titled himself "His Excellency," and he conducted what amounted to a royal court with levees in which the bewigged chief magistrate, garbed in breeches and stockings, would hold sway. The idea of such sycophantic toadying by such would-be courtiers nauseated Jefferson.

From his vantage point, Jefferson believed that Hamilton and the more extreme of his "Tory" Federalists wished for a monarch or at least lifetime chief executive, which amounted to the same thing. At the Constitutional Convention Hamilton had lobbied strongly for such an autocratic figure accountable to no elective process. As minister to France Jefferson was not one of the framers of the Constitution. If he had been there, he surely would have argued that too much power reposed in the presidency and that to check the potential abuse of such power the occupant should be restricted to one term.

Although he was not initially convinced that stronger central government authority was needed to assure the survival of the thirteen freed colonies, Jefferson eventually came around to accept the constitutional document and even gave it his lukewarm endorsement—but only after "the Bill of Rights" he helped draft was included in the whole constitutional package as the first ten amendments.

To Jefferson, the fight for independence had been much more than a war against George III. It had been a war against any arbitrary power that denied the natural rights of freedom of speech, freedom of press, freedom of assembly, and freedom of religion.

Now Hamilton and his ilk would jeopardize individual liberties, weakening the powers of the thirteen states by consolidating the central authority of the federal government. Federalists would exalt the president, raising him above the people into a remote and aloof personage.

If Jefferson was frank with himself, he would have to admit that Washington would have considered himself an "elective king" even in the absence of an Alexander Hamilton. Washington, after all, had only had one model for executive leadership—the eighteenth-century British monarch.

Jefferson had no fear of Adams becoming a king. He thought Adams was a decent if misguided man. Like the lawyer he was, Adams believed that the president was a trustee who acted in what he considered to be the best interests of his client, the people, but did not bear a responsibility to reflect their wishes.

In 1796, at the time of Adams's election, Jefferson had written to a friend that "the spirit of '76 is not dead—it is merely slumbering." But after four years of witnessing the Federalist administration from his high but impotent position as vice president, he came to believe that the continuation of Federalism would snuff out the revolutionary ideals of individual liberty.

Jefferson believed that what had happened in America was unique, and the political principles he and others had carved out in this new country in the New World represented a new and different kind of society. For Adams and Hamilton to erect on the foundations of this dream a pale imitation of the British government was a betrayal.

In December 1799, George Washington died from a chill he had developed in the holiday festivities. Jefferson, though at Monticello some seventy miles away, was pointedly not invited to attend the ceremonies.

Jefferson faced the new century with a vigor that belied his fifty-seven years. He seemed to inherit his rugged constitution from his father's side. His father, a sturdy pioneer of Welsh descent, was known for his legendary strength. Peter Jefferson the backwoodsman had married above himself into the aristocratic Randolphs of Virginia. Although the Randolphs looked down upon the rough-hewn farmer, his oldest son would always idolize his father.

Jefferson inherited not the delicate looks of the Randolph side but the raw-boned features of his father. The father would also bequeath to his son the anti-aristocratic bias of the frontiersman. But unlike so many of the backwoods strain, the elder Jefferson did not disdain the advantages of education. The provisions of his will insisted that young Jefferson be schooled in the classics. The result was that Jefferson became one of the most literate men of his time.

That was why the Continental Congress gave the thirty-two-year-old Virginian the task of drafting the Declaration of Independence. It also explains why he was chosen to follow Benjamin Franklin as minister to Paris during the Revolutionary War. When Jefferson was asked at that time if he had come to replace Franklin, he modestly demurred, saying, "No one can replace Doctor Franklin, I come only to succeed him."

Although the modesty was becoming, Jefferson had a mind that could shine even in the shadow of the legendary Franklin. The sojourn in France would forever shape his politics. Jefferson found France seething intellectually. As the agent of a revolutionary cause, he was welcomed by a land on the threshold of its own. Jefferson, who could read French, had been influenced by Rousseau, Montesquieu, and particularly Jean Jacques Burlamaqui's *Le Droit Natural*.

Two years before the Declaration of Independence, Jefferson had written his own personal manifesto of revolution: *A Summary View of the Rights of British America*. In intent and feeling it is not unlike Martin Luther's Ninety-five Theses, which he nailed on the castle door at Wittenberg.

Can any reason be assigned why 160,000 electors in the island of Great Britain
should give law to four million in the states of America, every individual of
whom is equal to every individual of them in virtue, in understanding, and
in bodily strength?

Jefferson became a revolutionary early in his life. At age twenty-two he
stood at the door of Virginia House of Burgesses when Patrick Henry
roared, "Caesar had his brother, Charles II his Cromwell and George the
Third"—at which point many of the members cried "Treason"—"and
George III may profit by their example."

It was this hatred of authoritarian control that was kindled by the Adams
administration's Alien and Sedition Act. The royalism Jefferson had spent
his life uprooting was not to be replanted, although it had been given a
new name: "federalism."

Jefferson the impotent vice president set out to activate his network of
followers. The result was America's first national presidential campaign.
Up to now the presidency was thought of an honor or title to be conferred,
not an office to be won. But Jefferson sought out those who would likely
be chosen as members of the Electoral College in their own community
and extracted their pledge of commitment to him. Of course, aggressive
canvassing was not considered proper by the powers-that-be in the big cities
of the Eastern seaboard.

Jefferson crisscrossed the fifteen states (Vermont and Kentucky were the
newly admitted states) sealing deals and cementing promises. One of the
deals he made, as previously mentioned, was his alliance with Aaron Burr
of New York City.

Jefferson was the first president who could be termed a professional
politician, and he proceeded to organize his national campaign profession-
ally. He commissioned the first campaign biography to be written, 5,000
copies of which were distributed. He even wrote the first political campaign
song. At rallies from Maine to Georgia Jefferson's partisans would gather
and sing:

> Rejoice, Columbia's sons rejoice,
> To tyrants never bend the knee
> But join with heart and soul and voice
> For Jefferson and Liberty
> From Georgia up to Lake Champlain
> From seas to Mississippi shores
> Ye sons of freedom loud proclaim
> The Reign of Terror is no more!

After waging the first state-by-state campaign, Jefferson was not surprised
by the news of November's balloting that a majority of the recently elected
members of the Electoral College were those sympathetic to the Jefferson-

Burr Republican slate. Jefferson was, however, dumbfounded when the vote resulted in a tie between him and Burr. Jefferson felt betrayed by Burr's attempt to exploit this technical impasse to elevate himself to the presidency instead of acceding to Jefferson, who, after all, was the agreed-upon candidate of the Democrat-Republican Party.

Amid rumors of various political plots, such as the Federalists throwing their votes to Burr in the House of Representatives or their installing Chief Justice John Marshall as an interim president, Jefferson rode from Monticello to the new capitol in Washington. On that December horseback journey, Jefferson tried to make some sense of the political maelstrom he was riding into. The members of the House of Representatives, who now had the responsibility of choosing the next president, were not only divided into Federalists and his party of Democrat-Republicans, but they were also subdivided into warring factions within themselves. There were the "High-Federalists," who regarded Jefferson as "the herald of French Revolutionary Jacobinism," and the more moderate Federalists, who might be inclined to accept Jefferson's victory at the polls. On the other hand, his own Democrat-Republicans were split into his followers and those of Aaron Burr.

In addition to himself and Burr, there were other principals who dominated the political scene: John Adams, the outgoing Federalist president; Alexander Hamilton, the de facto leader of the Federalist Party; and John Marshall, whom Adams had only recently, since the election, appointed as chief justice. Then there were Jefferson's political lieutenants, James Madison and James Monroe.

When Jefferson arrived in Washington, one of his first acts was to call on President Adams. The embittered Adams told him, "You threw me out, you threw me out!"

So Jefferson failed in his first objective of getting Adams to denounce the scheme of installing Marshall as an interim president. But Jefferson knew he could count on Adams's distrust of Burr and more importantly, Hamilton's hatred of the rival New Yorker. In addition, Jefferson was in the eyes of most of the country the legitimate winner. In other words, Jefferson held some winning cards, and he proceeded to play them coolly and astutely.

It was not to be, however, an easy battle. For days the balloting continued in the House of Representatives. Some members slept beside their desks as the all-night session in the House chamber grew hot and protracted. Jefferson, with Madison and Monroe buttonholing the congressmen, was edging Burr in the balloting but was falling short of the necessary majority.

Jefferson as the outgoing vice-president was the President of the Senate. From this ceremonial but strategic vantage point, Jefferson applied the carrot and stick to the reluctant Federalists. To the moderate Federalists he gave assurances that he would not try to undo Hamilton's national bank system and that he would not engage in any wholesale removal of Federalists from minor government offices. And to the extreme Federalists he held out a warning that if he were not installed there certainly would be a civil war and that following that war he would draft a new, more radical constitution. On the sixth day the Federalist opposition in the House of Representatives collapsed and provided the margin for Jefferson's election.

Jefferson was now president-elect over a young country that had split in disarray. In such civil discord, an inaugural address had to be more than a ceremony; it had to cement together the severed factions. Jefferson had but little more than two weeks after his February 17th election by the House of Representatives to prepare the address. This was somewhat less time than he had to draft the Declaration of Independence. As for that document, he employed no secretarial assistance nor did he consult any book or document.

At his lodging at Conrad and McMunn's near the Capitol, Jefferson wrote out in longhand successive drafts of what would be his first public utterance as president. Not since the Declaration of Independence twenty-five years before had he had an assignment of such momentous import and consequence. In a sense, the Declaration was the easier task. For Jefferson, a manifesto for rebellion flowed more smoothly from his revolutionary soul than did a reasoned call for reconciliation.

On Inauguration Day, Jefferson dressed plainly and walked from his boarding house to the Capitol with a group of friends. There was no procession. The only flourish was a company of artillery that paraded before him and discharged a cannon in salute.

He entered the North Wing of the Capitol, a building compound described by Henry Adams as "two wings without a body."

Inside the Senate chamber, Jefferson must have noted first the absence of President Adams. The disgruntled Adams, an aide told him, had bolted out of Washington in a 4:00 A.M. departure by carriage for Boston. This was more than bad manners on Adams's part—it was a deliberate political act that made Jefferson's task of promoting continuity and stability that much harder.

Relations with the other dignitaries of the day's ceremony were hardly less strained. Aaron Burr, the incoming vice president, had betrayed Jefferson in his double-crossing attempt to gain the presidency for himself. John Marshall, Adams's midnight appointment as chief justice, had the constitutional duty to swear in the new president.

Of all the actions by Adams, the post-election appointments of Federalist officials had most offended Jefferson. The appointment to the head of the judiciary of Marshall symbolized this "indecent conduct" by Adams.

Marshall, who was Jefferson's cousin (through the Randolphs) despised the president-elect. Marshall, who could hardly bring himself to speak to his cousin, ironically had the responsibility of swearing him in.

As Jefferson repeated the presidential oath recited by Chief Justice Marshall, he could look out and survey the audience, parts of which were decidedly hostile. Die-hard Federalists in the packed chambers waited with apprehension for the first words of this champion of revolutionary France.

He surprised them with this arresting statement: "We are all republicans, we are all federalists." The immediate unifying line did much to disarm the tension. When they heard the two terms, the audience no doubt pictured in their mind's eye the two words beginning with capital letters—in the names of the two major parties. Indeed, most editors would capitalize the words in later accounts.

Actually, the original draft shows that Jefferson wrote the words in lowercase. In a literal sense he was referring not to the names of the two parties but to two political science terms denoting two different philosophical approaches to government. It was Jefferson's novel insight that the two terms were not mutually exclusive. All Americans, he was saying, reject the concept of monarchy and the imperialistic tyranny of aristocratic rule. At the same time he was agreeing that some consolidation of government authority is necessary to hold together the fragile confederacy of the fifteen sovereign states.

Jefferson then added a sentence Miltonic in its simplicity and brilliance:

> If there be any among us who wish to dissolve this union or change its republican form, let them stand undisturbed as monuments of the safety with which error of opinion may be tolerated where reason is left free to combat it.

Jefferson's tone was dry and matter of fact, but the lucid analysis makes his Inaugural Address stand with the *Federalist Papers* as one of the seminal statements on American government. But the *Federalists Papers* did not discuss the Bill of Rights. What Jefferson was saying is that our political heritage is both the constitutional "union" and the "Bill of Rights" "republican form" of government.

Jefferson never had been an eloquent master of the spoken word, but for once his dry, dispassionate delivery enhanced the impact of his words. The tenor was not that of a rallying cry but that of reconciliation. The audience that strained to hear his measured sentences was more ready to ponder its message.

The more moderate Federalists were impressed by the magnanimity of tone. Not a note of chiding lecture or gleeful triumph intruded to sharpen any of his phrases into a partisan edge.

Yet in the olive branch extended to the moderate Federalists there was a "stick" apparent to those who would study the written text in later days. The audience heard "Federalists," but actually he was only saying that all Americans are supporters of the Constitution. In the same way he pledged to the Federalist opposition an administration that would respect their minority interests:

> Though the will of the majority is in all cases to prevail, that will, to be rightful must be reasonable; that the minority possess their equal rights, which equal laws must protect and to violate would be oppression.

Yet a closer scrutiny reveals a subtle if pointed reminder by Jefferson that his presidency would never resort to any legislation like the Adams administration's Alien and Sedition Act.

Jefferson took care to mute the revolutionary rhetoric that had filled his earlier letters and campaign talks. But he did not sacrifice to the interests of unity his Republican conception of the ideal government.

> A wise and frugal government, which shall restrain men from injuring another shall leave them otherwise free to regulate their own pursuits of industry and improvement, and shall take from the worth of labor the bread it has earned. This is the sum of good government and this is necessary to close the circle of our facilities.

What disdain Alexander Hamilton must have felt as he listened to Thomas Jefferson expound his philosophy of limited government! But the constituency that Thomas Jefferson championed—artisans, backwoodsmen, small farmers, and even plantation owners on the scale of Monticello—would have little need for a federal government that was anything more than a disinterested policeman or a remote and unexacting landlord.

If George Washington was the first who saw himself as an American, Thomas Jefferson was the first to see Americanism as democracy. In 1776, Thomas Jefferson wrote more than a rationale for rebellion—he introduced a revolutionary creed: "All men are created equal."

To Jefferson, a federal government that consolidated authority at the expense of the states or abridged liberties at the expense of individuals was betraying its special mission in history. And a federal government that saw its role as promoter of business and commerce in the coastal cities would reduce the influence of those who tilled their fields by hand. The "democrats" in Jefferson's day were the farmers and frontiersmen. They constituted a class unique to America, and, as such, they were to him the real Americans.

To constitutional purists, it comes as a surprise that Jefferson, the champion of limited powers to the federal government, would broaden that authority to negotiate the Louisiana Purchase. But Jefferson's belief in democracy pre-supposed a democratic way of life, and only in a nation of ample scope would his kind of Americans—the pioneers and future farmers—find the room to build their own future and carve their own destiny.

In iambic lines that almost suggest a patriotic hymn, he intoned:

This rising nation spread over a
wide and fruitful land
advancing rapidly to destinies
beyond the reach of mortal eye.

In words that Lincoln would later echo, Jefferson then described as "the world's best hope" this freedom offered in the open lands of this New World.

Some have characterized Jefferson's inaugural address the way future critics would assess Kennedy's: a triumph of style that promised more than the administration would deliver. But Jefferson's speech should be valued more for its immediate impact than substantive message. The speech brought stability to a divided nation on the verge of civil conflict. Jefferson the revolutionary triumphed as a reconciler.

3 _____

The Monroe Doctrine:
The Whispered Warning

We should consider any attempt on their part to extend their system to any portions of this hemisphere as dangerous to our peace and safety.

The Monroe Doctrine was hardly a doctrine, and it certainly did not originate with James Monroe. It was not really a doctrine because the United States could not enforce it, and the idea of a New World quarantine did not spring from the Monroe administration but from the British government.

Far from being the manifesto trumpeted by American politicians today, the Doctrine, as initially delivered, was little more than a memorandum and muffled at that. It was like a boy yelling "Don't mess around on my block" from the privacy of his own bathroom with the shower turned on.

Perhaps James Monroe was never meant to be cast in a heroic role. Our fifth president is called "the last of the Virginia Dynasty," but he falls a cut below his more noted predecessors. He could not claim like George Washington to be "the Father of his country," like Jefferson to be the author of the Declaration of Independence, or even like Madison to be the principal author of the Constitution. He does not truly rank as a Founding Father even though his chief qualification as a rising national politician was his close political association as a Virginian with Washington, Jefferson, and Madison.

James Monroe, whose father was Scottish and mother Welsh, came from plain, solid people who tilled their farm in Westmoreland County in the northern neck of Virginia.[1]

In 1774, at age sixteen, Monroe was a big and rugged boy for his age, and he left the family farm to study at William and Mary College in Williamsburg. There he was overwhelmed by the sophisticated and fashionable capital of the Virginia Colony. He arrived right when the Burgesses were still reeling from the impassioned pleas of orators like Patrick Henry, who called for freedom from the mother country. At any rate, the young Monroe developed a visceral distrust of England early on. He was not English but Celtic, and his family did not come from the gentry set who sent their sons to be schooled in England or who had their daughters outfitted with the latest French fashions.

So it was not surprising that in 1776 he eagerly volunteered for the Continental Army. His rapid rise in the military service led him to the rank of colonel, a title he would take more pride in than president.

Yet Colonel Monroe, as he liked to be addressed by his political followers and friends, was not considered particularly vain in an era when pomposity was more the rule than the exception. He did not tell war stories, and he never boasted of wounds he received at the Battle of Trenton or bragged of his associations with Washington and Jefferson.

It was not that he was, by nature, reticent or shy like Madison. On the contrary, he was a gregarious politician. Judge William Brooke, who practiced law with him, described Monroe in terms that might equally apply to Gerald Ford. "Though a slow man, he possessed a strong mind and excellent judgement."

In other words, Monroe was not a quick or imaginative thinker, but, through methodical application, he would gain detailed mastery of a subject. He was not an orator, but he always left his audiences impressed by his honesty of conviction.

One witness to a presentation he made at the Virginia Convention in 1788, where he opposed (like Jefferson) the newly proposed federal Constitution, commented:

> The speech of Monroe was well received. It made upon the house a strong impression which was heightened by the modesty of his demeanor, by the sincerity which was reflected from every feature of this honest face and by the minute knowledge which he exhibited of a historical transaction of surpassing interest to the south.

Not only mentally, but physically, James Monroe resembled Gerald Ford. The six-foot Monroe had a big, open, fair-complexioned face atop wide, rugged shoulders.

Monroe's country-boy heartiness would later contrast with his old-fashioned attire as president. As chief of state he insisted on wearing a broadcloth tailcoat, knee britches, and silver-buckled black shoes. But Monroe, who was the last president to dress himself in the formal eighteenth-century attire, was not affecting airs. His clothes, like his colonelcy, rendered mute testimony to his Revolutionary War service and his connection to the Founding Fathers.

At the time of the formation of the Monroe Doctrine, President Monroe was closing out his second term. He had been elected virtually by unanimous ballot in 1820 (one voter withheld his ballot so that only George Washington would have that distinction). Four years earlier, as James Madison's secretary of state, Monroe was the logical successor to his fellow Virginians. (Madison, after all, had been Jefferson's secretary of state, as Jefferson had been Washington's secretary of state.) In fact, the disgruntled members of the dying Federalist Party, such as Josiah Quincy, called the presidencies of Madison and Monroe "King James I and King James II."

But Monroe's climb to national leadership had not been smooth. As Washington's minister to France and, later, as Jefferson's minister to Britain, he stirred up controversy. President Washington recalled him in the first incident, and Jefferson received him coolly when he returned from the second mission. Henry Adams, the grandson of Monroe's secretary of state, John Adams, wrote that "Monroe was unparalleled . . . in the experience of being disowned by Presidents as strongly opposed to each other as Washington and Jefferson."[2]

Nevertheless, after each diplomatic setback Monroe returned to his home base in Virginia and ran for governor. For Monroe, it was a regrouping and a rebuilding of his political power. In all, he was governor for four terms; in between his state house tenures in Williamsburg, he sandwiched in his foreign ministries and his stint as U.S. Commissioner for the Louisiana Purchase.

Whatever finesse Monroe may have lacked as a diplomat, he was sure-footed in Virginia politics. If he was no intellectual like Jefferson or Madison, he was their superior in cultivating the support of courthouse politicians. His actions may have seemed rash abroad, but at home his moves were shrewdly tailored to political trends.

As president, Monroe selected his cabinet with great care. For secretary of state he chose John Quincy Adams, the son of the former president. It was an astute choice. Not only was Adams the ablest and most experienced diplomat in the land, but his choice for the head of the cabinet disarmed dissident elements in the North. Adams, who had ties to the dying Federalist Party, smoothed the ruffled feelings of New Englanders who were not overjoyed with the continuation of the Virginia Dynasty. In fact, Monroe made his first order of business, after selecting a cabinet, a presidential tour of New York and New England. He was the first president to do so since George Washington.

Monroe, like Ford, was not an insecure man. He was not afraid to fill his cabinet with talent that might make his own gifts seem pedestrian by comparison. Besides Adams, he chose William Crawford of Georgia to be secretary of Treasury and John Calhoun of South Carolina to be secretary of war. Both were considered presidential timbre and inspired their own political followings. The only figure of stature left out was Speaker of the House Henry Clay of Kentucky, who wanted to be secretary of state and refused any other offer.

The coalition nature of Monroe's administration has been characterized as "The Era of Good Feelings." Specifically, it alluded to the one-party hegemony of the Jeffersonian Democrat–Republican party which, in twenty years of controlling the Executive Mansion as well as Congress, had moved from its left-of-center position to the mainstream. The phrase "Era of Good Feelings" might also describe the rising American pride and nationalism sweeping the land in the years following the country's second conflict with Great Britain, the War of 1812.

But the powers of Europe, after the defeat of Napoleon, were also enjoying a time of increased cooperation and diplomatic comity. The royal houses of Europe subdued their rivalries in common kinship to protect the institution of monarchy. Then, the Congress of Vienna, the handiwork of Metternich and Talleyrand, reflected the spirit of the old order and was designed to bring peace and stability to Europe.

The peace in Europe, however, brought little peace of mind to American politicians of that day. The Napoleonic War, which so occupied European attention, had not only allowed the United States to develop as a young nation; it also had afforded the Latin American peoples of Mexico and Central and South America the opportunity to throw off the yoke of Spanish colonial rule and begin to form themselves into various national entities. Soldiers such as Simon Bolivar and José de San Martin were leading independence movements, emulating the heroic role of George Washington.

The United States had profited during the Napoleonic threat to Europe. Commercially, it grew as a shipping power, and geographically, it grew from the Louisiana Purchase territories, which a financially-pressed Napoleon had to sell to help pay for his costly war with Britain.

The United States, however, worried that the new resurgence of monarchy in Europe might rekindle Old World colonial ambitions and interference in the New World. One European country, although headed by a king, also felt mounting concern about the future of Latin America. That country was the constitutional monarchy of Great Britain, against whom the Americans had fought twice—once securing their political independence and then asserting their commercial and shipping rights.

The British foreign office was presided over by Stratford Canning, a left-of-center Tory who sympathized with the yearnings of peoples, like the Greeks, who were striving to free themselves from their autocratic Turk captors. But his high-minded concern for the new fledgling nations of Argentina, Chile, and Colombia was motivated by traditional British self-interest. British exports to South America in 1822 surpassed those of the

United States. British commercial houses were being established at a rapid rate in South American ports, and British mining concessions for extracting such ores as silver and tin were being granted. Bank of England loans were being steadily negotiated to put the new republics on solid footing. Yet, all of this heavy British investment in the future of South America could be jeopardized if Spain, backed by its royal allies of Austria, Russia, and France, reasserted its claim to its former colonies.

So on a hot lazy day in London, when most of the political and diplomatic officials were away from the capital, the American minister in London, Richard Rush, was startled by an inquiry delivered by a messenger from Stratford Canning in the British foreign office: Would the United States join Great Britain in a signed statement denouncing any attempt by the European powers to restore the rule of Spain in her last colonies?

Rush, the son of the revolutionary patriot Dr. Benjamin Rush, found himself in a dilemma. For one thing, he had no instructions from Secretary of State John Quincy Adams on how to treat such a diplomatic initiative. On the other hand, should he allow such a possible foreign policy break-through slip by while awaiting sea transit messages back and forth from Washington?

Rush decided that he might be justified in dealing on his own if he could persuade Britain to up the ante. He replied by asking whether Britain would be ready to follow the United States in recognizing Colombia, Mexico, Chile, and Argentina. Canning, however, would not commit Britain to an immediate recognition. Instead, he dangled a vague promise to do so in the future.

Canning was ready to issue a diplomatic signal but not a diplomatic snub, which might have provoked concerted action by the Holy Alliance of European powers.

When Rush's account of the diplomatic exchange reached Washington, it went directly to President Monroe because the secretary of state, John Quincy Adams, was vacationing in Massachusetts. Always cautious, Monroe immediately consulted his two mentors and predecessors, Jefferson and Madison.

Monroe was wary of any offer by Great Britain. To him, "Perfidious Albion" was an apt appellation for the former mother country. Ever since his family signed a remonstrance against the Stamp Act in 1774, Monroe had been an anglephobe, and his stint as Jefferson's minister to London had not ameliorated but aggravated those feelings. The unpopular treaty with Britain that he had helped negotiate was a memory he preferred to forget, and the English diplomat who drafted those provisions was none other than Stratford Canning, the bearer of the present diplomatic proposal.

To join the British in a warning against the Holy Alliance powers ran against the grain of Monroe's American fiber. After all, George Washington's parting testament was not to embroil American foreign policy in

European intrigue. That counsel, reaffirmed by Jefferson's stricture against "entangling" alliances, had voiced American suspicions about European intrigues.

Monroe, the first grass-roots politician to be elected president, subscribed to the average citizen's belief that America was a New World untainted by Old World corruption and cynicism. That same romanticism nurtured a sympathy for the new sister republics to the south. Canning's proposal, backed by the might of the biggest navy on the sea, could possibly offer insurance for the safety and security of those Latin American nations.

Monroe's immediate presidential predecessor, James Madison, suggested enlarging Canning's "avowed disapprobation" to include a declaration in behalf of the Greeks' quest for independence from the Turks. But Madison's predecessor Thomas Jefferson delivered more pragmatic counsel.

Jefferson analyzed both the role of the Americans and that of the British. The eighty-year-old "Sage of Monticello" saw that if America wanted to preserve the integrity of the New World, it could not, at the same time, take part in redressing the order of the Old. Jefferson told Monroe that U.S. foreign policy should demand not only the cessation of European interference in the Americas but also non-interference in Europe by the United States. To Jefferson, the advantage of the Canning proposal was not just the opportunity to block the Holy Alliance but, more significantly, the chance to limit the danger of English hostility. "Great Britain," Jefferson wrote to Monroe, "is the nation which can do us the most harm of anyone and, with her on our side we need not fear the World."

If there was any more experienced authority on Europe than the eighty-year-old Jefferson, it was John Quincy Adams, the son of the president whom Jefferson had defeated for reelection. The secretary of state had spent much of his formative life in Europe, initially as the son and secretary of his father in his diplomatic assignments. Then he earned his own foreign policy credentials as a minister to the Netherlands, Russia, and Britain. Adams was a diplomatic scholar who could speak many languages. In a cabinet meeting four years earlier Adams had outlined his view that the world "must be familiarized with the idea of considering our proper dominion to be the continent of North America."

John Quincy Adams was, throughout the Monroe administration, an unannounced candidate to follow him in the presidency. Although Adams may have occupied the premiership in the Monroe administration, others in the cabinet were ready to contest his succession. Secretary of treasury, William Crawford, was one, and secretary of war, John C. Calhoun, was another.

Few cabinet meetings in history have been more charged with the atmosphere of presidential politics as those November sessions, which were held on the eve of an election year in 1824. While Crawford generally approved of a joint initiative with Britain, Calhoun strenuously objected.

Calhoun, who would have the responsibility of running a war, feared provoking the Holy Alliance into an armed conflict.

Outside the executive branch, Henry Clay was less inhibited. The speaker
of the House, who had wanted to be chosen secretary of state, still hoped
to succeed Monroe as president. As speaker, he used his considerable oratorical talents to rally his followers. Clay's nationalistic "American System" of federal internal improvements such as roads, canals, and bridges
had its foreign policy counterpart. He envisaged smaller versions of the
United States blooming and flourishing in Latin America. Such romantic
projections may not have been down-to-earth, but they were practically
rooted in the political feelings of his fellow countrymen. "Let us," said
Clay, "become true Americans and place ourselves at the head of the American System."

John Quincy Adams, however, did not share such romantic sympathy
for sister republics to the south. A Calvinist by religion and Anglo-Saxon
by heritage, the New Englander put little stock in countries of Catholic
religion and Latin temperaments. It was one thing to tell Europe to keep
its hands off the Western Hemisphere, but it was another to join hands with
those weak Latin governments in the spirit of equality and fraternal affection.

Adams did not worry, like Calhoun, about the threat of European invasion; nor did he welcome, like Clay, the prospect of a Pan-American
crusade. To Adams, the first priority was to deter the European powers
from fishing in American waters. Russia was pressing claims in the Northwest from its base in Alaska. Even Britain, which suggested the Anglo-
American warning, was claiming far too much in the same area along the
Columbia River to suit Adams.

Adams had dealt with Canning before. In a conversation in 1821 with
the foreign office diplomat, he had accused the British of laying claim to
every place under the sun. "You claim India, you claim Africa . . . "

"Perhaps," replied Canning, "even a piece of the moon."

> No [said Adams]; I have not heard that you claim exclusively any part of the
> moon; but there is not a spot on this habitable globe that I could affirm you
> do not claim.

Yet Adams was not hostile to the Canning proposal. He did, however,
insist that the Americans go it alone. He lectured the cabinet:

> It would be more candid to outline our principles explicitly to France and
> Russia than to come in as a cock boat in the wake of a British man-of-war.

To those who shared Calhoun's fear of diplomatic isolation in case of a
Holy Alliance invasion, Adams had this to say:

I no more believe that the Holy Alliance will restore the Spanish dominion than the Chimborazo [mountain in the Andes] will sink beneath the ocean.

Adams's views prevailed in the cabinet. Richard Rush in London was instructed to decline Canning's proposal for a joint declaration. At the same time, however, he was to express general agreement with British policy with the exception that the United States believed Britain should immediately recognize the new nations in Latin America. On this point, Adams said:

We considered that the people of these emancipated colonies were, of right, independent of all other nations and that it was our duty so to acknowledge them.

But a message to London was hardly a manifesto. The cold formal language of diplomatic instructions could not allay the ardent nationalism as expressed by Speaker Clay.

President Monroe believed himself to be linear heir of George Washington and Thomas Jefferson. Now that his administration was drawing to a close, Monroe felt that something more like a pronouncement was needed to continue and enlarge on the foreign policy principles of Washington's Farewell Address and Jefferson's First Inaugural. But if Monroe wanted to be acclaimed as an advocate of Americanism, he did not want to be accountable as an architect of war. He remembered how northeasterners referred to the War of 1812 as "Mr. Madison's War." Monroe took seriously the characterization of his tenure as "the golden age of the republic."

Caught between the dangers of war and the demands of nationalism, Monroe vacillated. How could the President of the United States be both the keeper of peace and the champion of freedom? In the end the concern for peace yielded to that of posterity. So Monroe suggested issuing not only a non-interference warning but also support for the revolting Greeks as well.

Adams disagreed. Like Jefferson, he believed that American interference in Europe was just as wrong as European interference in the Americas.

The ground I wish to take [recommended Adams] is that of earnest remonstrance against the interference of European powers by force in South America, but, to disclaim all interference on our part in Europe; to make an American cause and adhere inflexibly to that.

The president at last yielded to his secretary of state on that point.

Monroe, however, did secure the cabinet endorsement of something more than a diplomatic instruction regarding the Latin American situation. Such a statement would not be addressed to kings abroad but to the Congress at home. It would be designed to fill the political need domestically without arousing hostility internationally. To do this, the presidential statements would be buried in a routine message to be delivered to Congress on December 2nd.

The secretary of state had his work cut out for him. In the fifty-two paragraph statement, only three paragraphs constitute what is known as the Monroe Doctrine. In this ponderous review of the nation's state of affairs, Adams inserted two warnings to Europe. The first "sandwiched-in" provision came in the seventh paragraph—the non–colonization section. A lengthy paragraph begins by discussing negotiations with the Russians and the British on "the respective rights and interests of the two nations on the northwest coast of this continent." The paragraph ends with this clause:

> that the American continents, by the independent and free condition which they have assumed and maintain are henceforth not to be considered as subjects for future colonization by any European powers.

In the statement up to the forty-ninth paragraph, the president's annual message dwelt on such important topics of the day as postal service improvements, repairs in the Cumberland Road, the protective tariff, the new U.S. Military Academy, and instructions to the U.S. Navy to seize ships engaged in the traffic of slaves. Then Adams sneaked in a mention of the Greek question:

> A strong hope has been long entertained, founded on the heroic struggle of the Greeks, that they would succeed in their contest and resume their equal status among the nations of the earth.

With that statement Adams watered down Monroe's original call for support to an expression of good wishes. American involvement in Europe's affairs was carefully proscribed in order to set up the warning to Europe not to meddle in the Americas.

The rest of the Monroe Doctrine continued in the fiftieth and fifty-first paragraphs. The key sentence in the fiftieth reads:

> We owe it, therefore, to candor and to the amicable relations existing between the United States and those powers to declare that we should consider any attempt on their part to extend their system to any portion of this hemisphere as dangerous to our peace and safety.

In the fifty-first paragraph, Adams lays down the rationale of this non-interference principle:

> Our policy in regard to Europe . . . is not to interfere in the internal concerns of any of its powers; to consider the Government de facto as the legitimate

government for us; to cultivate friendly relations with it, and to preserve those relations by a frank, firm and manly policy, meeting, in all instances, the just claim of every power; submitting to injuries from none. But in regard to these continents, circumstances are eminently and conspicuously different.

Then Adams expands on this non-interference principle:

It is impossible that the allied powers should extend their political system to any portion of either continent without endangering our peace and happiness; nor can anyone believe that our Southern brethren, if left to themselves, would adopt it of their own accord. It is equally impossible, therefore, that we should behold such interposition in any form with indifference.

The words were Adams's but the sentiments were those of Monroe and all Americans. If the British foreign secretary, Stratford Canning, first advanced the idea of non-interference by European powers in the Western hemisphere, it was his American counterpart, John Quincy Adams, who specifically originated and spelled out the non-colonization principle. The principle may have been triggered by Czarists' claims in the Northwest, but it was evolving into a slap at the British. An active candidate for the presidency, Adams was sensitive to those in the West who, like Andrew Jackson, had accused him of betraying interests to Great Britain and Spain in the Treaties of 1818 and 1819, which he had negotiated as commissioner. Adams saw in the writing of the presidential message a chance to squelch that criticism with a strong statement against further European colonization.

Stratford Canning was not happy to read reports from his minister in Washington about the presidential message. He had advanced a proposal in good faith to the Americans that they not only declined but stole as their own idea—when it was the Royal Navy that made such a proposal enforceable! To add injury to insult, they stretched and distorted the idea of non-interference in Latin America to mean an end to British colonization in areas like British Columbia, which was already part of the British Empire.

Canning put his best face on the development. He made public his earlier note to the French minister to show to South American countries that Britain had proposed the idea of non-interference first. Then he had the British recognize those Latin countries, saying, "I called in the New World to redress the order of the Old."

In this country, the response to the warnings to Europe was warm. For John Quincy Adams it meant he truly was confirmed as "the prime minister of the cabinet," and he consolidated his position as frontrunner for the presidency in 1824. But if John Quincy Adams gained a presidency, James Monroe attained immortality through the Monroe Doctrine.

No president, not even the venerable Washington, the learned Jefferson, or the saintly Lincoln, has a national sacred dogma attached to his name. By his decision to put the Latin American issue in a presidential message, he raised the flag of American foreign policy before the entire world and implanted that flag firmly in the American national consciousness.

The Monroe Doctrine owes its enshrined popularity to the mythical belief that the Atlantic and Pacific Oceans divide the New World from the intrigues of the Old. It was this belief—that God had singularly blessed this country—that inspired Washington's Farewell Address. The neutrality of Washington was then expanded into the hemispheric solidarity of the Monroe Doctrine.

For a century and a half isolationists and interventionists alike have invoked the Monroe Doctrine to oppose and support the League of Nations and the United Nations. Liberals cited it to advance Kennedy's Alliance for Progress in the 1960s, and conservatives cited it to propound Reagan's policy in Central America in the 1980s. Like Magna Carta, the Monroe Doctrine through the years assumed a mythic majesty far beyond what the participants had envisioned.

The historic manifesto of the Americas, interestingly, resembled the routing of a double play in baseball: Canning grabbed the foreign policy ball and tossed it to Adams at second, who pivoted and threw it to Monroe. Monroe then stepped on the presidential first base and registered the out. But no one expected it, at the time, to wind up in the diplomatic Hall of Fame.

What began as a groping response to a British foreign office proposal ended up as a presidential pronouncement. If Monroe only whispered the warning, he did so from the White House, with the imprint of the presidential seal. Originating as a domestic statement without standing of diplomatic accord or international law, it grew with the expanding might of the United States to become the mainspring of our foreign policy.

NOTES

1. His second cousin, who also hailed from the area, was Zachary Taylor, the twelfth president.

2. In all fairness, Jefferson had less of a complaint. He found it politically convenient to keep distance from Monroe's treaty with the British, which did not raise the issue of British impressment of U.S. sailors. On the other hand, Monroe had, in spirit, violated Washington's instructions of neutrality.

4

The Jackson Bank Veto: The War Against the Eastern Establishment

It is to be regretted that the rich and powerful too often bend the acts of government to their selfish purposes.

Andrew Jackson was, in a sense, the first "twentieth-century president." He was neither an exalted "father of his country" like George Washington, a philosopher-king like Thomas Jefferson, a benign judge like James Monroe, nor an academic dean like John Quincy Adams; he was, instead, a flesh-and-blood political leader who embodied the hopes and aspirations of his followers.

Like a Theodore or Franklin Roosevelt, Jackson personalized the presidency and forced the political debate to be a referendum on his personality. Andrew Jackson did not just preside over his country—he projected himself into the political fray. He parlayed his image, played to the press, and put together voting blocs. The power of the presidency was like a pistol—a weapon to be used and not just displayed on a shelf. Just as Jackson brandished the power of patronage, he wielded the power of veto—and he would use that veto to shape a campaign and reshape a political party.

To understand the political personality of Andrew Jackson, three facts in his background stand out. A Tennessean, Jackson was the first Westerner to be president. His roots were neither from the Virginia gentry nor the New England establishment—they were Scotch-Irish yeomanry. Second, he was the last president to be born an English colonial subject, and his earliest memories were of that conflict to free the colonies from that British yoke. Third, he was a general in the second fight against the British—the War of 1812, which the West fervently supported but many in the East opposed. General Jackson, who won his national fame in the battle of New Orleans, never overcame his bitterness against those New England commercial interests who threatened secession at the Hartford Convention, which had been convened to resist the war.

To Jackson, the royalists of England and the elitists of the East blended into one. He never forgot that he had won the popular vote in the election of 1824 only to lose in the House of Representatives to the New Englander, John Quincy Adams. Speaker of the House Henry Clay, a fellow Westerner like Jackson, had thrown his support to Adams in return for the job of secretary of state, and he would be regarded forever as a traitor by Jackson.

At first glance, Andrew Jackson seems like a gaunter edition of John Wayne, topped with an additional mane of gray hair. He was a six-foot-one frontiersman who had seen more than his share of fist-fights, duels, and hangings. Jackson, was, however, more complex than a caricature.

Born in a log cabin in North Carolina, he became the "Squire of Hermitage," a stately plantation in Nashville, Tennessee. If portrayed by the Eastern elite as an illiterate barbarian, he nevertheless read law as a young man and was elected a state judge.[1] A holder of slaves, he vigorously upheld the aspirations of the laborer, mechanic, and small farmer. A veteran Indian fighter, he was, interestingly, reverent about Indian customs and values. A believer in dueling to settle affairs of honor, he remained, however, a devout member of the Presbyterian Church. Opinionated and cock-sure in his views, Jackson not only tolerated those around him with a variety of opinions but actually encouraged his aides and advisors to express their differences.

Jackson judged a man more by his personality than his policies. He liked the rough-hewn and suspected the smooth-polished. The innate populism of his presidency would manifest itself right from the start. In his inaugural address of 1829, President Jackson questioned the constitutionality of the National Bank even though much of his cabinet favored the continuation of the National Bank in Philadelphia. No one should think, however, that the bank was even a minor topic of conversation in the inauguration festivities that year. The papers, except for those in Philadelphia, did not mention it.

Those periodicals hostile to the Jackson presidency were more aroused by the antics of his followers. Jackson partisans stormed the White House, breaking china, smashing crystal glasses, spilling punch, muddying the damask chairs, destroying sofas, and pulling down wall hangings. To escape the crush of the rioting celebrators, the newly sworn president had to crawl out of a rear window and find refuge in a nearby hotel. The Jacksonian revelers who felt that their hero had been cheated out of the White House in 1824 now flaunted the triumph of the Westerners against the East and the little man over the rich. One New England clergyman, shuddering at the mob scene, preached a sermon from Luke 19:41, "Jesus beheld the scene and wept."

Jackson, however, did not join the partying before or on inauguration day. He began his inauguration day by walking bareheaded down Pennsylvania Avenue from his hotel near 13th Street to the Capitol to take his oath. Then, after his address, he mounted his saddled horse and rode to the White House with a mob of carriages, wagons, and carts pursuing him in more of a chase than a procession.

Jackson was in a somber mood. His beloved wife, Rachel, had died barely a month before, following the dirtiest campaign in the nation's young history. There was the *Coffin Hand Bill* bearing the heading "Some Accounts of the Bloody Deeds of General Jackson." (It referred to the six militia men who were shot at his command when he was military governor in Florida.) Even worse were allegations that his wife was a bigamist and that he was an adulterer. Jackson had already killed one man (in a duel) who challenged the validity of his wife's divorce from the husband who had deserted her. He was quick to blame Adams and, even more, Adams's campaign manager, Henry Clay, for the gutter attacks. They were even to be held responsible for Rachel's death who, in his mind, had been sickened by the smears. Jackson, to whom chivalry toward women was not merely courtesy but a code, never forgot or forgave the slur on Rachel's sacred name.

Curiously, it was this quaint gallantry of a frontier man that caused the first rift in his administration. Jackson's old friend, John Eaton, whom he had named secretary of war, had married, with his encouragement, Peggy O'Neal Timberlake, the daughter of a Washington innkeeper. The pert Peggy, a young widow of a Navy purser who had recently died, had occasioned the wagging of Washington tongues by her obvious involvement with the older Eaton. That Eaton paraded the buxom Peggy to various functions was bad enough, but that he would actually marry the tavern hostess was unthinkable in the eyes of Washington society. A visitor to Washington at the time, who professed to be charmed by the gracious and courtly president, nevertheless said he "was under the government of Mrs. Eaton." Harriet Smith, another contemporary commentator, reported that Peggy was "the most malignant, ambitious and silly woman of all times."

Washington society, which had no First Lady to preside over it, was headed by Floride Calhoun, wife of the vice president, John C. Calhoun. Mrs. Calhoun, who came from old French Huguenot stock in South Carolina, refused to receive "the hussy" at her Dunbarton Oaks mansion in Washington, and all the other cabinet wives followed suit. When Emily Donelson, Rachel's niece, who did the hostessing duties at the White House, joined in the social boycott of Mrs. Eaton, Jackson even raged against her. He could not understand why she failed to see that the nasty stories against his old friend's young wife were a re-run of the slurs against her Aunt

Rachel. In the snub against Mrs. Eaton, Jackson saw the snobbery of the aristocratic East against the democratic West.

Into the social maelstrom Jackson's secretary of state, Martin Van Buren, insinuated himself. The widower Van Buren, who had no wife to account to for breaches of social etiquette, saw that it was to his political advantage to befriend the young Peggy Eaton. At the same time he convinced Jackson that the furor was being orchestrated not by the other wives but by Vice President Calhoun himself. Calhoun, Van Buren confided to the president, was trying to head off any possibility that Jackson would change his mind and run for reelection.

Calhoun had backed the older Jackson in 1828 with the tacit understanding that he would follow the Tennessean after one term. Most of the cabinet choices, with the exception of Eaton, were Calhoun's political allies. But the Calhoun succession, figured Van Buren, could be derailed.

Jackson's public break with Calhoun came at the Jefferson Day dinner on April 13, 1830. The annual celebration, in honor of its "patron saint," always had a states' rights flavor. Jackson, though, looked squarely at his vice president and toasted: "Our Federal Union—it must be preserved." The flustered Calhoun took a moment to recover and then responded, "The Union—next to liberty, most dear." The next spring, in a ploy that betrayed his "Italian" hand, Van Buren resigned as secretary of state, and Eaton did likewise as secretary of war. This allowed Jackson to call for the resignation of the rest of the cabinet, thus ridding his administration of the Calhoun influence.

The new appointments included Edward Livingston as secretary of state.[2] Livingston, who had been Jackson's aide-de-camp in the Battle of New Orleans, was probably closest to Jackson. Yet the choice that was closest in personality and background to the president was that of General Lewis Cass, the new secretary of war. Cass, who also entertained presidential ambitions, had been governor of Michigan as well as senior officer in the War of 1812. Levi Woodbury, who helped swing New Hampshire into the Democratic column, took the Navy Department. More questionable was the selection of Louis McLane of Delaware to be the secretary of Treasury, for McLane was friendly with the National Bank people in nearby Philadelphia. This was a strange selection by Jackson who, from his inaugural address, seemed to be hostile to the Bank charter. On the other hand, the new attorney general was Roger Taney of Maryland; he opposed the Bank. Taney, the first Catholic to serve in a cabinet, was a bid by Jackson to recognize that growing minority. The big void in the cabinet was the departure of Van Buren as minister to Britain. When the Clay-controlled Senate at first blocked the confirmation, Jackson warned, "In killing a Minister, they may have made a President."

The eventual exit of his chief lieutenant to London was more than compensated, however, by the rising influence of the "Kitchen Cabinet." The

Kitchen Cabinet did much more than privately advise Jackson—they served to advance his cause publicly. Never before had a public relations operation been run out of the White House. The most prominent member of this "Cabinet" was Francis Preston Blair, who lived across the street from the White House. Blair, whose influential family had forged political connections from Maryland to Missouri, published the national newspaper *The Washington Globe*, which was a mouthpiece for Jackson's policies. Blair, an editor by profession, occasionally drafted speeches for the president. Of more direct help to Jackson was the writing talent of Amos Kendall. Kendall, though, was more than Jackson's speechwriter—he was an alter ego. He was to Andrew Jackson what Harry Hopkins would be later to Franklin Roosevelt: a self-effacing courtier totally dedicated to serving his master.

The comparison to Hopkins extends even to the state of his health, which was perpetually ailing. The long hours in a day expanded in the service of Jackson were, if not the cause, certainly no cure for Kendall's apparent pain and suffering. Only in his forties at the time of the Jackson administration, Kendall appeared twenty years older with his premature white hair, sallow complexion, and stooped posture.

Although the spectral figure seldom appeared in public, most of Jackson's important state papers were drafted by "this twilight personage," as Harriet Martineau, the English author visiting this country, described him. "He is supposed to be the moving spring of the whole administration," Martineau added, "the thinker, the planner and doer . . . work is done of goblin extent and goblin speed which makes men look about them in superstitious wonder . . . he unites with great talent for silence a splendid audacity."

In general, the newly reconstituted Jackson cabinet favored continuation of the National Bank. The exception, of course, was Attorney General Roger Taney. In the "Kitchen Cabinet," Kendall was a fanatic on the subject, which was curious, considering that he was an Easterner and as a young man been a tutor to the family of Henry Clay, the foremost political advocate of the Bank. Born in Massachusetts and educated at Dartmouth, Kendall moved to Kentucky after completing his law studies. His first job there was with the Clays. Not only did he make the West his home, he also adopted Western politics with the vengeance of a convert. He gradually came to distrust and even despise the commercial East from which he had sprung.

It was Henry Clay, more than anyone else, who brought the Bank issue to a head. Clay was a Westerner, but first he was a nationalist who, for constitutional reasons, supported the Bank as a major instrument to consolidate federal power. Yet more significant were his political reasons. Clay saw in the renewal of the Bank charter a handy weapon with which to club Jackson to death politically.

The shake-up in the cabinet convinced Clay that Jackson, not Calhoun, would be the nominee of the Democratic Party in 1832. In December 1831,

Clay maneuvered to get himself the presidential nomination in his newly formed National Republican, or "Whig" Party, which held its convention in Baltimore. For his running mate he chose John Sergeant, a Philadelphia lawyer who had never held political office. The obscure Sergeant had two things to recommend him as a bright prospect for Clay: First, he was from the "Keystone State" of Pennsylvania, which had been a pivotal state in the election of Jackson four years earlier; second, he was chief counsel to the Bank, as well as a long time social companion of Nicholas Biddle.

No one could have offered a greater contrast to Andrew Jackson than Nicholas Biddle. In the prime of his manhood, Biddle was taking on an aging and ailing president whose haggard frame was racked by a constant cough resulting from a series of pulmonary hemorrhages. Biddle's languorous eyes manifested his innate aristocratic disdain, while Jackson's hawk-like eyes still gleamed with the acuity of a frontier scout.

Their backgrounds, too, were a study in comparison. Biddle, a scion of one of Philadelphia's oldest families, had studied in Europe, wrote poetry, and later edited *Portfolio*, a literary magazine of decidedly anti-democratic views. Jackson, who could not even remember the name of America's most famous author, Washington Irving, did little to conceal his contempt for culture.[3] The Eastern elite reciprocated by picturing Jackson as a jackass, which soon became the symbol of Jackson's Democratic party. "This worthy President," sniped Biddle, "thinks that because he has scalped Indians and imprisoned judges, he should have his own way with the Bank. He's mistaken." Finally, their personalities differed. Biddle was a polished financier who deftly manipulated behind the scenes. On the other hand, Jackson was a frontiersman who shot from the hip.

Yet, they both shared a strong will and stubborn conviction in the righteousness of their cause. At first glance Biddle might seem an effete example of Eastern breeding, but the world of finance had quickened his interest when, as a result of his family connections, he was made a board member of the National Bank in 1814. Biddle found in the National Bank a fertile field for his quick mind and thirst for eminence. Gradually taking control of the operations by using proxy powers to install board members friendly to his wishes, he then found a way to overcome the law that prohibited the National Bank from issuing "currency." He did this by issuing branch drafts signed by the presidents and cashiers of the Bank's branches. Actually, only the state banks could issue proper currency, but, through the forensic advocacy of the Bank's lawyer, Senator Daniel Webster, these banknotes were validated by the courts and became used as currency.

By 1832 over ten million dollars had been issued, mostly in five and ten dollar denominations. So the bank that had been founded principally as a depositor for federal revenues now had become the driving force in the commercial development of the young nation.

Andrew Jackson, however, did not share the Eastern investors' enthusiasm for the nation's new lending leviathan. His first messages as president revealed his distrust of the National Bank, and he remained non-committal on the issue of the Bank's charter, which would expire in 1836. In response to Biddle's queries he wrote, "I do not dislike your bank more than all banks, but, ever since I read the history of the South Sea Bubble, I have been afraid of all banks."[4]

In a real sense, the duel between the two men, Jackson the plantation farmer of the West and Biddle the financial wizard of the East, was a replay of the Jefferson–Hamilton conflict about the First National Bank. The safe course for Biddle would have been to pigeonhole the issue. After all, Jackson, who would be beginning his fourth and last year in office, had not yet committed himself on the re-charter question. But Biddle, who privately despised Jackson and the populist politics he championed, was persuaded by Henry Clay to force the issue into the open in the campaign year of 1832.

Clay reasoned he had everything to gain and nothing to lose by pressing for a vote to renew the charter. By his own count he figured he had just enough votes to pass the new act, though not without considerable opposition from certain legislators with rural, Southern or Western constituencies. If Jackson signed the bill, Clay would have the Bank people and Eastern money brokers indebted to him. On the other hand, if Jackson exercised the then rarely invoked power of veto, Senator Clay would have a tailor-made issue for the campaign: dramatic proof of the dictatorial style of "King Andy."

At first, Biddle was not totally convinced of Clay's strategy. He sent friends to sound out Louis McLane, the secretary of Treasury. McLane counseled against an application for recharter saying that Jackson would surely veto it. Yet eventually Clay, along with Daniel Webster, convinced Biddle that Jackson would not dare veto the application in an election year.

The application for re-charter came to the floor in the summer of 1832. There was never any doubt of its passage in the Senate, where Webster and Clay dominated with their oratory. Clay boasted, "Should Jackson veto it, I will veto him." In the House, however, anti-Bank forces led by a Jackson protégé, a young congressman from Tennessee named James Polk, made the outcome uncertain. But victory came on July 3rd, and Biddle hosted a gala dinner in Washington where both Bank supporters and Clay's backers for the presidency hailed their triumph. The celebrating congressmen and senators hated Jackson more than they loved the Bank. No wonder President Jackson would have the new Treasury building erected to block his view of the Capitol dome from the White House.

The political picture for Jackson seemed bleak. He could veto the Bank, but not without endangering his re-election. One who did not agree with that view was Attorney General Roger Taney, a bedrock Jeffersonian states-righter. He immediately wrote Jackson a legal memorandum recommending that the bill be vetoed as unconstitutional. Taney argued that the Constitution did not, in specific terms, authorize Congress to establish the National Bank.

A strict constructionist, Taney reasoned that the Bank did not meet the definition of "necessary" in the "necessary and proper" clause of the Constitution for the regulation of business.

When the president received his attorney general's memorandum, he immediately called Taney to come directly to the White House from Annapolis, where the attorney general had been arguing cases in front of the Maryland Court of Appeals. Jackson asked Taney to go over his reasons again for a veto message. To Taney, the flesh of the old warrior hung loosely on his frame, but the spirit of the sixty-four-year-old president showed no signs of sagging. The challenge to his leadership had fired the old man's defiance.

Jackson reminded Taney that others in the cabinet, particularly McLane and Woodbury, opposed a veto on constitutional grounds because it would bar him from agreeing to the re-application of the charter in 1836, when its statutory limit expired. Instead, they counselled a veto based on the reasoning that the re-application was premature and untimely. To Jackson, that sounded like waffling. He agreed with Taney that the bill should be vetoed because the whole concept of the Bank was evil. Taney was then instructed to prepare a veto message.

The scene for hammering out the language of the veto message was, perhaps, the weirdest ever occasioned in the drafting of a state document. Jackson was having his portrait painted by Ralph Earl, an itinerant portrait artist who had caught the fancy of Rachel Jackson while painting her at The Hermitage. Earl had married one of Rachel Jackson's nieces and moved to the White House to live with Jackson following his inauguration. Earl worshipped the president and felt it was his duty to paint as many portraits as he could to fulfill the rising demands for the upcoming presidential campaign. While Jackson posed in one corner of the room, Amos Kendall sat at a desk polishing up the draft language in another. Over Kendall's shoulder stood Attorney General Taney, who reminded the speechwriter of the pertinent legal points. In a third corner, another relative of Rachel Jackson, Andrew Jackson Donelson, the president's nephew by marriage and his White House Secretary by appointment, copied the completed and corrected pages of the Kendall draft for the official text of the presidential veto message.

The opening paragraph lead with the straightforward announcement "to return to the Senate, in which it originated, with my objections."

The next paragraph was the attorney general's constitutional objection, recast in Kendall's campaign rhetoric:

> The powers and privileges possessed by the existing bank are unauthorized by the constitution, subversive to the rights of states and dangerous to the liberties of people.

Then, in an egregious appeal to nativist prejudice, the message concocted the lie that American tax dollars would be lining the pockets of foreigners.

> By this Act the American Republic proposes virtually to make them a present of millions of dollars. For these gratuities to foreigners and to some of her own opulent citizens, the act secures no equivalent whatever.

The next paragraph, detailing the complicated financial structure of the Bank and its holdings, belonged to Taney. Yet the discussion of foreign holdings allowed Kendall to dangle the threat of subversion and foreign conquest:

> Is there no danger to our liberty and independence in a bank that in its nature, has so little to bind it to our country?
> Should the stock of the bank principally pass into the hands of the subjects of a foreign country, and should we unfortunately become involved in war with that country, what would be our condition?

The message then returned to the legal jargon of Taney, who cited the legislative history of the Bank and developed his interpretation that the constitutional word "necessary" means "needful," "requisite," and "essential." Again, Kendall capped the constitutional argument with political claptrap:

> So far from being necessary and proper . . . it is calculated to convert the bank of the United States into a foreign bank, to impoverish our people in a time of peace, to disseminate a foreign influence throughout every section of the Republic and in war, to endanger our independence.

In all, the speech, though fashioned in an artist's studio, was a cut-and-paste job, combining statutory description with street demagoguery. At the end, any constitutional pretext was abandoned to the cant of a campaign flyer.

> It is to be regretted that the rich and powerful too often bend the acts of government to their selfish purposes.

Kendall was sounding the trumpet of a class war, summoning the poor to overthrow the rich in language echoing Jefferson's Declaration:

> When the laws undertake to . . . grant titles, gratuities and exclusive privileges to make the rich richer and the potent more powerful, the humble members of society—the farmers, mechanics and laborers who have neither the time nor the means of securing like favors to themselves, have a right to complain of the injustice of their government.

Kendall distorted Taney's constitutional reasoning into political slogan-
eering:

> There are no necessary evils in government. Its evils exist only in abuses.
> Many of our rich men have not been content with equal protection and equal
> benefits, but have besought us to make them wider by Act of Congress.

The sentences were Kendall's salvoes launching a class war.

> We can at least take a stand against all new greats of monopolies and exclusive
> privileges, against any prostitution of government to the advancement of the
> few at the expense of the many . . .

The document was done on July 10, but the battle had just begun. Ahead
of Jackson lay both the battle to overturn the veto in Congress and the
presidential campaign in the fall. His former secretary of state worried more
about his old chief's physical survival than his political survival. On a visit
back from his ministry in London, Van Buren found his beleaguered captain
confined to bed. Jackson reached out for his lieutenant's hand with his right
hand and ran his left through his shock of white hair. "The bank, Van
Buren," Jackson whispered, "is trying to kill me, but I will kill it." Van
Buren later told his friends that "Iron Duke" was a more apt description
of the aging Jackson than "Old Hickory." Van Buren was likening Jackson
to Wellington, the leader of the Tory party in Britain whom Van Buren
met while minister in London.

If taken to the extent that Jackson had the arrogance of a ducal despot,
the Whigs in the Senate might have agreed with Van Buren. In the Senate
Daniel Webster thundered against Jackson's "arbitrary" and "mischievous"
use of the veto. "Such a universal power . . . is nothing but pure depotism.
If conceded to him, it makes him at once what Louis XIV proclaimed himself
to be when he said 'I am the State'."

The Bank charter had become the presidential campaign, and the race
had become a referendum on Andrew Jackson. In the Senate debate Thomas
Benton, a former Jackson foe, rallied Southerners and Westerners, saying,
"It was possible to be for *a* bank and for Jackson, but not for *this* bank and
Jackson."

Senator Clay then reminded Benton of the bitter words that he had used
once to denounce Jackson. A quarrel that Benton once had with Jackson
had turned into a gunfight, from which Jackson still carried a bullet. Benton
denied the precise charge and called Clay a liar. Clay then shouted "Calumny, calumny." When order was restored, Benton said stiffly, "I apologize
to the Senate for the manner in which I have spoken, but not to the Senator
from Kentucky." Clay rejoined, "To the Senate, I also offer an apology.
To the Senator from Missouri—none."

Amid such bitter tension, the Senate proceeded to vote, but could not muster the two-thirds majority needed to override the president's veto. The fight moved then from Congress to the country for the presidential campaign. The press divided pro and con. Newspapers that favored the Bank caricatured Nicholas Biddle as "Old Nick," complete with horns and tail, while those against the Bank pictured cartoons of "King Andrew I" draped in ermine robes upon a throne. Francis Preston Blair of *The Globe* naturally praised the Bank veto as "statesmanship" and Benton's impassioned defense as a "rout" and "carnage" of "the two twins," Clay and Webster. On the other hand, most of the national press and family periodicals like Philadelphia's *Saturday Evening Post* echoed Nicholas Biddle's views that the veto of the Bank Bill was "a manifesto for anarchy."

In financial terms, at least, Nicholas Biddle was not totally wrong. The National Bank, with its application for re-charter denied, died a slow death in 1836 when the president removed from it the deposit of federal revenues. The next year, the wildly speculative state banks, without a national bank to put on the financial brakes, unloosed a spate of expanded credit that incurred the Panic of 1837.

Andrew Jackson tore down the National Bank, but he built a national party that would not only sweep the country for his reelection in 1832 but also dominate American politics until the Civil War. His veto message helped rally divergent groups under the banner of the Democratic Party. Recent immigrants to the Eastern cities joined hands with the small farmers from outlying areas. Self-employed mechanics and craftsmen found common interest with the new factory workers in an expanding industrial nation. The South, like the West, distrusted the commercial East.

The Jackson veto message was a declaration of a class war. It was also a catalyst recasting the party of Jefferson that had been gradually co-opted by the establishment during the administration of James Monroe and John Quincy Adams.

Jackson's message in vetoing the application for the re-charter of the National Bank did not discuss the need for a national banking policy; nor did it analyze the merits of a national bank. It did not discuss the problem of financial speculation or weigh the arguments of soft money against hard. The message was not a financial accounting but rather a political counting of where the votes were.

It was not the secretary of Treasury, Louis McLane, who drafted this bank message but propagandist Amos Kendall, who was called "the most effective campaign writer until Horace Greely."[5] But if the style was Amos Kendall's, the sentiments were Andy Jackson's. Jackson had taken the veto dare of the Whigs and turned it back to defeat them. The box that the Bank proponents tried to put him in Jackson had overturned on top of them. Clay and the Whigs were smothered in the Electoral College, 219–49. The reelected Jackson saw himself as the champion of the underdog against the establishment and that his victory gave them hope. He undertook to carry the fight of the little people against the big interest and, by his triumph, lifted their aspirations. If in one sense the veto message was the cant of rank demagoguery, it was also a credo of raw democracy.

NOTES

1. When President Jackson was awarded an honorary degree at Harvard, well-wishers, aware of his unlettered reputation in Eastern circles, urged him to throw them a little Latin. He replied to their glee, "Sine qua non" and "E Pluribus unum." John Quincy Adams, his disgruntled predecessor, was outraged that his Alma Mater should give Jackson a degree and refused to attend the ceremonies saying, "As myself an affectionate child of our Alma Mater, I would not be present to witness her disgrace in conferring her highest literary honors upon a barbarian who could not write a sentence of grammar and hardly spell his own name."

2. The aristocratic and acerbic John Randolph of Virginia, who hated Jackson, said of the appointment of Livingston, "the most contemptible and degraded of beings, whom no human ought to touch unless with a pair of tongs."

3. Jackson, later in retirement, wrote Van Buren that "the Minister to Spain, that writer, ought to be replaced." He could not even recall the name of America's first great literary figure.

4. Speculative investment in a South Pacific venture had rocked the Bank of England in the eighteenth century.

5. *Anecdotes of Public Men* by John W. Forney. (1970.) New York: DeCapo Press.

5

Polk's Inaugural: Action as Eloquence

> It is confidently believed that our system may be safely extended to the utmost bounds of our territorial limits, and that as it shall be extended the bonds of our union, far from being weakened, will become stronger.

"Who is James K. Polk?" was the Whig's cry when he was chosen by the Democratic Convention in 1844. But Henry Clay, the Whig nominee, did not gloat when he heard the news from his son. His son made him guess the surprise choice of the Democrats. Clay asked, "Is it Van?" (Van Buren). "No," said the son. "Cass, then?" "No," smiled the son. "Not John Calhoun," countered Clay. His son thought his famous father would be delighted with the selection of the little-known Polk. But Clay muttered softly, "I'm beaten again." Clay, whose most quoted line is "I'd rather be right than be President," was right.

Clay was shrewder than the prevailing wisdom. Polk might have been an unfamiliar figure to the country at large, but he was not unknown by the Washington scene. A loyal Jackson lieutenant in the House, he built a following that later won him the speakership, a position more powerful than it is today. Interestingly, he was the youngest ever to be elected to the speakership, with the exception of Clay himself.

What Polk lacked in personality he made up in perseverance. What he lacked in charisma he made up in craft. In contrast to the high living, hard drinking, card playing Clay, Polk was an abstemious Calvinist who only found happiness in long hours of hard work. In his loner style, puritan disciplines, and pious righteousness, he was not unlike a latter-day Jimmy Carter.

Although he was equally as ambitious as Clay, Polk did not allow himself to dwell on the fantasy of being elected president. He did think that he had a chance to be named the vice presidential choice. In 1840, as governor of Tennessee, he had written to President Martin Van Buren suggesting himself for the second spot on the ticket. To Polk, the slating of a Tennessean with Van Buren from New York made sense. After all, Van Buren had been the running mate with the Tennessean Andrew Jackson in 1832, and Polk, who was nicknamed "Young Hickory," was a protégé of the still popular Jackson. To position himself for the vice presidency, Polk had run for governor in Tennessee, riding horseback over 1,300 miles across the state. Polk's bid, however, was spurned, and he always felt the Albany Regency—the Van Buren junta that controlled New York politics—was responsible. It was just as well because the incumbent Van Buren was rolled over by General William Henry Harrison.

The Whigs had learned their lessons from Jackson's success. They ran their own general complete with a catchy slogan—"Tippecanoe and Tyler too"—as a counterpoint to the foppish Van Buren, derisively nicknamed "Van, the dandy magician." They fashioned "Tippecanoe" Harrison as a log cabin dweller who would rather drink hard cider than brandy, and portable cabins with cider by the keg were rolled on wagons to campaign rallies. Since Harrison was not even born in a log cabin but in Berkley, one of the palatial mansions of Virginia, it was a piece of spectacular public relations that every modern image-maker of Madison Avenue would envy.

The only problem for the Whigs was that the aged general died after a week in office. Some say it was the strain of the three-hour inaugural address, the longest in history.

So John Tyler, called "The Accidental President," was now the president. Tyler, a Virginian, had been put on the ticket to balance Harrison, who was nominally from Ohio. Yet Tyler, in his politics, was closer to Southern Democrats like John Calhoun than to national Whigs like Henry Clay and Daniel Webster.

A disaster then befell the Tyler administration that would scramble the political situation for 1844, thus making the nomination of a "dark horse" like Polk possible. On a gala excursion down the Potomac on February 28, 1844, a new frigate, the U.S.S. *Princeton*, carried President Tyler, the cabinet, senators, diplomatic ministers, and their ladies on hand. The purpose of the cruise was to inaugurate the new cannon called the "Peacemaker." The gun, however, exploded, killing Secretary of State Abel P. Upshur, Secretary of the Navy John Gilmer, and a New York state senator. The daughter of the slain state senator, the beautiful Julia Gardner, a one-time actress, back-pedaled thirty feet in a dramatic swoon and fell into the arms of the widowed president. Shortly thereafter, he made her the First Lady.

arms of the widowed president. Shortly thereafter, he made her the First Lady.

The political loss of two key cabinet members made it necessary for Tyler to revamp his cabinet. He made John Calhoun his secretary of state, succeeding Upshur, and Southern Democrats, friendly to Calhoun's thinking, now filled the other slots, to the exclusion of all Whigs. Tyler now headed a totally Southern Democratic administration.

Tyler appointed Calhoun in the hope that he could engineer Tyler's nomination as the Democratic candidate in 1844. The president knew that the slave-holding Calhoun was anxious to bring the independent republic of Texas into the Union to counter the new free states being established in Michigan and Wisconsin.

What Tyler did not perceive was that Calhoun wanted to be president himself and that he had accepted Tyler's cabinet offer at the state department because it was the best forum in which to fulfill his own ambitions. Calhoun wanted to bring into the Union the independent Republic of Texas. He knew, however, that the annexation of Texas would inflame anti-slave sentiment in the North. Therefore, he joined his pleas for Texas with a claim to the disputed territory of Oregon. Calhoun saw himself as a blacksmith forging the linkage between the South and West—a coalition of expansionist sentiment that would propel him to the presidency.

In 1844 "expansionism" was firing the imagination of Americans with romantic visions of a United States stretching from Cuba to California. If juicy Texas was a fruit already on the ground waiting to be picked up, sweet Oregon seemed ready for plucking. And golden California was just about to ripen, not to mention tropical Cuba, only an arm's length from Florida.

But the sunny prospects for American expansion darkened the hopes of the two frontrunners for the presidency in 1844: Clay on the Whig ticket and ex-president Van Buren on the Democratic ticket. A year earlier the two rivals had concluded a secret deal to keep the slavery expansion issue out of national politics by postponing the annexation of Texas. By straddling the issue, both Clay and Van Buren hoped their Northern and Southern followers would stay in line.

On the eve of both conventions, the two leading candidates released letters stating their opposition to "the immediate annexation of Texas." As expected, Clay was nominated by the Whigs. But under the Democratic Convention rules, Van Buren faced the great hurdle of winning not a majority but two-thirds of the delegate votes. Although Van Buren led on the first ballot with 146, a majority of the 266 votes, he was still short of the 177 needed. Other favorite candidates were Lewis Cass of Michigan, Cave Johnson of Tennessee, James Buchanan of Pennsylvania, and, of course, John C. Calhoun of South Carolina.

James Polk, who was not even mentioned for president in the first seven ballots, was vying for a vice presidential nomination. His hopes were based on a deadlocked convention. Again, he had to deal with the "Albany Regency," which four years before had turned him down. The operative plan was to put forth the New Yorker Silas Wright for the presidency in case Van Buren could not put together the necessary two-thirds approval. Polk, in return for Tennessee's support and presumably Jackson's, would then be Wright's running mate.

Two things then happened to propel Polk from the standby candidate for vice president to the compromise choice for president. First, it turned out that Silas Wright did not want to be president. Second, the aging Andrew Jackson in Hermitage came out for Polk, whom he called "his boy." Jackson was a fervent annexionist and close friend of the Texas Republic president Sam Houston, who served with him in the War of 1812. When his old lieutenant and successor Van Buren stalled on the Texas issue, Jackson gave up on him: "Van has done himself in." To Polk's wife, Jackson said, "Child, I'm going to make Jamie the President if it is the last thing I do."

On the ninth ballot Polk won the nomination. He had been proposed to the Baltimore Convention by historian George Bancroft, who was a delegate from Massachusetts. Bancroft, though a New Englander, was close to Jackson and had written, at Jackson's suggestion, a campaign biography about Polk to be released before the convention.

James Polk was the first "dark horse" to be nominated for the presidency, but he was not an unknown horse. Although he had been a respected politician in Democratic circles, he had lost national standing in 1843 when he was defeated for reelection as governor of Tennessee. Yet Polk in 1844 had come back to be his party's nominee.

Polk may have lacked the sleeker line of Clay, but he positioned himself to run with the wind of expansionist sentiment. At the Baltimore convention, he fashioned an expansionist platform plank on both Texas and Oregon.

> That our title to the whole of the country of Oregon is clear and unquestionable, that no portion of the same ought to be ceded to England or any other power; and the re-occupation of Oregon and the re-annexation of Texas at the earliest practicable period are great American measures, which this convention recommends to the cordial support of the Democracy of the Union.

The syllable "re" prefixed to "occupation" and "annexation" was designed to counter attacks to outright aggression by anti-slave critics. In other words, the nation was only resuming possession of what once had been rightfully theirs anyway.

In the fall campaign, Polk rode hard on the expansionist issue while Clay backpedaled. If Clay was the better orator, Polk was superior at gut fighting. Polk would end his stump speeches with the campaign slogan of "54°40′ or Fight"—a claim that would grab Oregon territory all the way up to the Alaskan panhandle. Even then Polk only barely eked out a victory. In fact, Clay would have carried New York and the presidency but for the candidacy of a third-party nominee, James Birney, whose anti-slave ticket took 60,000 Whig votes away from Clay in that crucial state.

In late January of 1845, James Polk began his trip to Washington from Columbia, Tennessee. "Young Hickory" left with the blessing of "Old Hickory" in his ears. Jackson, upon hearing the news of Polk's election by the Electoral College, had thanked God that "He had permitted him to live long enough to see the country in safe hands." On the journey, Polk rode horseback to the Ohio River in Kentucky to catch a steamboat, then finished his trip to Washington on a newly laid railroad.

At age 49, Polk was the nation's 11th President and also the youngest. But he looked about ten years older. His original "Black Irish" looks had paled. His hair was prematurely white and his complexion sallow. At five feet eight inches he was not a commanding figure as he took the oath of office from Chief Justice Roger Taney, who Van Buren had appointed to the Supreme Court.

The Polks were welcomed about as warmly to the social fold of the Washington community as the Carters were in 1977. The God-fearing Polks frowned on frivolity and condemned both dancing and drinking. Fortunately for the more thirsty of Polk's Democratic partisans, the still-active but long-widowed Dolly Madison made her Octagon House behind the White House a "Wet House," where guests to the Executive Mansion could repair for stronger refreshment. Like Rosalyn Carter, Sarah Childress Polk was a close political confidant of her husband, the president. As the first president's wife to be a college graduate, Sarah Polk acted as her husband's secretary and shared his views as a strong nationalist and stern Calvinist.

On the bright, windy March day, Polk delivered his inaugural address atop the Capitol steps. In a speech with few perorations, he concentrated on priorities. Only in the beginning did Polk, a deeply religious man, leave concerns for spiritual heights.

> In assuming responsibilities as vast I fervently invoke the aid of that Almighty Ruler of the universe in whose hands are the destinies of nations and of men guard this heaven-favored land against the mischiefs which without His guidance might arise from a public policy. With a firm reliance upon the wisdom of Omnipotence to sustain and direct me in the path of duty which I am appointed to pursue, I stand in the presence of this assembled multitude of my countrymen to take upon myself the solemn obligation to the best of my ability to preserve, protect and defend the Constitution of the United States.

Then, following a dry analysis of federal-state relationships under the Constitution, Polk soared into another invocation by echoing the salute of his temporal deity, Andrew Jackson.

> Every lover of this country must shudder at the possibility of its dissolution and will be ready to adopt the patriot sentiment, "Our Federal Union, it must be preserved."

The rest of this comparatively brief inaugural was a recital of Polk's four-starred political agenda. First, he would pursue a Jacksonian monetary policy of no National Bank and no national debt.

> We need no national banks or other extraneous institutions planted around the Government to control or strengthen it in opposition to the will of its authors. Experience has taught us how unnecessary they are as auxiliaries of the public authority—how impotent for good and how powerful for mischief.
>   Ours was intended to be plain and frugal government, and I shall regard it to be my duty to recommend to Congress and, as far as the Executive is concerned, to enforce by all means within my power to the strictest economy in the expenditure of public money which may be compatible with the public interests. A national debt has become almost an institution of European monarchy . . . incompatible with the ends for which our Republican government was instituted.

Just as Polk's first domestic plank denounced the Clay policy of a national bank, the second opposed the Whig policy of higher tariffs.

> I have also declared my opinion to be "in favor of a tariff for revenue" and that "in adjusting the details of such a tariff, I have sanctioned such moderate discriminating duties as would produce the amount of revenue needed, and at the same time, afford reasonable incidental protection to our home industry" and that I was "opposed to a tariff for protection merely and not for revenue."

After nailing down his policies on the home front, Polk proceeded to lay the framework for his foreign policy: Texas and Oregon. Texas already had been creeping into the back door of the United States. A few days earlier, the outgoing president, Tyler, had maneuvered around the two-thirds vote requirement needed for treaty ratification. To outflank the Clay-controlled Senate, Tyler had his loyalists introduce a joint resolution to accept Texas. Since a joint resolution required only a majority, it passed easily, although its constitutional validity was uncertain.

In this third provision of his Inaugural, Polk vowed to make the Texas resolution reality.

> The Republic of Texas has made known her desire to come into our Union to form a part of our Confederacy and enjoy with us the blessings of liberty

secured and guaranteed by our Country. Texas was once part of our country—was unwisely ceded away to a foreign power—is now independent, and possesses an undoubted right . . . to merge her sovereignties as two separate and independent states in ours. I congratulate my fellow citizens on the entire restoration of the credit of the general government of the Union. . . .

He then introduced the theme of his inaugural.

It is confidently believed that our system may be safely extended, to the utmost bounds of our territorial limits, and that as it shall be extended the bonds of our Union, so far from being weakened, will become stronger.

In his fourth and final plank, Polk resumed his expansionist theme again, moving northwest from Texas to Oregon.

Nor will it become in a less degree my duty to assert and maintain by all institutional means the right of the United States to that portion of a territory which lies beyond the Rocky Mountains. Our title to the country of the Oregon is clear and unquestionable, and already are our people preparing to perfect that title by occupying it with their wives and children.

Polk then closed his speech, which was more of an agenda than an address, with another spiritual supplication "to that Divine Being who has watched over and protected our beloved country" to continue "His generous benedictions upon us, that we may continue to be a prosperous and happy people."

Polk, who could be fiery on the campaign stump, did not inflame his audience of over one thousand well-wishers. In his lawyer-like presentation of constitutional theory and international claims, the only emotion he betrayed was in his smoldering dark eyes.

Polk was probably the most secretive president until Richard Nixon. Besides his wife, only Cave Johnson, a lifelong friend from his early political days in Tennessee, was ever privy to any of his plans. Like Nixon, he found joy only in toil. He had been an exemplary student, winning honors in his study of law at the University of North Carolina, just as Nixon had done at Duke. And like Nixon, who linked himself to Dwight Eisenhower, Polk, too, attached his star to a popular hero: General Andrew Jackson. If the Californian a century later became known as "Tricky Dick," the Tennessean was called "Mendacious Polk." He not only kept his cards close to his vest, but he was not above springing a joker from his sleeve from time to time.

As a compromise candidate, Polk was constrained to select his cabinet with great care, balancing the various segments of the Democratic Party. James Buchanan, a rival candidate from Pennsylvania, became secretary of state; Robert Walker of Mississippi became secretary of Treasury; and William Marcy, who authored the political axiom "To the victors belong the spoils," was named secretary of war. Marcy was Polk's payoff to New York, a choice that did not totally satisfy the disgruntled ex-president Van Buren. Two personal choices by Polk included his crony Cave Johnson as postmaster-general as well as political counsellor and George Bancroft as secretary of the Navy. As the administration's resident intellectual, Bancroft would sometimes volunteer his speechwriting skills to Polk.

Buchanan and Marcy may have expected to dominate Polk, but the president soon made it clear that he alone would call the signals. In the first month of the administration, Mexico broke off diplomatic relations. Secretary of State Buchanan proposed that a circular note be sent to the diplomatic corps disclaiming any America intention of dismembering Mexico or acquiring New Mexico or California. Buchanan was afraid that Mexico, which angrily resented American annexation of Texas, would invite Britain to side with her in an eruption of hostilities. Britain, which was still wooing Texas as a potential ally and trading partner, had reason to oppose America because it was still making its inflated claims concerning the British territory of Oregon.

Polk dismissed the Buchanan proposal. He did not believe Mexico would begin a war, and he was not particularly worried if it did. Instead, he put into action his "stick and carrot" approach to force Mexico to the bargaining table. His stick was General Zachary Taylor, who marched with troops into Texas, and his carrot was John Slidell, who was dispatched to Mexico City with a checkbook.

Publicly, Polk demanded that the Rio Grande and not the Nueces River be named the Texas boundary line; he also insisted that millions of dollars be paid for the property damage suffered by American citizens living in Mexico during a succession of turbulent government overthrows. Privately, Polk wanted more. He coveted Mexico and, particularly, California. He was ready to pay for that territory, and the Mexican government could use the purchase money to satisfy our citizens' claims.

A more stable Mexican government might have been willing to negotiate the border dispute and property claims in a settlement reasonable and fair to both sides. In Mexico's eyes, however, Texas was still its territory, and the United States, by accepting Texas's invitation to annex it, was violating its sacred honor. On such a point of national pride, the Mexican president, José Joaquin Herrera—of shaky tenure—could not afford to be seen yielding to a gringo grab. So, the Slidell mission to Mexico City failed.

It was then only a matter of time before the presence of U.S. troops in the disputed Texas–Mexico border would lead to open hostilities. The unanswered question in case of war was the British role. Britain was not happy when Texas petitioned, for the second time, to be annexed by the United States. The first time was in the summer of 1844, when Clay and the Whigs, with aid from a few Northern Democrats, had managed to beat back annexation—only to have Tyler and Calhoun reopen annexation talks with the resolution next March, just before president–elect Polk was sworn in. It was in Great Britain's interest to have the newly formed republic under Sam Houston remain an independent nation. Britain offered to Texas important trading ties with guarantees for her security. Although Polk believed the British would begrudgingly accept America's annexation of Texas, he knew they would never agree to the 54°40′ Oregon territory.

It was necessary to settle the Oregon dispute with Britain before the war with Mexico erupted. The problem was that Polk had locked himself into the 54°40′ claim in both his party convention plank and his inaugural address. He had run as an expansionist, and now expansion fever was running high. A journalist named John O'Sullivan, in the *United States Magazine and Democratic Review*, had coined the phrase "Manifest Destiny," which epitomized to Americans their God–given right to all of North America.

Polk's settlement of the Oregon issue was a model of diplomatic duplicity. Privately, he instructed Secretary of State Buchanan to agree to the 49° parallel that the Tyler administration had offered earlier. But when that was rejected, he had George Bancroft help him draft for him the presidential message to Congress for December 2, 1845. In it Polk said "that the British pretensions of title could not be maintained to any of the Oregon territory upon any principle of public law recognized by nations."

When one timid Congressman told the president that his bold message could lead to war with Great Britain, the president replied that "the only way to treat John Bull was to look him straight in the eye: . . . that if Congress faltered or hesitated in their course, John Bull would immediately become arrogant and more grasping in his demand."

It was an early case of diplomatic brinksmanship, and it worked, at least to the extent of making Britain agree to the 49° border between the United States and British Columbia in Canada. But if the British were backing down, so was Polk, who had campaigned on "54°40′ or Fight." Again, Polk was at his deft best. He put the ball directly in Congress's court. He arranged for the British offer to settle the boundary dispute at the 49° to go directly to the Senate *before* he accepted it. In other words, he wanted to be in the position of considering the Senate's disposition of the treaty rather to give the Senate the chance to pick apart his recommendation. The Senate advised acceptance, and on June 14, 1846, the Oregon Treaty was signed. The 49° parallel was made the boundary, although Britain kept Vancouver Island and retained navigation rights in the Columbia River. Senator Thomas Benton, who agreed to the treaty, nevertheless shook his head and his wryly commented on all the jingoistic oratory that had gone on under the spell of "Manifest Destiny": "Oh mountain, that was delivered a mouse," Benton exclaimed, "thy name shall henceforth be 'Fifty four Forty'."

The final ratification of the treaty with Britain came none too soon: war

with Mexico had already begun. Polk had presented his war message to
Congress on May 11, 1846.

At first, key members of his cabinet opposed the idea of war. Secretary
of State James Buchanan and Secretary of Navy George Bancroft both felt
that Mexico should fire the first shot. Polk, however, had too long been
frustrated by his failure to bring Mexico to the bargaining table. His minister
to Mexico, John Slidell, had returned empty handed. Now that the British
threat in the Northwest had been dispatched with the new agreement,
California beckoned like a beautiful señorita, lonely and exposed.

Incredibly, on the night of the very day that the cabinet met to discuss
the Polk war proposal, dispatches arrived from General Zachary Taylor
reporting that Mexican forces had crossed the Rio Grande and attacked his
troops, killing sixteen of them. It was the "Pearl Harbor" that Polk, the
devout Presbyterian, had been hoping for and, perhaps, even praying for.

The next day, which was a Sunday, the pious Polk broke the Sabbath to
work with Bancroft on his war message to Congress, He wrote in his diary,
"I regretted the necessity which had existed to make it necessary for me to
spend the Sabbath in the manner I have."

The next day Congress heard Polk's message. "The cup of forbearance
has been exhausted," declared the president. "After reiterated menaces Mexico has passed the boundary of the United States, has invaded our territory
and shed American blood upon the American soil." As secretary of state,
Buchanan wanted to assure Britain that the intent of the message was only
to guarantee American property and rights and not to acquire California,
but Polk had a stop put to the covering diplomatic note.

In a burst of patriotic fervor, Congress endorsed the measure 40 to 2 in
the Senate and 174 to 14 in the House, but it was not long before the Whigs
found their voices. One freshman Whig named Abraham Lincoln, from
Illinois, made his famous but futile "spot" resolution demanding to know
the exact spot on which American blood had been shed. In New England,
Henry David Thoreau of Walden Pond, in protest to the war, refused to
pay his poll taxes and went to jail for a day. His resistance would result in
his provocative "Essay on Civil Disobedience." James Russell Lowell, another writer who opposed the war, wrote in his *Bigelow Papers*:

> They just want this California so's to lug new slave-states in to abuse ye and
> scorn ye and to plunder ye like sin.

Senator Tom Corwin, a Whig from Ohio, summed up the opinions of
the war protestors when he said:

> If I were a Mexican, I would tell you "Have you not room in your own
> country to bury your dead men? If you come in mine, we will greet you with
> bloody hands and welcome you to hospitable graves!"

If the war was unpopular with Northern Whigs, it was supported enthusiastically in the West. They did not buy the Eastern intellectuals' contention that Mexico was an innocent victim. What passed for government in Mexico was a state of anarchy where successive dictatorial chieftains evinced little interest in government except for cleaning out the state treasury. American citizens in Mexico were executed without trial, their property confiscated by government hooligans. Mexico had broken off negotiations with the Polk administration because it refused to recognize that the democratic population of Texas had a right to secede.

Actually, the state of anarchy in Mexico City encouraged dissolution of its remote parts. A series of junta leaders could not begin to administer the outlying provinces such as Texas or California, especially while fighting off coups d'états from rival factions in their own capitol. Polk sensed this opportunity and struck, signing the bill and finally completing the annexation of Texas on December 28, 1845. Then, when negotiations in Mexico City for purchase went sour, he began to send out feelers to California. In March he dispatched Captain John C. Fremont, the son-in-law of Senator Thomas Benton, on an expedition to California. The "Pathfinder of the West" declared the Bear Flag Revolution on June 14, 1846, taking possession of Sonoma as soon as he received word that the United States had declared war against Mexico. In short order, Commodore John Drake Sloan captured Monterey, the Mexican provincial capital of California, and declared California annexed to the United States.

In the Rio Grande valley, the war moved more slowly. The march of "Old Rough and Ready" Zachary Taylor was slowed by the trickle of reinforcements and supplies sent from Washington. Polk was jealous of the Whig general, who was increasingly criticizing him to the press, apparently positioning himself for a presidential race in 1848.

Polk's solution was to dispatch troops under a West Point general named Winfield Scott by boat to Veracruz, which lay in easy striking distance of Mexico City. On September 17, 1847, General Scott entered the "Halls of Montezuma" in Mexico City.

On Scott's heels Polk sent a foreign service officer, Nicholas Trist, to negotiate a peace. The terms under the Treaty of Guadalupe Hidalgo—February 2, 1848—secured the Rio Grande boundary with Texas and gained for the United States the territory of New Mexico and the California peninsula as far south as San Diego. In the agreement, the United States assumed the claims of those American cities whose property had been damaged and paid to the Treasury of New Mexico $15 million dollars to boot (or about three-fifths the amount Polk had originally instructed John Slidell to offer for those territories).

Polk rewarded General Scott and foreign service officer Trist, the victors of both battle and conference table, in a curious way: he relieved Scott of his general's command and dismissed Trist from the State Department.

Yet, despite the unloving idiosyncracies of this tight-lipped president, Polk stands as one of our most successful presidents. Shortly after his inaugural address, he confided to George Bancroft, his intellectual in residence and occasional presidential speechwriter, his four point administration program: annex Texas, settle Oregon, lower the tariff, and make the federal Treasury independent.

With regard to the last two, with the help of Secretary of Treasury Robert Walker, Polk succeeded in putting a lower tariff through the Congress and restored the Jackson bank policy in 1848 by repealing the Whig measures of the previous administration. He then joined the United States with Great Britain, which had repealed the Corn Laws in 1846, in the world free trade movement, and he reestablished the independent treasury system.

In his foreign policy, President Polk brought under the Stars and Stripes more territory than anyone else in the nation's history—including Thomas Jefferson with the Louisiana Purchase. His critics may call him "Polk the Mendacious," but he was also "Polk the Audacious."

Through a combination of deceit and daring, Polk earned the credit as the first president to master the art of realpolitik.

Other presidents may have had a more winning personality, but it was Polk's programs that won him success. What he lacked in style was more than made up by the substance of his accomplishments. He died a month after he left the White House, overworked in body and underappreciated in achievement. Yet Polk could take pride that he was the only president who actually delivered what he promised in his inaugural address. It was his actions that were eloquent.

6

The Gettysburg Address: The Great American Poem

We here highly resolve that those dead shall not have died in vain; that this nation, under God, shall have a new birth of freedom and that government of the people, by the people and for the people shall not perish from the earth.

In the middle of November 1863, thousands of men and women piled into the little town of Gettysburg to attend what they expected to be the finest speech they would ever hear in their lifetime. The orator for the occasion was America's most celebrated speaker, and they expected nothing less.

Yet they would leave the dedication grounds on that afternoon of November 19 disappointed. Little did they realize that they actually did witness not only the most memorable speech in their lifetime but in all history.

The orator who failed to meet the advance notice was not Abraham Lincoln but Edward Everett, the foremost platform artist of the day. The appearance of the president at the commemoration was only an afterthought. The only reason President Lincoln was asked to speak was that it would have been a breach of protocol not to ask the president of the United States to say a few words once he had already accepted the invitation to attend the dedication.

His decision to come to Gettysburg took the event's planners by surprise. President Lincoln rarely traveled outside Washington, except to consult with generals or to inspect troops on a battlefield. In fact, if Mrs. Lincoln had prevailed, the president would never have gone to Gettysburg since she had tearfully begged her husband to stay at the bedside of their sick son, Tad.

But if nothing momentous was expected from the president beyond the brief platitudes befitting the Chief of State in an ancillary role, Lincoln himself, from the day of the Gettysburg victory four-and-a-half months earlier, saw the occasion as an opportunity for this most profound message since his inauguration. When news of the Union victory at Gettysburg arrived in Washington, crowds gathered in front of the White House on July 6 to celebrate. President Lincoln welcomed the well-wishers but declined to say anything more than a few words.

> What has it been—eighty odd years—since on the Fourth of July for the first time in the history of the world a nation by its representatives assembled and declared as a self-evident truth that "all men are created equal" . . . Gentlemen, this is a glorious theme, and the occasion for a speech but I am not prepared to make one worthy of the occasion.

Lincoln made a vow to himself to make an address at another time telling what was unique about America. That time was the Gettysburg Battlefield dedication, and he distilled in that two-minute message a lifetime of his political thinking about the meaning of America.

The idea of a Gettysburg Battlefield cemetery dedication was borne of necessity. The thousands of bodies of the Union soldiers could not be shipped back to their native states for burial. On the first day of fighting alone, more than 17,000 men on both sides died. By the end of three days of fighting, the piles of strewn corpses amassed—often limbless, headless, and shattered beyond recognition. From Gettysburg went out the call for volunteers who would sort through this pitiful human debris and begin the painful task of boxing them for rail transport back to their homes. After a few weeks, however, the mountain of corpses to process, together with the stench of the summer heat's decay, proved too overwhelming.

The decision was then made to bury them at their field of sacrifice. Burial grounds already existed at Cemetery Hill, a place where the most intense fighting occurred, and it seemed a simple matter to bury the dead in the adjacent fields. From such exigency emerged the idea of a National Cemetery. When David Wills, who had headed the small volunteer burying force, said he would purchase some land, the first groundwork was laid for establishing a National Cemetery, a sacred memorial to those soldiers of the eighteen Union states who had participated in the battle. In Washington, President Lincoln was informed of these plans and approved.

By mid-August Wills had bought seventeen acres for $2,475.87 and plans for a national commemoration service were begun.[1] A new cemetery had to be dedicated formally, and such a ceremony demanded a eulogy for the fallen soldiers. The name of only one speaker suggested itself as worthy of such an august occasion: Edward Everett.

Edward Everett was more than a politician—he was a personage whose very presence gave stature to committees, lent weight to fund-raising appeals, and brought distinction to banquet halls. His public career as congressman from Massachusetts, senator, governor, minister to Britain, and secretary of state glowed with the eminence of a statesman; and it was undimmed by his unsuccessful campaign for the vice presidency in 1860.[2] Perhaps even more renowned was his academic career as a classics scholar, which reached its zenith when he became president of Harvard College, the nation's most prestigious institution. He was, in short, the culmination of the best breeding and schooling the Eastern establishment could offer, and every feature from his silken white hair, florid complexion, and handsome square face attested to the eminence of his rank and station.

If Doctor Edward Everett was a vision to behold on the podium, it was his voice that lifted his audiences' hearts—a mellifluous intonation shaped by classical rhetoric and trained in forensic dramatics. He knew how to lift and lower his inflection and when to roar with indignation or whisper in a sigh. Each chance in vocal modulation, each pause for a dramatic attention, and each gesture for theatrical effect was noted carefully on his text as on an actor's script and rehearsed until perfect in execution. So smooth was his style that even his conjurer's tricks—pulling out a silk white handkerchief to suggest the waving of a flag or jingling some coins in his pocket to connote the ringing of bells—not only enlivened but enhanced his performance. In his celebrated lecture on George Washington, which raised close to $100,000 for the good ladies of Mount Vernon, he even nudged a glass of water as he sipped so that "the crystal purity of Washington's character" was witnessed in the spilt droplet.

On September 23 David Wills, the head of the planning committee, tendered the invitation to Doctor Everett to be the speaker at the dedication ceremonies to take place in exactly a month. Even though Everett was the most heavily booked speaker in the nation, the committee thought the importance of the occasion would compel him to accept. The hopes of the committee hinged on his assent because, in their unanimous selection, there was no second choice.

Everett replied that he could not speak on October 23 because one month was scarcely time for adequate preparation. "I cannot safely name an earlier time," wrote Everett, "than the 19th of November. Should a postponement of the day first proposed be admissible, it would give me great pleasure to accept the invitation."

With the speaker and the date set, the Wills Committee proceeded with planning the ceremonies for the dedication of the National Cemetery at Gettysburg. As a matter of protocol, they mailed invitations to various government and military officials. To the astonishment of the planning committee, President Lincoln accepted! If the president was going to attend, he would have to be asked to participate. Yet remarks from a president, often addicted to jocular ramblings, could detract attention not only from

Everett but also from the solemnity of the occasion. David Wills now had a delicate task before him. In his letter of November 2 asking Lincoln to say "a few appropriate remarks," he stressed that the president's message be completely serious in tone suitable in nature to "kindle anew in the breasts of the comrades of these brave dead" a confidence that their sacrifices "are not forgotten by those highest in authority."

In the same mail, Wills sent a second more personal letter: "As the hotels in our town will be crowded . . . I write to invite you to stop with me— Governor Curtin (of Pennsylvania) and Honorable Edward Everett will be my guests at the time and if you come, you will please join them at my house."

Lincoln now had two weeks in which to prepare his remarks, in contrast to Everett who asked for two months. Yet what Lincoln would say, he had been preparing his whole life.

With the exception of the Bible, the first book to etch itself on Lincoln's mind was Mason Weem's *Life of Washington*. The biography, despite its "cherry tree" fable and other historical deficiencies, was inspirational. Like a story from the Bible, the boy read and reread this parable of patriotism. Years later Lincoln said about reading the book:

> I remember all the accounts there given of the battle fields and struggles for the liberties of the country, and none fixed themselves upon my imagination so deeply as the struggle at Trenton, New Jersey. The crossing of the river, the contest with the Hessians, the great hardships endured at that time, all fixed themselves on my memory more than any single Revolutionary event. I recollect thinking then, boy even though I was, that there must have been something more than common that these men struggled for.

Only a few books came into the possession of this backwoods lad, and those he would cherish as secret friends, stealing away from farm chores to find companionship on a quiet pasture hill or sneaking down the cabin ladder at night to reacquaint himself with favorite passages by the light of a dying fire. Certain sentences and words would capture him almost in a magic spell, and as his eyes alighted on those lines, his lips would roll the words once in his mouth.

One of these books, which Lincoln read at the age of twelve, was Grimshaw's *History of the United States*. The account begins with the discovery of America and the development of the colonies, climaxes at the Revolution, and ends with the War of 1812, which secured the independence of the new nation. The book, which denounced slavery, closed with this last paragraph.

> Let us not only declare by words but demonstrate by actions that "all men are created equal; that they are endowed by their creator, with the same inalienable rights; that among these are life, liberty and the pursuit of happiness.

"My mind," Lincoln once said, "is like a piece of steel—very hard to scratch anything on it, almost impossible after your get it there to rub it out."

One thing he never forgot happened when, as a young man, he worked on a Mississippi flatboat. Landing in New Orleans, Lincoln saw the pitiful sight of a mulatto slave girl paraded and pinched by prospective buyers as she was auctioned off. He vowed then, "If I ever get a chance to hit that institution, I'll hit it hard."

The riverboat job was Lincoln's first away from the farm; he was seventeen years old. When he returned he settled in New Salem, where he worked first in a mill and then a store. Borrowing books from the educated men of the town, he converted to memory much of the poetry of Robert Burns and the tragedies of William Shakespeare.

One day his boss, Squire Godfrey came into the store and found Lincoln reading instead of clerking and asked, "Abe, what are you reading there?" "I'm not reading," answered the nineteen-year-old Lincoln, "I'm studying."

As academic preparation it was certainly no match for that of the speaker at the Gettysburg dedication. Edward Everett had entered Harvard at age thirteen to study the classics. On the other hand, Lincoln, the son of a marginally literate frontiersman, far from attending university, only received a few years of formal schooling. The son of a clergyman in the cultural environs of Boston, Everett was awarded his own parish at age nineteen. Two years later, he preached a sermon as guest chaplain in the House of Representatives. At the same age Lincoln was selling groceries in a frontier town at the edge of the wilderness where there were no libraries and few families with books.

Unlike Everett, the young Lincoln did not pore over Demosthenes's speeches in Greek or Cicero's in Latin. Instead he studied closely the style of a circuit preacher addressing a congregation or a country lawyer talking to a jury. Billy Herndon, his law partner, marveled over Lincoln's ability to recall and recite from memory passages of a Sunday sermon or a legal summation that he had heard many years before. But if Lincoln had the ear of an actor, he had the heart of an activist—he yearned to be a leader, and politics was to be his stage. Like any politician, he loved to talk; but he also knew how to listen and how to translate constituent sentiments into cogent arguments.

It was this gift for plain speaking that elected him to the Illinois State House in his twenties. He was a legislator before he was a lawyer. In the reverse of the typical political path, the writing of laws led Lincoln to the study of law. He began with Blackstone. What fascinated the law student was the clear definitions of terms by the eighteenth-century English authority.

This master of jurisprudence had the ability to take a complex set of ideas or a confusing array of facts and turn them into clear principles of law. It was this clarity of logic and expression that Lincoln most respected in others and tried to develop in himself.

His first major address was not in the legislature but at the Young Men's Lyceum in Springfield in 1838. Although the twenty-nine-year-old Lincoln was considered the best stump politician in the state, an invitation to this more erudite forum was a high compliment to the backwoods legislator. The subject Lincoln chose was the fragility of democracy.

"To the father," Lincoln implored, "each generation owes the duty of transferring the blessings of liberty from one generation to the next." In biblical language that would foreshadow the Gettysburg Address, Lincoln suggested that the life of a democracy could be no less mortal than man: "The days of our years are three score years and ten." The paramount question, said Lincoln, "is the capability of people to govern themselves." Lincoln then asked,

> At what point is the point of danger to be expected. In answer, if it ever reaches us it must spring up amongst us. It cannot come from abroad. If destruction be our lot we must ourselves be author and finisher. As a nation of freemen, we must live through all fine or die by suicide.

As a legislator and as a lawyer, Lincoln developed a speaking style that was both pointed and pragmatic. He addressed the issue at hand—whether it was political or legal—without resorting to elegant adornment or emotional theatrics. The only relief to his straightforward and logical argument was a penchant for the picturesque anecdote or homespun analogy. He did not so much inspire audiences as persuade them. He preferred the gentle explanation to the fervent exhortation. Such an approach did not bring to Lincoln the reputation as an orator, even though he was one of the most popular political speakers in the state. For Lincoln there were few invitations to speak at commencements, dedications, or memorials that would lend themselves to philosophical sermons or emotional appeals.

In 1852 one such occasion did appear. Lincoln was asked to deliver the eulogy for Henry Clay at the state capital in Springfield. The forty-three-year-old Lincoln had left politics to concentrate on law. Hoping to be appointed to a top federal post by President Zachary Taylor, he decided not to run for a second term in Congress in the election of 1848. Instead, he devoted himself to promoting the Whig candidate General Taylor across the country. In New England he delivered a series of well-received talks on the campaign circuit, urging Whig listeners to stick with the Southerner Taylor and not to stray to the Free Soil ticket, which was headed by former president Martin Van Buren. The only offer to the disappointed Lincoln was the territorial governorship of Oregon, which his wife, Mary, persuaded him to turn down.

More than anyone else, Clay was responsible for Lincoln becoming a Whig. In Kentucky, where Lincoln was born in 1809, Clay was a legend, and Lincoln as a fellow Westerner attached himself to Clay's Whig banner in his first bid for political office. Clay, though a slaveholder in a border state, was a strong advocate of the federal union and had opposed the extension of slavery as destructive to that Union.

In the eulogy Lincoln commended Clay for "an eloquence" borne "of great sincerity and thorough conviction." "All his efforts were made for practical effect. He never spoke merely to be heard."

In describing Clay, Lincoln not only revealed how he himself spoke on a platform but, more significantly, how he himself felt about his country. When he said Clay believed that "the world's best hope depended on the continued Union of the States," he was voicing his own conviction.

> He loves his country partly because it was his own country, but mostly because it was a free country; and he burned with zeal for its advancement, prosperity and glory, because he saw in such, the advancement, prosperity and glory of human liberty, human right and human nature. He desired the prosperity of his countrymen partly because they were his countrymen, but chiefly to show to the world that freemen could be prosperous.

When Congress ratified the Kansas–Nebraska Act two years later, opening up slavery to the territories, Lincoln found in the issue a cause for all time. The new Republican Party in Illinois needed a candidate to oppose the author of the Act, Senator Stephen Douglas, and Lincoln eagerly accepted the challenge. He had finally found what his capabilities longed for: a crusade that would summon all his knowledge of government and law and all his belief in God and his country.

On June 16, 1858, at the state Republican convention in Springfield, Lincoln dramatically opened his acceptance speech for the Republican senatorial nomination with a biblical reference:

> A house divided against itself cannot stand. I believe this government cannot endure, permanently half *slave* and half *free*. I do not expect the Union to be *dissolved*—I do not expect this house to fall—but I *do* expect it will cease to be divided. It will become *all* one thing or *all* the other.

Between June and August, Lincoln debated Douglas seven times. The thrust of his talks was this challenge to the Democratic Senator.

> I should like to know if taking this old Declaration of Independence, which declares that all men are created equal upon principle and making exceptions to it, where it will stop. If one man says it does mean a negro, why not another man saying it does not mean some other man.

Lincoln lost the election even though he garnered more popular votes.[3] But Lincoln would later indicate to an associate that he was not devastated by the defeat:

> Walking home that night—the path had been worn pig-backed and slippery. My foot slipped from under me, knocking the other out of the way, but I recovered and said to myself, "It's a slip not a fall."

Lincoln was right. In losing to the famous Douglas, he won national prominence as one of the contenders for the Republican presidential nomination. He won that nomination at the convention when the favorite, William Seward, who was considered too close to the abolitionists, was blocked. And he beat Senator Douglas in the fall because the Democratic Party was split into Northern and Southern factions.

At the beginning of 1861, Abraham Lincoln, the new president-elect, bid farewell to his friends at the Springfield railroad station:

> I now leave not knowing when or whether I may return with a task before me greater than that which rested on Washington. Without the assistance of that Divine Being who ever attended him, I cannot succeed. With that assistance I cannot fail.

Wanting to accommodate demands of well-wishers in other sections of the country, Lincoln scheduled a roundabout train route to Washington for the inauguration that took him through Illinois, Indiana, Ohio, Pennsylvania, and New York. Most of the stops called for little more than brief extemporaneous remarks. The most poignant of these talks occurred on February 22, the date of Washington's birthday, when at the last minute Lincoln was asked to visit Independence Hall. More than any other talk Lincoln would ever give, those unprepared words from the heart at the site where the Declaration of Independence had been signed suggested the message of the Gettysburg Address two and a half years later. At this birthplace of our independence, Lincoln was thinking out loud his feelings about the meaning of America.

> I have often inquired of myself what great principle or idea it was that kept this confederacy so long together. It was not the mere matter of the separation of the colonies from the mother land; but something in that Declaration giving liberty, not alone to the people of this country, but hope to the world for future time.

Lincoln then asked:

> Now, my friends, can this country be saved upon that basis?

Unlike his short talk at Independence Hall, Lincoln had two weeks to prepare for his brief remarks at Gettysburg. But in those two weeks the president was pressed by feuding generals from the war front and restless congressmen at home. Far more urgent than writing remarks for a memorial service was preparing his annual message to Congress, which was due in the first week of December. 1863 had been a year of mixed results for the president: since the victories of Meade at Gettysburg and Grant at Vicksburg in July, the tide of the war had begun to shift in a hopeful way; but politically, support for the president had been ebbing. The radical Republicans, led by Thaddeus Stevens of Pennsylvania, were consolidating their control of Congress. They already had their candidate for the presidential election next year picked out: Salmon P. Chase, Lincoln's ambitious secretary of Treasury.

Lincoln, in an olive branch gesture, had invited some of the radicals to join him on the presidential train leaving Washington to attend the Gettysburg ceremony. Stevens, who was the Congressman from Gettysburg, contemptuously refused. To Stevens, Lincoln was already a lame duck chief executive. To a fellow congressman, Stevens gave his reason for turning down the invitation to attend the memorial services in his district: "Let the dead bury the dead."

The door to Lincoln's high-walled, dark-green-wall-papered office at the White House was a frail dam against the flood of insistent cabinet officers, complaining congressmen, and importuning office seekers. Amidst the repeated interruptions and distractions, Lincoln read battle reports, dictated letters, and signed commissions at his walnut desk. There was little time to work on the presidential message to Congress, not to mention his remarks for Gettysburg. Contrary to legend, however, Lincoln did not scribble the Gettysburg address on the back of envelopes on the train to the dedication.

It was a methodically prepared address written out in at least two, and possibly three, drafts in pencil on white lined commercial paper. When a sentence formed in his mind, he committed it to paper, then chewed on the pencil stub as he contemplated the next line.

Lincoln had decided early not to mention names or recount any battlefield action in his short remarks. Instead, he wanted to express what the battle had been about. Earlier in the fall he had told his young secretary, John Hay,

> For my own part I consider the central idea pervading this struggle is the necessity that is upon us of proving that popular government is not an absurdity. . . . If we fail, it will go far to prove the incapability of the people to govern themselves.

The speech was not completely finished by the time the presidential party boarded the special train on November 18 at the B&O depot. The president had left a hysterical Mrs. Lincoln, who pleaded with him to stay with their youngest son, Tad. Their middle son, Willie, had died a year-and-a-half earlier, and the grief had ravaged the father and pushed the mother over the brink into a continuing state of collapse.

Although Gettysburg is but sixty-five miles north of Washington, the War Department had charted a course that was just short of twice that distance. The route looked like three corners of an unfinished square—one and a half hours east to Baltimore, then north to Hanover, Pennsylvania, and then thirty miles west to Gettysburg.

On the six-and-a-half-hour ride, Lincoln presided at a long table set up in a crudely converted baggage car. As the train puffed its way through a succession of small stations, the president dished out stories from his bottomless well of anecdotes to his aides and members of the official party. At one stop between Baltimore and Hanover, a six-year-old girl lisped a presentation: "Here are some roses for you, Mr. President." "Well, you are quite a rosebud yourself," replied Lincoln.

When he was not chatting, Lincoln glanced at newspapers to learn not so much the latest war news, which he already knew from his daily telegraphed dispatches from the front, but for accounts of political happenings or human interest stories, which helped him keep a tab on the public pulse.

The track over a road bed that set the travelers' teeth rattling was far too bumpy to allow Lincoln the peace he needed to finish his remarks for the next day. If he did jot down notes on the back of an envelope, as one witness said many years later, it was probably to high-note a succession of key phrases as he tried to memorize and rehearse the delivery in his mind.

It was evening when the presidential train chugged into the little depot at Gettysburg. The town was chiefly distinguished for its carriage factory and a cluster of schools, including Gettysburg College and a girls' finishing school known as Miss Carrie's. Although the population of this county seat was a little over 2,300, close to that many people waited at the station to welcome the presidential party. Visitors had been spilling into the town for the last couple of days and had not been able to find beds. Instead, they slept on tavern floors, hotel lobbies, and even church pews. The torch-holding crowds surged toward the president, but he was able to make his way from the station through a gauntlet of honor guard soldiers to the town square, where the Wills House stood.

Waiting at the Wills House was a formal candelabra-lighted dinner for nineteen, including the French minister in Washington and a visiting French admiral. Edward Everett arrived later from Boston with his daughter, and Lincoln thanked him for kindly sending him an advance copy of his speech, which had arrived at the White House ten days before.

At 9:30, while throwing out some pleasantries to the high-spirited milling crowds outside the house, Lincoln received a telegram. His son's fever had broken, and he was recovering. It was a tired but relieved president who then climbed the stairs to his bedroom. The speech was still not finished, however, and at this bedroom desk he went over the working draft and penned the final sentences. During the process he would at times read out some lines to his valet, William Slade. "William, how does that sound?" he kept asking. Lincoln was not so much asking for advice as testing out the sound of the phrase as it rolled off his tongue. At 11:00 the light in Lincoln's window went out.

The morning of November 19 was cold and sunny. Little was left of the autumn foliage, which had been thinned by recurrent strong winds. If it was to be Edward Everett's day, it was also the shining moment for Ward Hill Lamon, Lincoln's old friend and former law partner from Illinois. To the disgruntlement of the planning committee, Lincoln had insisted on naming as chief marshal for the Gettysburg events the banjo-playing Lamon, whose main asset seemed to be his repertory of ribald ditties. Lamon had planted himself in the White House as head of the president's personal security detail, and he often slept nights outside Lincoln's bedroom door. Lincoln, who probably appreciated him more as a companion than as a custodian, had long wanted to reward Lamon in some way.

Chief Marshal Lamon had scheduled a parade, but the procession of the president and other dignitaries to the cemetery grounds hardly fifteen minutes distance away did not quite live up to the billing. President Lincoln rode a bay mare and looked distracted despite occasional efforts to give a wave of acknowledgment. His stove pipe hat, which he used as a briefcase to carry his address, made his six-foot-four-inch stature even more towering. The sad, gray eyes in a head above shoulders draped in a shawl suggested an age older than his fifty-four years.

At noon the ceremonies were supposed to begin. Up on the platform was a cushionless settee for the principal dignitaries. In the center position, Lincoln sat with Secretary of State William Seward on his left. The empty seat to the right waited for the overdue Edward Everett. At sixty-nine, the grand old man, who suffered from weak kidneys, had to make a comfort stop at a tent that was erected purposely for the aging orator's convenience.

The day had not begun auspiciously for Everett. He had risen after a fitful night at the Wills'. They had told him that the late arriving Governor Curtin possibly would have to share his bed because of the shortage of accommodations. It was bad enough to be asked to share a bed, albeit with a governor (who actually never did arrive), but the ultimate insult came when Everett made his late entrance on the platform and found that his name was not even listed on the program. Ward Hill Lamon had just listed "Oration" and beneath it "Dedication Remarks of the President of the United States." Lamon, however, had prominently listed himself as Grand Marshal. So Everett, on his own copy of the program, angrily jabbed a pen slash through Lamon's name.

The ceremonies officially opened with an invocation by the Reverend

William Stockton, chaplain of the Senate. John Hay later described the spiritual blessing, which was two to three times the length of Lincoln's remarks, "as a prayer which thought it was an oration."

Then came the moment the multitude of nearly twenty thousand was waiting for: the rising of the silver-haired orator Edward Everett to deliver what was anticipated as his supreme oration. Everett had spoken at countless anniversaries, funerals, memorials, banquets, dedications, commencements, and cornerstone layings, but this occasion was to be the culmination of his rhetorical career. He had spent the better part of the last two months preparing the address and rehearsing its delivery. The aging Everett only hoped his memory as well as his kidneys would hold out.

He looked at the blue heavens to see if it still described his opening line and then began: "Standing beneath this serene sky . . . " The words in measured delivery, he intoned. Each ornate phrase fell into place in a clause that eventually found its fit in an elegantly structured sentence. More than a few of his sentences were almost as long as Lincoln's entire 270-word address.

His oration conformed to the rule of classical rhetoric: an "exordium" (or introduction), "argument," and "peroration." In the opening Everett drew from his knowledge of ancient Greece to trace in detail the origin of memorial services to honor fallen warriors. He compared the two freedom-loving societies: Periclean Athens and the American Union. Classical allusion was piled upon historical analogy in seeming endless fashion.

With already forty minutes gone the audience was still enthralled by the sonorous cascade of phrases. The orator with a historian's eye and an actor's gesture then launched into a description of the day-by-day fighting in the Gettysburg struggle and the military strategy that shaped the battle.

The crowd, some of whom had witnessed that crucial engagement four months ago, listened as they would to a revered professor, who in this hour-long development of the "argument" laid upon a graphic account of the conflict a masterly analysis of the causes of the conflict.

Finally, the old rhetorician mounted his climatic peroration, closing it with thundering words: "In the glorious annals of our common country there will be no page brighter than which relates to The Battle of Gettysburg."

At the end, the audience, if stimulated, had not been stirred. The chiseled lines in his orotund tones had all the classic beauty of the antiquities Everett had spent a lifetime to study; but, like those smooth marble monuments, they were cold and lifeless. During the far from tumultuous applause the president congratulated the exhausted Everett. A five-stanza dirge by a Baltimore glee club followed. It was now the proudest moment in Ward Hill Lamon's life. In a stentorian roar he announced, "The President of the United States."

It was two o'clock. The president, by one account, whispered to Secretary of State Seward beside him: "It's a failure and they won't like it." Then he removed his gray shawl and fitted his steel-rimmed spectacles to the bridge of his nose. He held two pages of text in his right hand but did not look at it during his speech. Applause from the audience surged as he rose to his full height. Someone in the back then yelled, "Down in front." For the many thousands, the now-erect Lincoln at the platform presented their first glimpse of the president. If in death the martyred Lincoln was transfigured into a "Christ," in life he had been caricaturized by the press into a lanky, earthy, and often crude country bumpkin. The real Lincoln, despite his penchant for the often inappropriate joke, cast a somber look. The beard and deeply etched lines darkened his face, but his voice was resonant and clear. In a strident, flat Midwest accent like the actor who portrayed him, Lincoln began:

Fourscore and seven years ago . . .

Lincoln opened with the biblical phrasing from the 90th Psalm that he had used in 1838 in the Young Men's Lyceum. It must be remembered that Lincoln knew much of the King James version by heart, particularly Psalms, Proverbs, The Song of Solomon, and Isaiah, as well as the New Testament Gospels.

. . . our fathers brought forth upon this continent a new nation conceived in liberty. . . .

With echoes of nativity scenes from both Old and New Testament, Lincoln used the words "brought forth" and "conceived." The words "conceived in liberty" recall the Genesis account of Abraham who, with a concubine, "conceived in bondage" one child before siring his heir, Isaac. Lincoln, whose affectionate nickname by soldiers in the war was "Father Abraham," had been serenaded the night before at the Wills House by the outside crowd who sang the six-stanza hymn that ended with the refrain "We are coming, Father Abraham." Perhaps Lincoln saw in the term "Father Abraham" his own destiny as a father of a nation reborn and dedicated to the proposition that all men are created equal.

It is noteworthy that to Jefferson "all men are created equal" was a "self-evident" axiom, but to Lincoln it was a "proposition" still to be proved. William Seward, the only person Lincoln showed the draft to beforehand, objected to the word "proposition" as "inelegant," but Lincoln, from his early learning of Euclid's geometry, often used the word to advance a logical argument.

Now we are engaged in a great civil war, testing whether that nation—or any nation so conceived and so dedicated—can long endure.

Lincoln was comparing the Revolutionary War to establish independence
with the ongoing Civil War to preserve that Union. Lincoln was, in effect,
asking whether this experiment called democracy could survive.

> We are met on a great battlefield of that war. We have come to dedicate a
> portion of it as a final resting place of those who gave their lives that the
> nation might live.

Lincoln here expressed with poetic consonance ("gave" and "live") the
purpose of the occasion: the dedication of the National Cemetery. In the
early drafts the next sentence read "We meet to dedicate," but Lincoln, in
the final writing changed it to "we have come" to avoid duplication.

> But in a larger sense we can not dedicate, we can not consecrate, we can not
> hallow this ground. The brave men living and dead have consecrated it, far
> above our (poor) power to add or detract.

Lincoln's use of subtle rhyme ("dedicate" and "consecrate") explained
his avowal of the futility of doing anything in the way of a commemoration
service that would approach the significance of those fallen soldiers' sacrifice.
In the text Lincoln used at Gettysburg it was alliteratively written "poor
power," but during the delivery he omitted "poor."

> The world will little note, nor long remember what we say here but it can
> never forget what they did here.

The statement is ironic today, but the *New York Times* evidently concurred
when it said the audience "seemed to have agreed with President Lincoln,
that it was not what was said here but what was done here that deserved
the attention."

> It is for us the living, rather, to be dedicated here to the unfinished work that
> they have thus far so nobly carried on.

Lincoln's style of straightforward and quick-paced delivery employed no
gesture of hands and no change in inflection, but, according to observers,
at this point, Lincoln's clarion voice broke with emotion. The tenor of the
speech turned from eulogy to exhortation. If the audience ever sensed the
president's passion, it must have been as he issued this ringing summons:

> It is rather for us to be here dedicated to the great task remaining before
> us . . .

In his entire political career, Lincoln was dominated by only two objectives:
first, to prohibit the extension of slavery, and second, to preserve the Union.

Lincoln used the phrase "great task" several times in his career, that last being his first message to Congress, which read: "Let us proceed in the great task which events have developed upon us."

> ... that from these honored dead we take increased devotion to that cause for which they here gave the last full measure of devotion...

With "measure" Lincoln chose a Biblical word prominent in Shakespeare to express the ultimate sacrifice given by the Union dead.

> ... that we here highly resolve that those dead shall not have died in vain.

The declaration adds graceful alliteration to geometric logic: the "proposition" of democracy must be proved. The last phrase could have recalled the words of the first book Lincoln ever read, in which Parson Weems's George Washington is looking at the graves of Revolutionary soldiers and says "their deaths were not in vain."

> that this nation shall, under God, have...

While Everett was speaking, Lincoln penned a last minute addition to the text, "under God." When he uttered it, though, he inserted ungrammatically "under God" in the middle of "shall have." In the later copies Lincoln sent to Everett and the historian George Bancroft, he corrected it to "this nation under God shall have..."

Though not a religious man in a formal sense, Lincoln was deeply devout. After his breakfast and before going to his office, he used to spend about twenty minutes in the family library reading a passage from scripture, particularly from the Old Testament. Like Washington and Churchill, Lincoln believed that God had ordained for him a special role (in theology being the instrument of God's will is called the doctrine of Divine Providence).

Lincoln wrote just before his inauguration: "I know there is a God and that He hates injustice. I see a storm coming but if He has a place for me, I am ready." Yet his humility did not allow his belief in God to take on a messianic conviction. When during the war a delegation of clergy called on him and said of the Union cause "God is on our side," Lincoln replied, "No, the question should always be: Are we on His side?"

> ... a new birth of freedom...

The Biblical nativity analogy that began with "brought forth" and "conceived in liberty" is now completed. Lincoln, though a profoundly humble man, saw himself projected by destiny to be a father of his country, like

Washington. As Washington "brought forth" the nation from foreign bondage to freedom, so Lincoln would bring it forth from "domestic bondage" into more complete freedom. Like the Biblical patriarch for whom he was named, "Father Abraham" would sire a rebirth in freedom.

>   . . . that this government of the people, by the people and for the people . . .

This poetic trochee to describe democracy was not original with Lincoln. The friend of Thomas Jefferson, Judge Thomas Cooper, said something like it in 1794, and Daniel Webster used much the same definition in 1830. The most likely source was the Reverend Theodore Parker, who in 1854 said "government over all the people, for all the people and by all the people." Lincoln's law partner William Herndon had forwarded the New England abolitionist's sermon to Lincoln shortly thereafter. If Parker's phrasing took root in Lincoln's mind, he both adapted and improved it.

One thing, however, is sure. Lincoln did not stress the prepositions in the manner of later schoolboy recitals. The repetition of "people" with these different prepositions had more to do with poetry than polity.

>   . . . shall not perish from the earth.

"Perish" is both a poetic and biblical verb. It recalls Proverbs 29:18, a favorite verse of Lincoln: "Where there is no vision, the people perish."

Suddenly the speech was over.

The two-minute address of ten sentences of generally familiar Biblical words was completed before much of the audience could focus their attention. There was no applause. The crowd was either stunned by the unexpected brevity or, perhaps, by the prayer-like poetry. What they heard from their president was too short—and too simple.

Accepting the congratulatory handshake, Lincoln said to Everett, "I have failed, I failed and that's all that can be said about it." His two closest associates at the proceedings agreed. Seward, his staunch ally in the cabinet, said to Everett, "He has made a failure and I am sorry for it." His old friend Ward Hill Lamon, when asked for his reaction by Seward, replied, "I am sorry to say it does not affect me as one of his great speeches."

Yet there were more discerning listeners. Everett, himself a master of rhetoric, wrote Lincoln a few days later asking for a copy of the text, saying, "I should be glad if I could flatter myself that I came as near to the central idea of the occasion in two hours as you did in two minutes." His young aide, John Hay, who as a Brown student planned to be a poet, said, "The President in a fine free way, with more grace than his wont said his half dozen words of consecration."

Of course, there were some partisan newspapers who damned Lincoln. The *Chicago Times* called it "silly, flat and dishwatery." Some literary critics deemed otherwise. Henry Wadsworth Longfellow called it "admirable." Emily Dickinson's friend, Samuel Bowles of the Springfield *Republican*, called it "a perfect gem," and George William Curtis, who would become the famous editor of *Harpers*, said, "The few words of the President were from the heart to the heart. They cannot be read without kindling emotion."

Actually, its brevity rendered the address not only more beautiful but also more universal. Because the address was only 270 words, it was possible to reprint it in newspapers not only in this country but also in Britain. In an era when the daily newspaper was emerging as a phenomenon, the short address was printed and circulated to millions. Its very size would later encourage generations of school children to commit it to memory.

Yet not even the most prescient of literary men could foresee that in a hundred years the Gettysburg Address would be included in every anthology of English literature as America's sublime contribution to the world. They could not have anticipated the assessment of Lord Curzon, the British statesman, who praised it as the greatest speech ever delivered. It would take a bullet in a theater, a surrender at Appomattox, and the freeing of slaves in countless households across the land to enshrine the name of Abraham Lincoln and make his words eternal. Then by the accretion of time, myth, and legend a simple presentation became what Carl Sandburg called "the Great American Poem." The Gettysburg Address was now the American Creed.

NOTES

1. Later the seventeen acres were expanded to twenty-one at the suggestion of William Saunders, the landscape architect called in from Washington.

2. Everett had run with John Bell of Tennessee on the Constitutional Union Party ticket in 1860. The party, consisting of old-line Whigs, received 59 electoral votes in that four-party race, which split the Democratic Party into Northern and Southern Whigs and allowed the Republican Lincoln to win.

3. In those days the state legislature, by caucus, chose the U.S. senator. The 125,430 total of Republican votes for pro-Lincoln candidates exceeded the Democratic vote of 121,609 for pro-Douglas candidates.

7 _____

The Cleveland Tariff Message: The Battle Against Big Business

It is a condition that confronts us—not a theory.

Grover Cleveland is the only president to fail reelection but then win again. Actually, even in his defeat Cleveland gained the plurality. Since the development of the two-party system, Cleveland is the only president, with the obvious exception of Franklin Roosevelt, to win the popular vote for more than two elections.

Yet Grover Cleveland was not a popular president or an appealing leader. He had neither the looks to excite, the charm to persuade, nor the fame to impress people. In those post-bellum years when heroic service in the Union Army was a prerequisite for a presidential nomination, Cleveland had hired someone to take his place. In the midst of the Victorian era, when morality held a rigid sway, Cleveland became the first presidential candidate to admit fathering an illegitimate child. If Cleveland had been a sporting sort like a Henry Clay or John F. Kennedy it might have made him more intriguing. The bloated, mustachioed Cleveland, however, resembled a huge walrus on a cold rock. He was an image more dour than dashing, a figure more corpulent than charismatic.

Yet this plodding man would dominate an era in politics like an Andrew Jackson or a Franklin Roosevelt. For he offered to an age of rising wealth, developing industry, and expanding markets the one commodity that seemed scarce: honesty. His was an integrity so inviolable that it shone like a beacon in a political world where the corruption of big city machines and big business monopolies darkened the halls of democracy.

It was this rare honesty that propelled Cleveland in three short years from a city hall to the White House. A former sheriff who gained political prominence by hanging two murderers had now become president.

Money was the reason that impelled him to run for sheriff in 1870. For a job that required comparatively little time, it paid big money—about $40,000 in fees. To most aspirants the authorized fees did not represent the only source of financial enrichment. The office of the sheriff was the courthouse base of operations for all kinds of kickback deals, political bribes, and public graft. Into this unsavory den stepped the pure-minded Cleveland, who had a favorite saying from his mother: "Tis a sin to steal a pin and how much more a greater thing."

In his first days as sheriff Cleveland stopped a contractor who was delivering firewood to the county jail and measured the cordage himself. Finding it to be short, Cleveland decreed that future purchases would be made with public bidding. But if honesty pays, it does not always pay off in building political friends and support. Cleveland was criticized for hounding some staunch contributors to the Democratic Party. The pattern for his public career was thus established early.

Although Cleveland did not run for reelection, he had, however, proved his integrity and courage. What he would be remembered most for was springing the scaffold trap on two killers in performance of his sheriff duties. His reputation for honesty made Buffalo look to him as a mayoral candidate in 1880. The city had fallen into the venal clutches of an aldermanic "ring." Samuel Tilden, with whom Cleveland was increasingly compared, had built a national reputation by prosecuting corruption in New York City a few years earlier.

The forty-three-year-old Cleveland was notified of his nomination for mayor by the Democratic convention while arguing a case before the state supreme court. He was at first reluctant to leave his quiet, lucrative law practice for the stress and financial sacrifice the mayoralty would impose. But the old judge presiding over the case took him aside. "You better accept," he advised. "We are all interested in having good city government. You're an old bachelor and you haven't any family to take care of. It's your duty to run."

Little did Cleveland realized when he was sworn in as mayor on March 4, 1881, that exactly four years later he would be taking the oath as the twenty-second President of the United States. In Buffalo's city hall office he audited all disbursements, set up a commission to supervise public bidding, and vetoed every excess aldermanic appropriation—be it for personal livery service (the equivalent of today's limousine) or a donation for the Firemen's Benevolent Association. He became known throughout the state as "the Veto Mayor of Buffalo," a title that predestined his later hallmark as president.

His reputation as a reform mayor quickly lifted his name into speculation for governor. In 1882, the Republicans had nominated a candidate who was considered a puppet of the billionaire mogul Jay Gould. The Democrats sensed an opportunity but were split between two leading candidates, both of whom came from New York City. Finally they compromised and turned to Cleveland because he was both clean and from upstate.

As in the mayoral election and later in the presidential election, Cleveland took the governor's chair with the help of a big crossover of Republican votes. Even though his opponent, John Folger, had been a distinguished secretary of Treasury under President Chester Arthur, he could not shake the label of being the handpicked choice of Roscoe Conkling, who handled Jay Gould's political interests.

The day after Cleveland's election, a caller asked what would be his policies. "That's easy," he replied, "there's only one thing to do and that's to do it right." His first day as governor was symbolic. He announced that he would keep his door open at all times and transact the state business in public.

His strongest opposition in Albany came not from the Republicans but from the Tammany Hall Democrats of New York City. Tammany was a city political machine that wielded power not only in the state but also at the national level at Democratic conventions. Therefore it was widely believed that Cleveland, who now was being mentioned for president, would try to make his peace with Tammany.

But to the upstate Cleveland, Tammany smacked of everything that was politically evil in New York City: corruption based on exploitation of the immigrant Irish vote. He fought Tammany-backed bills; Tammany, in turn, tried to block confirmation of his appointments. Cleveland won most of the battles, often with the help of a young Republican legislator named Theodore Roosevelt.

Cleveland had been governor for hardly a year when Democrats in the nation began maneuvering to select their candidate for president. Any New York state governor was always a leading possibility. Samuel Tilden, who had been narrowly counted out in the dubious presidential election of 1876, was the expected nominee, but he declined because of health. Tammany tried to circulate the word that the Presbyterian Cleveland was an anti-Catholic bigot. Actually, Cleveland, popular with Irish voters in Buffalo, was hardly a bluenose. The bachelor lawyer liked to drink with the boys and once had been involved in a barroom brawl as a young "man-about-town." At any rate, the smear at the convention failed, and Tammany ended up having to vote for Cleveland because the unit rule in the state forced them to vote with the majority.

In one of the most famous nomination speeches in history, General Edward Bragg of Wisconsin, while putting forth the name Cleveland, pointed to the booing delegates from Tammany and said, "They love Cleveland for his character but they love him also for the enemies he has made." Again, it was his reputation for integrity that impelled the convention to turn to Cleveland as their standard-bearer against the Republican, James G. Blaine.

Blaine's reputation was less than pristine, and the minority Democrats would need the votes of independent Republicans or Mugwumps if they were going to wrest the White House from the Grand Old Party, which had ruled the country for nearly a quarter of a century. The Republican problem in electing Blaine was best illustrated by his old rival's refusal to campaign for the party ticket. Roscoe Conkling, the New York Republican lawyer, demurred, saying, "No, I've retired from criminal practice."

Blaine had everything Cleveland lacked: a distinguished appearance, a charming personality, and a silver tongue. The elegantly bearded Blaine not only looked like a statesman, but he also, as a former senator and secretary of state, had the qualifications—except for one thing: unqualified integrity. The state was set for one of the dirtiest presidential campaigns in personal mudslinging.

For almost a decade Blaine had been the dominant figure of the Republican Party. The elegant Blaine was described as "The Plumed Knight." But the knight's armor was besmirched in 1876 by the release of "the Mulligan Letters," which caused the Republican convention of that year, at the last moment, to turn to dark horse James Garfield. (Curiously, it was Garfield who gave Blaine the "knight" label in his elegant nominating speech that ironically led to his selection instead of Blaine's.) The correspondence which had been in the possession of a speculator named Mulligan, revealed a pattern of pay-offs to Congressmen for the support of the French company, Crédit Mobilier, a holding company for railroad expansion. It alluded to "influence peddling" on Blaine's part and revived the old stories of Blaine's involvement in Crédit Mobilier. By 1884 the furor of "the Mulligan Letters" had died down, and the Republican party rejected Chester Arthur, the weak president who had succeeded the assassinated Garfield, and turned to Blaine.

But after the Republican convention some leading Mugwumps unearthed new unreleased Mulligan letters relating more of Blaine's questionable railroad transactions. In one of the letters Blaine had penned, "Burn this letter." The resulting controversy put Blaine on the defensive.

The Blaine Republicans tried to paint Cleveland's opposition to the high tariff as hostility to the working man, but the smear did not stick. The country had wearied of the long rule of the Republicans who waved "the bloody flag" of Union victory to deflect attention from their abuses of power, such as Andrew Johnson's impeachment, the cruel military government of the South, the Whiskey Ring under Grant, the Crédit Mobilier scandal involving congressional Republicans, the disputed election of Hayes against Tilden in 1876, and congressional Republican opposition to civil service reform. By 1884 the economic issue of "protection" in government was no match for the political cry for "purity."

If the Republicans found the purity of Grover Cleveland's public life unassailable, his private life was another matter. The Republicans dug up one Maria Halpin, who claimed Cleveland had fathered her illegitimate son. Democratic leaders hoped Cleveland would deny the charge. Cleveland's blunt reply was, "Tell the truth." And the truth was that Cleveland had been involved with the attractive widow, and in 1874, when threatened with a paternity action, he assumed responsibility by agreeing to pay for the child's support.

Eventually, the defense of the scandal emerged from such Mugwumps as Republican Carl Shurz, the German-born friend of Lincoln, and Charles Curtis, the editor of *Harper's*.

> We are told that Mr. Blaine has been delinquent in office but blameless in private life while Mr. Cleveland has been a model of official integrity but culpable in personal relations. We therefore should elect Mr. Cleveland to the public office to which he is so well qualified to fill and remand Mr. Blaine to the private station which he is admirably fit to adorn.

Still the Republicans chanted:

> Ma, Ma, where's my Pa
> Gone to the White House
> Ha! Ha! Ha!

The Democrats answered:

> Blaine, Blaine, James G. Blaine
> The continental liar from the State of Maine
> "Burn this letter."

The stalemate continued until the eve of the election, when the minister of the Murray Hill Presbyterian Church in New York, the Reverend S. D. Burchard, assembled a meeting of clergymen to meet Blaine on the morning of October 24. At this session to endorse Blaine, Burchard called the Democratic Party the party of "Rum, Romanism and Rebellion." The charge infuriated the Irish Catholic voters whom Blaine had been trying to woo. Blaine, whose sister was a Catholic nun, was a vocal supporter of Charles Parnell, the leader of the Home Rule movement in Ireland, and was exploiting the old Tammany smears that Cleveland was "a Presbyterian Bigot."

On top of "Rum, Romanism and Rebellion" was "Belshazzar's Feast." That was the caption of the *New York World's* political cartoon describing dinner at the Delmonico Hotel (given on the same day as the ministers' meeting) by plutocrats Jay Gould, Charles Tiffany, Russell Sage, and Whitlaw Reid in honor of their guest and nominee, Blaine.

Because of the events of one day in New York, reform-minded Republicans switched to the Democrat Cleveland, and the Irish Catholics did not switch to Blaine. On election day, Cleveland carried New York State by 12,000 votes and thus the nation. The next day New York taverns were filled with celebrants who sang:

> Hurrah for Maria
> Hurrah for the kid
> I voted for Cleveland
> And I'm damn glad I did.

On inauguration day Cleveland presented a contrast to the outgoing President Arthur: The slim, handsome Arthur in reality represented the years of sloth and corruption; the obese Cleveland represented the cutting edge of reform. Yet Cleveland, in his address, symbolized the integrity and independence of his administration by not only writing his own speech, like Jefferson and Lincoln, but also by delivering it without a single note. He was the first and only president to do so. At the close of the address Cleveland struck the theme of his administration.

> The people demand reform in the administration of government and the application of business principles to public affairs.

But abstract principles do not apply easily to political facts. The Civil Service issue was a prime example. After 24 years out of office, the partisan Democrats thought all positions should go to Democrats. They flooded Cleveland with demands for 55,000 appointments, but the Reform Republicans, who backed Cleveland, expected him to be non-partisan and divide the appointments 50–50. Cleveland, whose first priority was administrative reform and executive reorganization, needed the experience of those who had proved to be hardworking and capable. Almost all of them were Republicans. Cleveland decided to oust only those Republicans in government who were either incompetent or politically active. Like most compromises, it satisfied neither side and angered both.

He did more than alienate the Democratic politicians and intellectual Republicans. Both, though influential, were few in actual numbers, at least compared to the Grand Army of the Republic (GAR)—the nation's most powerful lobby. For years the Republican Congress had fattened the pension rolls of Civil War veterans; it was estimated that one-fourth of the existing pension list was fraudulent. What had opened the floodgates for a spate of new claims was the notorious "Arrears of Pension Act," which allowed veterans to petition for disability even if they had failed to do so right after the war. The Pension Bureau tried to disallow some of the most outrageous claims, but Congress, backed by the GAR's agents in Washington, was overruling their decisions by rushing through hundreds of private bills to award pensions to specific constituents. One day alone two hundred and forty of these individual pension bills piled up on Cleveland's desk like autumn leaves through an open window. Cleveland, probably the most hardworking president since Polk, would work daily from about 8:00 A.M. to 2:00 A.M., examining the case made out in each bill, then having the facts double-checked. Many of the bills he vetoed. He became the biggest veto-signer in American history.

Perhaps the GAR thought that a president who did not serve in the war would bend over backwards in dealing with Civil War veterans. But instead of bending, Cleveland got his back up against that kind of suggestion. As mayor of Buffalo, he showed that when he vetoed an aldermanic appropriation for $500 for the local GAR Fourth of July Parade.

Cleveland not only vetoed the hundreds of pension bills but also took a perverse pleasure in publishing the details of the fraud perpetuated. One petition he vetoed said the claimant had fallen off his horse on the way to enlist. A Louisville policeman demanded a pension for the death of his son who died ten months after he deserted. A widow whose husband was killed on a ladder in 1881 said it had been caused by a flesh wound on the leg almost twenty years earlier! A widow of a captain who died of a stroke in 1883 said it had been triggered by a hernia twenty years before. One gallant former private said his acute eye disease was the result of a diarrhea attack from an army mess.

The vetoes by Cleveland only spurred the Republican Congress to greater efforts to wave "the bloody flag" of the Union cause. The Blair bill offered a government stipend to every injured veteran who had served at least three months and pensioned the parents of soldiers who had died. The bill would have cost $50 million a year.

To Cleveland, the bill was outrageous. It would have made the ninety-day soldier who had recently become a chronic alcoholic the legal equal of the man who lost a leg at Gettysburg.

Some thought otherwise. Former President Hayes called Cleveland a "penny-pincher." The *New York Times* accused him of sending "destitute aged mothers to the poor house in order that the Democratic Party may gain a reputation for economy."

Cleveland's answer: "The pension list should be kept a roll of honor." These words made sense, but it was the insensitivity of his actions that constantly exasperated his friends and infuriated his foes. Cleveland was not blessed with an overabundance of either tact or diplomacy. On Memorial Day in 1877, which was a Civil War holiday created to honor Union veterans, Cleveland announced he was going fishing. He also wrote a letter praising the erection of a monument to the Confederate general A. S. Johnston. Then he agreed to allow captured Confederate flags stored in a Washington Armory to be returned to their former owners. The decision was generous, but the timing of it—just before the Grand Army of the Republic's

national convention—was foolish. When the GAR delegates protested, he
enraged the members further by cancelling his scheduled appearance. If
Cleveland's motives in public service were pure, his understanding of public
relations was incredibly poor. The blunt honesty that was his virtue as a
statesman was also his fault as a politician.

To Cleveland, a principle could never be sacrificed to politics. A case in
point was his veto of the Texas Seed bill.

The bill appropriated ten thousand dollars to enable the U.S. Commissioner of Agriculture to distribute seed to certain Texas counties that had
suffered from a drought. Although the amount was trifling, such relief
raised an important principle. Cleveland, who had just vetoed the Blair
Dependent Pension Bill, saw in the Seed Bill a dangerous conception of
government. If distress was the determinant in providing aid, Cleveland
wondered where the government's responsibility to relieve human suffering
would end. If a natural disaster such as a drought demanded assistance,
would it not create a precedent to help out victims of countless other ca-
tastrophes such as floods, fires, hurricanes, tornadoes, and dust storms? To
Cleveland, the proper channel of relief was the state legislature or charitable
subscription. In his veto message, Cleveland wrote,

> It was wrong to indulge a benevolent and a charitable sentiment through the
> appropriation of public funds . . . I can find no warrant for such an appropri-
> ation in the Constitution and I do not believe that the power and the duty of
> the general government ought to be expanded to the relief of individual
> suffering which is in no manner properly related to public service or benefits.

At the same time, Cleveland made a public comment descriptive of his
philosophy and memorable for its phrasing:

> A prevalent tendency to disregard the limited mission of this government's
> power and duty, should, I think resteadfastly resisted to the end that the lesson
> should be constantly reenforced that *though the people support the government,
> the government should not support the people.* (Emphasis added)

Cleveland also did not believe that a central purpose of government was
supporting big business by protecting big tariffs. The dogma of the indus-
trialists and their political handmaidens who dominated Washington and
the state capitals was that what separated a booming America from depression and economic misery was the wall of high tariffs. Cleveland did not
share that conviction.

If he had been a Republican, Cleveland never would have received the
presidential nomination. Yet as a Democrat whose party strength lay in the
south and west, he could be a moderate on the tariff issue. Only a true
believer in protectionism could speak for the Grand Old Party. In the

previous election, Blaine had tried to scare the vote of the working man into the Republican column, but the tide of reform had been too strong. In his first message to Congress, he had pointed to the necessity of a downward adjustment in the tariff schedule; but it was not the only item in his agenda for administrative reform. It also included the strengthening of Civil Service, railroad financing, the coinage of silver, and a host of other problems, foreign and domestic. Yet one issue underlay the whole operation of government and determined the course of the nation. That was the national surplus in the Treasury. To today's reader, it seems laughable to term an excess of revenue a problem. Yet taking huge revenues out of general circulation and piling them in a golden heap in the Treasury could, in the long run, stifle economic growth and trigger a cycle of deflation and depression. The alternative was to give Congress a free hand to go on a spending spree for all kinds of schemes and projects. Cleveland rejected that policy because he believed that, as with the Civil War pension, programs once initiated are never terminated and actually only increase the demands for other products.

Thus, in a day before the income tax, when tariffs were the main source of revenue, Cleveland decided, in effect, to cut the taxes on consumers. It was, after all, the American family who bore the burden when they paid higher prices for goods protected by high tariffs. He decided to recommend a reduction of tariffs in the beginning of an election year. The controversial move was courageous. A range of other options would have reduced the surplus without stirring up a hornet's nest of angry furor by the manufacturing and industrial community.

The most popular option, of course, was the one Cleveland rejected: a massive pork barrel bill for building roads, bridges, coastal improvements, and federal buildings. But there were others that could have passed the Republican-controlled Senate.

Some Democratic leaders wanted to eliminate all internal revenue taxes on alcohol and tobacco. Others suggested cutting out the luxury tax on silk, French wine, and other such items.

A less rigid president might have accepted either proposal as a compromise. Even intellectual liberal Republicans who generally favored both Cleveland and lower taxes worried about pushing such a tariff reduction in an election year. The *New York Herald* wrote to Cleveland in 1887, "If you lose the election next year, you will put back tariff reform a dozen years," signing the letter "A Tariff Reformer."

To one fearful adviser, Cleveland lectured:

> Do you remember that I opposed a second term on the ground that human nature being what it is, the President would work for his reelection instead of the country?

And to another, he shrugged:

> What's the use of being elected or reelected unless you stand for something?

Cleveland worked on his message to Congress for the better part of three days, writing out in pen, on legal size paper, his tariff recommendation. In the reverse of the prevailing practice today, he scribbled out the rough draft and let his White House secretary, Daniel Lamont, whom he had brought from Albany, do the editing. In final form, it was a blockbuster filling eighteen pages of octavo size. Cleveland's speech also was precedent shattering because it was the first presidential message in the history of the republic devoted entirely to a single subject. He got to the heart of that subject at the very beginning:

> Our present tariff laws, the vicious, inequitable, and illogical source of unnecessary taxation, ought to be revised and amended . . .

He then assured Congress that he did not intend to let American manufacturers die from the exposure to European competition:

> It may be called protection or by any other name, but relief from hardships and dangers of our present tariff laws should be devised with special precaution against imperiling the existence of our manufacturing interests.

To those who contended that American workers would be thrown out of their jobs, he countered:

> . . . that a lowering instead of a repeal, would not be unsettling. To these the appeal is made to save their employment and maintain their wages by resisting a change . . . but the reduction of taxation should be so measured as not to necessitate or justify either the loss of employment by the working man or the lessening of wages.

Cleveland then advanced his central argument—that a high tariff was in effect a tax on necessities:

> Nor can the worker in manufactures fail to understand that while a high tariff is claimed to be necessary to allow the payment of remunerative wages, it certainly results in a very large increase in the price of nearly all sorts of manufactures which in almost countless forms, he needs for use of himself and family.

Then, in a radical motion, Cleveland denounced the high tariff as the tool of trusts or monopolistic cartels:

It is notorious that competition among our domestic producers is too often strangled by combinations quite prevalent at this time and frequently called trusts which have for their object the regulation of supply and price of commodities made and sold by members of the combination. The people can hardly hope for any consideration in the operation of these selfish schemes.

Cleveland closed in a much quoted line that attacked the doctrinaire protectionists who subscribed to the high tariff as an article of faith, as well as the idealistic free traders whose gospel was spreading from Britain.

Our progress toward a wise conclusion will not be improved by dwelling upon the theories of protection of free trade. *It is a condition that confronts us, not a theory.* (Emphasis added)

His final sentence ended:

I am so much impressed with the paramount importance of the subject to which this communication has so far been devoted, that I shall forego the addition of any other topic.

His focusing of this presidential message on a single problem is not the only reason that qualifies Cleveland's address as one of the most important presidential documents in history. Cleveland also deserves to be remembered as a great president for perceiving that a high tariff was not only a tax on necessities for the American family but also a tool big business cartels could use to gouge the consumer by squeezing our competition.

After a protracted debate, the Cleveland bill passed the House, but it never had any chance of emerging from the Republican Senate. But even if Cleveland resembled more a Sancho Panza than the Man of la Mancha, the quixotic attempt was not a total failure. He had targeted the Jay Goulds and other kingpins of big business and taken the protective tariff from the citadel of dogma into the open field of national debate.

As the captains of industry feverishly began amassing a political war chest for the presidential campaign of 1888, Cleveland remained unperturbed. For one thing, the old bachelor had married the beautiful, young daughter of his old law partner and friend, Francis Folsom. On June 2, 1886, the forty-nine-year-old Cleveland became the first president to marry in the executive mansion.

Frances Folsom Cleveland, who might be the most popular First Lady ever to grace the White House, brought for the first time a sense of rooted contentment to the bachelor politician's life.

The Republicans had nominated Benjamin Harrison, the grandson of William Henry Harrison. He was both a distinguished general and a high protectionist. In his behalf, the manufacturers papered the factories and homes with pamphlets and brochures detailing the horrors of depression and misery that would follow if the protective barricades of a high tariff were torn down. The disorganized Democratic campaign was no match for the oiled efficiency of the big business juggernaut. Cleveland lost the election, even though he won the popular vote by more than 100,000 votes.

In 1892, Cleveland returned to the White House on a surge of disgust against the monstrously high tariff written by Congressman William McKinley and the Republican administration. In the White House, Cleveland tempered that tariff. But his second term is know better for his stubborn defense of the gold standard against the strident demands of the "silver" Democrats of the west led by William Jennings Bryan. A true conservative, Cleveland despised the populists of the West as he did the plutocrats of the East. When the Democrats nominated the apostate Bryan after his "cross of gold" speech, he sat out the presidential election. "He was," as they said at the time, "still a Democrat but very still."

The poet and diplomat James Russell Lowell, who was a Republican, delivered a speech right after the announcement of Cleveland's tariff message. He called the "bluntly honest Cleveland the best representative of Americanism that we have seen since Lincoln was snatched from us . . . the President's chair has a *Man* in it and this means that every word he says is weighted with what he is."

In the tariff message, as in all his actions, Cleveland manifested a courage that never yielded an inch in the cause of truth and never surrendered an iota of principle to expediency. In a political age often blackened by corruption and chicanery, his honesty glowed like a light on a dark street.

8 _____

The Big Stick: Monroe Doctrine
à la Theodore Roosevelt

There is a homely adage which runs: "Speak softly and carry a big stick!"

Theodore Roosevelt was America's first global statesman. He came to the White House in the first year of the twentieth century, and eight years later, in 1909, his pyrotechnic leadership on the world stage had shattered the century cocoon of isolationism.

He built the Panama Canal, dispatched a modernized U.S. fleet around the world, negotiated an end to the Russo–Japanese War, forced the German kaiser out of Latin America, and arranged a summit conference trying to head off a European World War.

His critics called him an imperialist, but if that term implies a racist rationale, it does not apply to the first president to appoint a member of the Jewish faith to the cabinet and to invite the first black to dine at the White House.[1] On the other hand, if the term means that the Republican Roosevelt practiced a Bismarkian or Metternichean *realpolitik* like a Henry Kissinger or a Richard Nixon, he would have worn the label proudly. He did not shrink from the uses of power but revelled in its exercise.

Theodore Roosevelt was born not only with a silver spoon in his mouth but also with a majestic mace in his hand. Not since John Quincy Adams was a president more informed about world affairs, more experienced in dealing with world statesmen, or more articulate in defining the role of America in world diplomacy.

Roosevelt grew up among people who knew Europe at first hand. His great uncle, James, had lived in Paris, where he moved in fashionable circles and counted the queen of Spain and the marquis de LaFayette among his friends. Before the Civil War an uncle on his mother's side had lived abroad studying art and literature, and Theodore himself had visited two other uncles many times in London, where they made their home.

At age ten, right after the Civil War, Roosevelt's parents took him to Europe, where they spent a year traveling. Three years later, in 1870, Theodore again spent a year with his family visiting not only Europe but also the Middle East. That year Roosevelt spent much time in Paris and Rome and learned to speak German while living with a family in Dresden. His older sister, Bamie, upon whom he frequently depended for counsel, spent several years in the 1880s as hostess to their bachelor cousin Roosevelt ("Rosey") Roosevelt, when he was Secretary of the American Legation in London. "Rosey," the older half-brother of Franklin Roosevelt, had developed a special liking for Theodore and introduced him to many of the rising English politicians. One of them, Cecil Rice, who later became the British ambassador to Washington, served as best man at Roosevelt's wedding to Edith Carow in London.

During his visits with Bamie in London, Roosevelt not only dined and weekended with members of the British cabinet, judges of the High Court of Justice, and ranking lords of the Admiralty; he also sought the acquaintance of the leading historians and political philosophers such as John Morley, George Otto Trevelyan, and James Bryce.

Interestingly, one rising politician Roosevelt met only when he became governor was Winston Churchill, whom he resembled in many ways.[2] Like Churchill, he was born of aristocratic parentage and won public renown through military adventures. The Boer War in Africa for Churchill and the Spanish-American war in Cuba for Roosevelt made their names both household words.

Just as Churchill had to work to overcome the physical impediments of a severe lisp and stutter to fit himself for public life, Roosevelt had to surmount the handicap of a frail physique beset by asthma. Taking up boxing as a sport to recondition himself, at Harvard he won the lightweight championship. In the Dakotas, where he ranched in the 1880s, he won local fame when he knocked out a barroom bully who taunted him by calling him "four eyes." It was little known that Roosevelt was actually blind in his left eye because of a college boxing injury.

Senator Chauncey Depew once introduced Roosevelt as a "man of the West with an Eastern background." In that sense he was not unlike Churchill, who was described as "a British aristocrat who had inherited his mother's American temperament." Or, to put it another way, both had to the end of their lives the irrepressible exuberance, boundless energy, and insatiable curiosity of a little boy.[3]

Intellectually, Theodore was far more akin to Churchill than his cousin, Franklin. His scholarly history of the War of 1812 in 1882, which is still read by students of the war today, revealed not only his talents as a historian but also his geopolitical philosophy. Roosevelt, who became an assistant secretary of the Navy under McKinley, advocated a big navy. Like Churchill, who was in his career twice first lord of the admiralty, Roosevelt early subscribed to the philosophy of Alfred Mahon. Reviewing an advance copy of Mahon's book on sea power for the *Atlantic Monthly* in 1890, Roosevelt praised it in the highest terms. Later in the year Mahon, who was indoctrinating officers on his expansionist views at the Naval War College, was sidetracked for sea duty, Roosevelt lobbied vainly to block the posting. In frustration he exploded to Mahon, "Oh, what idiots we have to deal with."

Like Churchill, Roosevelt was an avowed imperialist. He shared with Churchill the view that the twentieth century was to be the Anglo-American era. In 1896 he praised a French commentator, Gustave LeBon, who described "the superior qualities" of the English-speaking nations that were destined to rule the world. Although he thought the English-speaking nations had a peculiar genius for self-government, his beliefs were not tinged by racism. In fact, he denounced the Aryan notions of Houston Chamberlain, whom he described as "an extremist whose doctrines are based in foolish hatred."

Also like Churchill, Theodore Roosevelt may have been impelled to seek a political career to avenge his father. Theodore Roosevelt, Sr. was, however, not a politician; rather, he was one of the gentry class who never let various civic pursuits interfere with his paramount duties as a father. Yet he did aspire to be appointed Collector of the Port of New York by President Rutherford Hayes. The Conkling Republican machine in New York blocked the appointment and young Theodore Roosevelt never forgot the slight to his father.

At Harvard he had not shown much interest in the Hayes–Tilden race in 1876, but four years later he was a reform candidate for the state legislature. The father he adored had died the year before. It is more than possible that the son, who never thought of himself as his father's mental or spiritual equal, chose politics for reasons of redemption as well as reform. He was pursuing the path denied to his father. Politics was a needed outlet for a son shattered by the sudden death of his father.

In Albany, the twenty-two-year-old Roosevelt quickly established himself as a leader of the Republican reformers. The nattily dressed Roosevelt was a conspicuous figure in his strident attacks against legislative pay raises, municipal trusts, and political corruption, even when it often involved Republicans. Often he found himself on the side of Governor Grover Cleveland. But Roosevelt was no Don Quixote. His ambition tempered zeal into pragmatism.

After two terms as state representative, Roosevelt, at the Republican convention of 1884, together with his friend Henry Cabot Lodge of Massachusetts, played a conspicuous role in denouncing the leading contender,

James Blaine. But when the tainted Blaine was nominated, Roosevelt did not join Carl Shurz and the other Republican reformers in supporting Cleveland. For this action he invited intellectual scorn. Unlike Nelson Rockefeller in the 1964 conclave that nominated Barry Goldwater, however, Roosevelt reasoned that participation as a delegate in a convention was an implicit pledge to support that convention's candidate.

It was a difficult time for Roosevelt personally even more than politically. When his wife Alice died in childbirth he left politics and bought a ranch in South Dakota.

There in the Badlands Roosevelt ranched, cowboyed, and sheriffed. As deputy sheriff of Billings County, he once rounded up three outlaws at gunpoint. He later wrote of his adventure for a magazine back East, taking care, he said ruefullly, not to put the pronoun "I" once in the narrative. His more important writing was his acclaimed book *Winning the West*, which established him as one of America's best narrative historians.

The cause that lured Roosevelt back to the East and politics was a hopeless run for Mayor of New York in 1886. He didn't win, but he burnished his Republican credentials in time for the Republican convention of 1888, which nominated Benjamin Harrison to oppose Grover Cleveland. Roosevelt threw his energies into the presidential campaign in the hope for a federal appointment. After many months, the only job he could secure was that of civil service commissioner, a position with minimal salary and no staff.

As civil service commissioner he would make up in publicity what he lacked in power. He fought Philadelphia department store magnate John Wanamaker who, as postmaster general under Harrison, doled out patronage jobs to Republican regulars. Before reporters Roosevelt attacked the integrity of the postmaster general, accusing him of "slanderous falsehoods" upon his character. For Victorian sensibilities, the real sensation of the press conference was his parting curse on the staunch Methodist churchgoer, "Damn John Wanamaker." The ensuing storm ignited popular support for the beleaguered Commissioner. Grover Cleveland, who came back to the White House in 1882, felt impelled to keep Roosevelt as commissioner even though the New York Republican had campaigned dutifully for Harrison.

Roosevelt, who had chased down bandits in the Badlands of the Dakotas, eventually wearied of tracking misappointed bureaucrats in Washington. In 1895 he traded his commissionership of the civil service for another commissionership that would better whet his sense of adventure. New York City had installed a police commission to investigate corruption and graft, partly because of reforms he had championed while in the legislature.

Roosevelt focused his indefatigable energies to the task. Soon no cop on the beat felt safe from the ubiquitous Roosevelt. The new commissioner would dart into a neighborhood taproom to evict from the barroom stool policemen who were drinking on the house while still on duty. He would descend upon other cops who chatted on corners with ladies of the evening.

The journalist Arthur Brisbane described the thirty-seven-year-old new police commissioner:

> Sing, heavenly muse, the sad dejection of our poor policemen. We have a real Police Commissioner. His teeth are big and white, his eyes are small and piercing, his voice is rasping. His heart is full of reform and a policeman in full uniform with helmet, revolver and nightclub.

Sometimes Roosevelt would make excuses to his hostess at a swank soiree, then reclaim the helmet and nightclub he had left with the butler in order to patrol the precincts until dawn, when he would fall asleep on his office floor. Other times, in the role of the storied King Haroun-Rashid of Morocco, he would stalk the streets incognito until he caught a policeman unawares in a corrupt act.

At the same time, he streamlined the force, setting up a school for recruits, putting the police on bicycle wheels, and establishing a telephone system from his office to the precinct stations. His own daytime uniform while administrating over the force was "modern" if not avant garde. He enlivened his black suit with a pink tasselled shirt, a blue sash taking the place of the more prosaic vest.

The results of his anti-corruption campaign did not quite match his pyrotechnic style. Roosevelt stumbled when he applied his reform zeal to the Sunday Blue Laws.

The community most unhappy with Roosevelt's crusade were the Germans; when they found their Sunday "beer gardens" closed, they were outraged. Even the mayor, who had appointed Roosevelt, sided with the German constituents: "I find that the Dutchman I had appointed is trying to turn all New Yorkers into Puritans." It was one thing to alienate the saloonkeepers, who were mostly Democratic in allegiance, but another to infuriate the good Teutonic burgers, who had always voted Republican.

When Roosevelt raided Sherry's, the elegant watering hole for the financial establishment, he added the powerful upper class to the opposition from the lower and middle classes.

It was time for Roosevelt to leave New York, which he did in 1897, when he finally secured, with the help of Cabot Lodge, an appointment as assistant secretary of the Navy by President William McKinley. Roosevelt had campaigned energetically for the Ohioan the year before.

McKinley was not eager to appoint the hawkish Roosevelt to such a sensitive position at a time his administration was trying to stay out of a war with Spain. The Spanish were in the midst of a conflict to hold onto their New World colonies. But finally the president, responding to the pleas of the New York Republican leader Tom Platt, appointed Roosevelt. Platt wanted the increasingly unpopular police commissioner out of his hair.

Roosevelt, an advocate for an expanded navy, soon revealed his philosophy in a speech to the Naval War College at Newport, Rhode Island.

> Peace is a goddess only when she comes with a sword girt on thigh. The ship of state can be steered safely only when it is possible to bring her against any foe . . .
>
> If we mean to protect the people of lands who look for us for protection from tyranny and aggression, we must have a strong Navy. Otherwise we should abandon all talk of devotion to the Monroe Doctrine or to the honor of the American name.

Under an indulgent Secretary John Long, Roosevelt worked to modernize the Navy in the same way he had on a smaller scale updated the New York City police force. To improve morale, he discouraged advancement solely by tenure and seniority and lobbied to build six battleships to increase the fleet's war preparedness on both oceans.

Roosevelt also promoted George Dewey to admiral of the Pacific Fleet, and dispatched Dewey to the Philippines. Dewey arrived in Hong Kong to learn that the U.S. battleship *Maine* had been destroyed in the harbor of Havana in Cuba on February 15, 1898. Roosevelt's cable to Dewey in Hong Kong was prescient.

> Keep full of coal. In the event of a Declaration of War, your duty will be to see that the Spanish squadron does not leave the Asiatic coast.

When President McKinley yielded to the demands of William Randolph Hearst's jingoist press and declared War in April, Dewey was right in position to destroy the Spanish fleet in Manila Bay.

To Roosevelt, America's entry into the war was long overdue. He had earlier described the vacillating McKinley as "one with all the backbone of a chocolate eclair." Roosevelt saw war as the only way to rid the Western Hemisphere of the remaining blight of European colonialism.

A full scale war, however, would not find Roosevelt long chained to an administrative desk in Washington. Although it could be successfully argued that Roosevelt's immense organizing talents might have been better employed in mobilizing the war effort, he resigned to field the First Volunteer Cavalry regiment. Certainly Roosevelt had compelling personal reasons to stay in Washington. His wife, who had recently given birth to their fifth child, Quentin, was severely ill. Yet Roosevelt confided later to his military aide, "I would have gone from my wife's deathbed to answer the call."

At San Antonio, Texas, the regiment drilled under its real commander, Colonel Leonard Wood. Wood, a professional soldier, was not amused when after weeks of rigorous training for the regiment, Roosevelt treated his troops to all the beer they could drink as they sang "There will be a hot time on the old town tonight."

The "Rough Riders," as Roosevelt called them, did possess a certain spirit. They were a motley collection of cowboys from the West, polo players, and steeplechase riders from Harvard and Yale, with many of the enlisted men being Negroes who left the streets of New York.[4] But they burned with the pride of an elite corps. In Cuba the culmination of their military involvement occurred in their attack against the Spanish defenses on San Juan Hill.

In what he would later call "his crowded hour" on the day of July 1, Roosevelt gave the signal for charge. Armed with extra spectacles in every pocket and festooned with a polka-dot blue handkerchief draped on his Spanish sombrero, Roosevelt led the bloody but victorious attack against the ensconced Spanish batteries.

Apart from the sinking of the *Maine*, Dewey's victory in Manila Bay, and Captain Walter Reed's fight against malaria, the Rough Rider's charge was the most remembered incident of the war. Roosevelt's fame, which in no small way was due to his friendship with war correspondent Richard Harding Davis, spread to the readers of the popular press.

The clamor for Roosevelt to run for governor of New York soon drummed into the ears of Boss Tom Platt, now the Senator from New York. The incumbent Republican governor had become unpopular through irregularities and extravagances revealed in Erie Canal construction contracts, but to the wary Platt Roosevelt was a "bull in the china shop."

Platt was eventually persuaded that the discordant notes of scandal could be drowned out by the rousing strains of patriotism. To audiences recently stirred by the glories of the recent war, Colonel Roosevelt proved to provide the right heroic note.

In a typical campaign rally at railroad stops across New York State, a bugler would sound the cavalry charge, and, as the notes died, candidate Roosevelt would begin the address: "You have heard the trumpet that sounded to bring you here. I have heard it tear the tropic down when it summoned us to fight at Santiago." He would close,

> We are face to face with destiny and we must meet it with high and resolute courage.

The campaign speech would urge voters to affirm the results of the war by electing a straight Republican ticket.

If little of substance was promised by the candidate, Roosevelt as governor compiled a solid performance in his two-year term. He improved civil service requirements, strengthened the franchise tax to control corporations, and enacted a tenement bill to relieve slum conditions in New

York City. As governor of the biggest state, Roosevelt was not unaware that the governor's house in Albany was one of the best stepping stones to the White House.

Roosevelt's timetable for a presidential bid was 1904, not 1900, when presumably McKinley would run for a second term. But Roosevelt's increasing independence, as Governor, from the Republican organization made Republican Boss Platt push him into national politics four years earlier. With Platt's behind-the-scenes urging, Roosevelt's name was circulated as a popular vice presidential candidate in the Republican convention of 1900 in Philadelphia.

Roosevelt had mixed feelings about the burgeoning speculation. On the one hand, he knew that a vice president had not been elected to the White House since Van Buren followed Jackson in 1836. On the other hand, Roosevelt could not bring himself to refuse the national spotlight by renouncing all interest in the vice presidency.

At the convention, Governor Roosevelt played the reluctant bride to the developing draft. The GOP national chairman Mark Hanna, who was President McKinley's mentor, tried unsuccessfully to block the move. "Do people realize that there is but one life between this madman and the Presidency?" But the convention, with some nudging by Republican bosses Platt from New York and Penrose from Pennsylvania, worked its popular will.

In the election campaign, Roosevelt crisscrossed the nation, logging 28,000 miles. It was more than any other presidential or vice presidential candidate had ever done, with the singular exception of the one who was his real adversary in the campaign: William Jennings Bryan. Adlai Stevenson, the Democrat's vice presidential nominee, was the actual opponent. But in a campaign where President McKinley did nothing more than issue pronouncements from his porch in Canton, Ohio, the burden of electioneering fell upon Roosevelt, whose principal assignment was to counteract Bryan's popularity in the West. Roosevelt said of his campaigning ability, "I'm as strong as a bull moose."

For Roosevelt, the campaign tour of the Rocky Mountain states, where he was welcomed by Rough Riders, was like a continual homecoming: RANGE GREETS ROOSEVELT, WYOMING IS STIRRED UP—ROOSEVELT ROUSES BUTTE. Finley Peter Dunne through the inimitable Mr. Dooley said, " 'Tis Teddy alone that's running and he ain't runnin', he's gallopin'."

Even in the West, where Bryan was idolized, the hero of San Juan was more than a match for the silver orator. The national plurality was 844,000, the greatest since Grant's reelection in 1872. In March, when Tom Platt was asked if he was going to Washington for the second inauguration of McKinley, he replied, "No, I am going to watch Teddy Roosevelt take the veil."

In the first few months, Roosevelt had little to do except preside over the Senate, which debated McKinley's appointments. When Congress broke, Roosevelt attended the Pan American Exposition at Buffalo, to which President McKinley telegraphed: "May there be no cloud on this grand festival of peace and progress."

No one could anticipate the thunderbolt that would shatter the convention and the nation when President McKinley himself came to the exposition on September 6. Leon Czolgosz, an anarchist, upon meeting the chief executive, pulled out a gun encased in a handkerchief and shot twice.

On the morning of the shooting, Roosevelt was attending an outing of the Vermont Fish and Game League at Lake Champlain. At dusk Roosevelt received a telephone message and hurried to Burlington to board a special train for Buffalo. When the president seemed to rally, Roosevelt, as a sign of confidence, left Buffalo to visit his family. The next day the president was dead.

The new president returned to Buffalo and first paid a call on Mrs. McKinley. Afterwards, he went to a friend's house, where most of McKinley's cabinet awaited. "I wish to say that it shall be my aim to continue absolutely unbroken the policy of President McKinley for the peace, the prosperity and the honor of our beloved country." The oath of office followed with Roosevelt adding his own redundant flourish: "And so I swear."

Despite the assurances for continuity, the forty-two-year-old Roosevelt, by the very dint of his vigorous personality, imposed a different imprint on national policy from the start. A creature of the American midlands, McKinley saw problems from the perspective of a small town lawyer whose chief clients were commercial interests. Roosevelt was a cosmopolitan aristocrat whose views had been shaped by wide reading and extensive travel abroad. Roosevelt also was an activist who saw the role of president as chief architect of American destiny; the stolid McKinley pictured himself as a benign chairman of the board who carried policies formulated by Congress and the right-thinking leaders of the business community. Theodore Roosevelt could not have forced himself to conduct a front porch campaign for the presidency even if political wisdom had dictated it. To Roosevelt, the presidency was "a bully pulpit" from which he should shape, not follow, American attitudes.[5]

One area where Roosevelt differed sharply from his predecessor was the American role in world affairs. McKinley had been pushed reluctantly by public opinion into the Spanish-American war. If Roosevelt had been president, he would have pushed for involvement. He would not have been as morally reluctant as President Wilson some years later or as politically careful as his cousin Franklin many years hence.

But although Roosevelt would not shrink from war, he was not an interventionist for reasons of territorial aggrandizement. He once told his friend, the German Ambassador Speck Von Sternberg, that America had as much interest "in annexation as a gorged boa constrictor might have in swallowing a porcupine." Instead, he saw the potential use of military force as a supplemental arm to world diplomacy. To Roosevelt, America had come of age as a mighty industrial nation, and America had to assert her rights on the world stage or risk losing them to the more internationally active European powers. As the leading democracy in the world, America had a duty to encourage the development of representative government and to safeguard the New World from European colonialism.

Roosevelt had been in office scarcely two weeks when his global attitudes were tested. The issue was the Philippines. One of his first pronouncements as president that September directed that "absolutely no appointment in the insular possessions will be dictated or controlled by political considerations." Roosevelt believed that the democratic heritage of the United States required that our administration of the former Spanish colony be exemplary. He also pledged that the United States make the Filipinos "fit for self-government after the fashion of the really free nations."

Early the next year Roosevelt dispatched to the Vatican his friend William Howard Taft, who had been a popular and able governor of the Philippines. Under Roosevelt's instructions, Taft was to negotiate the transfer of huge land estates owned by the Dominican Friars to the Filipino farmers. The discussions, which angered Catholics in America, dragged on for almost two years. But eventually a settlement was reached, with the United States agreeing to pay the church 50 percent of the appraised land value. In eight years, more than 50,000 Filipinos were tilling their own farms.

On a territorial dispute of a different nature, Roosevelt again found a quick settlement early in his administration. This time the dispute was with Canada. For many years Canada had been laying claim to the southern boundary of Alaska, which had been purchased by Secretary of State Seward right after the Civil War. The discovery of Klondike gold had stirred the issue to the boiling point. Great Britain, which had granted a self-government charter to the dominion about the same time as the Alaska purchase, suggested that the matter be submitted to an impartial tribunal for arbitration.

The British recommendation put Roosevelt in a box. On one hand, the United States had recommended during the Cleveland administration the arbitration method for Britain in the Venezuela dispute and could hardly reject the suggestion. But on the other hand, Roosevelt believed that the Canadians had no case, and thought the tribunal, in the interests of appearing fair, would trim the rightful dimensions of United States territory.

Roosevelt's strategy was to agree to a commission, but also to make sure it was stacked with his own men. For the London meeting the British chose their own Lord Chief Justice Alverstone to complement the two Canadian choices, who were, respectively, the lieutenant governor general of French

Quebec and a Toronto attorney. For his part, Roosevelt selected political friends Senator Cabot Lodge, Secretary of War Elihu Root, and George Turner, a former senator from Washington State.

While Roosevelt at home threatened "to run troops to the boundary line" if the negotiations failed to yield the right results, he sent Justice Oliver Wendell Holmes to London to persuade his fellow jurists and friend Lord Alverstone of the righteousness of the American claim.

As Roosevelt anticipated, the award gave the Americans almost everything they asked for. The British press angrily charged that Roosevelt had subverted the tribunal process. To Roosevelt, the American claim was solidly supported by all legal evidence, including extant maps. Roosevelt, however, was probably correct in speculating that an American delegation filled with American judges and international lawyers instead of Senators and Republican politicians would never have convinced the Republican Senate to ratify their arbitration award.

The Alaskan boundary dispute was not the only time Theodore Roosevelt waved the big stick of American power to force concessions by a European nation. The Kaiser's Imperial Germany actually was the first to feel the force of Roosevelt's assertive diplomacy.

Under its volatile despot Cipriano Castro, Venezuela had piled up immense debts to foreign creditors, particularly those from English and German firms. Even Roosevelt had called him "that unspeakable villainous monkey."

Originally, Germany had offered to submit claims to international arbitration, but the bantam dictator had arrogantly rejected the offer. He not only thumbed his nose at the foreign demands but insulted British sovereignty by seizing some of her ships in Caracas harbor.

By December 1902, the British and Germans, acting in concert, captured four Venezuelan gunboats and blockaded their harbors. The two governments then severed their relations with Venezuela. Roosevelt, who had already made George Dewey, the hero of Manila Bay, a four-star admiral with a new Caribbean command, dispatched him to sail to Venezuela.

The same day Dewey received his orders, Roosevelt instructed Secretary of State John Hay to call the German Chargé d'Affaires into the State Department for the deliverance of a stern warning that a congressional resolution was being prepared asking that the president uphold the Monroe Doctrine. Roosevelt was determined to force the Germans into arbitration, which the now frightened Castro was belatedly but eagerly embracing.

The Kaiser, whose brother, Prince Henry, had just completed a cordial tour in America, was astonished by the president's display of force. The showing of the U.S. flag in the Caribbean had its intended effect. The Kaiser agreed to let the United States act as arbitrator, and Germany backed away from making any landing in Venezuela.

Before the Venezuelan crisis, Roosevelt was sympathetic to European nations' rights to enforce the collection of any just debt incurred. The actions of the Kaiser's government, however, raised Roosevelt's fears that Imperial Germany might use such an incident to establish a naval base in Latin America. Years later he wrote, "I became convinced that Germany intended to seize some Venezuelan harbor and turn it into a strongly fortified place of arms."

It was not just Germany, however, but the possibility of any European power exploiting a debt crisis to take control of a Latin American nation that worried Roosevelt. The governmental instability of those nations impelled the president to reinterpret the Monroe Doctrine.

In Chicago on April 2, 1903, President Theodore Roosevelt used a banquet for business and civil leaders as the occasion to showpiece his extension of the Monroe Doctrine. Roosevelt was no orator of the William Jennings Bryan School of eloquence. In fact, he despised rhetorical flourishes. To Roosevelt, such an orotund style undermined a speaker's sincerity and credibility with his audience.

For this address, Roosevelt gathered all his files and correspondence on the Venezuelan crisis, together with a copy of the Monroe Doctrine, and made notes outlining the address. With the notes at his desk, he dictated the speech to his stenographer in the new West Wing of the White House, which he had decided to build shortly after he assumed the presidency. When the dictation was typed and corrected, he forwarded the draft to his secretary of state, John Hay, for review.

At the white-tie hotel dinner in the Auditorium (which is still standing and owned by Roosevelt University), the president was welcomed by Mayor Harrison and then introduced by Franklin MacVeagh, chairman of the committee and political ally of the president. In an auditorium that only holds five thousand, six thousand Roosevelt partisans rose to applaud. In his distinctive falsetto voice, he chopped out in a matter-of-fact tone the purpose of the address:

> Mr. Chairman, Ladies and Gentlemen: Today I wish to speak not merely about the Monroe Doctrine, but about our entire position in the Western Hemisphere . . .

His staccato delivery, which clipped off the consonants, became even more pronounced as Roosevelt quickly bore into the heart of the message:

> Our nation has insisted that because of its primacy in strength among the nations of the Western Hemisphere it has certain duties and responsibilities which oblige it to take a leading part thereon.

And then his voice rose in pitch.

We hold that our interests in this hemisphere are greater than those of any European power possibly can be, and that our duty to ourselves and to the weaker republics who are our neighbors requires us to see that none of the great military powers from across the seas shall encroach upon the territory of the American republics or acquire control thereover.

The audience enthusiastically roared their approval to Roosevelt's broadening of the Monroe Doctrine.

With the operative words "encroach" and "control," Roosevelt widened the application of the doctrine. No more did "interference" or "settlement" define the nature of intolerable European involvement. Any military action in the Western Hemisphere that would lead to a takeover or effective dominance of a nation's government would justify the United States in invoking the doctrine.

This policy, therefore, not only forbids us to acquiesce in such territorial acquisition, but also causes us to object to the acquirement of a control which would in its effect be equal to territorial aggrandizement.

Roosevelt paused to let the audience endorse his statement with their hands, then he moved to the proposed Panama Canal project. By implication, he seemed to be suggesting to his audience the dangers to our interests if a European country installed a naval base within sailing reach.

That is why the United States has steadily believed that the construction of the great Isthmian Canal, the building of which is to stand as the greatest material fact of the twentieth century—greater than any similar feat in any preceding century—should be done by no foreign nation but ourselves.

Roosevelt then detailed the terms of the treaty. Secretary of State John Hay consulted with Lord Pauncefote of Great Britain in December 1901. Britain awarded control of the canal project to the United States, along with the "exclusive right to regulate and manage it and becoming the sole guarantor of its neutrality."

He then proceeded to outline the treaty with the country of Colombia for completing the construction that had been initiated by a French Company.

In pardonable if hyperbolic self-praise, Roosevelt boasted that "those treaties are the most important that we have ever negotiated in the effects upon the future welfare of this country and mark a memorable triumph of American diplomacy—one of those fortunate triumphs which rebounds to the benefit of the entire world.

Next Roosevelt explained the diplomatic history leading up to the recent crisis in Venezuela. He even read in minute detail to the dinner audience the correspondence between his secretary of state and the German ambassador.

The purpose was to set the stage for reading again and emphasizing his presidential message of December 3, 1901, which was conveyed to the German government.

> The Monroe Doctrine is a declaration that there must be no territorial aggrandizement by any non-American power at the expense of any American power on American soil. It is in no way intended as hostile to any nation in the Old World.

Roosevelt once advised his friend William Howard Taft that "a speech should be a series of posters on the same subject in order to get the idea across and make it stick. . . . You have to iterate and reiterate until you are pretty well weary of the very sound of your own voice."

Roosevelt followed his own advice. He explained to his audience again the effect of this reinterpretation of the Monroe Doctrine:

> The concern of our government was of course . . . to keep an attitude of watchful vigilance and see that there was no infringement of the Monroe Doctrine—no acquirement of territorial rights by a European power at the expense of a weak sister republic—whether this acquisition might take the shape of an outright and avowed seizure of territory or of the exercise of control which would in effect be equivalent to such seizure.

With his eyes sparkling behind his pince-nez spectacles, his mustache bristling, and his teeth flashing as he inhaled, Roosevelt propounded his credo:[6]

> I believe in the Monroe Doctrine with all my heart and soul . . . but I would infinitely prefer to see us abandon it than to see us put it forward and bluster about it and yet fail to build up the efficient fighting strength which in the last resort can alone make it respected . . .

Roosevelt continued his sermon from "the bully pulpit."

> Boasting and blustering are as objectionable among nations as among individuals and the public men of a great nation owe it to their sense of national respect to speak courteously of foreign powers just as a brave and self-respecting man treats all around him courteously. To boast is bad and causelessly to insult another worse—yet worse than all is to be guilty of boasting even without insult and when called to the proof is unable to make the boasting good.

Here Roosevelt pulled out his brightest poster.

There is a homely adage which runs: "Speak softy and carry a big stick. You'll go far."

Roosevelt had first used the motto as governor to explain in a conversation how he handled Tom Platt's Republican machine. Shortly before he became president, he publicly introduced it to an audience at the Minneapolis State Fair, applying it as an apt axiom for the "New America of the 20th Century" and calling it a "West African saying." The truth, which Roosevelt didn't realize, was that something like it appeared in Benjamin Franklin's *Poor Richard's Almanac.*

The "big stick" was, of course, a modernized U.S. Navy, which Roosevelt asked his audience to support.

> If the American Nation will speak softly and yet build and keep at a pitch of the highest training a thoroughly efficient Navy, the Monroe Doctrine will go far.

After describing the needs of a modern navy, Roosevelt then concluded:

> If we have such a Navy—if we keep on building it up—we may rest assured that there is but the smallest chance that trouble will ever come to this Nation and that we may likewise rest assured that no foreign power will ever quarrel with us about the Monroe Doctrine.

As the speech ended, the thousands of dinner guests swarmed around Roosevelt in a burst of patriotic jubilation. Roosevelt had given vent to the new nationalism of the new century.

Two months later Roosevelt wrote a letter to be read by his Secretary of War Elihu Root at a dinner in New York. This corollary to the Monroe Doctrine stated,

> Brutal wrongdoing, or an impotence which results in a general loosening of the ties of civilized society may finally require intervention by some civilized nations and in the Western Hemisphere the U.S. cannot ignore this duty.

Later in December, 1903, in a presidential message to Congress, Roosevelt again clarified this corollary to the Monroe Doctrine, asserting that "America had no land hunger" and that interference would be a last resort and only because misdeeds had "invited foreign aggression to the detriment of the entire body of nations."

Under this corollary, Roosevelt sent troops to Santo Domingo the next year when revolution had reduced the nation to bankruptcy. Roosevelt was criticized again for imperialism when he helped the rebellious Panama province of Colombia secede in order to establish a more friendly nation to deal with in the construction of the canal. To those in Congress who denounced his high-handed actions in negotiating a treaty with the new government of Panama, Roosevelt replied: "I took the Canal Zone and let Congress debate and while the debate goes on, the canal does also."

Bluntness was always a Theodore Roosevelt hallmark, and on the podium his technique was plain, simple, and direct. Roosevelt seemed to follow another homely adage about public speaking, which dictates that you should tell an audience what you are going to say, say it, and then tell them what you have said. In his Chicago speech on the Monroe Doctrine, Theodore Roosevelt showed that he was obviously a disciple of this school. His style was strong emphasis of a single message in simple language.

But if such a direct style did not appeal to the classical rhetoricians of the day, it was ideally suited to the popular press that had become a staple of the American diet. Roosevelt was the first president to communicate directly with the American people, and they responded with an affection unsurpassed by any president.

Roosevelt was reelected in a landslide in 1904 and retired in 1909, leaving the presidency in the hands of his chosen successor and friend, William Howard Taft. Later a rift developed between the two men, and Roosevelt, in a later try for office, failed as a third party candidate in 1912.

But Theodore Roosevelt left an indelible stamp on American life. Under his leadership, the United States became a world power, ending its history as a second-class nation. Roosevelt perceived in the democratic promise of Abraham Lincoln the mission to carry American ideals to the rest of the world. He saw in the Monroe Doctrine the instrument to brandish that mission.

NOTES

1. On one occasion in the White House, Roosevelt even boasted to a Jewish visitor that he had Jewish blood in his Dutch ancestry.

2. Churchill traveled to Albany to meet Governor Roosevelt in 1900. At that time Churchill had just been elected to Parliament, and Roosevelt had just won the vice presidency. Roosevelt found the young visitor brash and conceited.

3. It is perhaps not coincidental that the Teddy Bear and the favorite character of the Teddy Bear world, Winnie the Pooh, took their names from Roosevelt and Churchill. A. A. Milne named the teddy bear of his son, Christopher Robin, "Winnie," for Churchill, in the 1920s. "Pooh" was his son's baby rendition of "bear."

4. At the end of the war Roosevelt paid special tribute to the "gallant Negro soldiers."

5. The term "bully pulpit" does not appear in any of Theodore's writings. It was quoted by an editor from a conversation he had with the president after he had left office. The words were used in the foreword to the speech collection published in 1930.

6. James Whitmore, who has played Roosevelt on stage, has testified that Roosevelt bared his teeth to take a deeper gulp of breath. It was a habit he had developed in his asthmatic years.

9 ⎯⎯⎯⎯⎯⎯

Wilson's Declaration of War: A Latter-Day Paul on Mars Hill

The world must be made safe for democracy.

If Theodore Roosevelt was a warrior, Woodrow Wilson was a priest. But, if a priest, he was not a pastor in the Roman Catholic tradition who ministered to his flock in the parish. Instead, he was like a Calvinist preacher who, in the stern language of Old Testament prophets, transmitted the gospel from God on high to his congregation. Woodrow Wilson was a parson's son who found in the mission of American democracy his messianic message. He entered political life to cleanse the American political temples of its corruption. He later stepped into the international arena to inject the democratic idealism of the New World into the corrupt power politics of the Old. He was a latter-day apostle Paul with American democracy as his gospel.

His religious zeal inspired his followers but infuriated his foes—for his opponents saw posturing in Wilson's piety. To them, Wilson was more hypocrite than hero: a politician who wielded his moralism to annihilate his foes and advance his own ambitions.

But if the preacher and politician in Wilson made him a paradox, he was neither the first nor the last American leader to use righteousness in his rise to power. Still, the contradictions in his background and record made those with political influence—whose support he needed to achieve his political goals—distrust him.

Wilson liked to portray himself as a Southerner. While a professor, he wrote a biography of George Washington, and as president he liked to cast himself as a continuation of "the Virginia Dynasty." But Wilson was hardly a Virginian. His birthplace in Staunton, Virginia, was more an accident of his father's pastoral calling.

Theologically, Wilson was not an Episcopalian but a Presbyterian, and the rigorous Calvinist upbringing of a child reared in a Scottish parson's manse made him far more spiritually akin to New England Puritanism than to Southern Anglicanism.

On the speaker's platform, Wilson projected the urbane polish of a British barrister. But his wit suggested a warmth that did not exist. Although women found him gracious and gallant, that charm did not extend to members of his own sex or to political peers.

Wilson carved out a role as a political reformer, but his nomination by the Democratic Party in 1912 owed much to the bosses of the big Eastern city political machines. He let himself be pictured as a pacifist with a moral loathing of war, but his niche in history is secured by his successful leadership in America's first World War.

His place in the hearts of men and women all over the world was not due so much to his victory in battle but to his defeat in peace. Like the apostle Paul, he tried to spread his gospel of democracy across the world. Many of his dreams for national self-determination were dashed by the Versailles Conference. The League of Nations, which he purchased at the cost of some of those dreams, was rejected by the U.S. Senate. The defeat broke him physically. The collapse would ensure for him a heroic legend— the martyred missionary of a righteous cause.

His father wanted him to be a preacher, and in 1875 he scraped up the money to send him to Princeton, then the "West Point" for future Presbyterian clergymen. Wilson remembered his years at Princeton as the nostalgic high point of his life. Interestingly, he was not a prize student. Perhaps it was because midway through college his intellectual interests shifted from theology to government. He began writing essays on political science, which were published in the *Nassau Literary Magazine*. In his senior year, he sold his first article, "Cabinet Government in the United States," to the *International Magazine*, the editor of which was future Senator Cabot Lodge.

At Princeton Wilson prepared himself to be a debater rather than a preacher. He organized and wrote the constitution for the Liberal Debating Club and, as its best debater, was made speaker of the prestigious Whig Society. This early experience helped develop Wilson's inordinate faith in the efficiency of debate framed on parliamentary rules under a charter. The seed had been sown for his later advocacy for a League of Nations.

A career in government in those days required the study of law. So, after graduating from Princeton in 1879, Wilson went to the University of Virginia Law School. During his first year, Wilson joined the Jefferson Debating Society and became its president. Then, revealing once again his fascination for tinkering with charters and parliamentary rules, he revised its constitution. After a year of law school, the high-strung Wilson collapsed with a nervous breakdown. He left law school and never went back. He tried practicing law in Georgia and was bored.

Wilson then married, and his new bride persuaded him to pursue an academic career. In the emerging discipline of political science, Wilson earned a doctorate at Johns Hopkins, then was appointed to professorships at Wesleyan, Bryn Mawr, and Princeton.

In 1896, when Princeton was celebrating its sesquicentennial, Professor Wilson was chosen to deliver the commemorative speech. In his talk, titled "Princeton in the Nation's Service," he said, "College professors could easily forget they were turning out citizens as well as directing pupils." In a stirring address that was as eloquent as it was erudite, Wilson captured the attention of alumni. From that day on Wilson, whose angular profile seemed to mark him for distinction, was viewed as a possible president of the college. Six years later the trustees installed the forty-six-year-old Wilson as president of his old alma mater.

In his inaugural address as college president, the embryonic statesman emerged from the scholar when he said "We are not put into this world to sit still and know; we are put into it to act." Wilson saw the presidency as a political forum. Not all of the audience was impressed. A delegate from a foreign country commented, "Wilson is quite all right and his ideas are not bad; but after all he is not God Almighty and Princeton is not a throne!"

Wilson soon found that he did not have a king's power. When he attempted to shut down the exclusive eating clubs and set up a preceptorial system like that in Oxford or Cambridge, he failed.

Wilson's first battle for democracy against the aristocratic establishment foreshadowed his later fight for the League of Nations. He staked out the high moral grounds for his crusade and carried the day—but not without a cost in alumni support.

Wilson also failed to achieve his plan for a graduate school, but he succeeded in burnishing his image as a reformer. And a reformer was just what the Democratic Party in New Jersey needed. A strong current was running against the Republican Party, which for many years had controlled the state house at Trenton. The Democratic city bosses of New Jersey believed that a college president unsullied by political battles was the sure ticket to victory.

Although Wilson had refrained from speaking out politically while president of Princeton, he had been accepting speaking invitations all over the state. His popularity as an after-dinner speaker grew. Compared with the political orators of the day, Wilson seemed more British than American. If his forensic style was more professorial than oratorical he had the academic trait of being succinct.[1]

He labored hard to achieve simple declarative sentences. This directness, combined with his aristocratic face and lank stature, commanded respect.

This is not to say that all the New Jersey politicians welcomed this transplanted Virginian. But a reform figure above the fray of state politics was intriguing. Wilson himself brought matters to a head with a surprise appearance from a nearby golf course to a Trenton caucus of Democratic political leaders.

"Gentlemen," he said, dressed with a gold sweater over a dark gray suit, "the time has gone by when you can play politics and fool the people; now it is a case of put up or shut up."

As a Democratic candidate, Wilson ran as "a progressive," directing his fire at big corporations and big city bosses. To Republican taunts that he was selected by those bosses, Wilson stated that he had "made no promises, made no deals and made no commitments." He even used his wit to affirm his purity. An inveterate limerick writer, Wilson fashioned this ditty comparing the bosses "to the young lady" and himself to the Princeton tiger:

> There was a young lady from Niger
> Who smilingly rode on a tiger
> They returned from the ride
> With the lady inside
> And a smile on the face of the tiger.

Wilson won in a record Democratic landslide, but he soon found that the Democratic city bosses who selected him had not forgotten his expedient disavowals of their support. The Democratic legislature put up their own candidate for U.S. Senate against Wilson. (This was before the 17th amendment was passed requiring direct election of senators.) Wilson, with his reform flag flying, took the issue to the stump: "The issue is between the people and the bosses." To the surprise of the regulars, Wilson won.

The victory caught the attention of the national press. He had hardly taken his oath as governor in 1911 when his name began to be boomed for the Democratic presidential convention to be held the next year:

In his inaugural address at Trenton, Wilson stated:

> We are servants of the people, of the whole people. Their interest should be our constant study. We should pursue it without fear or favor. Our reward will be greater than that obtained in any other service; the satisfaction of furthering large ends, large purposes, of being an intimate part of that slow but constant and ever hopeful force of liberty and of enlightenment that is lifting mankind from age to age to new levels of progress and achievement.

Wilson was aware that Theodore Roosevelt's chosen successor, President William Howard Taft, was alienating the reform element of the Republican Party. A successful Democratic presidential candidate would have to appeal to the "progressives" in the nation's majority party.

Wilson's reform agenda as governor pushed for an anti-corrupt practices bill, employers' liability, and a public utilities regulatory commission based on the progressive Governor Robert B. LaFollette's legislation in Wisconsin.

Wilson's strategy was to portray the Democratic Party as the "progressive party" and himself as the party's most "progressive" candidate.

The key to the Democratic presidential nomination lay in the party's dominant figure, William Jennings Bryan, who had thrice run unsuccessfully for president. As Woodrow Wilson correctly noted, "No one could be nominated without Bryan's approval."

The problem was that the intellectual professor had never been enamored with the evangelical populist, and Wilson's gibes about Bryan were a matter of public record. Wilson's chief rival for the Democratic nomination, however, did not excite Bryan either. He was Champ Clark, the speaker of the House, who commanded a network of fellow politicians across the country. To Bryan, Clark was a professional politician motivated by neither purpose nor program.

At the convention in Baltimore, Clark led Wilson on the first ballot by 100 votes. The other two candidates, Senator Underwood and Judson Harmon, ensured that the Democratic convention, with its two-thirds rule for nomination, would be a long, hot session.

Ironically, the difficulty for Wilson was the rift in the Republican Party. Theodore Roosevelt, who had challenged his erstwhile friend William Howard Taft for the nomination, had bolted the convention when the incumbent president was selected in a bitter fight. A split in the Republican Party made a Democratic victory likely. If any Democrat could win, the bosses of the Democratic Party preferred politician Clark to professor Wilson.

Bryan, who was pledged to Champ Clark, became increasingly dissatisfied with his choice as the voting continued for thirteen ballots. What bothered Bryan was the tainted support of Clark by some "Wall Street" delegates. On the fourteenth ballot Bryan may have reasoned that Wilson, if not a populist, was at least a progressive. So Bryan switched. A leather-lunged Clark delegate screamed at Bryan, who was unleashing his populist oratory on the floor, "You're not a Democrat!" Bryan shot back, "Three times more than six million Democrats have said I was. If you hand me up your name I'll strike it from the roll!" In the end, Bryan's followers in the West and South turned the tide. On the forty-sixth ballot, the trickle to Wilson turned into a flood, and Wilson was nominated.

At the time of the nomination, a Democratic senator told Wilson that the real battle that fall would not be against Taft but against Roosevelt, who had been nominated by the Progressives. But in the end, America's most popular political personality, with his "Onward Christian Soldiers" fervor, could only split the Republican vote in a three-way race. Shrewdly positioning himself in the middle between the conservative Taft and the "radical" Roosevelt, Wilson won in an electoral landslide with a little more than a third of the vote.

March 4, 1913, was a glorious day for the Democrats. Wilson was the first Democrat in the White House in sixteen years and only the second Democrat since the Civil War to be elected president. The new chief of state, in his brief inaugural address, struck a spiritual chord. The tenor was that of a preacher, not a politician:

> This is not a day of triumph; it is a day of dedication. Here muster not the forces of party, but the forces of humanity. Men's hearts wait upon us; men's lives hang in the balance; men's hopes call upon us to say what we do. Who shall live up to the great trust? Who dares fail to try? I summon all honest men, all patriotic, all forward-looking men to my side. God helping me, I will not fail them if they will be counsel and sustain me.

The new chief executive, who had written as a professor that the president must be like a prime minister, put his political science thesis into practice. He was the first president to enter the halls of Congress to announce his program. Working closely with Congress, he advanced measures to lower tariffs, enact a stronger anti-trust act, and establish the Federal Reserve.

Yet the shadow of tragedy darkened his administration in the second year of his term. In August, 1914, his devoted wife died; and in the same month the cataclysm of World War I erupted in Europe.

In the beginning Wilson, sharing the beliefs of leaders of both the Allies and the Central Powers, thought the conflict would end in six months. The nature of the new century's trench warfare, however, proved the experts wrong.

From the very onset, when the Imperial Germans invaded neutral Belgium, Wilson's personal sympathies lay with the Allies. As president, however, he adopted a position of official neutrality. In an appeal to the people, he stated:

> Every man who really loves America will act and speak in the true spirit of impartiality and fairness and friendliness to all concerned . . . The United States must be neutral in fact as well as in name during these days that try men's souls. We must be impartial in thought as well as in action.

Though the preponderance of public opinion favored the Allies, the sentiment did not translate into support for military aid, much less for intervention. Congressmen from the Midwest and West still religiously subscribed to George Washington's doctrine of non-involvement in European affairs. Furthermore, millions of German and Irish descent were sympathetic to the Central Powers.

But Wilson sensed early that the course of neutrality could be jeopardized on the high seas. The British blockade of German ports allowed American ships to land only in Allied harbors. The German Imperial High Command eventually took action to stop the one-sided trade of officially neutral America. The new U-boat was the German answer to the British blockade.

On May 7, 1915, the *Lusitania*, carrying American passengers, was sunk by a German submarine. Not until Pearl Harbor did a sinking more greatly shock the American people. Sentiment quickly solidified against Germany. Wilson at first responded with his ill-chosen phrase: "Sometimes a man can be too proud to fight."

The tone of his carefully drafted diplomatic protest was stronger. Wilson warned the Germans that "the United States would not omit any necessary action sustaining the rights of its citizens or in safeguarding the sacred duties of international obligation." William Jennings Bryan, Wilson's neutralist and isolationist secretary of state, objected to the wording and resigned. But the protest did not satisfy critics such as Theodore Roosevelt, who urged intervention. The fact that Bryan had resigned did not impress Roosevelt. "Both of them agree," Colonel Roosevelt charged, "that our policy should be milk and water. They only disagree on the precise quantity of dilution of milk and water in the measure." Even within Wilson's administration were those frustrated with the Wilson policy of neutrality. Colonel House, Wilson's principal aide and personal emissary to the Allies, for example, initially counselled entry into the war.

The mounting public outcry compelled Wilson to assert himself into international negotiation to protect American interests. He issued his call for "an open seas." At the same time, he began taking the steps for military preparedness so long demanded by Roosevelt and his other critics. Intervention, particularly on the eve of a coming presidential election, was ruled out.

In the 1916 election Wilson faced a united Republican Party behind a compromise choice. Justice Charles Evans Hughes, who was acceptable to both the Taft and Roosevelt wings, resigned from the Supreme Court and received his party's nomination. Hughes, the former governor of New York, had a record as distinguished as his bearded appearance. But his starched, pompous delivery was no match for Wilson's urbanity. In the end it was the Democratic Party campaign slogan "He kept us out of War" that might have made the marginal difference.

All through the campaign year he had continued his advocacy of "an open seas." The results were limited even if the British agreed to loosen a few of their blockade restrictions and the Germans moderated their submarine warfare. But now Wilson felt God's hand upon him. It fell upon him not only to end the war but to end all wars.

On May 27 of the election year, Wilson appeared with Senator Henry Cabot Lodge at a "League to Preserve the Peace" meeting to endorse the concept of a League of Nations. It was a plan that, though originally advocated by Roosevelt, had become the personal project of former President Taft. The spectacle of world war had caused a small band of political idealists to grow into an international lobbying group. President Wilson declared to the assembled delegates:

Only when the great nations of the world have reached some sort of agreement
. . . and some feasible method of acting in concert when any nation or any
group of nations seeks to disturb the fundamental interest, can we feel that
civilization is at last in a way justifying its existence and claiming to be fully
established.

Wilson then laid down the following principles:

"National Sovereignty," "Equal Rights for small and large nations" and
"Freedom from Aggression."

With these principles, Wilson urged support of three objectives: a negotiated end to the war, free use of the seas, and, significantly, an international tribunal.

Although Wilson had been vague about specifics, he felt it was necessary
three days later to calm growing isolationist fears. "I shall never myself,"
said Wilson in reference to George Washington's warning in the Farewell
Address, "consent to an entangling alliance but I would disentangle the
people of the world from those combinations in which they seek their own
separate and private interests. . . . "[2] It was an ingenious attempt to bridge
the isolationist and internationalist sentiments in an election year.

With the election won, Wilson could now afford to spell out details of a
League of Nations and his peace settlement package. In an address before
the Senate, he offered his final plea for mediation, which included five points:
Peace without victory; A League of Nations; American participation in the
League; Equality between nations; Self-determination; and freedom of the
Seas. Enumerating his points, the president closed with an appeal designed
to disarm his isolationist critics in the Senate. "I am proposing, as it were,
the doctrine of President Monroe to be the doctrine of the world . . . I am
proposing that all nations avoid entangling alliances which draw them into
competitions for power . . . "

The Germans answered Wilson's peace plan by resuming all-out submarine warfare against the British. Wilson responded by handing the German ambassador his walking papers and recalling our minister from Berlin.

For Wilson it was the time of his garden in the Gethsemane. Committing
America to war was an awesome and terrible act. He groped for any way
to avoid involving America in the European conflict. He tried sending peace
signals to Germany. He endeavored to negotiate secretly with Germany's
ally, Austria. He even considered armed neutrality as a possible response
to the resumption of German submarine action.

When the time came for his second inaugural address on March 5, 1917,
Wilson urged Americans to persevere in bringing "calm counsel to the issue
of war and peace. The shadows that now lie dark upon our paths will soon
be dispelled if we be but true to ourselves." Wilson, who could sound like

a mystic, was not without some Machiavellian considerations. As a politician, he was plugged into the prevailing isolationist sentiment. He echoed the worst of those fears by asking at a cabinet meeting "what effect the depletion of manpower" caused by American intervention "might have upon the relations between the white and yellow races." But the real problem for Wilson was both a moral and practical dilemma: if there was "peace without victory" how could a lasting peace be achieved?

Like Martin Luther, Woodrow Wilson wrestled with his decision. Entering the war would ensure victory but would endanger the post-war peace; not entering might be morally correct but would diminish America's authority on the world stage. Could a mightier justice be wrought through the sin of war?

By the end of winter, the resumption of German U-boat attacks on merchant shipping was unleashing a tide too powerful to contain. Wilson could not check it, but he might channel it for constructive ends. America, decided Wilson, would enter the war to end all wars. America would enter not as a mere contestant to share in the fruits of victory but as a crusader to stop injustice and impose a righteous settlement. To Wilson, the fight against autocracy was now more cleanly framed since Czar Nicholas had abdicated and Russia was withdrawing its armies. America would not join Britain and France as an ally but as an "associated power" on behalf of the world. Wilson, who had been trained in the law, saw America, in legal terms, as an "intervener" rather than an "original party to the dispute."

The loner Wilson sought his own counsel. He conferred with few except his White House aide, Colonel House, Secretary of War Lindley Garrison, and Secretary of State Robert Lansing, who had replaced Bryan. Then, armed with notes, Wilson began putting his thoughts on paper. As an academician, he was contemptuous of those who delegated the task of speechwriting to others. Actually, Wilson did not begin by writing out his speeches word for word. Instead, he outlined his points in a logician's argument. Wilson would then sound out this thinking on both his new wife, Edith Galt, whom he had married on the eve of the election year, and his press secretary, Joe Tumulty. Such a state document as a declaration of war, however, had to be written out. Wilson drafted the speech first in shorthand and then rewrote it in a mixture of shorthand and longhand. It took him two days, beginning at six in the morning, only taking time for lunch with his wife. When he finished the draft in late March, he typed it out himself. By this time he knew the contents like the palm of his hand.

April 2, 1917, was one of those glorious spring days Washington D.C. has patented. Blue skies and billowy clouds capped the Capitol as it awaited the president's appearance. On the Capitol steps the scene was far from tranquil, as angry socialist demonstrators made repeated attempts to bridge the cordon of policemen who were protecting the entrances. One of them broke free from the guards and assaulted Senator Henry Cabot Lodge, the

leader of the pro-war interventionists. The sixty-seven-year-old Boston
Brahmin dispatched the assailant with a well-placed right to the jaw. Tensions, even if they did not run along party lines, ran high. It was a day of
judgment. Journeying from the White House down Pennsylvania Avenue
to the Capitol for the convened joint session, Wilson was about to cross
the line from the side of the pacifists to that of the interventionists.

At 8:20 P.M. the president, with Tumulty, his wife, and Dr. Grayson,
his personal physician, entered the House chamber. He was escorted by a
body of cavalry to shield him from the anti-war protesters. On the floor
were seated not only congressmen, senators, and members of his cabinet,
but also members of the Washington Diplomatic Corps in evening dress.
An expectant hush followed the announcement of the President of the
United States, who mounted the rostrum of the speaker.

In a soft voice the president opened:

> I have called the Congress into extraordinary session because there are serious,
> very serious changes of policy to be made and made immediately; which it
> is neither right nor constitutionally permissible that I should assume the re-
> sponsibility of making.

The president then reviewed the history of his diplomatic negotiations
with the Imperial Government of Germany to safeguard freedom of the
seas for a neutral United States. "The new policy of the Germans," Wilson
noted, "would not be done by any government that had hitherto subscribed
to the humane practices of civilized nations."

The president in the role of the righteous prophet then hurled his judgment against the government of the Kaiser:

> The present German warfare against commerce is a warfare against mankind.
> It is a war against all nations . . . The challenge is to all mankind . . . Our motive
> will not be revenge or the victorious assertion of the physical might of the
> nation, but only the vindication of right, of human right of which we are
> only a single champion.

Wilson discussed and dismissed "armed neutrality" as an ineffectual
course of action. It was a course, said Wilson, that would "draw us into
the war without the rights of belligerents."

> There is but one choice we cannot make, we are incapable of making: we
> will not choose the path of submission . . .

As the *New York Times* reported, Congress did not wait to hear the rest
of the sentence. At the word "submission," Chief Justice White, who was
positioned in the front and center seat, exultant "with an expression of joy
and thankfulness on his face, dropped the big soft hat he had been holding

and waved his hands high in the air, brought them together with a heartfelt bang and the House and Senate followed him with a roar like a storm." The cheers drowned out the rest of Wilson's words "and suffer the most sacred rights of our Nation and our people to be ignored and violated."

Again, applause erupted when the president, in the most formal language, called for a declaration of war. Though the wording was dispassionate, the reaction was impassioned.

> With a profound sense of the solemn and even tragic character of the step I am taking and of the grave responsibilities which it involves but in unhesitating obedience to what I deem my constitutional duty, I advise that the Congress declare the recent course of Imperial German Government nothing less than a war against the government and people of the United States. That it formally accept the status of belligerent . . . and it take immediate steps . . . to exert all its power to bring the Government of the German Empire to terms and end the war.

Seldom has a call for a declaration of war been made in such a restrained fashion. No militant words or martial tone attended the president's request.

After outlining preparations for war, Wilson put forth the goal of that war: the forces of democracy against autocracy. Like the Apostle Paul in his Mars Hill address in Athens, Wilson had ascended Capitol Hill to expound in his declaration for war his gospel of freedom for the world.

> Our object . . . is to vindicate the principles of peace and justice in the life of the world as against selfish and autocratic power and to set up amongst the really free and self-governed people of the world such a concert of purpose and of action as will henceforth insure the observance of the principles.

Wilson then made clear that there was "no quarrel with the German People" who were thrust into a conflict "provoked and waged in the interests of dynasties or of little groups of ambitious men who were accustomed to use their fellow men as pawns and tools."

Wilson, now looking directly at his audience, raised his voice to that of a preacher. At this point the cool poise of the diplomat yielded to the passion of a disciple.

> The world must be made safe for democracy.

At first there was little awareness of the memorable sentence. One single exception was Senator John Sharp Williams. Alone, he clapped gravely and emphatically until the rest joined him in a mounting cascade of applause. Wilson then continued:

> Its peace must be planted upon the tested foundations of political liberty. We have no selfish ends to serve. We desire no conquest, no dominion. We seek

no indemnities for ourselves, no material compensation for the sacrifices we shall freely make. We are but one of the champions of the rights of mankind.

In the righteous language of the preacher Paul, Wilson envisioned the awesome task ahead:

There are, it may be, many months of fiery trial and sacrifice ahead of us. It is a fearful thing to lead this people into war, the most terrible and disastrous of all wars, civilization itself seeming to be in the balance.

Here Wilson offered his moral justification of the war: A plan to end all future wars by establishing an assembly of free nations. As Luther had wrestled with his decision to break with Rome, Wilson had struggled to work out an argument to contravene the sanctified precepts of neutrality laid down by Washington.

But the right is more precious than peace and we shall fight for the things which we have always carried nearest to our hearts—for democracy, for the right of those who submit to authority to have a voice in their own governments, for the right and liberties of small nations, for a universal dominion of right by such a concert of free peoples as shall bring peace and safety to all nations and make the world at last free.

Wilson was not only preaching his gospel of democracy to the autocrats of Germany and Austria but also to the Bolsheviks of Russia. The Russian Revolution had erupted in Saint Petersburg two months earlier. Czar Nicholas, who had allied his nation with the British and the French, had been overthrown by Lenin's followers. In a sense, Wilson could be said to be pitting the ideals of the American Revolution to those of the Russian Revolution.

Wilson closed with an invocation that began with words from Jefferson's Declaration of Independence and ended with the cry of Martin Luther.

To such a task we can dedicate our lives and our fortunes, everything that we are and everything that we have, with the price of those who know that the day has come when America is privileged to spend her blood and her might for the principles that gave her birth and happiness and the peace which she has treasured. God helping her, she can do no other.

The Chamber rose, according to the *New York Times*, in a "tumultuous" reception with Chief Justice White leading the applause from the front row. Even Henry Cabot Lodge, the most fervent of his critics, went over to shake the president's hand saying, "Mr. President, you have expressed in the loftiest manner possible the sentiment of the American people."

Only a few, such as Senator LaFollette of Wisconsin and other Midwestern isolationists, remained in their seats. In twenty-two minutes the president had proclaimed an act of war to crusade for world justice. Not until Churchill's speech in December, 1941, would a joint session of Congress be so uplifted and inspired.

The *Chicago Tribune*, comparing Wilson to Lincoln, called the speech "one of the great documents in the Liberty of the World." The *Baltimore American* said it would "go down in history as one of the profoundest and most impressive human appeals ever delivered." The poet Alfred Noyes termed the address "the most momentous declaration in the history of the world."

Across the world Wilson was hailed as a savior. "By a single statement" the *Philadelphia Inquirer's* London correspondent noted, "President Wilson has placed himself in the forefront as a world statesman and raised America to a leading place in the Council of Nations." When two days later a British member of Parliament made a casual reference to Wilson in routine remarks, the mere mention of his name caused the entire membership of the House of Commons to stand and cheer. The (London) *Daily Express* said his speech was the equal of the Gettysburg Address. Later there were reports of school children in Spain and other countries memorizing Wilson's words in classroom recitations. To this day grade school students in Korea memorize and repeat words from Wilson's address.

Wilson himself felt spiritually drained by the ordeal. When he returned to the White House he was pale and ashen. He sat silent with his aide Joseph Tumulty and then said, "Think of what it was they were applauding." No doubt the cheers of people who rushed out onto Pennsylvania Avenue as his entourage motored back to the White House were still echoing in his ears. "My message today was a message of death for our young men. How strange it seems to applaud that!" He then sank into his chair, laid his head on the table, and sobbed.

But Wilson, for all his soulful isolation, stood at the summit of his national popularity. Never again would the country stand so united behind him. The problems inherent in mass mobilization required him at the end of the war to demand war powers similar to that of Lincoln. But by then he was the target of Republican criticism for his management of the war.

Even as the war was ending in November 1918, Wilson was repudiated by a resurgence of Republican gains in the House and Senate. The preacher in his idealism had scorned the politicians and now was learning the price of his isolation.

At the Versailles Conference in France he again savored the cheers of the people, but the European politicians, like the Republican Senate, did not appreciate his pious pronouncements. Prime Minister David Lloyd George said the meeting with Wilson and Georges Clemenceau of Frances was like "being seated between Jesus Christ and Napoleon." Clemenceau, for his part, complained that "Wilson had 14 points when Moses only had 10."

The British and French, whose lifeblood had been drained by the war, resented America's leader, who demanded so much when his nation had contributed comparatively little, even though it represented the decisive difference. Wilson, who never had surrounded himself with strong personalities, now had to negotiate with Lloyd George and Clemenceau, who were masters of power politics.

His principle of "open covenants openly arrived at" was a chimerical idealism never to survive the closed doors of diplomatic horse trading. Wilson himself had to trade away many of his points for a just settlement of boundaries to ensure support for the League of Nations.

A weary Wilson returned to America to rally the people behind his League. The battle to win two-thirds of a Republican controlled Senate for approval of the treaty was uphill. Perhaps if he had taken some leading Republicans, such as ex-president Taft, with him to Paris or even had sat down to deal with Senator Lodge and others as he had with Lloyd George and Clemenceau, he would have achieved America's entry into the League. After all, Lodge was an internationalist who had advocated such a tribunal before Wilson. But so intense was his hatred of Lodge that Wilson scorned acceptance of any reservation to the League, no matter how trivial.

On his rail trip through the West, the fatigued Wilson subjected himself to eight or ten speeches a day. He collapsed from an embolism on September 26, 1919. His body, not his will, failed him. The rest of his presidency was shrouded in an array of White House announcements issued from a darkened room of a stricken president. His wife, who was derisively called "Mrs. President," stood guard and was the chief intermediary to the nation at large from a paralyzed president whose illness brought out a latent paranoia.

When Republican Senator Albert Fall, leading a congressional delegation, called on the president to check on his condition, the senator closed the awkward meeting by saying, "We're praying for you Mr. President." "Which way?" was the president's response.

Wilson lived out his presidency as a partially paralyzed wreck, but his endeavor to make the United States a member of the League of Nations died. Yet the internationalism based on democracy that he preached answered that of Lenin, who advocated dictatorship of the masses.

If Woodrow Wilson became a martyr to the cause of internationalism, it was he himself as much as his opponents who shaped the role. In him burned not only the moral principles of a prophet but the overwhelming pride. The vision of the preacher was undone by the pride of one who would not stoop to ply the politician's craft. Still, Wilson achieved sainthood in his defeated cause. In his declaration of war Woodrow Wilson tapped the roots of American idealism to preach democracy as a gospel for the world. He failed to see that this stubborn faith could be as insular as the isolationists he fought.

NOTES

1. Wilson, when asked once how long it took to prepare a five minute speech, replied, "Three hours." "Really," said the questioner. "How about a 30 minute speech?" Wilson paused and answered "An hour." "What about a two hour address?" "Well, I could deliver that right now."

2. Washington actually said "no permanent alliance." It was Jefferson in his first inaugural who used the adjective "entangling." Nevertheless, Wilson was invoking the oracle of "The Father of his country" to a nation that associated a policy of neutrality with Washington.

10 _____

The Sesquicentennial Address: The Sermon at the Shrine

Governments do not make ideals, but, ideals make governments.

John Calvin Coolidge was born on the Fourth of July: That fact, as well as the fact that two presidents, John Adams and Thomas Jefferson, died on the fiftieth anniversary of that patriotic milestone, may seem like little more than historical curiosity. Yet if those two aging Founding Fathers willed their feeble frames to live until that date, it can be equally asserted that the president who bore the name of the exponent of predestination felt the uniqueness of his birthday was just one augury of a political career that carried him to the White House.

Today Coolidge is remembered, if at all, as "Silent Cal," a cartoon caricature whose dry wit provided contrapuntal relief to the expansive era over which he presided. Forgotten is the legacy of a conservative idealist who trimmed government but never his principles.

For years, through the prism of iconoclasts like H. L. Mencken or historians like Arthur Schlesinger, Coolidge's resolve to balance the budget and reduce the national debt was derided as reactionary if not irresponsible. Today those actions win respect. Perhaps the least imperial of our twentieth century presidents invites a more sympathetic reappraisal in presidential history.

The Fourth of July arrival of Coolidge in Plymouth Notch, Vermont, in 1872 was singular in presidential history, but his rural background of Protestant pieties was not. Like most of our presidents, Coolidge was reared in a small town. Plymouth Notch in Vermont could have been the setting of a *Currier and Ives* print.

The New England town meeting was his early primer of government. Echoes of those debates rang in the ears of young Coolidge, the only son of Colonel John Coolidge, who for most of his life presided over those town meetings.

The result was that Coolidge grew up respecting the role of the politician. If the whole community looked up to Colonel Coolidge (the honorary title was bestowed by the Vermont government), his son's admiration was no less. In this, he was different from most of our presidents, whose aspirations were shaped by a strong mother in a family where the father was either weak or dead. Coolidge lost his mother at age twelve to tuberculosis. At such a formative age, the shock was traumatic for the introverted boy. Her picture would be the only one that adorned his desk in his White House years.

Perhaps if his mother had been alive, Coolidge would not have been sent to board at a nearby academy. For Colonel Coolidge, the decision made sense because in his active civic life he had little time to oversee the lad's studies.

The principal of Black River Academy was an Amherst graduate who pointed the young Coolidge in that direction. Coolidge won respect for his studious manner and was elected secretary of his class. In that role he delivered one of the graduation addresses—the first hint of the embryonic politician. That experience gave him the confidence to accept an invitation to delivery an Independence Day address at Plymouth. The speech was a paean to such New Englanders as James Otis, John Hancock, and John Adams.

As the first Coolidge to attend college, Calvin traveled to Amherst College in Northhampton, Massachusetts, in the fall of 1891 determined to exploit his educational opportunity. Not for him were the distractions of the newly organized fraternities or the attractions of the young ladies at nearby Smith College.

Even in his later years as president, Coolidge never felt comfortable in the social milieu. In his early manhood, such forays into the drawing room were painful. Amherst, though a small college, drew, along with Williams College, its rival, a sophisticated type of Easterner to its campus. Coolidge was a country boy among the more urbane Bostonians and New Yorkers. If he had excelled at games like others of his farmboy background, he might have bridged the gap. Instead, the slight and sallow Coolidge concentrated on his studies.

Coolidge studied languages—Latin, French, and Italian—as well as mathematics, rhetoric, and philosophy. The latter became for Coolidge more than just a course: it became a credo. The philosophy professor, Charles Garman, just like another government professor at Wesleyan at that time, Woodrow Wilson, taught that the purpose of education was to heighten the student's sense of public morality and foster his desire to serve society.

Coolidge wrote in his *Autobiography*, "We looked upon Garman as a man who walked with God." Garman, in the style of Socratic dialogues, made his students question and shape their own ideals. Coolidge wrote that Garman taught him to appreciate social stability, "weigh the evidence," and "carry all questions back to fundamental principles."

When Coolidge's academic awakening came in his junior year, his new intellectual sense of self carried over into other spheres. At the end of that year he finished last in the annual ritual walk across the campus with top hat and cane. As loser, he had to treat some seniors to a beer banquet followed by an address. His speech was a witty effort ending with the Biblical adage, "Remember boys, the Good Book says the last shall be first and the first shall be last." The prophecy struck no one at the time, including the speaker.

In discovering his drollery as a defense for diffidence, Coolidge found a path to popularity. In his senior year, he entered a newly formed national fraternity, Phi Gamma Delta. At graduation he was elected by his classmates to be the salutatorian. The occasion called for a humorous address, and Coolidge rose to the challenge and cleverly lampooned the foibles of various Amherst professors.

What Coolidge prized most in his Amherst years, however, was winning the Sons of the American Revolution Silver Medal for the best essay on the topic "The Principles Fought for in the American Revolution." He argued that this was the only country established upon an idea. The treatise won the Society's silver medal for the best collegiate essay in the country.

As a student, John Calvin Coolidge had, like Stephen Grover Cleveland and Thomas Woodrow Wilson, dropped his first name. His full name, however, was an apt one for the dour New Englander who believed hard work would bring its inevitable rewards.

Coolidge's industry, however, was not fueled by dreams of public fame. He did not choose law as a stepping stone to politics. Law was the obvious occupation for a college graduate who had been raised in the home of a minor magistrate, Justice of the Peace John Coolidge.

If Calvin Coolidge had envisaged a political career, he probably would have returned to Plymouth, where his family had roots and a recognized name. Instead, he accepted his first offer: a clerkship in a law office in Northampton.

His mentor, Henry Field, was a candidate for mayor at the time and so Coolidge had an immediate political baptism when he organized a ward for Field's successful campaign. Three years later in 1898, Coolidge was asked to run for councilman. He won and immediately began maneuvering for the city solicitor post, which was chosen by council.

This office, unlike councilman, was a paid position, and attorney Coolidge needed the additional stipend if he was to settle down and marry.

In the spring of 1904 he met Grace Goodhue, a music teacher in Northampton. They were married in October and honeymooned in Montreal. In the two-week jaunt Coolidge spent most of his time translating Dante's *Inferno* into English.

At their rented house in Northampton, Coolidge framed over his mantelpiece some less-august poetry:

> A wise old owl he sat on an oak
> The more he saw, the less he spoke
> The less he spoke, the more he heard
> Why can't we be like that old bird?

For Coolidge the poem was more reason that rhyme. Idle chatter served no purpose for him. In a political world where extroverts abound, Coolidge was an exception. As it was with George Washington, Coolidge's silence was perceived as strength. The Republicans nominated Coolidge for the state legislature in 1906, and he won by a margin of 264 votes. In his three terms, Coolidge kept his purse strings as tight as his lips on most issues. But on bills that did not require appropriations Coolidge was almost populist. He reflected the progressives' demand for reform in expanding the civil service, regulating the utilities, and limiting campaign spending.

Frustrated by his lonely weeks in Boston as a legislator, Coolidge decided to seek his political advancement at home. He campaigned for mayor of Northampton in 1909. His strategy was simply: he would give no speeches; instead, he would canvass door to door. At each house he would say, "I'm Calvin Coolidge, candidate for Mayor. I want your vote. I need it. I shall appreciate it."

In his two terms as mayor he simultaneously lowered the tax rate while reducing the town's debt. Despite his fiscal conservatism, he did, however, manage to raise teachers' salaries and expand the police and fire departments.

By 1911 it was Northampton's turn to have the state Senate seat in the capitol, and Coolidge was the logical nominee. He was pushed for the seat primarily because he did not seem to want it.

Coolidge arrived at the Capitol on Beacan Hill to find a few of his former legislative colleagues of the previous decade. As a freshman senator, one of Coolidge's greatest triumphs came in a task he was given because no one else would take it. He was appointed to negotiate an end to a six-week strike in the textile mills in Lawrence. His speedy resolution of the strike made the taciturn Yankee from the western part of the state a figure of respect with the Irish-American pols of Boston. His habit of never attacking Democrats won him friends in that party, which looked to him as a bridge to the Republican caucus.

His respect from both sides of the aisle enabled Coolidge to bring a trolley system to Northampton, overriding the veto of the Democratic governor. On other issues Coolidge was generally progressive—as long as it didn't empty the pocketbook. He sponsored and supported pensions for widows and minimum wage for women. For workers he favored workmen's compensation, and for the reformers he backed a state income tax, legalization of picketing, primary elections, and popular election of U.S. senators.

After two terms in the state senate Coolidge was tired of commuting to Boston. He was ready to quit until he learned that the president of the Republican-controlled state senate had decided to run for lieutenant-governor. Coolidge thought he might win enough votes in the caucus to land the prestigious post.

Unfortunately, after Coolidge had already filed his papers, Levi Greenwood, the president of the state senate, withdrew from the lieutenant-governor's race to run again for the state senate. Yet typical of the Coolidge luck, Greenwood, despite living in a heavily Republican district, was defeated by the invasion of suffragettes who had targeted Greenwood.

After learning of Greenwood's defeat on Wednesday after the election, Coolidge hopped on the first train to Boston to organize support in the caucus. As the new president of the senate, he delivered, upon his swearing in, a speech that was a credo:

> People cannot look to legislation for success. Industry, thrift and character are not conferred by act or resolve. . . . Self government means self support.
>
> Do the day's work. If it be to protect the rights of the weak, whoever objects do it. If it be to help a powerful corporation better to serve the people—whatever the opposition—do that. Expect to be called a stand-patter but don't be a stand-patter. Expect to be called a demagogue but don't be a demagogue. Don't hesitate to be as revolutionary as science. Don't hesitate to be as reactionary as the multiplication table.
>
> Don't expect to build up the weak by pulling down the strong. Don't hurry to legislate. Give administration a chance to catch up with legislation.

As the leader of the Republican opposition, Coolidge had delivered a masterful address. As the credo of a conservative Coolidge had eloquently captured in less than ten paragraphs that Yankee blend of pragmatism and skepticism.

As president of the state senate in 1913, Coolidge had to bring together the two factions of the Republican Party—the conservatives who had supported President Taft and the moderates who had bolted to support Theodore Roosevelt. As state chairman of his party's platform committee in 1914, he spliced both factions together under the theme "stability through moderation." Coolidge also displayed ability as presiding officer in the general court (the state senate) where he won a reputation for resolving issues speedily. He trimmed both the length and number of sessions. His expeditious dispatch of business was distinguished by his open mindedness and even humor. When one member complained that a colleague had told him to go to hell, Coolidge's reply was, "I've examined the Constitution and the Senate rules and there's nothing in them that compels you to go."

In 1916, Coolidge's career again advanced by his being at the right place at the right time. The Republican Party's losing candidate for governor, Sam McCall, had been promised the chance to run again two years later. However, Lieutenant Governor Grafton Cushing, thought he was the logical nominee. A vicious primary was the result with both sides lending their support to the neutral Coolidge for the vacated lieutenant-governorship.

The second position in the commonwealth is mostly ceremonial. It was an expedient slot for a son of western Massachusetts. In the campaign Coolidge willingly accepted playing second fiddle to McCall, who had won the primary. Touring the state together in an open roadster, Coolidge left the rhetorical jousting to the former Progressive McCall. When McCall finished stirring the crowds, Coolidge followed with a brief talk filled with names of local chieftains and party regulars.

As lieutenant governor, Coolidge enhanced his reputation for frugality. Once, a reporter entered his office on a wet snowy day. His wife suggested that the visitor could use a drink. Later three other reporters entered. Mrs. Coolidge poured them drinks and was about to refill the first reporter's empty glass when Coolidge said, "No, he already had his."

In 1918, McCall told Coolidge to announce his candidacy for governor because he intended to run for the U.S. Senate. Even though McCall later decided that the press of duties caused by World War I prevented him from making the Senate race, he did not renege on his commitment to back Coolidge for governor.

In the fall, while Massachusetts' most famous politician Henry Cabot Lodge was lambasting President Woodrow Wilson, Coolidge took an opposite tack: he attacked nobody. He talked little of himself or his party. Instead, he adopted a patriotic stance of supporting the war effort and the Democratic president. The strategy worked. He squeaked by his Democratic opponent by just 16,000 votes.

On New Year's Day, 1919, the cannon on the Boston Common boomed out its traditional twenty-one-gun salute announcing that the Commonwealth's forty-fifth governor had taken his oath. Coolidge closed his inaugural address on a moderate note:

> Whether we are to enter a new era in Massachusetts depends on you. The lessons of war are plain. Can we carry them into peace . . . ?
> Let there be a purpose in all your legislation to recognize the right of man to be well born, well nurtured, well educated, well employed and well paid. This is no gospel of ease or selfishness of class distinction, but, a gospel of effort and service of universal application.

As governor, Coolidge strove to increase the minimum wage and workmen's compensation law. He vigorously championed a raise in teachers' salaries but courageously blocked the veterans' lobby plan to give ex-soldiers state jobs without civil service examinations. His mildly progressive record was overshadowed by his handling of the Boston police strike of 1919. Again timing as much as tactics propelled the name of Coolidge into the spotlight.

American labor in 1919 was making demands for higher wages and shorter hours, which it had postponed during the war. In Massachusetts, Governor Coolidge had headed off a threatened strike of firemen in March. Later he helped secure an agreement to end a strike of the Boston Elevated Railway. Whether by direct action or by soft words to both management and labor, Coolidge deserved credit that year for maintaining labor peace.

In August, a satisfied Coolidge took off to vacation in Vermont. But then the police in Boston went on strike. At a time when Mitchell Palmer, Woodrow Wilson's attorney general, was gaining headlines by arresting anarchists, the police strike aroused fears.

When they actually did strike on Tuesday September 9, 1,117 of Boston's 1,544 officers walked off the job. At midnight riots erupted in Scollay Square, Roxbury, and South Boston. The mayor asked Coolidge for 3,000 state militia to help patrol the streets.

Pressures mounted for Coolidge to submit the policemen's demands to arbitration. Coolidge, as he wrote in his autobiography, "did not see how it was possible to arbitrate the authority of law." Instead, he issued a proclamation dispatching the state militia to Boston. Then he called on all loyal policemen to obey him and "aid in the maintenance of law and order."

For Governor Coolidge, his timing was a stroke of luck. The moment the striking policemen saw that continuing their strike would only further prejudice the public against them, Coolidge moved in and called them back to work on his terms: "The police have no right to strike."

In a telegram to national labor leader Samuel Gompers, Coolidge wrote, "There is no right to strike against the public safety by anybody, anywhere, anytime." The terse comment struck a national nerve. Public reaction was overwhelming.

Across the county Coolidge was hailed as a savior of the nation. He was hailed as "A St. George who has slain the dragon of anarchy." President Woodrow Wilson, campaigning for the League of Nations in Montana in 1919, took time out to praise Coolidge for stopping a "strike against revolution." America saw Coolidge as a victor in a second battle of Boston—although this time against Reds instead of Redcoats.

All of a sudden the nation wanted a closer look at this modest hero. As governor, he would only rent two rooms at $3.50 a day in a Boston hotel as his suite for receiving visitors; meanwhile, his wife stayed in half of a double house in Northampton with their two sons. Even Coolidge's wardrobe reportedly consisted only of a blue suit, a gray suit, and a white-tie ensemble for formal ceremonial occasions.

Because of the police strike, Coolidge may have become Massachusetts's most famous politician, but its most powerful politician was still Senator Henry Cabot Lodge, who spearheaded the fight against Woodrow Wilson's League of Nations. As the Republican leader in the Senate, Lodge had a deep stake in the coming Republican National Convention in 1920. Lodge did not want a Republican presidential nominee who favored the League of Nations.

The 1920 Republican National Convention was singular. Not since the previous century, when "King Caucus" controlled the slating of the Democratic Party's national ticket, had congressional politicians so completely dominated a convention's proceedings. There was, of course, no incumbent Republican president to influence the choice of platform and candidate.

Coolidge arrived in Chicago as a possible dark horse candidate. Coolidge, however, was caught between the crossfire of two Massachusetts politicians: Lodge, who opposed the League, and pro-league Murray Crane, the political leader from Western Massachusetts who had long been Coolidge's mentor. Privately sympathetic to the League, Coolidge remained publicly neutral, saying, "A governor does not take a position in foreign policy."

At the convention in Chicago, Coolidge was nominated for president by Speaker of the House Frederick Gilette of Massachusetts. Gilette said Coolidge was "patient as Lincoln, silent as Grant, diplomatic as McKinley, with the political instinct of Roosevelt." The reaction was polite.

The voting that followed the next day showed General Leonard Wood and Governor Frank Lowden of Iowa as the two leading candidates, with the governor of California, Hiram Johnson, pulling enough western votes to constitute a strong third. On the first vote, Coolidge won twenty-eight from Massachusetts and six from scattered states.

At that point the Senate leaders adjourned to their hotel suites in the Blackstone to plot their strategy. Lodge proposed Senator Warren Harding from Ohio as the best compromise candidate. The next day successive ballots pushed Harding over the top.

Coolidge later wrote in his autobiography that "a coterie of United States Senators" had manipulated the selection of Harding. Yet, but for the senatorial high-handedness, Coolidge might never had made it to the White House. Senator McCormick of Illinois, one of that "coterie," had suggested the name of Senator Irvine Lenroot of Wisconsin, a supporter of Theodore Roosevelt in 1912. As a moderate, Lenroot would balance the more conservative Harding. Harding was amenable because his personal choice, Governor Hiram Johnson of California, was not interested.

As Lenroot's name was put into nomination, a voice from the rear of the cavernous hall shouted "Coolidge, Coolidge." The cry caught on, almost drowning out a small demonstration for Lenroot. As the Lenroot rally fizzled, the chairman of the convention saw an Oregon delegate stand for recognition. Thinking he was seconding the Lenroot nomination, the convention chairman gave the Oregonian the floor. To the chairman's chagrin, Wallace McCamant of Oregon nominated Governor Coolidge.

Immediately, Massachusetts' delegation began to demonstrate, hoisting banners proclaiming "Law and Order," which they had earlier assembled in the hope of boosting their governor to the top spot. All at once the name of Coolidge caught hold. Many of the dissident delegates saw the Coolidge boom as a chance to register a protest against the backroom deals of a few imperious senators. Others, though they were staunch regulars, thought Coolidge, who hailed from Lodge's state, was the approved choice. Then there were those who saw a bandwagon forming and jumped aboard. Coolidge accepted the news of his nomination more with a sense of duty than delight.

The vice-presidential campaign he mounted was little more than perfunctory. As a candidate, Coolidge did less than the easy going Harding and far less than his Democratic Party counterpart, Wilson's former assistant secretary of the Navy, Franklin Roosevelt.

On November 2, Harding's fifty-fourth birthday, the Republican ticket won thirty-seven out of forty-eight states. Coolidge did not join in the jubilation. Victory meant leaving Boston and an office with much power and moving to Washington to an office with little more than protocol.

Washington was even worse than he expected. The vice president and Mrs. Coolidge did only the minimum of entertaining from their suite at the Willard Hotel. Still, a multitude of ceremonial events and social obligations required his attendance. The result was a crowded calendar and an empty life.

The sterility of Washington life made Coolidge yearn for his New England roots. In the summer of 1923, Coolidge and his wife were staying with his father at Plymouth Notch while their two sons worked as hired hands at nearby farms. On August 2 Coolidge retired early.

Colonel Coolidge, whose house had no telephone, was roused from his bed when he heard Coolidge's chauffeur knocking on the door. Accompanied by a newsman, the driver had ridden over bumpy roads to alert the vice president that Harding had died. The father awoke his son to tell him of Harding's death and that he was now president. The reaction of the awakened Coolidge was to offer a prayer for the country and himself. He then decided to take the presidential oath immediately instead of waiting until he reached Washington. He put in a call to Secretary of State Charles Evans Hughes, who verified the words of the oath. Hughes told him to do it before a notary. So, in a gaslit room, Coolidge's father swore in his son as the thirtieth President of the United States.

In front of his family and a few others, Coolidge drew up his five-foot nine-inch frame and repeated the words in the light of the lamp on top of the marble-topped table where the family Bible rested. The clock in the small fourteen- by seventeen-foot room read 2:47 A.M. The new president then went back to bed.

Coolidge, who had spent the day helping a neighbor rake hay, did not feel as Harry Truman did two decades later—that a truckload of hay had fallen on him. If the presidency was the ultimate in the succession of offices to which his political career had taken him, that responsibility, just as being mayor and governor, could be met by earnest application and honest adherence to God's and man's laws. The Bible—which in Vermont tradition he did not swear on—was open to his favorite verse from Micah: "To do justly and walk humbly in the path of the Lord."

Coolidge had been propelled to the White House by the sudden, premature death of a chief executive who had been the picture of robust hardiness. But, like the presidency of the state senate that fell open upon its occupant's unexpected defeat as state senator, or the governorship that was handed to Coolidge when McCall did not run for reelection—or the police strike that catapulted Coolidge into the national spotlight—Coolidge seemed to possess the one quality vital to a politician's career: luck. Coolidge, who was the only president to be born on the Fourth of July, was baptized in John Calvin's faith and received his name. Coolidge believed his fate was predestined.

President Coolidge inherited from Harding some of the most distinguished cabinet heads in history. Besides Secretary of State Hughes, it boasted Andrew Mellon as secretary of Treasury, Herbert Hoover as secretary of commerce, and Henry Wallace Sr. as secretary of agriculture.

Less worthy were Harding's friends Harry Daugherty as attorney general and Albert Fall as secretary of the interior, but the charges of cronyism had not yet ripened into corruption.

The first hint of what was to become known as the "Teapot Dome" had come to Coolidge's attention the year before while he was presiding over the Senate as vice president. Wisconsin Senator Robert LaFollette rose to demand an investigation of the leasing of naval oil reserves. The leases in Wyoming had been operating under the corporation name of Teapot Dome.

The Senate hearings, which probed into the dubious influence of Secretary of the Interior Fall in awarding the oil grants, did not get under way until two weeks after Harding's death. By early January of 1924, the investigation had uncovered the appearance of a bribe to Fall by Harry Sinclair, the president of Mammoth Oil Company, and by Edward Doheny of the Pan American Oil Company.

Although Coolidge had no knowledge of those dealings as vice president, the administration he now headed was tarnished by the breaking revelation of corruption. On January 24, he beat the Senate Democrats to the punch with this announcement:

It is not for the President to determine criminal guilt. . . . That is for the courts.
    If there has been any crime, it must be prosecuted. If there has been any property illegally leased, it must be recovered.

Despite Coolidge's statement, the Senate unanimously urged investigation into the roles Secretary of the Interior Albert Fall and Secretary of the Navy Edwin Denby played in awarding the leases. Coolidge, however, managed to stay in front of the investigation by appointing two lawyers in special counsel to investigate the matter. Yet he would not dismiss the cabinet officers before the evidence was in. Citing presidents Madison and Cleveland on the constitutional question of separation of powers, Coolidge said:

The president is responsible for his conduct relative to the retention or dismissal of public officials.
    I do not propose to sacrifice any innocent man for my own welfare nor do I propose to retain in office any man unfit for my own welfare.

Both secretaries—Fall, who was deeply implicated, and Denby, who seemed guilty only of poor judgment—resigned. Democratic attacks now focused on Attorney General Daugherty. From his own party, Senator Borah from Idaho demanded Daugherty's ouster. Coolidge decided to call Borah and Daugherty into his office. Hot words followed as Coolidge remained silent. Daugherty left, and then Coolidge said to Borah: "I guess you're right." When Daugherty refused to open his files to public scrutiny, Coolidge used that reason to fire him.
    Throughout the whole affair, Coolidge kept his head and his self-respect. He was cautious in acting, but caution when others are shooting off their heads is a virtue. In the Teapot Dome case, Coolidge used prudence to keep the executive branch from becoming a whipping boy for Congress. At the same time he worked to root out the wrongdoers. To this end he displayed more sense and skill than Harry Truman did in the corruption scandals of the 1950s or Richard Nixon in the Watergate conspiracy two decades later.
    The scandal that the Democrats hoped would propel them into the White House was deflected by Coolidge's unshakable integrity. That integrity was enhanced by his taciturnity. His brevity was just the opposite to the bonhomie of a Warren Harding. Although Coolidge had been a politician all his life, he didn't seem like one.
    In an ebullient profession, Coolidge was self-effacing. What a contrast he was to the hard sell the new medium of radio exemplified and new business service clubs like the Rotary Club exalted. In an age when both stocks and salvation were peddled, the Coolidge restraint seemed the sign of a statesman.

Coolidge was successful in upholding the integrity of the executive branch against the encroachment of congressional investigation, but the price was his relationship with Congress. His few legislative successes were negative. He vetoed a rise in veterans' pensions and a salary raise for postal workers.

He also managed to block a costly farm bill—the McNary–Haugen—that would have purchased surplus commodities at pre-war prices. The proposals closest to his heart, however—the bills to reduce taxes as well as the federal debt—were ignored.

The question in 1924 was whether the Republican leases would bypass President Coolidge in the nominating convention of 1924. After all, no "acting president," except Theodore Roosevelt, had ever continued in office.

Typically, Coolidge's public demeanor was one of disinterest. Privately, though, he chose as his chief White House aide C. Bascom Slemp. An astute party professional, Slemp freely dispensed patronage plums to the coterie of Southern Republicans who controlled the selection of delegates to the convention. Governor Pinchot of Pennsylvania, the former Bull Mooser, was a threat, as was the farmers' tribune, Frank Lowden of Illinois, who still smarted from his loss to Harding in 1920.

Coolidge's secretary of treasury, Andrew Mellon, who was from Pittsburgh, blocked Pinchot in Pennsylvania. As for Lowden, Coolidge dangled before him the embassy in London.

Two other possibilities were left in the field: an independent businessman who was encouraging a draft—Henry Ford—and a maverick Republican named Hiram Johnson.

Coolidge won Ford's support by backing the industrialist's bid to take over Muscle Shoals, the dam project on the Tennessee River begun by the Wilson administration.

Senator Johnson, however, refused to make way for the incumbent president. The old progressive Republican edged Coolidge in the South Dakota primary in March. But Coolidge blocked Johnson as he did the other progressive, Pinchot: he dispatched another cabinet secretary, Herbert Hoover, to divide Johnson's home-state delegation of California.

At the convention in Cleveland, Coolidge was nominated by his friend Marion Burton, former president of Smith College. Burton closed his tedious caricature of a speech fulminating, "That virile man, that staunch American, that real human being, CALVIN COOLIDGE."

The journalist William Allen White described the convention as "an outing of the chamber of commerce, and bankers and Rotarians" of which "Coolidge was the captain of the crew." But neither the captain nor the crew could decide on a first mate.

Coolidge chose Senator William Borah of Idaho, but Borah refused. The convention took the matter in their own hands and nominated Frank Lowden, who also refused. Finally, the GOP congressional leaders came up with the name of Charles Dawes, the former director of the Bureau of the Budget.

If the Republicans in Cleveland had difficulty in selecting a vice president, the Democrats in New York experienced disaster in choosing their presidential candidate. After 103 ballots in Madison Square Garden between the "wets," led by Governor Al Smith, and the "drys," led by William McAdoo, the exhausted delegates turned to Wall Street lawyer John W. Davis for president.

To balance the lawyer from "the House of Morgan," the Democrats chose Nebraska governor Charles Bryan, the younger brother of the three-time Democratic nominee William Jennings Bryan. The bizarre mating of capitalist with populist drained any enthusiasm for the Democratic cause.

The year had started with Democrats on Capitol Hill aiming their guns at the Republican administration over the Teapot Dome. By summer they had turned the guns on themselves in Madison Square Garden. Turning on their new radio sets to hear the proceedings, the people of the nations could not trust their governing to a party that apparently could not govern itself.

Those three saints of the industrial community—Henry Ford, Harvey Firestone, and Thomas Edison—visited Coolidge at the White House to offer their support. The luck that had marked Coolidge's public career held out. What looked like defeat for the Republicans in January turned out to be a debacle for the Democrats in November. One businessman, Elum Bliss, president of the Regal Shoe Company, caught the mood of the nation when he opined, "I prefer Coolidge to chaos."

Coolidge received about 16 million votes—twice as many as Davis and three times as many as Robert LaFollette, the candidate of the third-party Progressive ticket.

The election gave Coolidge the mandate he never had as president. The tax reform he had long championed now found congressional approval. He believed that a decrease in taxes would increase prosperity. Coolidge was a "supply-sider" before its originators had even been born. Accordingly, he scratched the tax on gifts, snipped the estate tax in half, and sliced the income tax for all.

Part of Coolidge's vision for prosperity rested on the development of commercial aviation. He pushed through Congress subsidization of the aircraft industry and establishment of the Civil Aeronautics Board.

Conversely, Coolidge held that subsidies for agriculture would be counterproductive. He torpedoed an attempt by the farm block to revive the McNary–Haugen bill, which would purchase produce at artificial prices and then dump the goods on the world markets.

Calvin Coolidge was no political philosopher, but neither was he a philistine, as he is frequently pictured. Unlike Franklin Roosevelt or John Kennedy, he wrote most of his major addresses himself, drawing from his grounding in the classics at Amherst College (which he never forgot). He was not a seminal thinker like Jefferson or Madison, nor was he a political scholar like Woodrow Wilson or Theodore Roosevelt; but then, he didn't pretend to be. His Yankee practicality made him prize deeds over words. When he chose to, he could express himself clearly and concisely.

A president who read Dante's *Inferno* in its original medieval Italian was hardly Sinclair Lewis's Babbit. Besides Dante, he also read history and biography for relaxation. Since his days of studying rhetoric at Amherst, he focused on the orations of the great. Although he was familiar with Lincoln's speeches, his favorites were by his fellow New Englanders—the orations of Daniel Webster and the lectures of Ralph Waldo Emerson.

He reread them when he was invited to speak at the Sesquicentennial in Philadelphia in 1926. Emerson had delivered the Centennial at Concord Bridge in 1875, and Webster had both delivered the Bicentennial of Plymouth Rock in 1830 and spoken at Bunker Hill in 1825, when the monument was laid for its fiftieth anniversary.

A Fourth of July address had, of course, a special significance to a president who shared his country's birthday. For one who now found himself by God's providence to be president he felt called upon to deliver a message that transcended the usual patriotic sentiments.

Coolidge saw an America in the full flush of prosperity enjoying the fruits of freedom but forgetting the faith in God that had inspired those resolves of freedom.

As the cherry blossoms imparted their pink glow to the Washington spring, Coolidge in his upstairs study pored over the words of Puritan preachers. He came to the conclusion that the Founding Fathers' love of freedom was inseparable from their religious faith. To Coolidge, the sources to read were not the natural law philosophers like Locke and Hume, who inspired Jefferson, but the Calvinist divines like Thomas Hooker and John Wise.

As a New Englander, Coolidge sensed that the drive for independence owed more to the Puritan theologians than the Enlightenment intellectuals. The latter might have given color to their thought, but the former was the substance of their creed and conviction—the warp and woof of their background and beliefs.

On his upstairs desk lay neat piles of extracts from selected sermons provided by the Library of Congress. In his tiny crawl, Coolidge penned the first draft of his address on yellow legal tablets. The draft was then typed by his secretary. Coolidge relied on neither a research assistant nor speech writer. He had dismissed Harding's speechwriter, Judson Welliver— the first to be solely employed for that purpose—the year before.

On July 4, 1926, Coolidge awakened to find his fifty-fourth birthday being rained upon. He, his wife, and his son John attended the First Congregational Church, and later they had a quiet dinner with Frank Stearns, an old family friend.

The next morning the president and Mrs. Coolidge were joined by Attorney General John Sargent as they drove to Union Station to catch the morning train to Philadelphia.

At his arrival in Philadelphia, Coolidge's limousine drove through pelting rain to South Philadelphia, where he was taken to the Exposition grounds near the Delaware River to view a miniature replica of colonial Philadelphia. The Coolidges did not leave the dry shelter of their car in their inspection of the exhibit.

More than 200,000 people braved the rain to greet the president. Many were small girls in white frocks holding flags, with their parents holding umbrellas over them.

At Memorial Stadium, Coolidge mounted a speakers' podium covered by an awning. He was introduced by Mayor Kendrick of Philadelphia.

Coolidge had titled his address "The Inspiration of the Declaration." It was more lecture than rhetoric and more sermon than a speech. He opened by saying,

> At the end of 150 years the four corners of the earth unite in coming to Philadelphia as to a holy shrine in grateful acknowledgement of a service so great, which a few inspired men have tendered to humanity, that is still the pre-eminent support of free government throughout the world.

In this sentence, Coolidge affirmed what Lincoln first said at Gettysburg and Wilson later expanded on during World War I—that America has a spiritual vocation as the first democracy. Almost a generation before the end of World War II, Coolidge was speaking of America's role as leader of the free world.

Continuing, he reinforced this idea of a holy mission:

> What people at home and abroad consider Independence Hall is a hallowed ground and they revere the Liberty Bell as a sacred relic.
>
> The pile of bricks and mortar, that mass of metal might appear to the uninstructed as useless now because of modern convenience, but, they are the framework of a great spiritual event.

That event was the "Declaration of Independence." It represented the movement of a people. It was not, of course, a movement from the top. To Coolidge, this was a central point. As an outsider amid the rich and sophisticated at Amherst College, Coolidge was proud of his own descent from the yeomanry stock of Yankee farmers. It was these sturdy but humble folks who strove for independence, not "the aristocracy," who had an "attitude of utter neutrality or open hostility."

> The American Revolution represented the informal and mature convictions of a great mass of independent, liberty loving, God-fearing people who knew their rights and possessed the courage to maintain them.

But Coolidge added that our forefathers fought for something more than independence.

> There is something beyond the establishment of a new nation . . . in the Declaration of Independence that was not only to liberate America but was everywhere to ennoble humanity.

Coolidge then restated the central theme of his address:

> It was not because it was proposed to establish a new nation but because it was proposed to establish a nation on new principles that July 4, 1776 has come to be regarded as one of the greatest days in history.

Those principles, said Coolidge, were that "all men are created equal, that they are endowed with certain inalienable rights and therefore that the source of the just powers of government must be derived from the consent of the people."

Like many past American orators, Coolidge restated the familiar Jeffersonian thesis. But then he shed the role of politician for professor, lecturing to his audience that the principle that sovereignty must rest with the people was not really a new idea. What was "revolutionary" was that "all men are created equal."

> The idea that the people have a right to choose their own rulers was not new in political history. It was the foundation of every attempt to dispose of an unpopular king. But we should search those documents in vain for an assertion of equality. The principle had not appeared before as an official declaration of any nation. It was profoundly revolutionary. It is one of the cornerstones of American institutions.

Coolidge then traced the development of this doctrine by New England's Puritan clergy. He cited first Reverend Thomas Hooker's 1638 sermon to the General Court. Next he cited the Reverend John Wise, a leader of the 1687 revolt against Edmund Andros, the royal governor of Massachusetts, and such eloquent preachers as Jonathan Edwards and George Whitfield.

> They preached equality because they believed in the fatherhood of God and the brotherhood of man. They justified freedom by the text that we are created in the divine image, all partakers of the divine spirit.

These puritans believed that authority came only from God. If kings did not have the divine right, men must have the political right to choose their own governments.

> Placing every man on a plane where he acknowledged no supervisors, where no one possessed any right to rule over him, he must inevitably choose his own rulers through a system of self-government. . . . These great truths were in the air that our people breathed. Whatever else we may say of it, the Declaration of Independence was profoundly American.

The rain-drenched crowds began to applaud the last line, but Coolidge, without a pause, then uttered a stern reminder to those then enjoying the fruits of an unprecedented prosperity:

> The Declaration is a spiritual document. It is a declaration not material but of spiritual conceptions. Equality, liberty, popular sovereignty, the rights of man. . . . They have their roots in religious convictions. . . . Unless the faith of the American people in these religious convictions is to endure, the principles will perish. We cannot continue to enjoy the result if we neglect and abandon the cause.

In a memorable line, Coolidge then compared the difference between our American Revolution and the recent Marxist one in the Soviet Union headed by Comrade Lenin.

> Governments do not make ideals, but ideals make governments.

The government, Coolidge contended, cannot dictate ideals, for that responsibility rests with the people.

> There is no method by which that burden can be shifted to government. It is not the enactment, but the observance of laws that creates the character of the nation . . .

Some in the audience thought they heard an allusion to "Teapot Dome" as Coolidge continued:

> Ours is a government of the people. It represents their will. Its officers may sometimes go astray, but that is not a reason for criticizing the principles of our institution. The real heart of the American government depends upon the heart of the American people.

Coolidge then sought to remind his audience that the Founding Fathers were men of deep spiritual convictions.

While there were always among them men of deep learning, and also those of comparatively large possessions, the mind of the people was not so much engrossed in how much they knew, or how much they had as in how they were going to live.

Coolidge closed much as he began—as a preacher speaking to those who had made their pilgrimage to a national shrine. His sermon was an implicit contrast between the American and Russian revolutions. The message he wanted to leave with his audience was that ours had religious roots. If theirs was based on materialism, ours, said Coolidge, was founded on a "great spiritual development."

We live in an age of science and of an abounding accumulating of material things. These did not create our Declaration. Our Declaration created them. The things of the spirit came first. Unless we cling to that, all our material prosperity, overwhelming though it may appear, will turn to a barren scepter in our grasp. If we are to maintain the great heritage which has been bequeathed to us, we must be like minded as the fathers who created it. We must not sink into pagan materialism. We must follow the spiritual and moral leadership which they showed.

The wet, weary audience applauded mostly out of respect for the president and relief at his conclusion.

Late that afternoon Coolidge returned to Washington. The rain had not dampened his satisfaction in delivering what he thought was his greatest address.

By contemporary standards, the speech might seem more preachy than presidential. Yet that role is not inappropriate for one who is chief of state as well as chief executive. Theodore Roosevelt, after all, had called the presidency a "bully pulpit," and to Coolidge the Sesquicentennial was an occasion for a sermon.

It was neither the first nor the last time a president would deliver a spiritual warning. The professorial Woodrow Wilson and the born-again Jimmy Carter come to mind. The best comparison, however, may be to Eisenhower. Although Eisenhower was not quite so didactic, Coolidge did, like Eisenhower, believe that the foundation of American's political and economic freedoms was its belief in God. Coolidge, who like Eisenhower presided over a post-war prosperity, was afraid that the material benefits of a free economy were making people forget its spiritual roots. That fear was the focus of his address.

If Coolidge labored alone over this address, he did have guidance. In a sense, Coolidge was still a star pupil writing to please the professor he revered, Charles Garman. Public service, no less than the ministry, was a spiritual calling and in this the highest of his nation's offices, Coolidge endeavored to produce a speech worthy of the professor's precepts.

President Coolidge's beliefs had not changed in the three decades since he had risen from solicitor to mayor, from state legislator to governor, and from vice president to president. His belief that no man was above the law had remained. To him, the Constitution was as sacred as the Ten Commandments. He would not nor could not be an imperial president. When Coolidge said in 1928, "I do not choose to run," it was not so cryptic as characteristic of personal beliefs that disdained the leadership personality cult of a contemporary Mussolini.

Unlike the two Roosevelts he fell between, he did not exalt or expand the power of the presidency. His character and credo forbade such a role. He had a Yankee's revulsion for grandstanding and a conservative's respect for the separation of the executive, legislative, and judicial powers. Yet restraint can produce accomplishments no less than activism. His removal of the federal debt while reducing taxes was a triumph that grows greater each year as the deficit exceeds $1 trillion. He showed that special interest groups like the farm block could be combatted and that the budget could be trimmed. It is not surprising that Ronald Reagan would restore the portrait of Coolidge to a premier niche in the White House.

Coolidge, like most presidents, did not get along with Congress, but he never allowed his relations to diminish his respect for their prerogatives. His actions underscored his belief that Congress, no less than the president, represented the people's will. Because of the 1929 stock market crash that occurred the year he left the White House, Coolidge's conception of the presidency would be condemned as narrow and short-sighted. In the depths of the Depression his statement that "the business of the government was business" would turn sour. But in defense of Coolidge, he only mirrored the prevailing wisdom of his day. The Democrats, after all, had nominated a Wall Streeter to oppose him in 1924. Even Governor Roosevelt in the 1920s was not suggesting anti-trust suits or measures to tighten regulation of banking and the securities market. Republicans as well as Democrats believed that business was the engine of economic progress.

But if Coolidge did not stretch to the fullest the power of the presidency, neither did he abuse that power. The wire tapping by Nixon as well as by Roosevelt, Johnson, and Kennedy would have been distasteful to him. Neither did he intern citizens of Japanese ancestry like Roosevelt, appropriate a steel mill like Truman, hound steel executives with IRS agents like Kennedy, or participate in a coverup like Nixon.

Coolidge was like a sea captain who ran things by the a book—and that book was the Constitution. Perhaps Coolidge lacked the foresight of a prophet, but this son of a New England town meeting presider did possess the faith in the American democracy—a faith as bedrock as the Vermont hills from which he sprang.

Coolidge was no visionary, but he was an idealist; and his compass was the Constitution. He was faithful to his vows and to the people who elected him. It was his fidelity that restored the tarnished presidency he inherited and reflected the mandate he represented. Oddly, this frugal Yankee amid an expansive era was a man to fit his times. He did what people wanted, and he did it honestly and well. He did not glorify himself or the presidency, but on the 1926 Fourth of July celebration he did exalt the ideals that made this country great.

11 _____

Franklin Roosevelt's First Inaugural: The Rhetoric of Recovery

Let me again assert my firm belief that the only thing we have to fear is fear itself.

Franklin Delano Roosevelt was more than a president—he was a presence. In the 1930s his reassuring patrician tones were a familiar voice in American homes. He was the first president to project his personality into the family living room. If radio in that decade became the focal centerpiece of furniture, Roosevelt, more than any commentator or entertainer, commanded its air waves. His intimate chats were models of conversational intimacy. They invited a credibility lacking in the frenetic cant and histrionic excesses of the typical politician heard at a local courthouse rally. Roosevelt seemed more real to them, and his presence, still attested today by a yellowing photograph of that regal profile in countless Appalachian and African-American homes more than a half-century later, represented a source of hope.

When President Franklin Roosevelt took his inaugural oath in March 1933, America was stricken with its worst economic crisis in history. If, as historians suggest, the recovery by the United States during his administration was accomplished more by the mobilization for World War II than by his New Deal programs, he did permanently restructure government foundations and reshape the presidency as an institution. The agency for this political revolution were the rapidly expanding powers of the federal government. The catalyst for that expansion was the charisma of Franklin Roosevelt, whose voice radiated his innate buoyancy and self-confidence. The president became more than just chief of state or chief executive. The president emerged as "chief guarantor" of economic hopes and opportunities.

Franklin Roosevelt, who marshalled the war against depression, had little in his childhood that suggested darkness and despair. Nor was the promise of dynamic leadership evident in this solitary youth, whose afternoons, following morning sessions with tutors, were filled with riding horses on sunny days or poring over his stamp collection on less hospitable ones.

In both of these pursuits he was joined by his aging father, who, like three generations before him, was a country squire administering the tract of acreage bordering the Hudson River north of Poughkeepsie, New York. James Roosevelt, a widower, had taken as his second wife, Sarah Delano, a handsome woman twenty-six years his junior.[1]

Fair-haired and blue-eyed, young Franklin was born on January 30, 1882. He was always the centerpiece of his parents' life. Some thought Sarah Delano Roosevelt doted on him, but actually she disciplined him. She might have indulged her penchant for combing his golden curls or clothing him in a Lord Fauntleroy suit, but she kept him to a strict allowance and made him take full care and responsibility for the Irish setter an uncle had given him. If she afforded him their class advantages of French and German tutors as well as frequent travel in Europe, she kept close supervision on his lessons and instructed him in their tours of European museums and historic sites.

For a possessive mother, the decision to send her only child to Groton, Endicott Peabody's Anglican and ascetic boarding school in Massachusetts, must have been a decision made by her head not her heart. At Groton, Franklin showed his first political interest by arguing on the debate team for the independence of the Philippines. The teenaged Roosevelt, while not a brilliant student, had an innate curiosity in the world whetted by both his hobby of stamps and love of the sea. In his last year at Groton, he even made plans to sneak off on a fruit peddler's cart to Boston and enlist in the navy for the Spanish-American War, but a felicitous outbreak of measles confined him to bed on the day he was supposed to depart.

Notwithstanding that aborted adventure, no cloud darkened the sunny life of Roosevelt until his first year at Harvard. His father, who had long suffered from a heart condition, died. Perhaps even more traumatic than the not unexpected death of his ailing parent was his failure to be taken in by the Porcellian, Harvard's most elite club, which interestingly had accepted his more flamboyant cousin Theodore many years before.

Roosevelt, though tall at six-foot one-inch, had too slight a frame at 150 pounds for the football team. Rowing and tennis were his sports. The pursuit, however, that demanded most of his energies during his Harvard years was his work at the *Crimson*, the university's daily newspaper. As a "compet," or tryout, in his first year, he scored a major coup by knocking on President Lowell's door for an interview and discovering that the university president favored McKinley over Bryan in the 1900 presidential election. The Democrat Roosevelt was disappointed by the news, but he was delighted by his scoop, which was picked up by national newspapers.[2] The irregular interviews, which violated university precepts, no doubt helped propel Roosevelt in his senior year to the presidency of the *Crimson*.[3]

In the summer of 1903, before his last year at Harvard, he met at North East Harbor Eleanor Roosevelt, the niece of his distant cousin who was now president. It was the first love for both of them. It also was a match in contrasts, pairing the handsome Franklin with the homely Eleanor and counterpointing his debonair charm with her diligent earnestness.

Although his mother tried to forestall the romance with a Caribbean cruise, Franklin was undeterred. He chose Columbia Law School over Harvard because it enabled him to be near Eleanor, who lived in New York City. On St. Patrick's Day in 1905, they married in New York. Her uncle, Theodore, who was in the city to participate in the Irish parade, gave his niece away. "It's good you'll be keeping the name Roosevelt" joked the president, who commanded the spotlight away from both the bride and groom.

Franklin Roosevelt did not finish Columbia Law School. Instead, he clerked for a Wall Street law firm where, after he passed his bar examination, he specialized in admiralty. The law, as in Woodrow Wilson's case, did not enthrall him. Even if he did choose a branch that suited his maritime interests, Roosevelt looked forward to the weekends when he could return to Hyde Park.

In 1910, a political opportunity arose for Franklin in much the same way as it had for his cousin Theodore three decades before. The political powers that be offered him the state senate nomination for the Poughkeepsie area. No doubt the Democratic Party leaders offered him the bid because of his familiar name.

Yet Franklin Roosevelt as a Democrat in Dutchess County had about as much chance to win as his cousin Theodore as a Republican had been given in New York City.

Despite discouragement from his law firm, Franklin Roosevelt accepted the challenge. He was the first New York politician to campaign by automobile. Down dusty back lanes he rattled in his two-cylinder red Maxwell, calling on Republican farmers who had never seen a politician at their doorsteps. Although the accent was Groton, his manner and language invited an easy accessibility that did not talk down to the voters. Like his cousin Theodore before him, he ran "against the bosses," confounded the experts, and won narrowly.

In Albany he found the Democratic caucus dominated by the Tammany boss Charles Murphy. The machine wanted to reward a longtime regular, Bill Sheehan, with a U.S. Senate seat. Like Governor Woodrow Wilson in

New Jersey, Roosevelt favored a constitutional amendment for direct election of senators and deplored the caucus process that allowed a few bosses to handpick a senator who would represent millions.

Roosevelt persuaded seventeen fellow Democratic senators to boycott the caucus and so not be bound by the inevitable caucus decision to vote for Sheehan. Although eventually the caucus did choose Sheehan, the Democrats, lacking the holdout votes of Roosevelt and his coterie, did not have the requisite constitutional majority to elect him to the U.S. Senate. Against overwhelming pressures to end their walkout, including some threats to cancel some of the legislators' mortgages, Roosevelt kept his group together and outlasted the siege. After over sixty ballots, the boss of Tammany offered the white flag of truce and negotiation. A compromise candidate, Judge James O'Gorman, was agreed upon, and Roosevelt was hailed as a young knight following the tradition of his famous cousin.

The defeat of the "Tammany Tiger" triggered the development of three relationships that helped shape Roosevelt's life. First, it marked the beginning of a friendship with Al Smith, a seven-term assemblyman from New York City. Second, it brought his name to the attention of Louis Howe, a gnome-like reporter, who soon agreed to manage State Senator Roosevelt's campaign for reelection. Third, it pulled reformer Roosevelt toward the political star of New Jersey, Governor Woodrow Wilson, who was increasingly being mentioned as a presidential candidate in 1912.

But for Roosevelt to play any role in the coming presidential campaign, he had first to secure his own reelection. The Democratic senators who had stood with Roosevelt against Tammany were on Tammany's "hit list," with Roosevelt's name at the top. Roosevelt, who had barely won two years before in a heavily Republican district, seemed especially ripe, and Democratic regulars supplied a covert nudge for his Republican opponent. To make things worse, as campaign time approached, Roosevelt contracted pneumonia. Howe, who early saw national potential in the young patrician politician, took the unheard-of step of putting full page ads in the country weeklies proclaiming the Democrat Roosevelt as a friend of the farmer and foe of the machine. It worked, and Roosevelt actually increased his vote margin by a thousand or so votes.

In June of 1912, State Senator Franklin Roosevelt traveled to Baltimore for the Democratic Convention. The state Democratic organization was committed to the leading contender, Speaker of the House Champ Clark of Missouri, but Roosevelt had already given his word to Woodrow Wilson, and he challenged Tammany by organizing a few rallies and displaying the New Jersey governor's banner in New York.

At the convention hall, he took a leaf from Abraham Lincoln's book and packed the galleries with some of his pro-Wilson friends armed with faked credentials. The ploy proved helpful in halting the Clark steamroller. Just when the Clark vote was steadily increasing on each roll call, a Roosevelt-led demonstration interrupted the balloting. The break allowed the old warrior William Jennings Bryan to stiffen the resolve of weakening Wilson delegates by declaiming a diatribe against the "Wall Street Bosses" associated with Clark.

President-elect Wilson noted with approval Franklin Roosevelt's loyal electioneering in a campaign that had pitted the governor against Roosevelt's cousin Theodore as well as President Taft. Accordingly, Wilson offered Roosevelt a top assistantship in the Treasury or the customs job in New York. To Wilson's surprise, Roosevelt rejected them, but he did accept the position of assistant secretary of Navy.

Perhaps Franklin Roosevelt wanted to follow in the political footsteps of his "Uncle" Teddy. What is certain is that Roosevelt from his early days of childhood had always heard the call of the sea. He had fed those dreams by amassing in his lifetime the richest private collection of naval lore in the United States.

Roosevelt began his duties in the Navy Department office in what is now the old Executive Office Building next to the White House. Meanwhile, Winston Churchill as First Lord of the Admiralty was ensconced at Whitehall streamlining the British navy on the eve of the coming European conflict.

Although growing European hostilities seemed far away to America, Roosevelt worked in harness with Secretary of Navy Josephus Daniels to expand and modernize the American fleet. Like his cousin, Roosevelt staunchly advocated a large, powerful navy even before America entered the war. A first priority was navy personnel. After hacking away at deadwood in the senior officer ranks by pushing them into retirement, Roosevelt halted the time-honored judicial practice of sentencing wayward youths into navy enlistment.

Even more significant was Roosevelt's cutting costs and red tape in procurement contracts. He made himself a frequent inspector of the country's shipyards. One of the managers with whom Roosevelt developed a close association was Joseph Patrick Kennedy, who supervised Bethlehem Steel's main plant. Even before President Wilson's mammoth naval appropriation bill was finally enacted in 1916, Roosevelt gambled by lining up contracts for materiel ahead of time without legal authorization.

His reputation as a take-charge executive was sufficient enough for the anti-Tammany forces to ask him to be a candidate for the U.S. Senate in 1916. The machine Democrats countered by drafting James Gerard, Wilson's distinguished ambassador to France. Though the thirty-four-year-old Roosevelt showed surprising strength in the upstate districts, he lost by 75,000 votes.

Roosevelt could shrug off the defeat because a return to his duties at the Naval Department promised greater responsibility and action as the nation geared up for the inevitable involvement in the European conflict. When

America entered the war in March 1917, Roosevelt devoted much of his energies to find a new mining device to end the German U-boat menace.

Roosevelt discovered an eccentric inventor who had devised an electrical submarine trap. Despite the skepticism of the British high naval command, Roosevelt pushed the project forward. The new mining instrument, which the British admiralty later admitted was one of the most effective new technological developments in the war, sank more than 200 German submarines in the North Sea.

In July 1918, Assistant Secretary Roosevelt crossed the Atlantic to Britain in a destroyer, the new anti-submarine vessel his department had launched. While there he met Prime Minister David Lloyd George and King George V, who told him he had just received a letter from cousin Theodore informing him of his son's death in France.[4]

After the war Democratic politicians began maneuvering to find a successor to the stricken President Wilson. Roosevelt was committed to his friend Alfred E. Smith, the governor of New York. Although the Irish Catholic governor had little national support, Roosevelt dutifully made a nominating speech in his behalf.

James Cox, a newspaper publisher in Ohio, was nominated perhaps because he had no association with the controversial Wilson and his League of Nations crusade. Smith and his Democratic followers in New York were afraid that the mounting sentiment for a return to Republicanism would overwhelm the state Democratic ticket.

Thinking the Roosevelt name might hold New York State, Smith decided to push his ally as a running mate for Cox. So he made a nominating speech for his old Albany colleague for vice president just as Roosevelt had done for him a few days earlier for president. The magic name of Roosevelt aroused dispirited convention delegates, who were gloomy about their prospects with a lackluster Cox in the face of a Republican tide.

After the nomination, Governor Cox and Roosevelt made their duty call at the White House to visit the ailing president. Wilson pleaded with the two candidates not to straddle the League of Nations issue like the Republicans but to press it resolutely. They agreed.

For the campaign Roosevelt commandeered Louis Howe, who had been his aide at the Navy Department, to map out the strategy and schedule. The chain-smoking Howe engaged a special train on which Roosevelt would crisscross the nation, chugging more miles than any other candidate in history—including his cousin Theodore who had died the year before. No doubt it was during this one-thousand speech campaign to every section of the country that the idea of his own candidacy for the White House first took root. The enthusiasm of crowds at rail stations made Roosevelt imagine momentarily that the Democratic ticket might have a chance, but two weeks before the end Louis Howe took him aside and told him the facts. "They like you, Frank, but you're not the issue. What really matters is that they like Harding and don't like the League."

On election day, a war-weary nation overwhelmingly chose Senator Warren Harding and "the normalcy" he pledged. Roosevelt sent his congratulations to his opposite number, Governor Coolidge of Massachusetts, and made preparations to return to private life.

Entering banking in New York City, Roosevelt kept his name in circulation by championing a host of volunteer activities, including the Boy Scouts and the Woodrow Wilson Foundation.

Despite his unsuccessful vice presidential campaign, Roosevelt was still somewhat of a national figure within the professional ranks of the Democratic Party. His continuing popularity made him a target of investigations by the Republican Senate in Washington. Their findings purported to show that he sanctioned entrapment procedures to weed out homosexuals in the navy. That summer of 1921, Roosevelt had to return to Washington from Campobello, his vacation retreat off the coast of Maine, to clear his name.

Drained by the experience, Roosevelt sailed back to the island on a New York friend's yacht. The storm-tossed cruise turned out to be hazardous, and Roosevelt had to take the helm for long, exhausting hours. Physically spent by the ordeal, he nevertheless ran off with his sons to see a forest fire after he arrived. Then he took a dip in the bay's icy water. That night he complained of aches. The next morning his left leg refused to move at all. Doctor W. W. Keen of Philadelphia was summoned from his Maine summer home to look at Roosevelt.[5] If poliomelitis had been diagnosed immediately, the spread of paralysis in his legs might not have occurred.

At Hyde Park the crippled Roosevelt found himself emotionally buffeted between two forces vying for control of his life. At one side was his mother, who wanted her son to resume the placid life of a country squire like his father. She had always thought politics was an unworthy profession for someone of his class and station.

On the other side was the chain-smoking, hard-drinking Howe, who, to Franklin's mother, embodied all that was unsavory about political life. Howe, who had bet his career on the star of Roosevelt, was not about to see his life's work wasted. He found an unlikely ally in Eleanor Roosevelt.

Eleanor Roosevelt had considered divorce when her husband's affair with his Naval Department social aide, Lucy Mercer, was revealed. In the aftermath, a modus vivendi was reached in which each would pursue their separate interests. Howe had directed her inexhaustible energies to women's causes. Shy at first, she had, under Howe's tutelage, begun to accept speaking engagements. By 1921 she had become a personality in her own right. To give that up to play nursemaid to an invalid for the rest of her life was unthinkable.

As Roosevelt learned to stand with braces and move about with assistance,

Louis Howe became his legs for his continuing involvement in many activities. Roosevelt restricted himself to public ceremonies where his presence and remarks were demanded. One effect of the disease was to make the president a more productive executive as he was, by necessity, confined long hours at his desk. The invention of the telephone allowed him to use his hearty, distinctive voice to keep in touch with political friends in the state. It was just as important as the radio would be a decade later in communicating to the nation.

In 1924 Roosevelt catapulted back to the national stage he had left after his campaign for vice president four years earlier. Again it was the Democratic Convention that provided the opportunity. Governor Alfred Smith went to the convention as a leading candidate for the nomination. His principal opponent was William McAdoo, Wilson's son-in-law who had served as secretary of treasury in that administration. It was an epic confrontation: the cities versus the country, the "wets" against the "drys," the ethnics against the nativists, and the Catholics and other minority religions against the Protestants.

Smith's backers and their allies in other city organizations did their best to impose their New York City idol on a reluctant South and West. The convention was held in their home ground of Madison Square Garden, and they had slated as their nominating speaker the greatest orator of the day, Bourke Cockran.[6] Cockran, Churchill's biographer tells us, was the former congressman and trial lawyer who taught Winston Churchill how to speak. Cockran, however, died the day before the convention opened. In one of his last conversations, he called Roosevelt and said, "Frank, get out of your bed and make the speech." Smith, who had been screening several candidates for the nominating speech, was receptive to the Cockran suggestion. A Protestant Roosevelt with some ties to the South and farming areas made political sense. When Smith called Roosevelt, he replied "All right, Al, as long as I don't have to audition."

At Hyde Park, away from the scorching temperatures inside Madison Square Garden, Roosevelt reworked a draft that Louis Howe submitted to him. An outside suggestion came from Governor Smith himself, who liked Judge Proskauer's description of him as "the Happy Warrior," from Wordsworth's poem.[7] Initially, Roosevelt demurred, musing that the illusion to an English poet was a shade too precious for the Irish Catholic hero of the East Side tenements.

A more difficult problem was logistical. How could the crippled Roosevelt made his way down the aisle of the arena? A wheelchair was out of the question, and a long walk, even with the support of his son, through milling delegates offering their greetings would be too exhausting. Roosevelt's decision was to be carried to his seat on the platform hours before the delegates assembled.

When his name was called out, Roosevelt made his way to the podium, leaning on his sons James and Elliot for support. At the last moment he swung himself forward by his crutches and grabbed the edge of the speaker's stand.

Out from the loudspeakers rolled the ringing voice whose majestic cadence warmed the hearts of even those who opposed Roosevelt's candidacy. It was not the organ-stop oratory of William Jennings Bryan or the preaching eloquence of Woodrow Wilson but rather simple phrasing in patrician tones delivered in a style both intimate and informal.

> You equally who come from the great cities of the East and from the plains and hills of the West, from the slopes of the Pacific and from the homes and fields of the Southland, I ask you in all sincerity, in balloting on that platform tomorrow, to keep first in your hearts and minds the words of Abraham Lincoln "With malice towards none and charity towards all."

Lincoln's words, which Roosevelt himself added to Louis Howe's draft, stirred applause. Then he came to the closing paragraph:

> He has the power to strike at error and wrongdoing that makes his adversaries quail before him. He has a personality that carries to every bearer not only the sincerity but the righteousness of what he says. He is "the Happy Warrior" of the political battlefield.

Though the bells and claxons signalled a wild demonstration for Governor Smith, it was Roosevelt who was the most popular figure of the convention. But Roosevelt's speech, even if one of the best nominating speeches in history, was not enough to crack the convention deadlock. After a record-breaking 103 ballots, the bankrupt convention made its futile compromise choice: John W. Davis, a New York City lawyer who conveniently was born in the hills of West Virginia; and as his running mate, Charles Bryan, the plodding younger brother of William Jennings Bryan.

The race against Calvin Coolidge, who had succeeded president Harding when he suddenly died in Alaska, was hopeless. Of more concern to New York Democrats was the gubernatorial race, where Republicans were running Theodore Roosevelt, Jr., son of the late president, against Governor Smith. The still ailing Franklin dispatched his wife Eleanor to campaign against her first cousin while he confined himself to a radio address on behalf of Davis.

Smith won, and Franklin Roosevelt retreated to Warm Springs, Georgia to recuperate in its invigorating waters and begin a regimen of restrengthening his body by regular swimming.

It was in Georgia that Franklin D. Roosevelt would make the fateful decision that led to his presidential candidacy. He had returned to Warm Springs after chairing Governor Smith's successful convention campaign for the nomination. Then, in the weeks thereafter, he worked by telephone to kindle support for Smith from his political friends and contacts in the West and South.

Smith faced an uphill race in running against the Republican nominee Herbert Hoover, humanitarian hero of post-war relief in Europe. Hoover, who had served as Harding's and Coolidge's secretary of commerce, had pre-empted the nomination when Coolidge said cryptically, "I do not choose to run."

For Smith to have any chance of beating Herbert Hoover, he had to carry his home state of New York. Unless there was a strong slate in the state races, even that was doubtful. So Smith urged Roosevelt to run for governor, but he refused.

Roosevelt was not being coy. His doctors had said he had a chance to walk again without braces or even a cane if he stayed several years in Warm Springs and followed the prescribed exercise regimen. For one thing, Roosevelt did not believe he had to have the governorship before he could make a run for the presidency. He was already a popular personality among those who attended Democratic conventions.

In Syracuse, where the state Democrats were meeting in September, the situation was growing desperate. With no other politician approaching Roosevelt's popularity available to accept the nomination, Smith authorized a draft to be mounted for the absent Roosevelt. But would he accept?

Roosevelt's whereabouts in Georgia could not be established to find out his answer. If Roosevelt continued his refusal in the face of the draft, the Democrats would adjourn without a candidate. Finally, Al Smith turned to Roosevelt's wife. She knew her husband was attending a picnic near Warm Springs. She left word to call. When Roosevelt returned the call, she handed the phone to Governor Smith. To reporters in Syracuse who questioned Governor Smith on Roosevelt's fitness, he replied, "The Governor of New York does not have to be an acrobat."

The governorship of New York does not require an athlete, but the campaign did require a high degree of stamina. Against the Republican tide, which had rolled over Smith in the nation as well as the state, Roosevelt squeaked through a victory.

Roosevelt went to Albany not as a reformer but as a preserver of Smith's progressive record of accomplishments. Unlike the combative Smith, Roosevelt was more conciliatory in dealing with Republican legislative leaders.

Roosevelt, whose eye was now on Washington, had little desire to be controversial and collect enemies who would roadblock his national ambitions. Just occupying the governor's chair of the nation's largest state was enough to propel him into the inside rail position for the Democratic nomination in 1932—provided, of course, he was reelected in 1930.

The only cloud darkening the chances of the attractive and appealing governor was the issue of his health. Howe dispelled that by having Roosevelt qualify for a half-million–dollar life insurance contract and then announcing it to the press.

Roosevelt need not have worried about his election prospects. By 1930 the Wall Street Crash of the year before had soured the chances of his Republican challenger. He was reelected by an unprecedented landslide. The next two years saw Roosevelt assemble a team for a national race.

A key political operative was Jim Farley, who used his travels as a potentate for the Elk's to make political soundings. For issues Roosevelt relied on his "Brain Trust," recruited out of Columbia University, that consisted of Raymond Moley, Rex Tugwell, and Adolph Berle. From the Smith administration he inherited Judge Samuel Rosenman, who had acted as legal counselor. Rosenman carefully organized the various issues into big red manila envelopes.

If the nomination had required only a simple majority of the convention delegates in Chicago, Roosevelt would have glided in, but the two-thirds number specified by Democratic rules made the frontrunning governor an easy prey for convention intrigue.

When Roosevelt's strength crested on the second ballot, Joseph Kennedy, whom Roosevelt had befriended in his navy days, called William Randolph Hearst in California. Hearst, who had been aided by Kennedy in some financial deals, was backing Speaker of the House Jack Garner for the nomination. The isolationist Hearst liked "Cactus Jack" for his anti-League views. Kennedy pledged to Hearst that Roosevelt would oppose the entrance of the United States into the Geneva organization despite his wife's active advocacy.[8] Hearst feared the consideration of other potential candidates more favorable to the League, such as Newton Baker, Wilson's former secretary of war, or Al Smith, the nominee of the previous convention. So he swung California's forty-four votes to Roosevelt in return for Garner's vice presidential nomination.

For his acceptance speech, Governor Roosevelt broke precedent by dramatically flying from Albany to Chicago to deliver his address personally. To the tune of "Happy Days Are Here Again" (which Roosevelt had picked to replace "Anchors Aweigh," which had greeted him at previous conventions) the enthusiastic delegates uproariously cheered their standard bearer in what promised to be a Democratic year.

Roosevelt had two acceptance speeches in his hand. The first was Howe's draft, and the second was that of Ray Moley's as edited by Rex Tugwell. Curiously, Roosevelt began with Howe's draft—the speech he hadn't read—saying that his appearance underscored his commitment not to be bound "by any absurd traditions" in meeting "the national crisis." Then, seeing Moley's puzzled frown in front of him, he switched to the speech he had scanned.

> Ours must be a part of liberal thought planned action of enlightened international outlook, and of the greatest goal to the greatest number of citizens.

Roosevelt then asked: "What do the American people want more than anything else? Work and Security..."

In his golden ringing tones he then delivered his clarion promise:

I pledge you, I pledge myself to a New Deal for the American People.

The phrase that Rosenman had adopted from Moley brought the convention to their feet.[9] The cavalier attention to the speech, which Roosevelt with his usual aplomb delivered without a hitch, reinforced the view at the time that Roosevelt was a playboy in politics. Walter Lippmann described him as "a nice young man who wanted to be a President" with a "mind that was not clear."

But if Roosevelt was not forthright in his statements that announced new programs yet denounced Hoover for runaway spending, he had sights clearly aimed at the White House. In Roosevelt's mind, Hoover was one of those management efficiency types more suited to running corporations than the country.[10] To Roosevelt, the cold and dour man in the old-fashioned collar seemed not to understand the plight of the average man, who was bewildered and frightened by the worsening economic crisis.

The keynote of his campaign, despite the inconsistencies of platform and personal pledges, was "a New Deal" for the "forgotten man."

In a March address, Roosevelt had resurrected William Graham Summer's phrase in a line pointing to "the forgotten man at the base of the economic pyramid." Although it angered conservatives, the term caught the public imagination. Upon hearing it, Al Smith, his embittered rival and former friend, burst out with, "This is not the time for demogogues."

Even though some Republicans pinned their frail hopes on linking Roosevelt to the corrupt Mayor of New York, Jimmy Walker, there never was much chance for Hoover's re-election.[11] Roosevelt, who had more experience than any of his advisors in national politics, defied conventional wisdom by running his own campaign. If he was intellectually shallow, he was no political lightweight. As Louis Howe commented, "Never in forty years of experience have I known of a Presidential campaign being so completely controlled, dominated and directed by the candidate himself."

At eleven o'clock wizened Louis Howe, who had watched the returns alone, opened an old bottle of sherry in his desk. He had put it away twenty years ago in Albany after the Sheehan fight, and it was not to be opened until Roosevelt was elected president. Carefully, Howe lifted his glass to Farley and said, "To the President of the United States."

It is hard to second-guess Roosevelt's strategy. He won with over 57 percent of the vote cast. Hoover received only fifty-seven electoral votes. At the Biltmore in New York, the victorious Roosevelt kissed his mother, saying, "It is the greatest day in my life." There was never a stronger popular mandate in American history for a new program or policy or a clearer repudiation of laissez-faire. As Will Rogers put it, "The little fellow felt that he never had a chance and he didn't until November 8th and then he grabbed it."

The chance Hoover grabbed on November 8 was the hope to persuade Roosevelt to join him in sponsoring some economic initiatives in the interregnum before March. The wily Roosevelt, to Hoover's anger, refused to dilute the opening thrust of his presidency by any mutual cooperation.

On March 4 the lowering skies and icy March winds could not chill the enthusiasm of thousands of exuberant Democrats who roamed the streets to cheer Franklin Roosevelt. Elsewhere in the country there was little to cheer about. That winter depression had stalked more deeply into the heart of America. Hoover's hope that "the corner had been turned" had been cruelly shattered by the soaring unemployment statistics and by the rumbling currents of discontent that erupted into a maelstrom of violence. In the farm belt, agitators talking of revolution tipped over milk trucks and stormed banks, and in city streets, the grim looks of despair could be read in the hungry, hopeless faces of those in unemployment lines. The whole financial structure of the nation tottered toward collapse. The failure of thousands of banks caused governors of twenty-two states to close banks in late February.

On Inauguration Day the crowd massed in front of the Capitol grew still as they awaited the appearance of the president-elect. When he entered to proceed up the ramp on the arms of son Jimmy, there was a burst of applause as the Marine Band played the last bars of "Hail to the Chief." In the front rows, Mrs. Woodrow Wilson stood to raise a handkerchief; Bernard Baruch, a dollar-a-year Wilson adviser, threw up his hat; and Josephus Daniels, Roosevelt's old boss at the Navy Department, pounded vigorously with his cane. Amid the swelling applause, a few rays of sunshine burst forth upon the inaugural stand.

The bearded Charles Evans Hughes, who had so narrowly lost some sixteen years ago, read the oath as Chief Justice. Breaking tradition, Roosevelt repeated the whole oath instead of just saying "I do." The family Dutch Bible, which had belonged to the common ancestor of Franklin and Theodore Roosevelt, lay open to the thirteenth chapter of First Corinthians. "For now we see through a glass darkly; but then face to face; now I know in part; but then shall I know even as also I am known. And now abideth faith, hope, charity, these three but the greatest of these is charity."

Six days before, in his Hyde Park study Roosevelt had gone over the Raymond Moley draft, which had been edited and shortened by Sam Rosenman. On a lined legal-sized yellow pad, he made notes and additions. As he waited in the Senate chamber before proceeding to the inaugural stand, he penned an opening line to his finished text. "This is a day of consecration."

But as he stood at the stand, after the waves of cheers died, after his oath of office, he amended that opening in a ringing voice:

This is a day of national consecration.

As millions huddled around radio sets, Roosevelt then issued his trumpet call.

> First of all let me assert my firm belief that the only thing we have to fear is fear itself—nameless, unreasoning, unjustified fear which paralyzes needed efforts to convert retreat into advance.

At the word "fear" a gust of wind shook the microphone with a knock that reverberated into the listeners' living rooms. The phrase, which Sam Rosenman borrowed from Henry Thoreau, reassured Americans as no sentence ever had. Then Roosevelt flung back his head and intoned:

> In every dark hour of our national life a leadership of frankness and vigor has met with that understanding and support of the people themselves which is essential to victory. I am convinced that you will again give that support to leadership in these critical days.

There followed an adagio provided by Moley delivered in softer tones:

> Values have shrunk to fantastic levels; taxes have risen; our ability to pay has fallen. Government of all kinds is faced by serious curtailment of income; the means of exchange are frozen in the currents of trade; the withered leaves of industrial enterprise lie on every side; farmers find no market for their produce; the savings of many years in thousands of families are gone. More important, a host of unemployed citizens face the grim problem of existence and an equally great number toil with little return. Only a foolish optimist can deny the dark realities of the moment.

In two biblical allusions Roosevelt then denounced Wall Street and big business in lines that he himself added:

> They have no vision and when there is no vision the people perish. The money changers have fled from their high seats in the temple of civilization.

The partisan crowd responded by giving its first sustained burst of applause. Roosevelt continued:

> This nation asks for action and action now. . . . We must act and act quickly. We must move as a trained and loyal army willing to sacrifice for the good of a common discipline because without such discipline no progress is made, no leadership becomes effective.

In an untypically grim tone for Roosevelt, he directed a challenge to Congress:

> I shall ask the Congress for the one remaining instrument to meet the crisis—broad Executive power to wage war against an emergency as great as the power if we were in fact invaded by a common foe.

The crowd then thundered into its longest applause of the day. His wife later remarked that it scared her to hear how close the country was to accepting a dictatorship.[12]

The unsmiling president closed with a firm warning:

> We do not distrust the future of essential democracy. The people of the United States have not failed. In their need they have registered a mandate that they want direct vigorous action. They have made me the present instrument of their wishes. In the spirit of the gift, I take it.

In that dire moment the people wanted action, and the new president gave it to them. The first thing he did was to order a banking holiday throughout the nation. Within a week he had declared a national emergency and received from Congress almost unlimited power over banking transactions. In the next one-hundred days, he took the country off the gold standard. He cut the pay of one million government employees and thereby achieved a 25 percent reduction in government expenditures. He enacted Federal Aid for the unemployed and established the Agricultural Adjustment Administration for the control of agriculture.

The dramatic statements as well as the swiftness of his actions overwhelmed the constitutional and economic fallacies that lay within some of these acts. But the assurance of his words coupled with the appearance of his activity lifted the people out of the slough of despair.

It is just possible that without the vigorous leadership of Franklin Roosevelt America might have been receptive to a demagogue such as Senator Huey Long, Father Coughlin, the anti-Semitic commentator, or perhaps to Army Chief of Staff General Douglas MacArthur, who at Hoover's orders had put down the demonstration of the Bonus Army strikers the previous year. Certainly Roosevelt believed as much.

The Depression decade was a time for a charismatic personality, as Hitler in Germany and Mussolini in Italy, among others, proved. For a physical cripple such as Roosevelt, voice was a integral part of that appeal, and the introduction of the radio carried Roosevelt's words to every home in America.

Unlike Churchill, Roosevelt did not himself draft his major addresses or his "Fireside Chats." But he had, as Reagan would have later, an ear for the rhythm and cadence of a well-turned phrase or sentence. Roosevelt too, like Reagan, viewed leadership as theater.

His presidency was far more than the totality of all of its legislative acts and executive orders—it was a personality people could trust and believe in. Roosevelt, as Reagan would a half-century later, defeated an incumbent president who was an engineer both by background and frame of mind, as well as a decent man with profound religious faith. Each challenger was a candidate who, as governor of the nation's most populous state, offered the rhetoric of hope to a troubled citizenry.

No man has ever personified the federal government like Franklin Roosevelt. Washington might have been an elected king, but Roosevelt was more than a monarch—he was a patriarch from whom all blessings flowed. If the people saw him as a paternal figure, much of that feeling was evoked by his patrician voice, which radiated assurance and concern. The first of such occasions was his inaugural address in 1933. It struck the national chord of a listening nation and symbolized for many the hope of recovery.

NOTES

1. Sarah Delano Roosevelt's progenitor in America was a French Huguenot emigrant to Massachusetts in the seventeenth century. He spelled his name "de la Noyes."

2. Even though his distant cousin Theodore was on McKinley's ticket as vice president, Franklin adhered to the Democratic tradition of the Hyde Park Roosevelts.

3. Other notable editors include former Secretary of Defense Caspar Weinberger and author David Halberstram.

4. He also met Winston Churchill, who forgot the meeting, much to Roosevelt's annoyance, when they had their secret conference in August 1941 on a ship in Newfoundland Bay.

5. W. W. Keen, a Philadelphia surgeon, had performed the successful removal of cancer from President Grover Cleveland's jaw in a secret operation on a boat in the Chesapeake Bay. It is ironic that he would be better remembered for his initial incorrect diagnosis of Roosevelt. To his credit, Keen did track down two specialists who quickly saw that it was infantile paralysis.

6. Cockran, who was an intimate friend of Churchill's mother, became the revered father figure in Churchill's life. Three times he was a keynoter to the Democratic National convention. His speech opposing Cleveland in 1888 is best remembered. Taft and Wilson both called him the outstanding orator of the day.

7. "This is the Happy Warrior, this is he whom every man in arms would will to be."

8. Roosevelt, to his wife's chagrin, had ducked the issue as governor saying it was not a New York State matter.

9. Moley was perhaps influenced by the title of a Stuart Chase article in *The New Republic*: "New Deal for America." The phrase first appeared with Mark Twain.

10. Interestingly, in 1920 Roosevelt had written Hoover suggesting that he run for president on the Democratic ticket. Hoover was then completing his war relief work in Europe.

11. Although the Seabury Committee documented charges against Mayor

Walker, Roosevelt refused to condemn personally his Tammany ally. Finally, to the relief of Roosevelt, Walker resigned and took an extended trip to Europe.

12. Edmund Wilson, in an article in *The New Republic*, saw in it "the warning of dictatorship."

12 _____

Harry Truman's Acceptance Address: The Turnip Day Talk

Senator Barkley and I will win this election and make the Republicans like it—don't you forget that.

It was the fate of Harry S Truman to follow a legend as president, but he would weave his own folk tale in his 1948 upset victory. Yet his stature in history owes more to his courage as a statesman than to his cunning as a politician.

Today Truman's administration is remembered for his forthright confrontation of the Soviet threat. During his presidency there were put in place the building blocks of foreign policy that checked the advance of Soviet imperialism in Europe, such as NATO, the Truman Doctrine, and the Marshall Plan. But what made Harry Truman a hero in this country's political history was his underdog campaign in 1948. It was not his role as head of the free world but as the little guy who fought against great odds. That struck a common chord with the man in the street who daily battled the tasks of feeding his family and paying the mortgage.

Today it is forgotten that Harry Truman was, upon leaving office in 1953, the most unpopular president of this century.[1] The occupant of the nation's highest office seemed almost a personification of the courthouse politico. The salty earthiness that suggested an unbefitting lack of dignity is now hailed as the embodiment of homespun integrity.

Truman's rise to the presidency supports the American dream that any child can grow up to be President of the United States of America, but it is also every mother's wish that her child does not dirty himself in professional politics that would lead to high office. Harry Truman embodied that paradox.

Harry Truman's mother certainly did not want him to become a politician—rather, she hoped he would become a pianist. Like Franklin Roosevelt, Truman had in his mother a woman equally strong-willed and devoted to his development.

A boyhood contemporary who later became a foe said that Vivien Truman, Harry's older brother, "did all the hard work of the house." His mother, who had studied music in college, wanted Harry to be a musician, and he "did what his mother wanted him to."

While other boys called Harry "four-eyes" and "sissy" for not playing their sports, the thick-lensed Harry practiced the piano.

As a young boy in Independence, Missouri, Truman was more an Horatio Alger hero than Mark Twain's Huck Finn. A bookish lad with a frail frame, he eschewed sports to concentrate on his studies. In his spare time he worked as a handyman in the local drugstore. Contrary to his later reputation as a scrappy political battler, Truman was considered a "mama's boy" who ran away from any neighborhood fight, unlike his contemporary Eisenhower who was growing up some hundred miles to the West.

Yet Truman did aspire to an appointment to West Point. It was not that he wanted to be a soldier but because it offered a free college education. But although Truman did not dream of a military career in his youth, it was in the Army that he first realized his potential for leadership.

After some unrewarding years as a bank clerk and farmer, Truman found his military service as an officer in France in World War I a challenge.[2] His company, which mostly consisted of Irish Catholics from the back streets of Kansas City, was not impressed by their bespectacled commander. They staged a mule stampede in the stables and then a riotous demonstration in the barracks. A calm but stern Captain Truman told the soldiers, "I'm not here to get along with you—you're here to get along with me. And if there are any of you who can't, speak up and I'll bust you back now."

At his first glimpse of war at the Battle of St. Mihiel, Truman didn't see action (although Brigadier-General Douglas MacArthur of the 42nd Division distinguished himself in that engagement). Later, though, Captain Truman did see his share of gunfire and emerged from the war with both respect from his company and for himself.

The camaraderie at the front ripened into his first nucleus of political support. When Truman returned home, he quickly joined the newly formed American Legion. One of his fellow Legionnaires from the war was Sergeant Eddie Jacobson.[3] Their mutual success in a canteen operation in France led them to form a partnership in a haberdashery after the war, but the undercapitalized clothing store failed in the recession of 1921.

In the meantime, Truman married Bess Wallace, the daughter of one of Independence's oldest families. Mrs. Wallace had opposed the match as beneath her daughter's class, and the collapse of his business no doubt confirmed her original judgment.[4]

It was not surprising that Truman, who was better at making friends than money, accepted an invitation to run for county judge in 1922. The office, which was equivalent to a county commissioner and more administrative than legal, was suggested to him by Jim Prendergast, a fellow artillery officer in France. Jim was the nephew of Tom Prendergast, the boss of the Kansas City Democratic Party.

Truman's first speech as a candidate was a disaster. On the platform at Lee's Summit he could not manage to say a word after he was introduced. Instead, he fled the podium and did what he knew best—mingled with the crowd and talked to each constituent, one by one. When he did finally muster up the courage in the next appearance to give a thirty minute address, it was a painful ordeal and even more painful for the audience. Nevertheless, through his associations as a Legionnaire, Mason, and Baptist—or as his various occupations as a farmer, railway dispatcher, and merchant—he knew more people than the other five candidates. All he had to do was solidify those contacts by crisscrossing the county in his yellow roadster.

Truman's tenure as a county judge was brief. He was defeated for re-election two years later. First, the Prendergast tag did not help him in the county outside Kansas City; even more important, the Democrat label was the wrong one in the year of President Calvin Coolidge's landslide election.

Truman was not about to quit politics. Taking a job as the local Automobile Association secretary, Truman circulated the county preparing his comeback in 1926. This time, with the strong financial support of the Prendergast machine, he aimed for the politically key position of chief presiding judge.

He won, but the price for his emergence as a major professional politician of the area was his identification with the unsavory Prendergast organization. But whatever revelations surfaced about payoffs and kickbacks in the Kansas City Democratic administration, no scintilla of scandal ever touched Judge Harry Truman's name.

In eight years, he established a record as a competent administrator and tireless advocate for modern planning techniques in county government operations. No item escaped his notice. He even scouted for the right sculptor to erect a statue of his favorite hero, Andrew Jackson, to adorn the new courthouse of Jackson County. As a history buff, he researched and checked every detail from selection of uniform to size of horse. The courthouse had been built by the bonds Judge Truman had persuaded the county to issue.

When the U.S. Senate seat opened in 1934, Judge Truman, originally aiming for a congressional seat, shifted his sights for the upper house when the organization slated another for Congress.

With Boss Prendergast's blessing, Judge Truman filed for the Senate contest against two congressmen. Truman was the underdog. He was little known outside Kansas City, and where he was known he was viewed as Prendergast's pawn. The respected St. Louis *Post Dispatch* called Truman "a Prendergast office boy" and "puppet." Truman countered by charging that his opponents "had been in Washington so long that they had forgotten the Missouri point of view." Despite the odds, Truman squeezed out a narrow primary victory by painting himself as the most pro-Roosevelt candidate across the state while letting the machine pile up a record vote in Kansas City.

When Truman was sworn in at age fifty in January 1935, he neither looked like a senator nor felt very comfortable as one until the Senate Democratic whip told him one day, "Harry, the first six months you're here you'll wonder how the hell you got here and after that you'll wonder how the hell the rest of us got here."

If the Senate is divided between showhorses and workhorses, Harry Truman was definitely the latter. Rare were the occasions when Truman spoke on the floor or missed a committee hearing. The Railroad Committee was the particular focus of his legislative interest. Such modest deportment and steadfast diligence endeared him to the more senior members of the "club."

A regular Democrat, he supported President Roosevelt on his court packing scheme in 1937 and everything else. The only exception was when Roosevelt attempted to pick his own man, Alben Barkley, as majority leader. On this issue Truman sided with the Senate "establishment."

Perhaps for that reason Roosevelt seemed to encourage Governor Lloyd Stark to oppose Truman in 1940. Roosevelt several times invited Stark, a millionaire orchard grower, to sail down the Potomac on the presidential yacht, while the uninvited Truman fumed. Funds were scarce for the underdog against an odds-on favorite who could finance his own campaign. In Washington only financier Bernard Baruch sent a check to the Truman campaign, for he thought FDR's hosting of Stark represented a presidential purge. Few of Truman's friends thought he had a chance against the millionaire Stark, particularly because an ongoing investigation was returning criminal indictments against Prendergast and some of his associates in Kansas City. The St. Louis *Post-Dispatch* exulted, "Harry Truman, the erstwhile Ambassador in Washington of the defunct principality of Prendergastia, is back home appraising his chances of being re-elected. They are nil. He's a dead cock in the pit."

Truman knew his enemies were right if he faced Governor Stark in a two man race. So he plotted to arrange that mutual friends induce Tom Milligan to enter the primary. Milligan, the brother of the congressman Truman had beaten for the Senate in 1934, was the prosecutor who convicted Tom Prendergast of income tax evasion and election fraud. Since Lloyd Stark was riding high on the Prendergast scandal, Milligan was asked why he shouldn't reap the benefit as the one who actually had put the old boss behind bars.

The three-way split, in a replay of 1934, gave Truman a fighting chance. Nevertheless, it was still the swaggering Stark's race to lose and he rose to the occasion. Stark, who earlier had implied interest in running for president, or vice president in 1940 if Roosevelt chose to run for a third term, presented an inviting target.

Senator Bennett Clark, who six years earlier had opposed Truman, now shed his neutrality to attack Stark, whom he despised.

> It is hard to estimate the political situation in Missouri just now since Lloyd's ambition seems to be like the gentle dew that falls from heaven and covers everything high and low. He is the first man in history who had ever tried to run for President, Vice President, Secretary of War, Governor General of the Philippines, Ambassador to England and U.S. Senator all at one and the same time. At the same time it is rumored that he has accepted candidacy for both the College of Heraldry and the archbishopric of Canterbury.

The primary race ended with the pompous Stark being deflated by the plodding Truman. The fall contest was a walk in the Roosevelt reelection year. The next four years saw Truman win national prominence as chairman of a committee investigating war contracts. Without his committee work, speculation about him as a possible running mate for Roosevelt four years later would not have surfaced. Henry Wallace, Roosevelt's secretary of agriculture had been picked to replace John Nance Garner in 1940, but Southern leaders as well as some of the big city machine bosses such as Ed Flynn of New York were uneasy with his leftist views.

Truman naturally dismissed such talk. He wrote to Harry Watner, a friend in Missouri, "I have worked nine years learning how to be a U.S. Senator and I see no reason in the world to throw it away. The Vice President simply presides over the Senate and sits around hoping for a funeral."

Others were less reluctant. One was Senator Alben Barkley of Kentucky, the other Jimmy Byrnes of South Carolina.[5] Byrnes was a former senator whom Roosevelt had appointed to the Supreme Court and then drafted to be a kind of "assistant president" as head of the Mobilization Board.

Truman publicly discouraged consideration of him as vice president, but Robert Hannegan, the new Democratic national chairman, privately laid the groundwork for his candidacy. In his contacts with political leaders, Truman's old political ally from Missouri suggested the name of Truman, implying that Barkley was too old and Byrnes too conservative for organized labor.

Of course, the president could have settled speculation by announcing his choice, but Roosevelt was never known for directness or candor. While he agreed with party leaders that Wallace would probably have to be dropped from the ticket, he could not bring himself to tell Wallace. His personal favorite was William Douglas, whom he had appointed to the Supreme Court.

As Democratic delegates prepared for the journey to the July national convention in Chicago, rumors were rife, and maneuvering mounted. Wallace, the embattled vice president, solidified his labor support and extracted from the president a letter expressing delight if the convention nominated him. To counter the growing insider reports fed by Hannegan, which mentioned Senator Truman as the likely choice, Jimmy Byrnes telephoned Truman to ask him to deliver a nominating speech in his behalf. Truman, who had been pushing the candidacy of Speaker of the House Sam Rayburn, agreed—since the Texan had withdrawn his name.

At the convention, Hannegan had one ace up his sleeve. At a White House meeting two weeks earlier he had elicited from Roosevelt a letter, dated July 14, in which Roosevelt stated that he would be glad to run with either Harry Truman or Bill Douglas and that either man could bring real strength to the ticket. Actually, the names of Truman and Douglas were reversed in the original letter, but Hannegan, according to Margaret Truman, had the secretary retype the letter putting Truman first. Furthermore, he had the letter postdated for the beginning of the convention. At the same time Hannegan got CIO political operative Sidney Hillman to pledge support for Truman if Wallace failed to be nominated.

The first ballot saw Wallace outdistance Truman, but a scattering of favorite sons denied the vice president a majority. On the second ballot, one of the favorite sons, Governor Bob Kerr of Oklahoma, shifted his votes to Truman. Kerr, to whom the Democratic National Committee gave the choice keynote speaker assignment, was ordered to switch. Kerr, who had hoped for lightning to strike himself after his magnificent address, dutifully obeyed. The Kerr move signaled a trickle of switches that gradually ripened into a trend. At the end of the count, the vote stood at 477½ for Truman and 473 for Wallace. It was enough to trigger a massive change of votes by many states. By the end of the changes, Truman was the winner 1031 to 105. His acceptance speech was modest and brief.

> You don't know how very much I appreciate this very great honor which has come to the state of Missouri. It is also a great responsibility which I am perfectly willing to assume.
>
> Nine years and five months ago I came to the Senate. I expect to continue the efforts I have made there to help shorten the war and win the peace under the great leader Franklin D. Roosevelt.

After the convention President Roosevelt called Truman to the White House and instructed him to plan an extensive campaign schedule. The campaign burden had to be assumed by the vice presidential candidate because the wartime president had to limit himself to only a few campaign appearances.

The "Bobtail Special," his campaign train, proved to be a dress rehearsal for his "whistle stop" train four years later. One memorandum governed the conduct of the vice presidential candidate. Among the points were these:

• Don't explain why you were chosen at Chicago or that you did not desire to be the candidate.

• There is no need to commend Wallace . . .

• Avoid having your picture taken with Negroes or city bosses.

• Make your speeches, particularly those on radio, short. Speak slowly and give the impression you have a lot of common sense.

• Avoid storytelling. Make your hearers believe you a solid, practical, clear-thinking American.

• Have an assistant check speeches for grammar and for doubtful words—mark pronunciation.

• Speak of "progressive legislation" instead of "New Deal" which has been deluged with criticism.

Although Truman delivered hundreds of speeches, the most remembered address was one of the few Roosevelt himself made. It was the famous "Fala" speech, in which Roosevelt replied to a charge by Governor Dewey of New York that a destroyer had been sent specially to pick up his Scottish terrier: "These Republicans, not content with attacking me, my wife or my sons—no, not content with that—they now attack my little dog Fala . . . "

In a campaign climaxed by Roosevelt's triumphant open limousine ride down Fifth Avenue on a cold, wet October day, the Democratic ticket handily beat back the Republican challenges of governors Thomas Dewey of New York and John Bricker of Ohio.

The new vice president did not even move his office in the Senate Office Building—he just changed his sign atop the door. He had little to do except preside over the Senate. Although he attended some cabinet meetings as a formality, Truman's views were not asked; neither was he ever briefed on issues of foreign policy or national intelligence.

On April 13 Vice President Truman left his Senate-presiding duties to walk over to Sam Rayburn's Capitol office for one of the speaker's "Board of Education" meetings, after which some of the key leaders would repair for some "Bourbon and Branch." It was there that Truman received a call to come directly to the White House through the front door.

At the White House Truman was met by Eleanor Roosevelt, who said, "Harry, the President is dead." "What can I do to help?" asked Truman. "No," replied Mrs. Roosevelt gravely, "What can we do to help you?"

Truman later confided to a friend that he felt the way he did in his youth "when a cartload of hay fell upon you." The inaugural ceremonies were stalled until a Bible could be located. Finally, someone found a red Gideon in Appointments Secretary William Hassett's office, and Truman was sworn in by Chief Justice Harlan Stone with only family and friends present.

A few days later, after the funeral rites for President Roosevelt were completed, the new president addressed Congress. He closed:

> I have in my heart a prayer. As I have assumed my heavy duties, I humbly pray, Almighty God, in the words of King Solomon: "Give therefore thy servant an understanding heart to judge the people, that I may discern between good and bad; for who is able to judge this Thy so great a people."

The ending set off a standing ovation.

When Truman took office, the Allied troops were already crossing the Rhine, but the end of the war with Japan was not yet in sight. More important than the conclusion of conflicts both in Europe and Asia was the beginning of the Cold War with the Soviet Union, about which Truman had neither understanding nor briefing.

One of his first decisions was to replace Edward Stettinius as secretary of state with Jimmy Byrnes. Byrnes had accompanied Roosevelt to Yalta and had taken extensive notes. After Byrnes' report of his perceptions of Stalin, Truman decided to appoint him.

A major consideration in his choice of Byrnes was the fact that Stettinius, who never held an elective office, was first in line to succeed Truman under the old Presidential Succession act.[6] Truman felt that Byrnes had more qualifications and experience than any one in the country. The problem was that Byrnes agreed and did not hide his feelings.

On Truman's sixty-first birthday, he announced the conclusion of war with Germany. The end prompted the Potsdam meeting of the "Big Three" in July (where Clement Atlee, in the midst of the conference, replaced Churchill, whose Conservative Party was not reelected to power). At the meeting, Truman had a chance to size up Marshal Joseph Stalin for the first time. "He reminds me of Tom Prendergast," Truman naively confided to a friend on his first impression. But beneath the facade of Old World manners, the diminutive dictator was implacable on the issues of Berlin, Poland, and other matters.

One afternoon, after he had toured Berlin to observe the destruction, Truman returned to find an excited Henry Stimson, the secretary of war. Stimson handed him a telegram:

TOP SECRET

Mr. Stimson:

OPERATED ON THIS MORNING. DIAGNOSIS NOT YET COM-
PLETE BUT RESULTS SEEM SATISFACTORY AND ALREADY EX-
CEED EXPECTATIONS. LOCAL PRESS RELEASE NECESSARY AS
INTEREST EXTENDS GREAT DISTANCE. DR. GROVES PLEASED.
HE RETURNS TOMORROW. I WILL KEEP YOU POSTED.

This was the first word from General Leslie Groves' office that the atomic
bomb test had been successful. The local press release meant that a cover
story would be issued that an ammunition dump had exploded accidentally.

Truman wanted to inform Stalin of the bomb, but, at Churchill's suggestion, he included the report of the new weapon casually in the midst of
a long conversation so that Stalin missed the potential significance.

When the new bomb exploded on Hiroshima a month later, the war with
Japan ended. Truman has been castigated by historians for deciding to use
the bomb. But for Truman—even though he agonized over the conse-
quences of using such a cataclysmic weapon—his reasoning was simple: It
would save a million lives, not only the lives of Americans who would be
killed in the costly invasion of the island of Japan but the Japanese as well,
who would defend themselves in a suicidal frenzy. The bombs that exploded, first in Hiroshima and then in Nagasaki, caused the Japanese government to sue for peace and ended the war.

Despite his inadequate preparation and training to be leader of the free
world, Truman did not brood over his background or dither over a decision.
He placed a sign in the Oval Office that said, "The buck stops here." Then
he placed on his desk this quotation from fellow Missourian Mark Twain:
"Always do right. This will gratify some people and astonish the rest."

Shortly after Truman entered the White House, Roy Roberts of the Kansas City *Star* offered to an eager public a profile on the president about
whom they knew little. Roberts suggested that he was a limited man who
"when approaching fifty was still looking at the rear end of the horse as he
plowed the corn rows."

Too many reporters were misled by the contrast between the plain Harry
S Truman and the patrician Franklin D. Roosevelt. They saw in his folk-
siness an inability to lead and read in his inelegance an incapacity to command. Those who served under Captain Truman in France could have set
the press straight. The clerkish captain they had tried to haze quickly let
them know who was in charge.

Despite his apparent unpretentiousness, Truman had a fascination with
regalia and ritual. After all, he was a thirty-third degree Mason who cherished his military experience. But if he was always respectful of rank, he
expected others to honor his own rank; and if he was often loyal to a fault,
he in turn demanded loyalty in others. Thus, while his dismissals jolted
those cabinet officers he fired, it should not have come as a surprise that

President Truman would fire those who questioned his ability or competence.

After Stettinius, the next to leave was Attorney General Frances Biddle from Philadelphia. He was replaced by the more compatible Tom Clark from Texas. Biddle was miffed when what he thought was his *pro forma* resignation was accepted. Later in the year Harold Ickes left. The cantankerous secretary of the interior had publicly attacked Truman's choice for secretary of Navy, Ed Pauley, as too close to the oil interests.

The biggest thorn in the Truman side was Henry Wallace, the secretary of commerce. Wallace, a pet of the ideological left, criticized Truman's foreign policy as threatening to the Soviet Union. In 1946 at Madison Square Garden before an audience packed with Communist sympathizers, Wallace stated that he wanted the U.S. to disband its armed forces and share atomic secrets with Russia. He had "cleared" the speech with the president—but not the version he delivered.

When Truman privately reprimanded Wallace, Wallace leaked the details of the meeting in a way favorable to himself. Even though Wallace's departure risked alienating the leftish wing of the Democratic party, Truman asked Wallace to resign.

As the year 1946 began, the honeymoon engendered by the initial swell of sympathy for the new president had long since elapsed. In his January message to Congress, he repeated his list of domestic priorities, such as a "full employment" law, a massive public housing program, a Federal Election Protection Commission, and more regional river valley developments like the Tennessee Valley Authority (TVA). Republican Assistant House Minority Leader Charles Halleck said it was "a call for more billions and bureaucrats." Political insiders as well as congressional leaders who once had painted Truman with the coloration of a Southern Democrat were rudely jolted.

Together with the Marshall Plan, the president enunciated the Truman Doctrine to combat Soviet adventurism in the Balkans:

> It must be the policy of the United States to support free people who are resisting attempted subjugation by armed minorities or outside pressures.

To implement the doctrine, Truman asked for $400 million in aid to Greece and Turkey, the countries most menaced by Russian's imperial ambitions.

The initiative in our foreign policy abroad did not necessarily translate into popularity back home. For one thing, foreign aid, particularly the Marshall Plan, cost billions in taxpayers' dollars; and, for another, the success in rebuilding Europe was overshadowed by the ascendancy of Mao Tse-tung and his Communist Party in China.

By 1948 any residue of affection for the "accidental" president had been eroded by the publicly aired squabbles between Truman and Republican congressional leaders such as Senator Robert Taft and Speaker of the House Joseph Martin; by the attacks by labor leaders such as bushy-browed John L. Lewis and George Meany; and by the parting salvoes of exiting cabinet members such as Henry Wallace and Jimmy Byrnes.

In the spring of 1948, President Truman received only a 38 percent approval rating of the Gallup Poll. The president just didn't seem presidential. His features were ordinary, his appearance was pedestrian, and his voice was flat and shrill. To say Republicans believed 1948 looked like a good bet to regain the White House is an understatement. Even the Democrats believed Truman's chances were hopeless.

Some of them, like Franklin Delano Roosevelt, Jr., hoisted the name of General Dwight Eisenhower, the country's most popular war hero. Joining the Roosevelt boys were Jacob Arvey, the Chicago boss; William O'Dwyer, mayor of New York; Frank Hague, mayor of Jersey City; John Bailey, Democratic leader of Connecticut; and Senator Claude Pepper, a partisan of Henry Wallace. These and others were writing letters, issuing statements, and forming ad hoc groups to draft Eisenhower. Of course, no one knew where the general stood on the issues or even whether he was a Democrat, but that did not deter leading Democrats lending their names to a draft movement. *The New Republic* noted, "Democratic politicians are not concerned about Eisenhower's views. What they want is a winning candidate who will carry local candidates to victory."

When Eisenhower finally closed the door on the draft, the Americans for Democratic Action (ADA), a liberal splinter group, tried to drag Justice William Douglas off the bench. ADA president Leon Henderson said, "The Democratic Party must choose Douglas or invite a disaster that will impair the future of progressivism in America."

At this point, Truman bowed to pressure from Democratic National Chairman J. Howard McGrath and agreed to call Douglas to ask him if he would consider running on the ticket with him. Douglas refused, reportedly saying to onetime New Deal brain truster Tommy Corcoran, "I would never take a Number 2 to a Number 2 man."

In July delegates were pouring into a sweltering Philadelphia for the Democratic National Convention. The heaviness of the humidity was exceeded only by the weight of gloom. On July 13 spirits were lifted shortly by the organ-stop oratory of Alben Barkley, who roused the convention with a "William Jennings Bryan" keynote address attacking Republicans and big business.

Back at the White House, Truman wryly listened to the report of Barkley's success. He knew that Barkely wanted the nomination for himself and had angled for the keynote slot in order to trigger a presidential draft movement. Truman's old friend, Leslie Biffle, secretary of the Senate, was even buttonholing other Senators in behalf of the seventy-year-old Kentuckian.

Truman deflated the Barkley boomlet by a few phone calls to some convention lieutenants. Then at seven o'clock he boarded the train at Union Station bound for Philadelphia. During the ride he reread the memorandum his young aide Clark Clifford had prepared for him.

Clifford had originally joined the White House staff as a naval aide, but the smooth Missourian had proved himself skillful in negotiating the labyrinthine paths to power. He had outlined to the president the hard realities of his chances for reelection.

It was like a football game, Clifford explained, when in the last minutes the losing team has to gamble by throwing a long pass. In this situation, the long pass was to call the Republican Congress back into session. The purpose would be to put the Republicans on the defensive by forcing them to support or oppose the various interest groups that comprised the old New Deal coalition.

The Republican platform had been written to the specifications of Governor Thomas E. Dewey and not Senator Robert A. Taft, who for the second time had lost the nomination bid to the New Yorker. Truman had to make it appear that the Republican Congress was rejecting the Republican platform. Of course, if the Republicans in the Eightieth Congress even passed modest increases in Social Security, the minimum wage, farm subsidies, or veterans' benefits, any hope of a Truman upset was dashed.

In addition to being a blueprint for victory, the Clifford memorandum was an outline of the points the president was to make in his acceptance speech later that evening.

It was not a prepared speech but rather some conversational talking points. Clifford and other Truman advisers had come to realize that Truman could not deliver a prepared text in the polished manner of Franklin Roosevelt. If Roosevelt caressed each word in unhurried cadence, Truman rapidly spat out the words as if he were anxious to be done with speechmaking. On April 17 Truman had read a prepared text to the American Society of Newspaper Editors in Washington. The speech drew only a flicker of polite applause from the crowd. But afterwards, instead of sitting down, the president started telling this influential group exactly what he thought of the international situation in his own earthy language. The result was a sustained standing ovation.

It was a major discovery. What the prepared text gains in elegant phrasing and quotable lines it loses in spontaneity unless the speaker has the acting abilities of a Roosevelt or Reagan. Of course, White House advisers and State Department diplomats are understandably nervous when a president speaks "off-the-cuff" on diplomatic or politically sensitive issues. In addition, handouts of an advance text ensure maximum coverage.

Yet Clifford recommended that the advantages were well worth the risk for an underdog candidate whose peppery personality lost its homespun tang when filtered through the process of reciting a speechwriter's draft.

This experiment meant more work for Truman because he had to work out his own way of expressing the "talking points" prepared for him. But the more he put into preparing the talk, the more believable he was in delivering it.

Although the president arrived at Philadelphia's Civic Center well before 10 P.M., it was not until 2:00 A.M. that he was finally escorted to the speaker's platform. Because of delaying actions by disaffected Southern delegates, Truman did not even receive the nomination until 1:45 A.M. In 1932 Roosevelt was the first presidential candidate who had ever addressed the convention, but Truman became the first incumbent president to do so. It had the effect of jolting the convention delegates in the late hour.

When the bank played "Hail to the Chief," the Wallacites released a flock of doves from inside a floral liberty bell. They were trying to convince the party and country that peace with Stalin could be won by appeasement. One bird started to perch on Speaker Sam Rayburn's bald dome as he was trying to introduce Alben Barkley, who would then present Truman. Another blundered into the balcony and dropped dead on the floor, causing one delegate to compare Truman with the dead pigeon that lay before him.

Standing before the delegates wilted by the sweltering heat and battered by the charges traded between the Wallacite North and Dixiecraft South, the president seemed the only crisp figure as he jauntily appeared in his starched shirt, double-breasted white suit, and bow tie.

As he waited for the soggy crowd to settle down, the sixty-four-year-old Truman had the vitality of man half his age. He knew they needed a dose of his enthusiasm, and he gave it to them in his first sentence:

> Senator Barkley and I will win this election and make the Republicans like it—don't you forget that!

A surge of emotion swept through the crowd. People who moments earlier had been too tired to stand when the president was introduced now were on their feet shouting their heads off.

Then he proceeded to list the benefits that had been won by the Democratic administration for the American people—social security, minimum wage, unemployment compensation. To remind the farmers who might still be listening to him on the radio, he said:

> Never in the world were the farmers of any republic or any kingdom as prosperous as the farmers of the United States—and if they don't do their duty by the Democratic party they are the most ungrateful people in the world.

Then to union workers Truman pointed out that wages and salaries had increased from $29 billion in 1933 to $128 billion in 1947.

> That's labor and labor never had but one friend in politics and that is the Democratic Party and Franklin D. Roosevelt. And I say to labor what I have said to the farmers: They are the most ungrateful people in the world if they pass the Democratic Party by this year.

Truman next tore into the Republican Congress:

> The Republican Party favors the privileged few and not the common everyday man. Ever since its inception, that party has been under the control of special privilege and they concretely proved it in the Eightieth Congress . . . they proved it by the things they failed to do.

Truman followed with a litany of Congressional failures.

Toward the close of the speech, the president pulled his trump card from his sleeve:

> On the 26th day of July, which out in Missouri we call "Turnip Day," I am going to call Congress back in and ask them to pass laws to halt rising prices, to meet the housing crisis—which they are saying they are for in their plat-form.
>
> At the same time I shall ask them to act upon other vitally needed measures such as aid to education which they say they are for, a national health program; civil rights legislation; a higher minimum wage, new veterans' benefits . . . additional farm subsidies . . .
>
> Now, my friends, if there is any reality behind that Republican platform we ought to get some action in a short session of the 80th Congress. They can do this job in 15 days if they want to do it. They will still have time to go out and run for office.

As he ended, the delegates—and even some reporters—rose to cheer the plucky president. He may not have a chance to win, but he was going to put on a fight that would give the American people their money's worth.

The call for Congress to come back in session did momentarily worry the Dewey campaign managers. His top lieutenant Herbert Brownell tried in vain to persuade Senator Taft to put a Republican stamp on some of the less controversial and less costly of the Truman agenda items. Taft answered, "We're not going to give that fellow a nickel."

As long as public opinion polls showed a twenty-to-thirty point gap between Governor Dewey and Truman, there was no reason to be alarmed. Dewey, with his operatic baritone of a radio announcer's voice, intoned platitudes of piety and unity. He was trying to offer a leadership profile of poise and dignity in contrast to the squabbling and splintered Democratic Party.

The Southern Democrats had walked out of Philadelphia after Hubert Humphrey, the mayor of Minneapolis, secured an FEPC [civil rights] plank in the platform. Under Governor Strom Thurmond of South Carolina, the "Dixiecrats" fielded their own candidate for president under the "States Rights" banner. Many of the leftwing Northern Democrats bolted to push the candidacy of Henry Wallace as the Progressive Party candidate for president. Of the two, the Wallace threat worried Truman most because the defections could switch states like New York, Pennsylvania, and California to the Republican column.

The Truman team countered by chartering a campaign train. As a vice presidential candidate four years before, Truman had electioneered by train, and he thought the nostalgic informality and close proximity to the crowd agreed with his chirpy style. The fuel for this "whistlestop" tour was the unacted-on-message that President Truman sent to the reconvened Eightieth Congress.[7] When Congress adjourned on August 12, Truman then had his campaign slogan: "That no good do-nothing Congress."

Aboard the *Ferdinand Magellan*, the presidential train, Truman often began his campaign remarks on the back of the rear car announcing, "I'm Harry Truman—I work for the government and I hope you'll let me keep my job on the 2nd of November." After the cheers mingled with laughs died down, he would unloose his attacks on the Republican Party as "the tools of Wall Street and Big Business." For populist demagoguery, his speeches were pages from the Bank Veto Message of his favorite president, Andrew Jackson, who had excoriated the Whigs and business interests. Often a partisan in the crowd would yell out "Give 'em Hell, Harry." "No," the president would answer, "I just tell the Republicans the truth and they think it's Hell."[8]

Perhaps never before had a chief of state let himself appear so "unpresidential." Feisty instead of formal, grinning more than grave, Truman looked like he was having the time of his life to the surprise of reporters who were traveling on the *Magellan*. There was nothing he enjoyed more than poking fun at the pompous Dewey. He described Dewey as "some kind of doctor with a magic cure for all the ills of mankind" and asked his listeners to imagine that "we the American people" were visiting him for "our usual routine checkup." The president would tell the crowds this story, imitating both the smooth doctor and confused patient.

"You been bothered much by issues lately?" asked the doctor.

"Not bothered exactly," the patient replied. "Of course, we've had a few. We've had the issues of high prices and education and social security and a few others."

"That's too bad," says the doctor. "You shouldn't have so many issues."

"Is that right?" replied the patient. "We thought the issues were signs of good health."

"Not at all," says the doctor. "We shouldn't think about issues. What you need is my medicine of soothing syrup—I call it unity."

Truman twirled an imaginary moustache and imitated the doctor edging up a little closer. "Say, you don't look good."

"Well, that seems strange to me, Doc," the patient replied. "I never felt stronger, never had more money and never had a brighter future. What is wrong with me?"

"I never discuss issues with a patient," the doctor replied, "but what you need is a major operation."

"Will it be serious, Doc?"

"Not very serious. It will just mean taking out the complete works and putting in a Republican administration."

To Truman, Thomas E. Dewey was a glossy portrait waiting to be punctured. A study in dignity, the moustached New York governor conducted himself as if the election had already been won. After all, *Newsweek* magazine reported interviews with fifty potential experts across the country: Every one of them concluded that a Dewey victory was a certainty. The only political suspense remaining was the composition of Dewey's cabinet. Periodicals ran features on John Foster Dulles and Herbert Brownell, who were expected to be, respectively, Dewey's secretary of state and attorney general. They appeared in newsstands the same week one of President Truman's radio network broadcasts were cut off in mid-sentence because of insufficient funds to pay for it. The week earlier the Truman train ran aground in Oklahoma. The *Magellan* did not pull out until Governor Roy Turner, a political ally, passed the hat. Meanwhile, the Dewey juggernaut rolled on, described by Drew Pearson as "the most skillful and astute campaign in recent history."

Dewey had reason to be confident. He headed a unified party and had presided over the nation's largest state with a record distinguished for its honesty and progressivism.

There was, however, a cold artificiality in his personality that prompted Theodore Roosevelt's daughter Alice to describe him as "the little man on the wedding cake." One Republican politician reported that "it was hard to tell which was the more chilling experience—to be snubbed by Dewey or to have shaken his hand." The polished and urbane Dewey, who had been a brilliant prosecutor before becoming governor, did not suffer fools or incompetence gladly. When an engineer of a campaign train carrying him in Beaucoup, Illinois, suddenly rolled back, the candidate shouted within earshot of the press: "Someone ought to shoot the engineer." Reverberations of that incident did not enhance Dewey's image with organized labor.

But if the stately Dewey seems stuffy in retrospect, it must be remembered that many Americans, after years of Roosevelt, were accustomed to a more elegant presence in the White House than Truman and his White House staff of poker-playing cronies from Missouri offered. The pundits as well as the pollsters sensed this trend and predicted defeat. The increasing number of crowds turning out to hear the president speak at whistlestop appearances were discounted as a testament to the office and not the man.

Truman's campaign ended in St. Louis. There the speechwriters in the train had pooled their best lines and drafted a blockbuster for the president to use. In the 356 speeches Truman gave while logging 31,700 miles, the staff regularly supplied the "talking points" with comments of particular local interests as well as some choice zingers. But Truman ignored this eclectically woven masterpiece and spoke off the top of his head at Kiel Stadium in St. Louis.

> People are waking up, that the tide is beginning to roll and I am here to tell you that if you do your duty as citizens of the greatest Republic the sun has ever shone on, we will have a government that will be for your interests, that will be for the peace of the world and for the welfare of all people and not a few.

The president voted at 10 A.M. in Independence. Instead of staying up for returns, he retired at 10 P.M. At that time commentators, notably H. V. Kaltenhorn of NBC radio, were still predicting a Dewey victory in the face of early Truman pluralities. "When the farm vote is heard from," intoned Kaltenhorn in his guttural German accent, "Governor Dewey will be elected the next President." Yet his Midwestern states, Illinois and Ohio, as well as the late reporting California, went for Truman, giving him 304 electoral votes. When his campaign train returned to Washington, the victorious president, holding aloft the *Chicago Tribune*'s front page heading "Dewey President," was met by a flood of Johnnie-come-lately Democratic politicians, who pressed into his staff's hands a pile of back-dated checks. The Washington Post building emblazoned a sign: "MR. PRESIDENT, WE ARE READY TO EAT CROW WHENEVER YOU ARE READY TO SERVE IT."

In his "Turnip Day Acceptance Speech" Truman had found a formula to reassemble the New Deal coalition that had elected Roosevelt for four terms. While labeling Dewey as the "candidate of the special interests," Truman targeted his appeal to the lobbies of organized labor, the Farm Bureau, the veterans, government employees, and pensioners as well as Jewish and Negro organizations.[9]

Like "Old Hickory," "Give 'em Hell, Harry" sandbagged the opposition party by setting them up as "the party of privilege" and knocking them down with a strong dose of populist demagoguery.

The Truman who emerged at Union Station was no longer "the accidental president" who had been overwhelmed with his sudden burden of responsibilities. Freed from the shadow of Roosevelt, he now basked in the glow of vindication and victory. The manner of the man changed with the mandate. He began to rely less on the experts and more on his instincts. The presidential personality that had once seemed insecure now radiated a cocksure appreciation of his own political judgment and wisdom.

As a result, Truman became a stronger leader in foreign policy abroad but more vulnerable at home. This was the dichotomy of a leader who always practiced statesmanship in world affairs but often descended to rank partisanship on domestic issues. The Cold War initiatives he championed, such as the Marshall Plan to rebuild Europe, the Truman Doctrine to safeguard the Balkans, and "Point Four," a proto–Peace Corps program to send farm technology to starving nations, insured for him the recognition of history and the gratitude of the free world.

But in the laurels of his unexpected victory were also the seeds of his second–term unpopularity. In the end, the qualities of loyalty that propelled an undistinguished party workhorse from county judge to senator to vice president proved his undoing. Many of the mediocrities he appointed seemed to have as their chief qualification service in past campaigns and residence in Missouri. Some of them were indicted and prosecuted for payola, influence-peddling, and favoritism in contract awarding.

Today only those who were his contemporaries can recall that he left the White House as the century's most unpopular chief executive. Instead, he is nostalgically remembered as the plucky president whose upset victory against the predictions of the press and pollsters was a testament to the gutsy, plain-speaking virtues the average American would like to see in himself. The "Turnip Day Talk" was vintage Truman. By the tenor he took and the tactic he employed he laid the basis for a victory. As a winner, not only did he extend the coalition continuation of the Democrats as America's majority, but he also changed the character of that party's foreign policy leadership from one-world idealism to Cold War Realism.

NOTES

1. In January of 1953 Truman had an 18 percent approval rating in the Gallup Poll compared to 22 percent for Richard Nixon in 1974. Both presidents, despite titanic achievements in foreign policy, were beset by domestic scandals. Truman, of course, was not forced to resign, although, like Nixon, some of his White House staff and appointees went to jail. There was even a bill offered in the House of Representatives asking for his impeachment. Unlike the one for Nixon, it never cleared the Judiciary Committee.

2. One of his boarding house companions as a bank clerk in Kansas City was Arthur Eisenhower, older brother of Dwight.

3. Jacobson, who later became a supporter of Chaim Weizman, the Zionist leader of Israel, played an instrumental role in influencing President Truman to recognize Israel in 1948.

4. Mrs. Wallace never quite reconciled herself to her son-in-law, even though

he and her daughter lived in her house and later she lived with them in Washington. She even voted for Dewey in 1948.

5. For one who never became president, James Byrnes had probably the most impressive public service credentials in American history. From state legislature in South Carolina, he was elected to Congress and then the Senate, where he was assistant majority leader. After being appointed to the Supreme Court, Byrnes went to the White House as head of War Mobilization. After the war, he would be secretary of state and later governor.

6. James Byrnes had served as congressman and senator from South Carolina. As Senator he was elected as assistant majority leader. President Roosevelt appointed him to the Supreme Court just before the war. During the war he made him head of War Mobilization, a job pundits described as "Assistant President." In 1950, the former secretary of state would be elected governor of South Carolina.

7. Truman adopted the term proudly after Senator Taft used it as an epithet. He had said the president was off campaigning at some "whistlestop." Many medium-sized cities were outraged by the downgrading description.

8. When I approached Mr. Truman in April 1960, he said much the same. Truman, who was dining with Senator Stuart Symington of Missouri, gave me this advice: "Read American history and tell the truth. All you Republicans said I was giving 'em Hell, but I was only telling the truth and they thought it was Hell."

9. Despite opposition by the State Department, Truman made the United States the first nation to recognize Israel at the same time it declared itself a state.

13 _____

Eisenhower's Farewell Address: An Old Soldier's Warning

In the councils of government we must guard against unwarranted influence, whether sought or unsought, by a military-industrial complex.

Like George Washington, Dwight David Eisenhower departed from a two-term presidency as he entered—with the undiminished esteem and affection of the American people. Like Washington, Eisenhower was not a superb strategist, but he did possess, in full measure, the qualities of command. But if Eisenhower was not brilliant, he inspired a devotion that was ardent. A sense of presence only partly explained his appeal. For his ruddy face, broad smile, and bald head radiated a glow that would light up a dark room. More important was his projection of character, which was expressed in a self-effacement shaped by years of self-restraint. Whether innate or acquired, this modesty and discretion stood him well as a government bureaucrat in Washington and as a military diplomat in Europe.

It was no accident that Eisenhower's eight years were the most prosperous and peaceful in American history. He was the last president who balanced most of his budgets (six out of eight), and his fiscal restraint generated an economy that witnessed record lows in inflation and highs in productivity. At the same time, his presidency enjoyed the highest prestige abroad, as Eisenhower both protected the interest of the free world and preserved a stable peace.

Until recently historians generally did not award Eisenhower high marks for presidential leadership. Perhaps they confused activity for action and intellectualism for intelligence.[1] In his climb up the military bureaucratic ladder, Eisenhower learned to work his will by giving credit to others. Those who worked under him saw little of the genial "Ike." One former staffer told this writer, "He was a five star general—I was a private—and he and I both knew it." He could tell reporters he was reading Zane Grey westerns, but the country boy style masked both a burning drive and political shrewdness.[2]

Eisenhower could switch from the general to genial Ike in a split second. One moment he was a frowningly intense executive, and the next, if he stepped before the public camera, he could grin like a Huck Finn as if painted by Norman Rockwell. But underneath the famous "Ike" smile was "Eisenhower," which in German means "maker of iron."

Even in Eisenhower's youth his smile hid a competitive zeal and a fierce temper. By some accounts the greatest duel in Abilene since its legendary shoot-outs in its "Wild West Days" was a fist fight between Dwight Eisenhower of the Southside of town and Wesley Merrifield of the Northside. After both were exhausted, the battered Wesley gasped, "I can't lick you, Ike," and the equally bloody Ike gasped back, "And I can't lick you."

Much of this fierce drive he channeled into sports like football and baseball. This drive for excellence carried over in school, where he developed a phobia about misspelled words (to which tongue-lashed White House speechwriters would later attest). Besides the precise subjects of spelling and math, his favorite course was history. Although there is no indication that his schoolboy dream was a general's star, his fascination with the careers of Caesar and Alexander was so intense that his mother often locked up his history books so Dwight could spend time on other subjects.

His decision to go to a service academy was one of economics: It was his only chance for a college education. It also gave him a chance to play football. But an attempted tackle of the legendary Jim Thorpe ended the career of someone the *New York Times* called "one of the most promising half-backs in the East."

A disappointed Eisenhower threw his energies into coaching the junior varsity team. He proved so adept that when war came in 1917, Eisenhower found himself confined to Texas training infantry. His experience as a coach made him a superb instructor, but training troops was like scrimmaging all week without being allowed to play the game on Saturday.

Although he pestered the War Department with requests for overseas duty, the only travel order Captain Eisenhower received sent him to Fort Leavenworth to instruct provisional second lieutenants. There he found time to take a course in the first tank school.[3] The training helped him win a slot at Camp Meade in Maryland to head a tank battalion scheduled to be shipped to France. He did such a superb job that, to his dismay, he was sent not overseas but a few miles north to Camp Colt in Gettysburg, where he was asked to reorganize its armored units into a tank corps. There, on the historic field of Pickett's charge, a restless Eisenhower relentlessly drilled his charges.

Once, when some of his soldiers were getting drunk at a local hotel, Eisenhower stationed guards at the tavern. The local congressman, who was a friend of the innkeeper, threatened to have Eisenhower replaced. "You do that!" shot back Eisenhower. "Nothing would please me more than to be taken out of here. I want to go overseas!"

Just when Eisenhower was about to embark for France at the rank of lieutenant-colonel, the Armistice ended the war on November 11, 1918. Eisenhower could hardly believe it. A career professional soldier had missed action in the greatest war in history!

After the war Eisenhower was assigned to Panama under the tutelage of General Connor, the early apostle of tank warfare. Connor arranged for him to go to the General Staff School at Fort Leavenworth, where Eisenhower placed first in his class.

From such a premier ranking his next assignment to prepare a guidebook for American battlefields in Europe must have seemed anti-climactic. Possibly the only reason Dwight accepted it was because it enabled him to be close to his younger brother Milton, who was one of the key bureaucrats in the Agriculture Department. With a talent for uncluttered prose, Major Eisenhower finished the rush project a month before deadline.[4]

The published work, which pleased his superiors, singled him out as excellent material for a staff officer. He was then assigned to the prestigious Army War College in Carlisle, Pennsylvania. Again, his grades gained for him not a base command but another book to write. He was asked to rewrite the military guidebook on the terrain of Europe.

His return to Washington in November 1929 coincided with the Wall Street crash. In the depths of the Depression, he had the surrealistic task of enlisting skeptical businessmen to develop plans for military industrial expansion.

His lucid proposal brought him to the attention of Douglas MacArthur, who was then chief of staff. MacArthur liked the clean-writing major, who shunned the spotlight.

Eisenhower became MacArthur's chief of staff in the Philippines in 1935. Eisenhower, who wrote all MacArthur's speeches, said later of the general's fondness for self-promotion, "MacArthur had an 'eye' problem. He was addicted to the perpendicular pronoun."

When war did erupt, Eisenhower was back in America at Fort Sam Houston in Texas. On Sunday, December 7, he was attending to a pile of paperwork in Fort Sam Houston. He came home at noon for a nap after lunch when the telephone rang reporting the news of Pearl Harbor.

Five days later General George C. Marshall summoned him to Washington to become assistant chief of the War Plans Division. The meeting with Marshall was formal and brief. "What should be our general line of action in Asia?" Eisenhower was given two hours to prepare his report. Eisenhower proposed abandoning the Philippines and building a Pacific base in Australia. If MacArthur was angered by his former subordinate's recommendation, Marshall appreciated it for its cold realism.

Later that month Marshall took him to the White House when Roosevelt met with Churchill and then, in January, to the first wartime conference with the British military high command. It was apparent that the English officers liked the affable American colonel with his unpretentious poise. Perhaps Marshall, a model of courtesy and demeanor in the Lee tradition, saw something of himself in the younger Eisenhower, who refused even privately to indulge in anti-British gibes.

The choice of Eisenhower to head the European theater of operations astonished the world and, even more, the hundreds of generals who out-ranked him. To those who had been in and out of Marshall's office it was no surprise. Eisenhower had been tagged as "Marshall's fair haired boy."[5] Eisenhower reflected Marshall's views that Europe should be the first priority and that an allied invasion of France could take place as early as the fall of 1943. When Roosevelt would not let Marshall leave Washington, Marshall chose Eisenhower.

In July of 1942, Major General Eisenhower went to London to assume command of the Allied Forces. The first invasion of American troops would take place, however, in North Africa. Eisenhower's talents for tact and diplomacy were fully taxed as he tried to hammer out a common allied strategy reconciling two different approaches to the war. The Americans wanted an early invasion of France to relieve the strain on Russia, whereas the British general staff feared that a premature landing would result in disaster. Churchill, already looking to post-war politics, was anxious for a Mediterranean invasion to free the Balkans from German rule before the Russians arrived. The compromise was a North African campaign to set up an Italian invasion for 1943 and then a landing in France the following year.

From an anonymous military bureaucrat in early 1942, Eisenhower had become, in two years, "Ike," the most recognizable soldier in the world. It was hard to imagine that a couple of years earlier a wire service caption of a picture taken during maneuvers in Louisiana had identified him as "Lt. Col. D. D. Eisenbeing." By the time of the D-Day invasion in June 1944, the most familiar grin in the world belonged to Eisenhower.

The broad-beamed Eisenhower smile kindled an affectionate response not only back home in America but in Britain as well. He seemed to embody the best of America: a down-to-earth manner, an up-in-spirits attitude, and a level-straight integrity.

Although Eisenhower knew when to flash his grin for cameras, the regular guy he seemed to be was not an act. No general was ever more concerned about the morale of his men. Indeed, he considered morale, along with intensive drilling, the two most important things a commander could instill in his men.

When other generals asked enlisted men about their unit, training, and weapons, Eisenhower asked where they were from, how their families were, and what they planned to do after the war.[6] Eisenhower opened up an officers' resort to enlisted men and moved out of a sumptuous suite at the posh Claridge's in London to share a room with Harry Butcher, his public relations assistant, at a less elegant hotel.

All Britain took this unpretentious general to their hearts. They noted with approval his speech to a Sandhurst graduating class to regard their duties to their men like "heads of a family." Word also circulated about his sending home an American officer for cursing a British officer. Actually, the Englishman had pleaded with Eisenhower not to reprimand the American. "He only called me a son-of-a-bitch—we all know that can even be an affectionate term." Eisenhower answered, "My information is that he called you a British son-of-a-bitch. My reprimand stands."

If his popularity was insulation, Eisenhower needed every bit of it to hold the alliance together, as British interests jockeyed against American and as generals vied against each other for power and command. No other general except Marshall could have commanded the respect of both the swashbuckling George Patton and the vainglorious Bernard "Monty" Montgomery, not to mention Prime Minister Winston Churchill, who believed his training as soldier and war historian qualified him as a military strategist.

The Americans eventually acceded to their senior partner in the war against Hitler. They agreed to an American landing in North Africa. It was Eisenhower's first battle command, and he did not emerge with glory. But it was the lack of political, not military, experience that almost cost him his command. Eisenhower cut a deal with the hated Admiral Darlan, commander of the Vichy France, to ensure an unopposed invasion of North Africa. Although General Marshall later estimated it saved about 10,000 casualties, the alliance with a Nazi collaborator like Darlan struck a sour note with commentators back home.

The D-Day landing in Normandy in June 1944 was, without a doubt, the most gigantic military undertaking ever attempted. The successful movement of armies, tanks, and weaponry across the Atlantic to secure a beachhead on a hostile, fortified shore was not only a tactical triumph but a logistical miracle as well. All the decisions for that vast operation funneled through one man—General Dwight David Eisenhower.

To those critics who said Eisenhower as a military man lacked broad based political experience to be successful as a president, the answer is that Eisenhower's tenure as leader of the free world began not in 1953 but in 1944. Eisenhower's Allied command over a military and civilian operation exceeded in numbers the government establishment Roosevelt found when he came to Washington a decade earlier. As supreme commander, Eisenhower was called on to negotiate diplomatic and political arrangements with heads of government and sovereign states. Not only did he have to work with a strong-willed Churchill, he had to mollify a temperamental DeGaulle. He had to effectuate concordats with the Vatican and mediate between factions of exiled governments.

The skills Eisenhower displayed in organizing the landing were more than logistical—they were political and diplomatic. Like George Washington before him, he knew how to lead, and he made his subordinates submerge their ambitions in pursuit of a common goal. He not only had the Americans swearing by him but the British, too. Said Churchill to the House of Commons in February 1944:

> General Eisenhower has built up a uniform staff in which every place was filled with whomever was thought to be the best man, and they all ordered each other about according to their rank, without the slightest regard to what country they belonged to.

Although Eisenhower, as supreme commander, personally made the major decisions on strategy, tactics, and personnel, he learned, like all successful leaders, the art of delegating authority. Many of the decisions involved assignment of tasks, constructed of artificial harbors, provision for assault techniques, occupational currency, and logistical methods. Here Eisenhower's role was more supervisory than direct.

But someone had to give the vast bureaucracy a sense of direction and priorities. Someone had to be able to apply all the information assembled. Someone had to make sure each role meshed into the whole. That man was Eisenhower.

On June 4 the joint Allied staff met in the mess room of Southwick House, a lovely country estate just north of Portsmouth. The wind and rain rattling the French windows in staccato beat also shook the Allies confidence as they gazed at the other wall, where a map of Southeast England and Normandy was dotted with pins outlining the position of Allied and German units. If Eisenhower delayed the landing plans, it would mean postponing the campaign until June 19, the next time for favorable tides.

Whatever Eisenhower decided, it would be a risk. He began pacing the room, head down, chin in his chest, hands clasped behind his back. At 9:45 P.M. Eisenhower looked out into the driving rain and gave the order to go.

As the invasion went ahead in the early dawn hours, Eisenhower scribbled a press release to be used if necessary. Such acceptance of blame—rare among leaders—reveals the essence of Eisenhower.

> Our landings have failed and I have withdrawn the troops. My decision to attack at this time and place was based on the best information available. The

troops, the air, the Navy did all that bravery and devotion could do. If any blame or fault attaches to the attempt it is mine.

The invasion at Normandy, however, caught the Germans by surprise and was a singular success. Once the full panoply of the Allied might was brought to bear upon the European continent, Germany's defeat was inevitable.

Of the major decisions remaining, the most crucial was the conquest of Berlin. Roosevelt, at Teheran, along with Eisenhower, overruled Churchill and agreed to allow the Soviets to enter Berlin first. To get to Berlin before the Red Army would have required an extraordinary and costly effort. Eisenhower acquiesced to Roosevelt's decision that the Soviet entry into Berlin in 1945 was a small price to ensure their cooperation in the post-war era. Eisenhower was wrong, but this decision was based on his soldier's philosophy of obeying the commander-in-chief and of attaining an objective with the minimal sacrifice of his men's lives.

At the Potsdam meeting, President Truman, in an afternoon automobile excursion while touring bombarded sites, said to Eisenhower, "General, there is nothing that you may want that I won't help you get. That definitely and specifically includes the Presidency in 1948." A stunned Ike laughed and said, "Mr. President, I don't know who will be your opponent for the Presidency but it sure as hell won't be I." (He thereby endeared himself not only to Truman but to legions of grammarians as well.)

As the filing date for the New Hampshire primary neared, Eisenhower did send a letter to the editor of the *Manchester Union Leader*:

> Politics is a serious, complicated and, in its true sense, noble profession. In the American scene I see no dearth of men fitted for national leadership . . . my decision to remove myself from the political scene is definite and positive.

When Eisenhower wrote that letter in 1948, he truly believed that he closed the door forever on the presidency. Like every analyst in the country, he believed Truman would be defeated. The Republican victor, whom he thought would be Dewey, would run for reelection in 1952, and in 1956 a sixty-five-year-old Eisenhower would be too old to mount a campaign.

The presidency he did accept was head of Columbia University. When he was first approached by the trustees in 1947, he told them "You got the wrong Eisenhower." Some of the disaffected academicians spread the story that Dwight was chosen instead of Milton because of some telephone communication mishap! If his Columbia years were not Dwight Eisenhower's finest hours, the tenure was not without its successes and accomplishments. His fame brought money to a financially embarrassed institution, and his administrative skills put the university in sound fiscal order.[7]

Eisenhower was no academician, but he also was not the anti-intellectual his critics suggested. Actually, his decision to include Marxism as a course of study prompted diatribes from the right wing. Eisenhower responded that "there would be no intellectual iron curtain at Columbia," and he refused to interfere with the rights of students to form radical clubs and promote left-wing politics.

By 1950 Eisenhower could no longer conceal his boredom with the endless meetings of academic life, where more was deferred than decided and more argued about than acted upon. When President Truman offered him the supreme commandership of the newly organized North Atlantic Treaty Organization (NATO), some commentators thought Truman was cleverly removing from the political scene his greatest obstacle for reelection in 1952. Governor Thomas Dewey, who already had announced his choice for the Republican nomination, scoffed at the report. "It would increase his qualifications, if that's possible." Additional support from the Republican party's Eastern establishment came from Senator Henry Cabot Lodge, the grandson of the senator who had opposed Wilson's League of Nations. Lodge, however, was very much an internationalist and told Eisenhower in a November 1951 meeting that, unless Eisenhower agreed to run, Senator Taft would be the candidate—and a losing one.

Eisenhower was by roots and inclination a Republican, but by experience and outlook he was an internationalist. From either viewpoint the election of Truman or Taft was unacceptable. For the first time Eisenhower began to hear the magic word "duty" that Dewey, Lodge, and others pressed into his ears.

On January 6, 1952, Republican Senator Henry Cabot Lodge of Massachusetts entered Eisenhower's name in the New Hampshire primary, but Eisenhower did not return from Europe to campaign.

Eisenhower never lusted for the White House. If he had, he could have had the Democratic nomination in 1952, if not 1948. He believed that Taft's isolationism was too big a price to pay to end Truman's populism. At the same time, every instinct of the professional soldier warned him against revealing an interest in the nomination, much less an open declaration. Yet, he could, in the tradition of his hero George Washington, respond to an honest draft by the people as a matter of duty.

The outpouring of votes in the New Hampshire primary and then the massive write-ins for him in the Minnesota primary convinced Eisenhower that his duty lay in responding affirmatively to the popular mandate. He began preparing to wind up his duties at NATO for his return to the United States. Truman, who had announced his decision not to run after Senator Estes Kefauver beat him in the New Hampshire primary, accepted Eisenhower's resignation with "sadness."

On June 4, Eisenhower flew to Kansas. At the Kansas City airport, Dan Thornton, the folksy governor of nearby Colorado, slapped Eisenhower on the back and said "How ya, pardner." For a moment Eisenhower froze in distaste, then he rejoined, "How ya, Dan." The transition from general to presidential candidate had begun.[8]

From an artistic viewpoint, Eisenhower's opening speech was not a forensic success. The language was as soggy as the rain-drenched crowd that waited for him in Abilene Stadium. Eisenhower inveighed against disunity, inflation, overtaxation, bureaucracy, and communism, and the *Chicago Tribune* dismissed the speech as "five star generalities."

The press conference the next day was, however, a ten-point strike. James Reston of the *New York Times* wrote that Eisenhower outdid the master, Franklin D. Roosevelt. "He has that easy grace that marks a great athlete," said Reston. "He has the most expressive face and hands in American public life and yet there is a restrained toughness in his expressions and his gestures that appeal to the intellectual and worker alike."

To the majesty of a George Washington, Eisenhower added the frontier town modesty of a Gary Cooper. Even in his most inarticulate ramblings of homespun pieties there was a sincerity and idealism of Owen Wister's "Virginian" that transcended the cant of the professional politician.

Delegating the convention maneuverings to Dewey and Lodge, Eisenhower took to the hustings proclaiming, "I'm going to roar out across the country for a clean, decent convention. The American people deserve it." Eisenhower was careful to distance himself from the dirtywork in Chicago, where Taft, the embodiment of integrity, was savaged by the Dewey and Lodge operatives. Taft offered a compromise that would divide the disputed delegations equally for the two factions. Dewey and Lodge, who knew the arrangement would probably give Taft a first-ballot victory, rejected the compromise offer.

Once Lodge and New Hampshire governor Sherman Adams engineered the passage of the "Fair Plan Amendment," the rest of the convention was anticlimactic. The delegates (with the contested delegates not voting) rejected the Credential Committee's report and seated the Eisenhower delegates. The result set the stage for a first-ballot victory, which came about when Warren Burger, a lawyer member of the Minnesota delegation, rose to switch his state from favorite son Stassen to Eisenhower.

Watching his victory unfold on television from his Blackstone Hotel suite, Eisenhower immediately pushed his way past weeping Taft workers into Taft's Hotel to pay a call on the defeated senator. "This is not time for conversation on matters of any substance; you're tired and so am I. I just want to say that I want to be your friend and hope you will be mine. I hope we can work together." It was a typical Eisenhower gesture—one that represented not only good will but good politics.

Accepting the nomination, Eisenhower said,

Ladies and gentlemen, you have summoned me on behalf of millions of your fellow Americans to lead a crusade—for freedom in America and freedom in the world. I know something about the solemn responsibility of leading a crusade. I have led one. I take up this task, therefore, in a spirit of deep obligation, mindful of its burdens, of its decisive importance, I accept your summons. I will lead this crusade.

Eisenhower's Democratic opponent was Illinois governor Adlai Stevenson, whose acceptance address was one of the most eloquent speeches in American history.

In early September, the Scripps-Howard chain, which like most newspapers in the country favored Eisenhower, criticized the campaign for "running like a dry creek."

Stevenson charged that General Eisenhower was a "captive candidate," if not of the Taft philosophy then perhaps of the Dewey organization. But Eisenhower, as supreme commander of the biggest military operation in history, had learned the art of delegating responsibility. That meant listening to those who had expertise in their field. That reliance resulted in his only regret of the campaign, when he reluctantly agreed to delete praise for General Marshall in a campaign speech while on the same platform with Senator Joseph McCarthy in Wisconsin.[9]

If there was any remaining doubt about the outcome of the election, it was resolved when Eisenhower, on October 24, pledged "I shall go to Korea." That announcement galvanized the American public, which had become increasingly disillusioned with the Korean "conflict." President Truman had entered Korea in June 1950, when Communist troops from the North invaded South Korea.

On election day the voters responded by giving Eisenhower an overwhelming mandate of 442 electoral votes, including victory in four states in the Democratic South.

For Inauguration Day on January 20, 1953 the president-elect replaced the silk top hat with the homburg. Although he discarded the cutaway morning coat, traditional elegance was found in the lines of his inaugural address. Emmet Hughes, the former *Time* writer, put into stylish prose the beliefs of Eisenhower about America's leadership of the world:

> We are called as a people to give testimony in the sight of the world, to our faith that the future shall belong to the free . . .
> We are free men. We shall remain free never to be proven guilty of the one capital offense against freedom, lack of staunch faith.

If the halting delivery of the new president was sometimes unequal to the crafted lines of his speechwriter, Eisenhower was his most poignant in the short prayer he composed himself after attending services at the National Presbyterian Church.

> Give us, we pray, the power to discern clearly right from wrong and allow all our words and actions to be governed thereby.

Especially we pray that our concern shall be for all people regardless of station, class or calling.

Eisenhower's first order of business was to bring an end to the Korean War. Right after the election, the president-elect went to Korea to study the military implications of American involvement. With the threat of atomic weapons, he was able to force the North Korean Communists to the peace table in the spring. By July Eisenhower was able to secure peace and a signing of an armistice treaty that guaranteed South Korea's border on the thirty-eighth parallel.

If most Americans generally rejoiced in the treaty, it did not please members of the right-wing China Lobby. "Softness on Communism" had been a favorite theme of Congressional Republicans, and Eisenhower's withdrawal from Korea confirmed their suspicions about the president.

The Korean War, the Stalinist repression in Eastern Europe, the conviction of State Department aide Alger Hiss, and the trial of the Rosenbergs for passing nuclear secrets to the Soviets had aroused fear of Communist tyranny and subversion. Senator Joseph McCarthy was exploiting these anxieties with reckless attacks on those in government whose past associations linked them with left-wing groups.

In a June commencement speech at Dartmouth College, Eisenhower told students, "Don't join the bookburners"; but still he refused to make a direct attack on McCarthy. It was Eisenhower's personal code "never to engage in personalities." His political instincts told him that if he attacked the senator he would raise him to the president's level, thereby giving him the publicity and attention he sought. He also was convinced that the end of the Korean War would cool the hysteria that fueled McCarthyism.

By 1954 McCarthy's popularity was at an all-time high. Half the American public, according to a Gallup Poll, rated him favorably. A right-wing populist, McCarthy drew his strength from those with Eastern European background as well as Protestant fundamentalists. Still, Eisenhower told his advisors such as brother Milton and press assistant Jim Hagerty, "I will not get in the gutter with that guy." "I am convinced," he said, "that the only person that can destroy McCarthy is himself."

Eisenhower proved right. In 1954 McCarthy directed his committee to investigate Communist influence in the Army. Joseph Welch, a counsel for the Army, brought out that McCarthy had falsified evidence and received stolen classified government documents. Eisenhower commanded his chief of staff Sherman Adams to work behind the scenes with those Republican Senators opposed to McCarthy. A Senate committee selected to investigate McCarthy's conduct recommended "censure," and he was reprimanded in a Senate vote. It was not the frenetic attacks from the left but measured criticism from his peers and conservatives in the Republican-controlled Senate that finished McCarthy as a force in American politics.

A country weary of the partisanship of Truman, the divisiveness of the Korean War, the excesses of McCarthy, and the surge of rising costs turned to a hero who transcended politics and offered unity. By the beginning of his third year in the White House, Eisenhower had brought military peace and political stability to a grateful nation.

Eisenhower was now free to concentrate on what he always regarded as his premier responsibility as president: leadership of the free world. In the summer of 1955, Eisenhower flew in the presidential plane *Columbine* to Geneva for the first summit meeting. No peacetime president since Woodrow Wilson had gone to Europe, and the stage was set for an international drama.

On the fourth day of the conference, Eisenhower electrified the world. Speaking in the elaborate council chamber of the defunct League of Nations, he made a disarmament proposal that was at once bold and radical.

> I propose . . . to give each other a complete blueprint of our military establishments . . . to provide within our countries facilities for aerial photography to the other country . . . and make more easily attainable a comprehensive system of inspection and disarmament.

In his attempt to persuade Khrushchev and the Soviet leaders to accept the "Open Skies" plan, Eisenhower's gesture established him as the world's foremost statesman and champion of peace. Said *Le Monde* of Paris, a traditionally anti-American newspaper: "Eisenhower has emerged today as the type of leader humanity needs today." Even nonaligned nations that had embraced the tenets of Marxism criticized the Soviet's rejection of the peace initiative. Still the world warmed to the "Spirit of Geneva," seeing in the meeting between the big powers a hope for lessening world tensions.

When Eisenhower returned to begin a delayed vacation of fishing and golfing in Colorado, a Gallup Poll greeted him showing that 74 percent of the American public approved of his performance. But the holiday was not soon enough. On September 24, Eisenhower was felled by a severe heart attack in the bedroom of the Doud House in Denver. Not since FDR's death was a nation so jolted. A nation suddenly realized its dependence on a president who had become a symbol of world peace and national unity. Even if Eisenhower fully recovered, there seemed little likelihood of his accepting a second term the following year.

Ironically, Eisenhower, who before the heart attack had all but ruled out a reelection bid, found his convalescence a frustration worse than the burdens of office. The enforced idleness made him realize that the retirement he had long yearned for was better in fantasy than in fact. In February, when doctors gave him a clean bill of health, Eisenhower made his decision.

Again Eisenhower had as his opponent Adlai Stevenson. But in 1956

Stevenson's eloquence descended into inconsistency prompted by desperation. One day he was a dove calling for a nuclear test ban and an end to peacetime draft, and the next day he was a hawk attacking Eisenhower's cutback in defense and "bailing out" of Korea. For Stevenson to attack the popular Eisenhower personally was an error, but to attack him on matters of war and peace was an egregious blunder.

If there was any doubt about Eisenhower's preeminence as leader of the free world, it dissolved in the closing days of the campaign, when British parachuters landed in Egypt and Russian troops rolled into Hungary to put down a popular rebellion. Eisenhower denounced moves of both ally and adversary. But the decisions to refrain from military involvement in both the Middle East and Eastern Europe were painful. On one hand, by refusing to aid the beleaguered freedom fighters in Budapest he snuffed out any hopes of Hungarian independence from Moscow. On the other hand, by asking for a cease-fire in the United Nations he strained the alliance of United States' staunchest ally. The cease-fire was passed by the General Assembly.

Yet the country must have agreed with Eisenhower's restraint in meeting world crisis when war threatened. In 1956 Ike won the largest popular vote in American history, carrying 41 states with 457 electoral votes.

The millions of Americans who trusted Eisenhower did not hold the same faith in the Republican Party. For the first time since Lincoln, a winning Republican presidential candidate failed to carry both houses of Congress with him. The political deadlock between a Democratic Congress and a Republican chief executive caused some analysts to predict that Eisenhower, who was prevented from running in 1960 by the twenty-second Amendment, would be an impotent president in his second term.[10]

The Eisenhower who pushed through in 1957 the first civil rights act since the days of Reconstruction was no lame duck. In fact, he seemed more of an eagle, as federal troops swooped down on Little Rock in September of that year to enforce integration of the school system, which was being blocked by Arkansas governor Orval Faubus. Government-sanctioned segregation in the South was overturned in 1954 by a Supreme Court decision led by Chief Justice Earl Warren, an Eisenhower appointee.[11]

On the foreign front, in July 1958 the president also dispatched troops to Lebanon. Landing 1,400 Marines on the Beirut airfield was Eisenhower's answer to the plea from Lebanon's beleaguered president, who feared a leftist takeover. As he had done similarly in Guatemala in 1954, the president's quick dispatch of forces stabilized the country.

In October, when a resolution in the U.N. Assembly was passed saying that Arab states would respect the independence of other nations in the Middle East, Eisenhower withdrew the Marine garrison. In ordering the surgical strike, the former general outlined two considerations: if a nation had "too little popular support," the U.S. government "should not be there" and that any military commitment should be brief and temporary to prevent erosion of popular support (as in Korea). Such had been the rationale for his refusing to help France beat back Ho Chin Minh in 1954.

The congressional elections of 1958, however, did not turn on Eisenhower's commitment to secure freedom both at home and abroad. Rather, the issues were an economic slump and a political scandal involving his chief aide, Sherman Adams, who had accepted expensive gifts from Boston textile tycoon Bernard Goldfine. For the first time, the Eisenhower administration seemed on the defensive, and Democrats gained thirteen new senators and forty-eight new congressmen.

The overwhelmingly Democratic Congress on Capitol Hill saw at the other end of Pennsylvania Avenue a Republican president shorn of the services of his chief of staff, Sherman Adams, who resigned, and his secretary of state, John Foster Dulles, who was dying of cancer. Yet in his last two years Eisenhower proved he still wielded power.

On the domestic front, Eisenhower held the line on spending by blocking Democratic proposals for housing, health care, and education. Internationally, Eisenhower faced down an ultimatum by Khrushchev to open West Berlin to Soviet patrols from the East.

The name of Eisenhower was still the most popular in the world. When he went to France in 1959 to meet DeGaulle, a million people in Paris greeted the "liberator of Europe." Following his triumphant tour of Britain and Germany, as well as France, he returned to host Chairman Khrushchev at Camp David. In December of 1959, Eisenhower embarked on the most spectacular diplomatic tour undertaken by a U.S. president. He visited eleven nations in three continents. In India, millions welcomed him with placards proclaiming him "the Prince of Peace."

In 1960 Eisenhower was scheduled to visit the Soviet Union, but on May 1st something happened that made the Soviets withdraw the invitation. An American reconnaissance U-2 plane piloted by Gary Francis Powers was shot down over Soviet territory.

Along with the plane was shot down Eisenhower's trip to Moscow and the hopes for the ongoing summit meeting taking place in Geneva, as well as the forthcoming Asian tour to Japan, the Philippines, Taiwan, and South Korea. Communist-backed demonstrations in Tokyo, as well as other capitals, against Americans had poisoned the atmosphere.

The biggest disappointment in 1960 to Eisenhower, however, was not the diplomatic setback but the narrow political defeat of vice president Richard Nixon by Senator John F. Kennedy. He told his family it was the "blackest day of his life." Although Nixon was not his ideal candidate, he did prefer him to Governor Nelson Rockefeller or Senator Barry Goldwater. (Actually, if he could have picked the nominee, it would have been Robert Anderson, the taciturn lawyer who had succeeded George Humphrey as secretary of treasury.) What depressed Eisenhower about the Republican defeat was the implicit repudiation of his eight-year record. What angered him was the demagogic exploitation of a fake "missile gap" by Senator Kennedy while he, in helpless frustration, was relegated to a modest role in the campaign. As far as Eisenhower was concerned, Kennedy was an appealing young man whose inexperience in defense and foreign-policy matters was monumental.

The "missile gap" was the most blatant charge in the winning Kennedy theme of "getting the country moving again." The attack against an administration presided over by a universally admired military leader would not have found ready acceptance if the Soviet launching of the space Sputnik in 1957 had not aroused public concern about United States' slippage from its technological edge.

The sudden emergence of the Soviet satellite circling in space sent shock waves throughout the nation. Americans, who had long taken for granted their nation's leadership in science and technological innovation, now demanded that a greater priority be given to science in the educational curriculum of its high schools and universities. It was unthinkable that Russia should beat America in the space race to the moon.

It was this popular restlessness with an administration that had long since spent its crusading zeal of eight years to "clean up the mess in Washington" that led to the country's rapture over the young president-elect. Perhaps the Republican defeat served to make Eisenhower a little more determined to put in his final say during his last days in public life.

Malcolm Moos, a White House speechwriter, was the first to make a written suggestion to President Eisenhower that he deliver a "Farewell Address." Moos had come to the White House in Eisenhower's second term through the recommendation of the president's brother, Milton. Milton, at that time president of Johns Hopkins University in Baltimore, had been impressed by Moos, a political science professor. A Minnesotan whose father was a Theodore Roosevelt Republican, Moos had written a history of the Republican Party.

Moos, like any speechwriter, had studied the background and philosophy of the principal for whom he worked. He found out that Eisenhower's hero was that greatest of soldier-statesmen, George Washington. Eisenhower, who was familiar with Washington's most influential statement, the Farewell Address, readily adopted Moos's suggestion.

If George Washington had been stung by the suggestion of Jefferson, among others, that his presidency was too monarchical, Eisenhower also was annoyed by the attacks of Kennedy and his followers in the media. In both situations, the adulation of a military hero had slipped to more human proportions through the erosion of political controversy.

The approach of a new century in Washington's case or a new generation of leadership as exemplified by Kennedy at the end of Eisenhower's presidency made both presidents seem almost anachronisms in a rapidly changing society. Eisenhower, who as a young officer championed the tank when his superiors still thought in terms of the horse, was sensitive to the charge that he was not alert to changing technology.

To Eisenhower, however, the turn to technology as a panacea to all problems was a disturbing phenomenon. He and Sir Winston Churchill had discussed this in 1959 when the aging British statesman had visited the Eisenhowers. Both leaders, whose roots were in the nineteenth century, agreed that the modern technology of the twentieth century was a mixed blessing, bringing with it the enhancement of material benefits but the erosion of individual dignity and rights as well. According to the president's grandson David, both men were concerned that Britain and the United States were democracies whose political institutions would be tested by the mass urbanization of the twentieth century. Eisenhower, in the odyssey of his own life, had witnessed the shift of American values from small town to suburb, from the rooted identity of neighborhood to the rootless sprawl of the metropolis with the concomitant loss of individual identity.

Eisenhower had told Moos in a memorandum of his desire "to have something really significant to say when I leave the White House." That mandate became more specific as it filtered through Milton Eisenhower to Moos. Dr. Eisenhower had reacted even more strongly than the president to journalistic criticism of his older brother.

The first draft Moos sent to the Oval Office assumed a far more defensive note than the final version. The president himself edited out a more explicit response to the notion of a "missile gap" and eliminated a lot of techno-logical language.

At the same time the president was talking to Robert Anderson, his secretary of Treasury. Anderson had come to Washington first as secretary of the Navy, then moved up to secretary of defense before succeeding George Humphrey at Treasury in the last two years. A Texan, Anderson had impressed Eisenhower with his analytical mind and astute judgment. Although Anderson had enjoyed a stint in the Texas legislature before building his law career, he seemed to Eisenhower as one who understood politics without being seduced by its glamour. Eisenhower, who had never suffered from "Potomac Fever," had disdain for those who allowed am-bition to cloud their judgment.

It was from Anderson that Eisenhower first heard the phrase "military-industrial complex." Actually, the man who coined the term was Ralph Williams, a navy officer who helped as a speechwriter when Anderson headed the Navy Department. In the closing days of the administration, Williams was assigned to the White House, where he also was asked to submit his ideas.

The phrase first appeared to describe the impact of military installations on public schools. In 1957 those school districts were asking for federal compensation to handle the influx of students at schools near military bases.

That disruption led Anderson to ponder the effect of massive outlays of spending on American institutions in general. He foresaw sociological problems that would result in the burgeoning industrial leviathans spawned by military defense contracts.

This thinking nicely dovetailed with Eisenhower's own anxieties that the inventor and the entrepreneur, whose genius and drive had built the greatness of America, would be crowded out by the gigantic corporation, whose economic power dwarfed that of most nations. It was no anomaly that the supposedly "big business" administration of Eisenhower pursued the most vigorous anti-trust policy of any administration in history. Eisenhower, who counted many top corporate leaders as close friends, was not friendly toward conglomerate mergers.

By January Moos's draft had absorbed the Ralph Williams injections and had been thoroughly reviewed by Milton Eisenhower. Only minor reediting was supplied by the president as he substituted an occasional word or deleted excess sentences. A succession of four corrected texts cycled between Moos and the president.

The Farewell Address was scheduled for the evening of January 17. It was to be delivered at 8:30 P.M. from the White House. Dressed in a somber gray three-piece suit, Eisenhower arrived at the studio room in the West Wing fifteen minutes early. Donning his clear-rimmed glasses, he read the text over again. He had practiced it with the actor Robert Montgomery, his television advisor. Although the effect of his slight stroke in November 1957 still made him stumble over a few words, Eisenhower was not nervous.

The routine announcement of the address had been swallowed up by the fervor surrounding the last cabinet appointments being announced from president-elect Kennedy's house in Georgetown. From the White House window, the stands for the parade four days later could be seen on Pennsylvania Avenue.

As the light blinked for the introduction of the President of the United States, Eisenhower straightened his tie and coughed into a handkerchief:

> This evening I come to you with a message of leave taking and farewell and to share with you, my countrymen . . .

Eisenhower's tone was low-key and intimate. His tenor was that of observation, not oration. He proceeded to praise Congress, an institution that every president since has more castigated than commended:

> My own relations with the Congress which began on a remote and tenuous basis when long ago a member of the Senate appointed me to West Point, have since ranged to the intimate during the war and immediate post war period and finally to the mutually interdependent during these past years.

Eisenhower himself had chosen the word "intimate," and he underlined it
in his text. He went on to say it "had cooperated well to serve the national
good rather than mere partisanship."

The old soldier then alluded to the horror of war:

> We now stand 10 years past the mid point of a century that has witnessed
> four major wars among great nations—three of those involved this country.

The Russo-Japanese War of 1905 was the exception in the conflict that
included two World Wars and Korea.

> Despite these holocausts, America is today the strongest, the most influential
> and the most productive in the world.

Then Eisenhower struck the theme of his address in this underlined words:

> Understandably proud of this pre-eminence we yet realize that America's
> leadership and prestige depend not merely upon our unmatched material
> progress, riches and material strength but on *how* we use our power in the
> interests of World peace and human betterment.

During the war Eisenhower had been closer to Roosevelt than Churchill
in his assessment of Soviet imperialism and the prospect of post-war cooperation. Yet he, who had felt a genuine warmth toward a fellow general
like Marshall Zhukov, had sadly come to realize in full measure the im-
placability of Soviet intentions regarding the destruction of Western democratic ways.

> We face a hostile ideology global in scope, atheistic in character, ruthless in
> purpose and insidious in method.

The danger it posed was of "indefinite duration." In the continuing crisis
of the Cold War there would be many calls to find "a miraculous solution"
by spending ever increasing sums on research and development of new
weapons. The word "balance" was the touchstone of his middle-of-the-
road philosophy, and he urged that every such proposal "must be weighed
in the light of need to maintain balance ... between cost and hoped for
advantage."

In developing that theme, Eisenhower first established the priority of
seeking peace through strength.

> Our arms must be mighty, ready for instant action, so that no potential
> aggressor may be tempted to risk his own destruction.

But in mobilizing the manpower and maintaining the weaponry necessary to combat a global challenge, Eisenhower feared a monster in the making. He made the point with a biblical allusion:

Until the latest of our world conflicts the United States had no armaments industry. American makers of plowshares could, with time as required, make swords as well. We have been compelled to create a permanent armaments industry of vast proportions.

Then in ringing phrases Eisenhower delivered the most quoted words in his career of service to the country. The sentences summed up his deepest feelings and gave voice to his greatest fears.

This conjunction of an immense military establishment is new in the American experience. The total influence—economic, political and even spiritual—is felt in every city, in every state house, every office of the federal government. We recognize the imperative need for this development. Yet we must not fail to comprehend its grave implications.

Then the old general delivered his direct warning:

In the councils of government, we must guard against the acquisition of unwarranted influence, whether sought or unsought, by the military-industrial complex.

Eisenhower himself had inserted "whether sought or unsought" in last minute editing to soften the effect. He did not fear the rise of some American version of military fascism. What troubled him was the emergence of a powerful military spending lobby fueled by big business.

Seven junior officers—six navy and one army—would follow the five-star general to the Oval Office. Perhaps, their limited experience at a less than exalted level made them more compliant to the recommendations of Pentagon generals and admirals.[12] Eisenhower knew from firsthand experience the recurring Pentagon problem of endemic waste and inflated estimates.

Yet Eisenhower's volcanic temper would have erupted if he could have heard the "doves" of the 1970s quote him to support some kind of unilateral disarmament vis-à-vis the Soviet Union. Eisenhower wanted a defense second to none. Such a weapons system, however, should be tailored to the leadership of the free world, not the lobby of big business defense contractors.

As the last president who made an effort to balance the fiscal budget each year, he foresaw the disruptive impact of a mammoth defense-spending ticket. But he also perceived the more subtle dangers of the "military-industrial complex" in a free society:

> The potential for the disastrous rise of misplaced power exists and will persist. *WE MUST NEVER* let the weight of its combination endanger our liberties or democratic processes. We should take nothing for granted.

Eisenhower, with the capitalization and underlining he added, showed that he sensed the development of that "iron triangle" of the Pentagon, congressional committee chairmen, and defense industry lobbies, whose pressure would smother the unorganized citizenry's common sense and sound judgment.

Then Eisenhower delivered a second warning that, if it is not so popularly remembered, was equally prophetic. The new age of technology and the rise of the massive corporation in financing the development of such sophisticated instruments and weaponry would serve to stifle the individual entrepreneurship that forged America's economic greatness.

> Today the solitary inventor tinkering in his shop has been overshadowed by task forces of scientists in laboratories and testing fields.

Eisenhower could see the individual's role dwarfed and the purpose of the university distorted by the awarding of massive contracts by big government and by business.

> The free university has been . . . the fountainhead of new ideas and scientific discovery. But now research springs not so much from individuals engaged in random pursuit of knowledge, as from public agencies in grim pursuit of specific, predetermined results. For every blackboard there are hundreds of new computers.

Eisenhower agreed with Churchill's remark, "We need engineers in the world—not a world of engineers" as well with his brother Milton, who wrote, "Modern men worship at the temple of science, but science tells him only what is possible not what is right." For that reason he warned "that public policy could itself be the captive of a scientific technological elite."

The old soldier, however, reserved his sternest words for those who would let their children or their children's children shoulder the cost of deficit spending. Here he was warning his Democratic successor of the economic cost of political promises made in the course of the recent campaign.

> You and I and our government must avoid the impulse to live only for today, plundering for our own ease and convenience, the precious treasures of tomorrow.

The last president to send fiscally honest budgets to Congress held conservative economic views that seemed almost quaint to the academic opinion of his day, but now he seems a Cassandra whose dire warnings have been fulfilled by trillion dollar deficits.

> We cannot mortgage the material assets of our grandchildren without risking the loss also of their political and spiritual heritage.

Eisenhower's matter-of-fact delivery assumed almost a plaintive note as he pleaded to television listeners.

> We want democracy to survive for all generations to come—not to become the insolvent phantom of tomorrow.

Eisenhower followed this admonition with an apology—his failure to achieve mutual disarmament.

> I wish I could say tonight that a lasting peace is in sight. Happily I can say that war has been avoided.

The old soldier then ended his presidential service as he began—with a prayer, that he himself composed:

> We pray that peoples of all faiths, all races, all nations, may have their human needs satisfied; that those now denied opportunity shall come to enjoy it to the full; that all who yearn for freedom may experience its spiritual blessings; that those who have freedom will understand its heavy responsibilities; that all who are insensitive to the needs of others will learn charity; that the scourges of poverty, disease and ignorance will be made to disappear from the earth and that in the goodness of time all peoples will come to live together in a peace guaranteed by the binding force of mutual respect and love.

To this final text he penned in his own postscript,

> (Now on Friday noon I am to become a private citizen of the United States. I am proud to do so. I thank you and good night.)

NOTES

1. In 1967 a general, while discussing the criticism of Vietnam, told Eisenhower, "Herodotus said about the Peloponnesian War, 'One can't be an armchair general 28 miles from the front.' " Eisenhower expressed interest, "Herodotus was it? The Peloponnesian War?" Afterwards he turned to his son and an aide and commented, "Well, it wasn't Herodotus but Aemilius Paulus and it wasn't the Peloponnesian War but the Punic War with Carthage." When someone asked why he didn't correct the general he replied, "I got where I did by hiding my ego and hiding my ambition."

2. He liked to convey that picture of himself as he told some little league players, in my presence: "There were two boys at a swimming hole on the last day of

summer. The blond-haired kid asked the darker one, "What do you want to be when you grow up?" The boy answered, "President of the United States." And then he asked his fair-haired pal, "What do you want to be?" He answered, "Pitcher for the New York Yankees." "Well," continued Eisenhower, "both boys failed in their dreams. One became President—President of an Abilene dairy—as for the other one . . . that was me."

3. It was there that he met George Patton and, like Patton, became an early apostle of tank warfare.

4. The academic world always downgraded Eisenhower's intellectual talents. Yet Eisenhower wrote his best-selling *Crusade in Europe* without the held of a ghost writer. The same could not be said of Kennedy's *Profiles in Courage*. Eisenhower was mocked by the press for his rambling prose in press conferences. Yet his lack of clarity was sometimes deliberate. Once when questioned by a reported on a NATO commander's field authority to dispatch missiles, Eisenhower responded in a way that would make Casey Stengel seem lucid where the subject could never find the predicate. Afterward Eisenhower turned to his press secretary Jim Hagerty, "I guess those fellows will never figure out whether those commanders have the authority or not."

5. The late John McCloy, who served as assistant secretary of war told this writer that Eisenhower convinced three men simultaneously that he was "their boy": MacArthur, Marshall, and Roosevelt. MacArthur hand-picked him for the Philippines. FDR thought of him as his monitor on the politically ambitious MacArthur. At the same time he was Marshall's protégé.

6. A year later, on the night before the allied forces crossed the Rhine, a restless supreme commander found himself walking in the misty dusk. He encountered a nervous soldier starting to light up a forbidden cigarette. He said to the private, who did not recognize him, "Soldier, why don't we both walk along the river together and we'll both draw strength from each other."

7. One of the immediate benefits was his persuasion of football coach Lou Little not to leave for Yale. "Lou," said the football-knowledgeable Ike, "You're one of the reasons I came here." More pleasing to the academics was his convincing of Nobel Prize winning physicist Isador Rabi to stay at Columbia instead of leaving for Princeton to be with his friend and colleague Albert Einstein.

8. Years later, in 1964, I observed a similar insight into the real Eisenhower behind the smile—a visitor had asked the general how he saw himself as one who had been a soldier, diplomat, educator, and president. Eisenhower replied, "Just plain Ike." Later the visitor, as he left, said "Goodbye, Ike." The general's face steeled before he managed to summon his familiar smile.

9. Of course, Governor Stevenson in Mississippi had endorsed the race-baiting Senator James Eastland while tailoring his remarks to the states'-rights audience.

10. It is altogether possible that Eisenhower would have acceded to his party's demand to run again. This is the opinion of his son and others. The amendment that restricted presidents to two terms was widely regarded as the Republican Eightieth Congress' posthumous revenge on FDR. Ironically, it served to prevent the Republican party's two most popular presidents from running again—in 1956 and in 1988.

11. Eisenhower, who warmed to the genial personality of Governor Warren, was cool to the judicial activism of Warren on the Supreme Court.

12. In 1965 I found myself as a voluntary "sergeant at arms" for the Republican National Committee at a meeting of a National Policy Committee where Nixon, Dewey, Goldwater, and some former cabinet members were reviewing various Republican policy positions to be endorsed. Former President Eisenhower presided. A Republican congressman read a summary of a white paper criticizing President Lyndon Johnson for stripping our defense. An angry Eisenhower challenged some of the statistics provided by the Pentagon: "Congressman, generals lie!"

14 ―――――

The Kennedy Inaugural: A Young Warrior's Call to Arms

And so, my fellow Americans, ask not what your country can do for you; ask what you can do for your country.

John Fitzgerald Kennedy flashed like a meteor across American skies. From the brilliant eloquence of his inaugural address to the traumatic shock of his assassination, American hopes soared in rapt gaze of this incandescent star and then were dashed in darkness. His vibrant presence signalled not only a new decade but also a new political age of television when style became as important as substance.

It was his charismatic style, which combined debonair poise with elegant phrase, that lifted expectations to a stratospheric high. The performance, however, was never to equal the promise. His admirers will blame an assassin's bullet, but hindsight historians will note that his record of legislation did not match the rhetoric. His legacy was more symbolic than substantive. Like a prince in a storybook of yesteryear, Kennedy embodied in his presidency the idealism of the young—not just in his own country but around the world. Although recent revelations about his White House years, including squalid reports of his sexual adventures, have somewhat tarnished the glitter of his knightly armor, it is his image, perhaps more than any other contemporary world figure, that still kindles idealism around the world.

John Kennedy was more than a politician; he was a star. If he was the first president to possess a Hollywood glamour, he was also the first who could be said to be, in a sense, a son of Hollywood. His father, Joseph Kennedy, had been a movie producer in his formative years in the late 1920s.

It is true that young John Kennedy did not grow up in Beverly Hills, but neither was he raised in Boston, where he was born in 1917. John and his brothers and sisters were not to sink roots in the city of their parents. Instead they would call home a succession of mansions on Park Avenue in New York City; in Palm Beach, Florida; in London, England; and in Hyannisport, Massachusetts. The cosmopolitan addresses were a far cry from the towns of Independence or Abilene, where Truman and Eisenhower grew up.

John Kennedy was not only the first president to be born in the twentieth century; he was also the first Catholic president. Yet he was not a cultural Catholic like Al Smith, who was a native of New York's East Side and imbued with the values of an Irish neighborhood and community. John Kennedy did not receive the typical Catholic education. He prepped at Choate, which Adlai Stevenson had also attended. Then in 1935 he went on to Harvard, from which both his father and his older brother, Joseph, had preceeded him.

"Jack" Kennedy, like his brother Joe, was schooled in the Ivy League and reared away from Irish Boston because his father did not want his sons to suffer from the social barriers he had encountered. His children's friends were more from the social register than from South Boston.

Joseph Kennedy, whom Roosevelt appointed to head the newly formed Securities and Exchange Commission (SEC) in 1934, had later jumped at the offer to become ambassador to the Court of St. James in London for similar reasons. The result was that John Kennedy seemed, because of his education and travels, more WASP than Catholic and more English than Irish.

The flag Joseph Kennedy raised for his children was family. The values and loyalties he imbued were those of the clan. The father was the chieftain, and his oldest son, Joseph, Jr., was the prince and heir. Not only was he given the rights of accession but also the ambitions of his father.

Ambassador Kennedy yearned to succeed Franklin Roosevelt in the White House in 1940, but Roosevelt's third term blocked any chance. A bitter Kennedy came home from London with the intention of supporting the Republican, Wendell Willkie. Only a last-minute meeting with FDR at the White House turned a planned radio speech for Willkie into one for Roosevelt. The president had dissuaded Kennedy by hinting that his time might be 1944.

The ambassador's eldest son was the answer to a father's fantasy. Joe had the rugged frame to play on Harvard's football team and the jaunty good looks that propelled him to class leadership. Beside him, his younger brother Jack was a scrawny, almost sickly figure. Jack had first gone to Princeton for a year to escape comparison with Joe, but then he yielded to paternal pressure and followed Joe to Cambridge. But in no way could Jack equal the record of Joe, who was a campus celebrity. The junior Kennedy didn't even try. He did not distinguish himself scholastically until his final year, when he wrote his senior thesis on British foreign policy leading up to the war. The tract incorporated his father's views on British impotence without echoing his isolationism.

It was the first time Jack really won his father's admiration, which had been reserved mostly for Joe. His father pushed the buttons available to a multimillionaire's touch and turned his son's paper into a popular best seller. He asked the help of *New York Times* editor Arthur Krock, who both reshaped the awkward prose and picked the title *Why England Slept*. Then he called on Henry Luce, the publisher of *Time*, to write a glowing introduction. Joseph Kennedy wrote Jack, "You'd be surprised how a book that really makes the grade with high class people stands you in good stead for years to come."

Jack's more bookish nature might have led him to a career in journalism, but the wartime crash of his brother's plane on an English coast changed that. Now it was Jack who became the bearer of his father's dreams.

Before the crash of Joe's B-17 bomber, Jack had narrowly escaped death in his own ordeal. In 1943, as a skipper of a torpedo craft in the Solomon Islands, Kennedy let his fast P.T. boat be trapped by a Japanese destroyer, whose gunfire sliced his boat in two. One injured crewmate would have drowned but for the efforts of Lieutenant Kennedy, who dragged him safely to shore. Later Kennedy and his men, in a tale made for Hollywood, got a message to rescuers by etching on a coconut shell. His wartime adventure triggered into action the public relations firm Ambassador Kennedy kept on retainer in New York. Their releases were picked up by some national wire services. John Hersey read one of them and then wrote a fuller account of the saga for the *New Yorker*.

If it were not for the death of his brother and ambition of his father, John Kennedy would never have sought a political career. Of course, he had the hero's credentials to win in that first post-war election of 1946. What he lacked was a congressional district.

Kennedy's father decided on the seat in Cambridge, where the colorful James ("The Last Hurrah") Curley was retiring in hopes of becoming mayor again. The father rented a suite in the Bellevue Hotel for his son to use as a residence. Charges of carpet-bagging fell short since Jack's maternal grandfather, John ("Honey Fitz") Fitzgerald, for who he was named, was living in the same hotel in retirement. "Honey Fitz," a former mayor and congressman, was still a legendary name in the district, perhaps even more than Ambassador Kennedy, son of state Senator Patrick Kennedy. As James Curley—who was once a political foe of both the Kennedys and Fitzgeralds—remarked at the time, "Just the name of John Fitzgerald Kennedy is enough to carry that district."

In both the primary and general elections John Kennedy won in a landslide. He arrived in Washington in 1947 looking so young for his twenty-nine years that he was mistaken for a page boy by older House members. Neither his years in the war nor months in the campaign had shaped any political philosophy. His views reflected a strange amalgam of constituents' needs and his father's opinions. Domestically he generally voted with the other urban Democrats, but in foreign policy he often fought the Truman–Acheson policies.

Liberals approved of his support of public housing and his opposition to the Taft–Hartley labor law. Yet rightwingers rejoiced when he lambasted Truman for the loss of China to the Communists. "This is the tragic story of China," he said in Salem in 1948. "What strong men had saved, our diplomats and our President have frittered away." The speech echoed one a year earlier where the *Boston Herald* carried this headline of his speech to a Polish group: "KENNEDY SAYS ROOSEVELT SOLD POLAND TO THE REDS."

Kennedy's record in the House did not endear him to the Cambridge academic community, but it did solidify him with Irish–Catholic voters who sympathized with Senator Joseph McCarthy's crusade against "Communists in the State Department."[1]

Few senators offered a greater contrast to "Tail Gunner" Joe McCarthy, the junior senator from Wisconsin, than the aristocratic Henry Cabot Lodge from Massachusetts. Lodge, a leading member of the Republican Party's Eastern internationalist wing, had been spending a lot of his time away from his Senate duties importuning General Eisenhower to run for president. The bearer of a familiar name in Massachusetts history, Lodge had won by over a million votes in 1946 and did not consider himself vulnerable.

Jack Kennedy and his father thought otherwise. In the early 1950s while Lodge was flying across the country and to Europe building interest in the Eisenhower nomination, Kennedy was crisscrossing Massachusetts to Elks Lodges and Legion Halls promoting himself.

Lodge's absorption in the Eisenhower campaign proved to be his undoing. Not only did his absenteeism prevent him from attacking Kennedy's thin legislative record, but, more importantly, his defeat of Taft at the Chicago Republican National Convention allowed Kennedy to woo Taft die-hards.

To that task the ambassador addressed himself, employing his conservative friends in the Taft camp to advance the Kennedy case with right-wing publishers of conservative dailies and weeklies across Massachusetts. On the left, Jack stressed his ties with organized labor and courted the skeptical ADA (Americans for Democratic Action) and their friends in the academic community.

While the wife and daughters of the former ambassador to Great Britain organized hundreds of receptions for constituents to be presented to and regally feted by the "First Family" of the Boston Irish, the patriarch himself mobilized a team of high salaried campaign strategists, precinct organizers, and speech writers. Never had so much money been spent in a Massachusetts campaign. After all, Kennedy was running against the Eisenhower tide.

For the father the possibility of a late appearance by Joe McCarthy at the side of fellow Republican Lodge hovered over the campaign like a shadowy specter, but, McCarthy, who might have been influenced by Joe Kennedy's contribution to his own hotly contested reelection in Wisconsin, never showed.

In the end Kennedy edged Lodge by 70,000 votes in the face of the Eisenhower landslide. The proud Lodge was unseated, which avenged a loss by Jack's grandfather, "Honey Fitz" Fitzgerald, to Lodge's grandfather some four decades previously. Lodge's wry comment gave one explanation of his defeat. "It was those damned tea parties."

At the age of thirty-six, John Kennedy was a freshman senator and beginning to emerge from the parental cocoon. In his six years in the House, Kennedy had displayed more skill as a campaigner than as a congressman, and, as a bachelor, he fit the role of playboy more than statesman. On September 12, 1953, he formally changed that status by wedding the daughter of an aristocratic Catholic family. Jacqueline Bouvier Kennedy was a stunning bride twelve years younger than the Senator.

But more than the entrance into marriage was the escape from death that quickened his sense of purpose. Jack Kennedy had long suffered from a back ailment that forced him to resort to crutches. An operation to fuse the degenerating discs in his back was dangerous because of his affliction with Addison's disease, which made surgery a life-threatening procedure.

Kennedy, who played it safe on political issues, risked all when it came to his life. Despite odds that were no better than fifty-fifty, he arranged for the operation. "I'd rather be dead," he exclaimed, "than spend the rest of my life on crutches." The comment of his political aide Larry O'Brien summed it up. "Jack, it will either kill you or cure you." It almost did kill him. Last rites were even administered, but the senator rallied.

The survival shaped in him a sense of destiny. The presidency was always a family goal, but now he began to contemplate the role that level of leadership demanded. He was more than just his father's son. If fate had decreed that he would live, Kennedy felt he must have something unique to give.

In his long months of recuperation, Kennedy turned his curious mind to the subject of leadership. With the help of his new aide, Ted Sorensen, he canvassed historians on those legislators who had defied their constituents' wrath to vote their conscience. If most of the first rough draft was penned by Sorensen, the selection of material, its organization, and final editing bore Kennedy's hand. The book, titled *Profiles in Courage*, was not only a best seller in 1956 but was a Pulitzer Prize winner. For the third time in his life a book carried John Kennedy to a new plateau of recognition.

Why England Slept engineered his first national recognition. The Hersey article about P.T. Boat #109 enshrined him as a war hero. And now *Profiles* established him as something more than the average politician.

In preparing *Profiles*, Kennedy had begun to value the Senate as an institution. Kennedy, whose favorite historical personality was British Whig Prime Minister Lord Melbourne, had come to respect the traditions of "the club" even if he did not reveal the capacity for behind-the-scenes work that would invite the laying on of hands by its ruling elders such as Senator Dick Russell or Walter George.

Nevertheless, the cabal of Democratic Southern Senators much preferred Jack Kennedy of Massachusetts to Estes Kefauver of Tennessee even if the populist loner was a fellow Protestant from the South.

At the 1956 Democratic Convention in Chicago, Adlai Stevenson, who had earlier hinted that the Catholic Kennedy would make an ideal running mate to solidify the Democratic city labor vote, suddenly decided to make no recommendation and let the delegates choose.

Despite his father's opposition, Jack entered the vice presidential lists. Kefauver, because of two strong campaigns for the presidency, had a national organization already in place. Kennedy, nevertheless, almost won because he enlisted the help of conservative Southern power brokers who detested Kefauver. Just as he was thirty-eight votes short of a majority, Senator Albert Gore, who was also an aspirant, switched to his fellow senator from Tennessee, and that triggered a tide for Kefauver.

The loss of the vice-presidential nomination in 1956 steeled Kennedy's resolve to run for the presidency in 1960, when the magic name of Eisenhower would no longer be on the Republican ticket. Senate duties yielded to the priority of fielding a national organization for a name that now had national recognition.

Of course, he first had to win reelection in 1958 to the Senate—and win overwhelmingly. Outside of Massachusetts, operatives such as his brother-in-law Stephen Smith began to sound out those contacts made in the abortive vice presidential sortie. In addition, his younger brother Bobby was establishing connections with the AFL-CIO.

Bobby, as counsel for the Senate Government Operations Committee, had become close to Walter Reuther, the big union's head. After graduating from the University of Virginia Law School in 1953, he had been hired by the Senate committee with the help of a call by his father to Senator McCarthy.

Senator John Kennedy was one of the few Democrats who did not vote against McCarthy. Although he had the valid excuse of being in a hospital bed at the time of the censure, he could have "voted" by pairing himself with one of the absent Republicans.

With the demise of McCarthy as a political influence, the Senate committee, now headed by the conservative Democrat John McClellan of Arkansas, turned the spotlight to the corruption of organized labor. Bobby Kennedy, as a hard driving counsel, centered his focus on the Teamsters.

The terrier appearance of Bobby before the nationally televised Teamster hearings made the name of Kennedy a household word. Meanwhile, Ted Sorensen was blazoning the byline of John F. Kennedy as he ran a cottage industry of ghostwritten articles for national magazines such as *Readers' Digest* and Sunday periodicals with titles such as "Can You Retire at 65?", "A City Senator Looks at the Farm Problem," and "What is Happening to our Fishing Industry?"

On the academic front, the senator persuaded a skeptical James Mac-Gregor Burns of Williams College to begin an in-depth biography to be ready by the 1960 campaign.[2] Burns, whose authoritative biography of FDR had been nosed out by Kennedy's *Profiles* for the Pulitzer Prize, was head of the ADA in Massachusetts and a former Democratic candidate for Congress.

If there were intellectuals who questioned Kennedy's enthusiasm for liberal causes, there were bosses who doubted his electability as a Catholic. To that end the Kennedy operatives such as Larry O'Brien and Kenny O'Donnell argued that Kennedy's Catholicism would actually be an asset, for it would mobilize massive turnouts in metropolitan Eastern states.

The landslide reelection win by Kennedy in 1958, even if against a political unknown, suggested proof that he could attract those independents who had voted for Eisenhower. The Kennedy strategists reasoned that the appeal of Ike transcended ideology. It was popular trust in an idol who had led his nation through war and then peace.

Kennedy now maneuvered to present himself as a hero for a new generation. The other presidential possibilities for 1960 all had histories that shaped a defined political role: Senator Lyndon Johnson was the Senate majority leader; Hubert Humphrey was a New Deal populist; and vice president Richard Nixon was a fighter against communism both at home and abroad. In the Gallop Poll surveys of 1959, Kennedy registered higher support levels than any of them. He was popular because he didn't seem political.

His appeal suggested Hollywood more than Washington. His picture on the cover of such women's magazines as *Redbook* and *McCall's* sold as many copies as did that of Grace Kelly or Marilyn Monroe. As his father said, "Jack draws a greater crowd at a fund-raiser than Cary Grant or Jimmy Stewart." Kennedy and his advisors exploited this phenomenon. With his wife, Jacqueline, as a charming hostess, the senator appeared on Ed Murrow's "Person to Person" TV show, where he recited Alan Seager's "I have a Rendezvous with Destiny." Later, when Caroline was born, he posed for a full photographic spread in the *Ladies' Home Journal* performing household duties.

Kennedy was both a curious observer and a willing participant in the making of this mythomania. As Norman Mailer suggested, he understood the concept of "superman arriving at a supermarket." Kennedy learned from his father that what counts is not what you are but what you seem to be.

Kennedy was the first to marshal an array of quotations to parade before a political audience. Previously, Republicans and Democrats might have heard an obligatory reference to Lincoln or Jefferson, and a century ago an occasional allusion to the Bible was noted.[3] But Kennedy cited poets such as Tennyson and T. S. Eliot, philosophers such as Socrates and Spinoza, and historians such as Thucydides and Gibbon.

The lines came not from Kennedy's readings but from a notebook of quotations that Ted Sorensen had compiled for use in speeches. Their purpose was more for image than illustration.

Similarly, Kennedy often ended his addresses with a patriotic vignette from history. Sorensen writes in his own book, *JFK*, how he would signal some of the often-used anecdotes with just a picture of a "candle" or a "sun." These would cue Kennedy to tell the story of Colonel Davenport before the darkened legislature in Hartford in 1780 or Benjamin Franklin's closing remarks to the Constitutional Convention in 1787 alluding to a design of the sun on the presiding chair.

If John Kennedy represented "the new politics," Hubert Humphrey, his principal opponent in the 1960 primaries, was the favorite of the liberals. Yet in polls that pitted a Hollywood personality against a New Deal populist, Kennedy easily outdistanced Humphrey as well as other unannounced candidates, such as Lyndon Johnson and Stuart Symington. The only unresolved factor in the political equation was the effect of Kennedy's Catholicism in the minds of Protestant voters.

In New Hampshire the French and Italian Catholics turned out to help give Kennedy, their New England neighbor, the expected big victory margin. In Wisconsin, however, Hubert Humphrey from adjacent Minnesota was called the state's "third senator." The open checkbook of the Kennedy campaign more than made up the difference. Humphrey took the offensive calling Kennedy an "amoral politician" who had been "soft on McCarthyism" and "weak" on civil rights. Kennedy, in 1958, had voted with the South on many civil rights issues. Yet Kennedy surmounted the attacks to win with 56 percent of the vote.

Although the Kennedy bandwagon was now in full swing, Senator Humphrey still hoped he could stop it in West Virginia. For one thing, in that state, Republican Catholics could not cross over to vote in the primary election as they did in Wisconsin. The heavily Protestant state was also where Franklin Roosevelt was "God" and the "New Deal" philosophy of Humphrey was "gospel." The Humphrey team played at rallies his campaign song to the tune of "Give Me That Old Time Religion."

Kennedy countered by recruiting Franklin D. Roosevelt, Jr. to attack

Humphrey for dodging military duties. In a state that boasted the highest percentage of enlistments in World War II, the charge stung Humphrey. Perhaps even more telling was Roosevelt's letter sent to West Virginia voters—sent with a Hyde Park postmark.

On the May 10th primary, Kennedy's massive win buried the religious issue. *Baltimore Sun* reporter Howard Norton said, "It just proves you can't trust the bigots."

The Kennedy bandwagon had reached high gear by the Democratic Convention in Los Angeles in July. The only danger could be an ambush led by Senator Lyndon Johnson. The Texan announced his presidential candidacy when Congress adjourned in June and came out blasting at Kennedy's call for President Eisenhower to apologize to Chairman Khrushchev for the downing of the U–2 plane. Kennedy had said a statement of regret could reinstate the scheduled summit talks. Johnson thundered to audiences, "Do you want a leader who wants to apologize to the Soviets?" The Senate majority leader, who had played statesman-too-busy-for-political-hucks-tering, now spewed off salvoes that Kennedy was a "no-show" senator, a crippled invalid, and son of a Nazi-appeasing father.

The liberals in the party did not totally trust Kennedy. Eleanor Roosevelt expressed their thoughts when she alluded to Kennedy's book: "Jack ought to show a little less profile and a little more courage."

The favorite of the intellectual left was still Adlai Stevenson. The two-time loser, however, could not bring himself to announce his candidacy openly, and the Kennedy forces, who controlled the convention, denied the former Democratic standard bearer the customary invitation to address the delegates. When Adlai Stevenson entered the convention hall to take his seat among the Illinois delegation, he was greeted by a tumultuous reception the likes of which had not been seen since the Willkie draft by Republicans in 1940.

Later in the week the only eloquence of the convention came when Senator Eugene McCarthy, in nominating Stevenson, electrified the audience by imploring, "Do not make him a prophet without honor. Do not reject this man."

Stevenson had the decibels, but Kennedy had the delegates. At the end of the first ballot, Wyoming's votes put Kennedy over the top.

The celebration by Kennedy followers had hardly begun when it soured amid the suspicion of a sellout. Kennedy was planning to ask Lyndon Johnson to be his running mate. To the liberals it was scarcely better than teaming up with Richard Nixon. The Texan represented everything the Northern wing of the party detested: states' rights, courthouse politics, and oil money.

Kennedy's brother, Bobby, was apoplectic. How could John ask the man who called him a cripple and his father a fascist to be the vice presidential running mate?

Despite the opposition by organized labor and the Americans for Democratic Action, Senator Kennedy liked the idea for one reason: it shored him up in the South, where his support was weak. The Democratic court-house cabal in each state ran the Kennedy–Johnson campaign in the South, which freed Kennedy to concentrate on the key Northern states.[4]

In a close race, the first real shift toward Kennedy came in the wake of the first presidential television debate. The Kennedy forces were amazed that Nixon accepted their challenge, for Kennedy did not have to "win" but only hold his own against Nixon, who as vice president was running as a "quasi-incumbent."

If experience was Nixon's chief asset, the viewers did not sense it. Whether it was because Nixon was recovering from an illness or because of poor makeup, a pale, nervous, and perspiring Nixon was seen defensively re-sponding to attacks by a rested, confident Kennedy.

A vigorous Kennedy had found his theme: "Let's get this country moving again." The slogan, which was suggested by his adviser Walt Rostow, seemed to project Kennedy's personality appeal in a campaign with few issues.

One of those issues, however, served to emphasize the Republican charges that Kennedy was too young and inexperienced to run the nation. Quemoy and Matsu were two islands off the shore of the China coast that had always been part of Formosa. When Kennedy suggested that the islands were not worth defending, he gave the vice president the opportunity to remind voters what happened when Dean Acheson said in 1950 that "Korea was not in the perimeter of defense."

In a succeeding debate, Kennedy managed to outflank Nixon on the right by urging the government to intervene in Cuba and remove the threat of Castro Communism. A shocked Nixon, who knew Kennedy had been briefed by the CIA on a future invasion plan, could only backpedal.

The Kennedy money trained a new kind of political operative called the "advance man," whose job was to schedule Kennedy's appearances to fit television deadlines for the six o'clock news, then mobilize enthusiastic crowds for the camera's eye.

But the biggest boost for the Kennedy campaign arose from a minister's statement that was a throwback to the 1884 "Rum, Romanism and Rebel-lion" charge that had helped elect Grover Cleveland. Norman Vincent Peale, the Protestant preacher, released a statement signed by other clergymen questioning the Catholic Kennedy's ability to separate matters of church and state.

Before a group of ministers in Houston, Kennedy brilliantly acquitted himself by pledging to resign in the unlikely circumstance of religion ever conflicting with his constitutional oath.[5]

Another minister also figured strongly in the outcome of the closing days of the campaign. The Reverend Martin Luther King had been jailed in Alabama for protesting segregation. King, a registered Republican at the time, appealed in vain first to Nixon and then to Kennedy. The senator heeded his campaign advisers in the South, but Bobby defied his instructions and signed in his brother's name a telegram urging release. The action unleashed in Northern cities a massive turnout by blacks who had earlier questioned Kennedy's commitment to civil rights.

In the closest election in history, the telegram to King could have supplied the marginal difference in big cities such as Chicago and St. Louis, whose huge pluralities nudged Illinois and Missouri into the Kennedy electoral column. Disgruntled Republicans, however, pointed to the massive irregularities in the voting tabulation in the machine-controlled precincts in those same big cities.

At three in the morning Nixon's press secretary read a provisional statement indicating the vice president's defeat. Bobby Kennedy, with the family in Hyannisport, snapped his opinion of the Nixon non-appearance: "He is going out the way he came in—no class."

Class or style was a major priority as president-elect Kennedy assembled his governing team. Kennedy had read Richard Neustadt's recently published book, *Presidential Power*, and asked the author's advice on the transition. Neustadt's scorn for Eisenhower and reverence for FDR shaped theories on the presidency that fit nicely into Kennedy's preconceptions. Great presidents, wrote Neustadt, are both artists whose medium is power and actors who master the theater of office. To govern is to continue to campaign from the best of all stages or platforms: the White House.

The first forum was the presidential inauguration and particularly the inaugural address. Kennedy had found his theme in the course of the campaign. 1960 was the centennial year of Lincoln's election, and speechwriter Ted Sorensen capped Kennedy's airport remarks with quotations by the martyred president. One of his endings, which alluded to the Cold War, went this way. "A hundred years ago Abraham Lincoln said, 'This nation cannot endure half slave and half free' and we, like Lincoln, will rise to the challenge."

Although the main body of Kennedy's campaign remarks recited promises in civil rights, education, and health that presaged a war on poverty, it was the Cold War that more excited his vision of leadership. He transmitted to Sorensen this direction for an inaugural address. Kennedy saw himself as embodying a new generation that had come of age in the World War II conflict, and he asked Sorensen specifically to convey the passing of the torch.

In a sense, Sorensen was an ironic choice to write a martial summons. Sorensen, a conscientious objector in World War II, reflected his Nebraskan heritage. His hero was Republican Senator Robert LaFollette, who had blended a domestic policy progressivism with a foreign policy pacifism.

In December, Sorensen closeted himself in his Arlington, Virginia apartment to hammer out the first draft. Kennedy had specifically asked him to read Lincoln's Gettysburg Address to extract its secret. Sorensen found that the answer lay in its economy of expression. For other homework, he took with him copies of previous inaugurals from the Library of Congress. Only the rhetoric of Wilson's first inaugural seemed to offer inspiration.

Although Sorensen was a lawyer by profession, he had a poet's love for and fascination with words and their sounds. At parties the introverted, bespectacled legislative aide would amuse guests with rhyming ditties. In his draft of the inaugural, he reflected this ear for iambic rhythms and parallel structuring. Fortunately, he had a principal in Kennedy who, unlike Eisenhower, did not disdain the rhetorical flourish.

Sorensen's thirty-paragraph draft was taken by the president-elect to Palm Beach for his Christmas vacation. Kennedy read the draft aloud, noting with approval the parallel phrasing that crafted elegance through epigram.

He had only two major corrections. First, he substituted "adversary" for "enemy" in a line that alluded to the Soviets. The second objection had more to do with politics than diplomacy: He thought the address unduly roused expectations that could not be realistically met in two terms, much less one. Therefore, he inserted a paragraph that emphasized a beginning rather than a fulfillment of goals.

The day before his swearing in Kennedy paid his second visit to President Eisenhower. The first in November was more in the nature of a courtesy call. A somber but cordial Eisenhower sketched a *tour de horizon* of foreign policy problem spots around the globe: Cuba, China, Laos, and Berlin.

As Kennedy left the White House, a raging storm was starting to drop eight inches of snow on Washington, blotting out the green dye Interior Department workers had sprayed on the lawns to give the yellowing grounds a rejuvenated look. Now flame throwers from the Pentagon had to be called in to melt the ice on the streets and sidewalks around the capitol and parade route. Despite the cold and the inconvenience of the unabating storm, the white blanket gave a pristine glow to the Washington spectacle of a young president and a new administration taking office.

Kennedy, who had talked about the beginning of "a golden age of poetry and power," had asked Marian Anderson to sing the National Anthem and deputized Frank Sinatra to bring in a galaxy of stars to sing at the various inaugural galas.

The poet to express such an era was the New Englander Robert Frost. Kennedy, who often quoted Frost's "promises to keep and miles to go before we sleep" as an exit for campaign remarks, had commissioned Frost to compose a poem to be read at the inaugural. If the aging bard in the wind and blinking snow had difficulty in reading his piece, it was the idea more than the message that counted.

Nothing could detract from the spectacle of the new president resplendent in his top hat, cutaway coat, and striped trousers. Kennedy had chosen the formal attire to represent a clean break with the prosaic street clothes and

homburg hats of the Eisenhower administration. (No one was more delighted with the sartorial switch than former Ambassador Joseph Kennedy,
who sported the same cutaway to his son's inaugural that he wore to his
presentation at the Court of St. James.)

As he was sworn in on his family Bible (Douay) by Chief Justice Warren,
the new chief executive looked nothing like the scrawny twenty-nine-year
old who had taken his congressional oath fourteen years before. The maturing years, not to mention daily shots for his Addison's disease, had filled
out his face, and television also served to add weight to an appearance that
up close, seemed less forceful.

Kennedy certainly offered the most handsome presence since Harding,
and his style suggested the most lively administration since Theodore Roosevelt. He opened loftily in lines that owed much to Wilson's first inaugural.[6]
The voice was high and the accent a medley of Boston Brahmin and Irish,
which muted the "r" of American English.

> We observe today not a victory of party but a celebration of freedom.

Like other presidents before him, he then spoke of the constitutional
requirement of oath. He used that reference to invoke our revolutionary
beginnings and his generation's response to that heritage.

> We dare not forget today that we are heirs of that first revolution. Let the
> word go forth from this time and place, to friend and foe alike, that the torch
> has been passed to a new generation of Americans—born in this century,
> tempered by war, disciplined by a hard and bitter peace, proud of our ancient
> heritage and unwilling to witness or permit the slow undoing of those human
> rights to which this nation has always been committed, and to which we are
> committed today at home and around the world.

The biblical subjunctive reflected Kennedy's primary directive to Sorensen
to write that the post-war generation had come of age.

Then Kennedy, in dithyrambs reminiscent of Churchill's wartime eloquence, delivered a call to arms.[7] If taken literally, it explains and predicts
his administration's involvement in Vietnam a year and a half later. Neither
Truman nor Eisenhower previously—nor Johnson nor Nixon later—ever
suggested interventionism on such a large scale. The internal rhyme and
alliterative phrase was more poetic than practical.

> Let every nation know, whether it wishes us well or ill that we shall pay any
> price, bear any burden, meet any hardship, support any friend, oppose any
> foe, to assure the survival and success of liberty. This much we pledge and
> more.

If Kennedy countenanced military intervention, he now coupled it with diplomatic initiatives. In three successive paragraphs he advanced the concept of the Peace Corps in the Third World, the Alliance for Progress in Latin America, and a new reliance on the United Nations.[8]

> To those in the huts and villages of half the globe . . . We pledge our best effort to help them to help themselves . . . not because the community may be doing it, not because we seek their votes but because it is right. If a free society cannot help the many who are poor, it cannot save the few who are rich.

Although Kennedy did not mention by name what later would be called the Peace Corps, he hit upon its idealistic appeal with an aphorism that has the beauty of a biblical beatitude. In the second foreign policy commitment, he offered his own update of the Monroe Doctrine, as did both Theodore Roosevelt in 1904 and FDR in 1938 with the Good Neighbor Doctrine.

> To our sister republic south of the border we offer a special pledge to convert our good words into deeds—in a new alliance for progress. And let all our neighbors know, we shall join with them to oppose aggression or subversion anywhere in America.

For his third commitment, Kennedy applied Lincoln's phrase about the meaning of our democracy to the United States.

> To that world assembly of sovereign states, the United Nations, our last best hope in an age where the instruments of war have far outpaced the instruments of peace . . .

The next line is where Kennedy softened Sorensen's "enemy" to "adversary."

> Finally to those nations who would make themselves our adversary, we offer not a pledge but a request that both sides begin anew the quest for peace.

From the arms race Kennedy moved to the arms talks with the Soviets, coining the catchy parallelism. This is perhaps the second-most-quoted inaugural line.

> So let us begin anew remembering on both sides that civility is not a sign of weakness and sincerity is always subject to proof. Let us never negotiate out of fear. But let us never fear to negotiate.

Sorensen's musical ear allowed Kennedy to follow a lyrical aphorism with a feminine internal rhyme.

Let both sides explore what problems unite us instead of belaboring those problems that divide us.

As they did so often in campaign remarks, Unitarian Sorensen and Catholic Kennedy then invoked the moral authority of the Old Testament.

Let both sides unite to heed in all corners of the earth, the command of Isaiah— to "undo the heavy burdens . . . [and] let the oppressed go free."

Then Kennedy, wary of the high expectations of his inaugural rhetoric, revealed his own poetic touch in fashioning an escape clause. It imitated the Churchill line, "It is not the end, nay not even the beginning of the end. . . ."

All will not be finished in the first hundred days. Nor will it be finished in the first thousand days, nor in the life of this administration, nor even perhaps in our own lifetime on this planet. But let us begin.

Kennedy then returned to his generational theme.

Since this country was founded, each generation of Americans has been summoned to give testimony to its national loyalty. The graves of young Americans who answered the call to service surround the globe. Now the trumpet summons us again—not a call to bear arms though arms we need—not as a call to battle though embattled we are—but a call to bear the burden of a long twilight struggle . . . a struggle against the common enemies of men: tyranny, poverty, disease and war itself.

Like a young King Harry at Agincourt, Kennedy echoed Shakespeare in his summons to his contemporaries to mount the challenge of the Cold War.

In the long history of the world, only a few generations have been granted the role of defending freedom in its hour of maximum danger. I do not shrink from this responsibility—I welcome it. I do not believe that any of us would exchange places with any other people or any other generation.

Then Kennedy, stabbing his finger in the air as his nasal twang pierced the heavy January cold, laid the prefatory groundwork to call attention to the climactic peroration.

An so, my fellow Americans . . .

Then he paused to build audience anticipation.

Ask not what your country can do for you—ask what you can do for your country.[9]

An electrified audience clapped their numb hands to warmth. No other presidential line has quite so kindled American idealism. Three long minutes later, a dimming applause was reignited by its twin refrain.

And so my fellow citizens of the world: ask not what America will do for you, but what together we can do for the freedom of man.

To close, Kennedy offered a Churchillian valedictory.

With a good conscience our only sure reward, with history the final judge of our deeds, let us go forth to lead the land we love asking his blessing and his help, but knowing that here on earth, God's work must truly be our own.

The hordes of Democrats and Kennedy partisans who braved the frigid January winds to participate in what they thought would be a milestone event in American history were not disappointed. Kennedy not only rose to the occasion but transcended it in eloquence that yields only to the sublimity of Lincoln's second inaugural.

It was television, however, that transformed a constitutional ceremony into an inspirational creed for the nation's young. Kennedy had directed it to his contemporaries of returning veterans, but its message would more make its mark on that generation's explosive crop of children.

The volunteers for the Peace Corps, the demonstrators for civil rights, and later the student militants against Vietnam would see themselves as missionaries of that message.

Kennedy, by his elegance of style and eloquence in speech, had cast a new image of the politician. Politics had become public service. What had been the province of cigar-smoke lobbies of courthouse and state capitols became the preoccupation of campus and classroom.[10] Idealism, when coupled with the impatience of youth, would prove to be a volatile combination.

Television had turned politics into theater, and Kennedy was the first to exploit that phenomenon. In the 1930s it was the motion picture house that manufactured legends bigger than life, but in the 1960s it was the television screen.

If the glamour of Hollywood offers escape, that of Washington gives rise to expectations. The stuff of dreams can become a source of disillusion.

Kennedy's actual performance was mixed. The early disaster of "the Bay of Pigs" invasion in Cuba in the spring of 1961 was followed by the deliverance from a Soviet missile threat in that same country in the fall of 1962.

At his summit meeting with Khrushchev in Vienna in the summer of 1962, Kennedy, in the eyes of such observers as Dean Acheson, seemed uncertain and unprepared. Yet in October during the missile crisis, he made Khrushchev back down and remove the Soviet missiles in Cuba on the promise that the United States would dismantle their missiles in the Soviet backyard of Turkey. The next year Kennedy secured what his administration considered to be their greatest foreign policy achievement: the nuclear test-ban treaty.

No doubt, the presidency for the young chief executive was a maturing process. His admirers on the left suggest that, had he lived, he would have ended the Vietnam involvement and concentrated on such domestic priorities as civil rights and poverty legislation. Nevertheless, it was Kennedy who first committed troops to Southeast Asia, and it was not Kennedy but his successor Johnson who bulldozed through Congress the massive war on poverty program and the civil rights acts.

The singular domestic achievement of Kennedy was an economy-stimulating tax cut, which two decades later inspired President Reagan to do likewise. What is remembered about the Kennedy administration is the inspiration he evoked by asserting "Ich bin ein Berliner" at the Berlin Wall and by signing into the law the Peace Corps act that engaged the idealism of youth.

Any accountability of the president's record was ended by the tragedy in Dallas. John Kennedy is primarily remembered for those eloquent words on Inauguration Day: "Ask not what your country can do for you—ask what you can do for your country." Like a wedding day picture of a radiant bride soon to suffer an untimely death, Kennedy's martyrdom preserved the hope and promise of a dream yet to be fulfilled.

Revisionist biographers may cite CIA plots against the lives of Castro in Cuba or Diem in Vietnam, the wire tapping of Martin Luther King by the president's brother Bobby, the attorney general, or even his tawdry liaisons with Marilyn Monroe or mafioso moll Judith Exner. Yet they can never dim the symbolic appeal of hope that his magical presence and eloquence inspired on Inauguration Day. At a time when politics became theater, Kennedy became its first star.

NOTES

1. According to Robert Richards of the *San Diego Union*, in 1950 John Kennedy came to the office of fellow congressman Richard Nixon of California and handed his staff a check for $1,000.00 for his campaign against left-leaning Helen Gahagan Douglas for the U.S. Senate.

2. As a student at Williams College, I remember an infuriated James MacGregor Burns returning from an ADA meeting in Boston in 1954 where Kennedy, the featured speaker, had recommended that the ADA disband. I was babysitting for the Burns children while Burns and his wife took the three-hour ride to Boston.

3. Ted Sorensen told me that about half of Kennedy's campaign talks contained

a scriptural citation from the Old Testament. They were supplied, said Sorensen, by a Rabbinical scholar from a Jewish institute.

4. In December 1959 Vice President Nixon predicted to me that the only combination that could defeat him was a Kennedy–Johnson slate that would corral both northern Catholic Democrats and southern Democrats, both of whom had been shown by the polls to have strong leanings for the Republican vice president.

5. Kennedy asked his speechwriters to come up with some Catholics who died in the Alamo. Although many Irish names were sprinkled in the list of defenders, none could be cited as Catholics. Sorensen found a way out by having Kennedy recite a litany of Irish names and then add, "No one asked what church they attended." Kennedy also exploited the same emotional vein by saying "No one asked my brother Joe what church he went to before he went on the bombing mission that would cost his life."

6. "This is not a day of triumph but a day of dedication."

7. "Fill the armies, rule the air, sweep the mines, plough the land, build the ships, guard the streets, succor the wounded, uplift the downcast and honour the brave."

8. In a conversation with me, Sorensen took great pride that no other president before or since specifically singled out the United Nations as a priority in foreign policy.

9. Although Sorensen did admit to me that in rereading presidential speeches he found a few by Harding unexpectedly worthwhile, he said he did not know of the Harding speech of 1921. "In the great fulfillment, we must have a citizenship less concerned about what the government can do for it and more anxious about what it can do for the nation." It was an addiction to parallelism, not plagiarism, that guided the Sorensen pen.

10. A Pennsylvania state legislator when Kennedy was assassinated, I was asked to give the eulogy at the State House memorial service. I quoted Simonides: "Go, stranger, and to Sparta tell/that he in faithful public service fell." I said that Kennedy "ennobled the profession of politician" and that "because of his vibrant example countless young would be inspired to enter public service."

15 _____

President Nixon's Toast
to Chairman Mao:
The Beijing Breakthrough

While we cannot close the gulf between us, we can try to bridge it so that we may be able to talk across it.

Richard Milhous Nixon has dominated the political scene of postwar America. Just as Roosevelt was the towering figure of the Depression and World War II, so Nixon has been the most influential political personality in the years since.

From the congressional investigation of Alger Hiss to that of Watergate almost three decades later, the name of Nixon has produced a ton of newspaper headlines. (The Nixon Library at Yorba Linda, California, features a wall with sixty *Time* magazines with Nixon on the cover.) In six out of seven national elections, Nixon as vice presidential candidate, presidential candidate, or recently pardoned ex-president was the chief political issue.[1]

His resiliency has astonished friend and foe alike. From the self-inflicted wounds of his gubernatorial defeat press conference, he emerged from political death to be elected president in 1968. Even today, despite the ignominy of resignation and pardon in 1974, he has again resurfaced from political exile to surpass former presidents Ford, Carter, and Reagan as the elder statesman whose counsel is most sought by world leaders.

Nixon was a leader uncharismatic in appearance, awkward in movement, sometimes didactic in delivery, and occasionally pious in posture. Yet by strength of mind and singleness of purpose he made himself a political force and a shaper of events. That drive, which propelled him to the top of

American politics at an early age, also spawned legions of Nixon–haters on the political left.

Yet the perception of Nixon as a right–wing ideologue has been ridiculed by "movement conservatives." His proposals and programs put him to the left of any Republican president this century, including Theodore Roosevelt. Indeed, it can be argued convincingly that Nixon's record falls to the left of John Kennedy's. The establishment of the Environmental Protection Agency, the elimination of the draft, the implementation of "affirmative action" (e.g., the Philadelphia Plan), the massive funding for the arts, giving the vote to the District of Columbia, the installation of wage–price controls, and the recommendation to Congress for a family assistance program (a welfare reform proposal deemed too radical by congressional Democrats) were hardly priorities in a right–wing agenda.

Nixon's rhetoric, opposite that of Kennedy, was tuned to the ears of the right, but his record was that of a pragmatic centrist. (Kennedy's major domestic accomplishment was a tax cut for business, which Reagan emulated in 1981.) The great accomplishments of Nixon, however, were in the field of foreign policy, where he foresaw the opportunity and then forged the opening of relations with China in 1972. Even Nixon detractors must conceded that the rapprochement with China, which split the shaky Sino-Soviet alliance asunder, was the diplomatic coup of the century.

Outside the United States, where the presidency is seen through the prism of foreign policy, the accusations of presidential misconduct are writ small and foreign policy achievements loom large. Accordingly, Nixon is viewed as the most skilled innovator and practitioner of diplomatic initiatives in recent years. The restoration of relations with China, détente with the Soviet Union, and truce in the Middle East all enhanced his reputation as the ablest of statesmen on the world scene.

Perhaps Nixon's personality might have been better suited for a European parliamentary government, where a bent for political intrigue and veiled maneuvering is not only accepted but admired. If it is easy to envision Nixon as prime minister, it is equally hard to conceive of Reagan, Carter, or Kennedy advancing to parliamentary leadership.

The American president is also chief of state, and in this role, Nixon lacked the telegenic ease and public charm of Roosevelt, Eisenhower, Kennedy, or Reagan.

Nixon was miscast for a career in American politics. He was an introvert in an extrovert's profession. A loner might succeed as a prime minister but falter in the chief of staff role of president.

At first glance, Richard Nixon's background falls into the traditional patterns of most U.S. presidents. He grew up in a small town, albeit Southern California, where the Protestant ethic of midwestern roots was strong and in a family whose mother firmly instilled those pieties.

Nixon was neither a natural leader as a boy like Eisenhower nor a ready joiner like Truman in his early manhood. He was not athletic like Ford or handsome like Reagan. A shy, introverted Nixon concentrated on his studies, excelling first in high school, then at the local Whittier College, and finally at Duke Law School. William Y. Elliot, a renowned international law professor at Duke in 1959 called Nixon, who competed in his class with thirty-five Phi Beta Kappas, as "the finest student he ever had."[2] One law review article won the attention of Supreme Court Justice Robert Jackson.

Brilliance of mind, which even his enemies impute to Nixon, does not necessarily make a person popular with his peers. Woodrow Wilson, the only president of this century who might be considered to be more of an intellectual than Nixon, was not easy to like.

Outside of Wilson, the only other world leader of this century that Nixon possibly could be compared with is Margaret Thatcher. Just as Thatcher reached out to working classes to build a party dominance, so Nixon with his appeal to "the silent majority" widened the base of the Republican Party that is the framework of the current Republican Party's national dominance.

Thatcher, like Nixon, is a loner. Like Nixon, she was reared in a grocery store with a perfectionist parent she tried to please by scholastic success. (The parent Thatcher strove to please was her father.) The great influence on Nixon was his Quaker mother, whom his cousin, the writer Jessamyn West, describes as "a strong-willed saint." Her son inherited her resolve.

But what an admirer may call a singleness of purpose, a detractor calls unadulterated ambition. An ambition that is not masked in geniality is all the more naked.

In little more than twelve years Nixon rose from congressman to his party's presidential candidate. Although Kennedy also enjoyed a meteoric rise, it is Nixon who is pictured as opportunistic if not ruthless.

His critics charge that Nixon only decided to be a Republican when he answered a want-ad for a congressional candidate. Actually, Nixon grew up in a Republican family whose father's proudest memory was a handshake with presidential candidate William McKinley in Ohio in 1896. Unlike a majority of wartime voting servicemen, Nixon voted for Dewey in 1944. In the same year he sought out the former governor, Harold Stassen, in an island encounter to ask his support if he entered politics. A year-and-a-half later Nixon, like Kennedy and many other returning veterans, did seek and win the congressional nomination in his home area.

Democrats bitterly speak of congressional candidate Nixon's hatchet-job of Democratic incumbent Jerry Voorhees. What actually took place was that Nixon, in a debate confrontation, rose to challenge Voorhees when the Democratic congressman denied that he had been endorsed by a leftist pro-Communist action committee. Nixon, who had a copy of the newspaper endorsement in his pocket, stood and read to the audience his proof. Congressman Voorhees was damaged by Nixon's confrontation, but that was not what cost him his House seat. Voorhees, like twelve other California Democrats, lost because of the Republican landslide of 1946, the greatest Republican victory in history for a congressional election. The Republicans captured both House and Senate.

It was not his defeat of Voorhees but the prosecution of Alger Hiss that first made Nixon the target of the left. Although today historians agree with the Court's verdict that the former State Department political adviser lied about his association with the Communist Party, criticism of Hiss was unpopular in 1947. Against the warnings of some senior Republicans such as Congressman Karl Mundt of South Dakota and Dewey adviser John Foster Dulles, Nixon persevered in the politically risky investigation of Hiss. That success in exposing Hiss brought him national fame—but at the price of suspicion and enmity from the press and the liberal academic community.

Yet no historian has suggested that Nixon in the hearings by the Un-American Activities Committee trampled on Hiss's constitutional rights. The treatment of Hiss, a prominent diplomat, was fair and proper. Hiss was later sent to jail when federal courts found him guilty of perjury.

Hiss's conviction, and even more importantly, the conviction of the Rosenbergs for delivering atomic secrets to the Soviets, triggered a wave of anti-Communist sentiment in the early 1950s. No longer was the Soviet dictator Stalin affectionately remembered as "uncle Joe," the American ally in World War II. Now he was the tyrant brutalizing Eastern Europe with his Soviet troops and sending aid to his Communist allies in Red China and North Korea who were killing American soldiers on the Inchon Beachhead and on Pork Chop Hill.

It was Senator Joe McCarthy, not Nixon, who made himself a national sensation by charging that there were Communists in the State Department. Three years after the Hiss investigation, McCarthy's excesses served to erode the credibility of "anti-communism" as a legitimate political issue.

It is forgotten today that before the rise of Joe McCarthy it was President Truman who instituted the loyalty oaths in the federal government; that it was Mayor Hubert Humphrey who founded the Americans for Democratic Action to fight the pro-Soviets in the liberal wing of the Democratic party; or even that it was Congressman John Kennedy in 1950 who blamed Secretary of State Dean Acheson for losing China to the Communist world.

In 1950 Nixon revived the left's hatred by defeating Helen Gahagan Douglas (wife of actor Melvin Douglas) for the Senate seat in California. It is claimed Nixon won by smearing Douglas with the mailing of a "pink sheet" listing Douglas's pro-Soviet votes.[3]

Interestingly, Douglas first raised the pro-Communist issue about Nixon in the general election. On a yellow sheet (for cowardice), Douglas pointed to a vote in which Congressman Nixon had voted the same way as Vito

Marcantonio, an outspoken pro-Soviet Representative from New York City. Douglas had emerged victorious from a bruising primary battle with Sheridan Downey. Downey, a conservative Democrat, had charged in the Democratic primary that Congresswoman Douglas had voted often with the notorious Marcantonio.

During that Democratic primary Nixon had laid low—not knowing who his opponent would be. Upon winning, Douglas hoped to preempt a Nixon attack by her "yellow paper" charge implying that Nixon on one procedural vote was undermining our soldiers in Korea. The charge angered Nixon, who had a far better record in supporting President Truman's foreign policy initiatives than Mrs. Douglas.

In response, Murray Chotiner, a Republican campaign operative on loan from Governor Earl Warren, prepared on Nixon's behalf a pink sheet with all the votes listed by House bill—number and date. Actually, during the campaign Nixon never voiced the word "pink" to describe Douglas, but she did refer to "Nixon and his brown shirt [Fascist] followers," and accused him of anti-Semitism (which a California Jewish Fair Elections Committee later repudiated).

The thrust of Nixon's campaign attacks was Douglas' failure to support wholeheartedly President Truman in his anti-Communist foreign policy. Nixon was one of the first Republican congressmen to support Truman's foreign policy initiatives such as the Truman Doctrine, the Marshall plan, and later NATO. He was justly proud of his role on the Herter Committee, a select group of Republicans who visited Europe and reported findings to support the foreign policy of the Democratic president.

Nixon, unlike most of his Republican colleagues, was an internationalist. His first speech upon returning from the Pacific was an address to a Pasadena, California, Kiwanis Club. Still in the navy, he spoke to the luncheon audience in uniform. The prescient talk outlined the shape of U.S. foreign policy for the post-war years. The Soviet Union, which was then still an ally, would be the paramount adversary. Nixon called for collective security in Europe. The free society would eventually prevail against communism by being just that—free.

Those internationalist credentials made Nixon acceptable to the Eastern wing of the Republican Party. Governor Dewey, the titular head of that wing as well as twice the Republican presidential candidate, sought out the newly elected senator from California as he was organizing the campaign for General Eisenhower. Nixon had the four criteria Dewey was looking for: acceptability to the Taft wing (because of his anti-Communist reputation in the Hiss case); an internationalist on foreign affairs; geographic desirability of being from California; and the youth to complement the appeal of the older General Eisenhower.

For Nixon, at age thirty-nine, after five years of political office, to be chosen as his party's nominee for vice president was just short of amazing. Yet more incredible was his successful battle in keeping that nomination. Today the phrase "the Checkers speech" trivializes a rhetorical tour de force.

Nixon's troubles began when the left-leaning *New York Post* headlined as news a dead story about a "secret Nixon Senatorial fund" to pay for such expenses as campaign mailings. It was "secret" only because Nixon insisted—to prevent undue influence—that the identity of the donors should not be known by him. (One of the donors was Herbert Hoover, Jr.) The Los Angeles paper that had previously uncovered the existence of the fund had found nothing improper in the financial arrangement.

Yet at a time when the "mink coat" corruption of the Truman administration was a major weapon in the arsenal of General Eisenhower's campaign, Tom Dewey, Sherman Adams, and other handlers of the Eisenhower campaign panicked and pressured Nixon to step down as the candidate. Nixon fought back by requesting the Republican National Committee to schedule him time for a nationwide television address. On his flight back to California from campaigning in Oregon, he began writing out notes on airline stationery. He would detail his own finances, then challenge the others—including Eisenhower by implication—to do likewise. Stevenson and Eisenhower were much wealthier than Nixon, who owned little more than the mortgage on his own house. On the hustings the best defense is to go on the offensive, but Nixon calculated that the nature of television demanded that he avoid the shrillness of partisanship.

Nixon knew that Senator Sparkman employed his own wife as a secretary and sensed that Governor Stevenson must be hiding something because he alone among the national Democrats had not joined in on the attack on him. Researchers from the Republican National Committee proved his hunch was correct.

As a lawyer, Nixon jotted down his notes realizing that he would be talking to a jury who would be watching from their living rooms. Nixon could make his struggling finances an asset by establishing a bond with all other American families in similar circumstances.

On television he opened by baring his financial soul. He had submitted all his tax records after an audit by a national accounting firm and now called on all other candidates to do likewise. Eisenhower, who had enjoyed certain tax write-offs on his bestselling book, *Crusade in Europe*, broke his pencil in fury when he heard Nixon's challenge.

Then Nixon wielded a Ciceronian "praeteritio." He brought to his audience's attention the existence of an Illinois fund of Governor Stevenson and running mate Sparkman's employment of his wife in his Senate office. But Nixon stopped short of passing judgment. A less-adroit politician would have lambasted the Democratic candidates for those questionable practices. Nixon, however, never lost sight of his goal. His primary objective was to redeem himself. If he had tried to savage the Democrats, he would have undermined his own credibility.

Nixon, who alone wrote the talk, jotted down at the last minute the idea of mentioning the cocker spaniel, Checkers, which had been a gift to his daughters. Remembering Roosevelt's use of Fala in 1944, he said, "And I'm not going to return Checkers." If Nixon critics choose only to remember the mawkish line, they fail to appreciate one of the most effective speeches in political history. Nixon turned the tables on his opponents. The overwhelming approval by viewers, who sent in their telegrams and contributions, turned Nixon from a liability to an asset on the ticket. Only Theodore Roosevelt in 1900 or Franklin Roosevelt in 1920 had equaled vice presidential candidate Nixon as a drawing card in 1952. The Eisenhower–Nixon ticket won in a landslide, and the new vice president was for the first time in many years a national if controversial figure.

Eisenhower's relationship was correct, but distant. Yet Eisenhower, to his credit, made Nixon the first active vice president. Under Eisenhower's direction, Nixon created today's role of the vice president. Eisenhower's assignment of vice presidential duties to Nixon enabled him to establish himself as his party's candidate to succeed Eisenhower in 1960. When Eisenhower gave his nod to the Nixon renomination for vice president in 1956, albeit belatedly, he was annointing Nixon for 1960.

Eisenhower respected Nixon's intelligence and loyalty. Yet during all his years in the White House Eisenhower did not take Nixon into his circle of close advisers. For one thing, the age gap between the general and the former junior Naval officer was too great. For another, Eisenhower had the military dislike of the professional politician.

Unlike his predecessors, Eisenhower mobilized the services of his vice president. After all, the vice president held, under the constitution, the second office in the nation. He was, in a sense "the deputy chief of state." And because the president, by power of his office, is the "head of his party," Nixon could become the "deputy head of party." In these two roles Nixon would serve as the first modern vice president.

Not until George Bush would a vice president travel so widely and to so many nations as the president's emissary. In the course of those travels, Nixon met heads of state such as Churchill, Adenauer, Tito, Nehru, DeGaulle, and even Ho Chi Minh in Hanoi (in 1954). Two of his trips helped establish Nixon in his countrymen's eyes as a courageous advocate of American ideals. In Caracas, Venezuela, he survived a rock-throwing mob organized by Communist agitators. In Moscow, he stood toe to toe with Khrushchev in an impromptu debate that developed in a model kitchen at an American exhibition. His courage in the first and coolness in the second won him the respect of the former general, who appreciated steadiness under fire. More importantly, Nixon's missions abroad burnished the young vice president's international credentials as a potential presidential candidate.

If Nixon profited by being Eisenhower's emissary abroad, the assignment as chief spear-carrier for the Republican Party was a mixed blessing. On one hand, he collected chits from Republican politicians for his attacks on Democrats at Lincoln Day dinners and campaign rallies. Yet those same speeches stereotyped him as a hatchet man. Nixon was too shrewd not to sense the end result. He could win the Republican nomination in 1960 only to lose the election. Once Nixon had made up his mind to seek the presidency—soon after he was reelected vice president in 1956—he sent word that he wanted to scale down his partisan campaigning. Sherman Adams, Eisenhower's chief of staff, rejected the plea.

Eisenhower deliberately insulated himself from the brunt of partisan attack by creating lightening rods in his administration. Dulles as secretary of state, Ezra Taft Benson in agriculture, and Nixon in Republican Party campaigning were some of the lightning rods Eisenhower created to deflect criticism away from himself.

The simplistic version of the 1960 campaign is that Nixon blew his lead in the debate with Senator John Kennedy. Kennedy evinced a "presidential poise" against a nervous Nixon and so demolished the supposedly more experienced Nixon. Why, the pundits asked, did Nixon risk his lead by even agreeing to the debate?

When Nixon agreed to the debates, he was behind in the polls.[4] The post-convention upswing had not yet been recorded. The high point of the Nixon campaign had been his July convention acceptance speech ("I have seen the American dream because I've seen it come true in my own life"), which according to Theodore White was far better received than the one by Kennedy in Los Angeles the month before. Nixon always saw himself as the underdog in an election in which registered Democrats overwhelmingly outnumbered Republicans. He reasoned that the debates were the only way to reach independents and Democrats.

Although those who listened on radio thought Nixon had "won" the debate, those who watched on television saw a pale, perspiring, gaunt Nixon who had just emerged from a hospital bed. The contrast in appearance cost Nixon the debate. Although Nixon more than held his own in the following three debates, the damage in the first and most watched debate gave Kennedy momentum. Nixon never quite caught up.

More appearances by President Eisenhower might have made the difference, but in a private visit Mrs. Eisenhower called on Mrs. Nixon to ask that her husband be limited to two or three appearances.

Eisenhower said later that Nixon's narrow defeat was the second saddest day of his life—next to his son's death. In fact, President Eisenhower, through his Attorney General William Rogers, wanted to contest the vote frauds in Illinois, Missouri, and Texas. In a magnanimity that is little heralded, Nixon refused, saying that proof of ballot manipulation would only undermine the credibility of the United States as leader of the free world.

Nixon never should have run for governor in 1962. He should have foreseen that Californians would resent his using Sacramento as a stepping-stone back to Washington. In a slip of the tongue, Nixon had pledged: "When I become President of California. . . . "

Nixon's California race for governor was, next to Watergate, the most wretched chapter in his political life—beginning with the challenge to him by the John Birch hard-right in the Republican primary and culminating with his tirade against the media in the post-defeat press conference.

To his friends, Nixon's outburst was the reaction of a sleepless, frustrated candidate. To his enemies, it was the real Nixon. Yet most columnists failed to realize that Nixon had sensed a growing undercurrent against the press that Eisenhower would tap two years later in his speech to the Republican Convention or that George Bush in 1988 would exploit in turning the tables on Dan Rather. If Nixon did decide to run again, the press would have to guard against seeming biased. The pundits in writing Nixon off also failed to give much attention to his press conference criticism of President Kennedy's handling of the Cuban missile affair. Nixon was determined to remain the opposition's voice in foreign affairs.

When Nixon moved to New York City in 1963 to practice law, he apparently had given up his presidential ambitions. After all, New York was the political domain of his rival Governor Rockefeller. Kennedy's assassination and the rise of the radical right caused Nixon to reassess his presidential hopes. He might position himself as a long-shot deadlock choice if Rockefeller and Goldwater canceled themselves out. At the convention, Nixon played the senior party statesman role trying to bridge together the Rockefeller and Goldwater wings.

Nixon campaigned loyally for the sure-to-lose Goldwater while Rockefeller sulked in his Albany tent. Nixon understood that Rockefeller's refusal to campaign would prevent his nomination in 1968.

He also assessed correctly that after the Goldwater debacle in 1964, Republicans were bound to win back in 1966 some of the congressional seats lost in the Democratic landslide. Nixon could position himself as the biggest beneficiary of such a Republican victory. As he crisscrossed the nation boosting congressional candidates, Nixon sensed President Johnson's unpopularity as well as his own surprising reservoir of strength with the district Republican leaders who would go to the Miami Convention in 1968.

Nixon was delighted when at the close of the 1966 Congressional campaign, President Johnson called a press conference to denounce him as "a chronic campaigner [whose] problem is to find fault with his country and his government during the period of October every two years." Johnson's attack handed Nixon the national credit for the Republican victories.

The Republicans picked up forty-six seats in the election. The biggest winner was the Republican not on the ballot that year: Richard Nixon. Nixon now sensed a 1968 presidential victory within his grasp. Not only could he be nominated, but President Johnson could be defeated. Johnson was increasingly an unpopular president saddled with an unpopular war.

The press had written off Nixon's chances when he moved to New York in 1963. ABC had run a television special, "The Political Obituary of Richard Nixon," in which Alger Hiss was the guest commentator.

Nixon chose to practice law in New York City because it was, as he said, "the fast track" where law and finance had global interests. On behalf of legal clients, Nixon could travel to Europe and Asia, where he could refurbish his international relationships. No American had as many influential contacts with world leaders except Eisenhower.

One of these was President Charles DeGaulle, who while hosting private citizen Nixon in 1963, predicted the former vice president's return to national office. Nixon received more respect abroad than he did at home. To such parliamentary nations Nixon was "an opposition leader." The foreign press featured his views as front-page treatment, which then was relayed in the American press.

Nixon's years in New York were a happy time for Nixon and his family. Free from the daily scrutiny of public life, he could enjoy the life of a reflective private man.

Nixon was always bored with the small talk that is the stock and trade of the more typical Rotarian politician like Gerald Ford. He preferred discussions on a set agenda with experts. Even more appreciated were memoranda to which he would pen a reasoned answer point-by-point. In the century of the telephone, Nixon is a throwback to an Adams or Jefferson, who penned serious letters of substance. A book sent to Nixon by author or friend would get a five-page letter offering a critique of the book's thesis.

Nixon, who could be stiff in superficial chitchat, was warm in a working relationship. Curiously, for one who fought the press, Nixon enjoyed the company of writers. Bright journalists, such as William Safire, Pat Buchanan, and Ray Price, who reflected an ethnic as well as philosophical diversity, came to work for Nixon in those New York years as he prepared for the presidency in 1968.[5]

Ray Price, a Yale graduate and former New York *Herald Tribune* editor (he wrote the editorial endorsing Johnson against Goldwater in 1964), was quintessentially Ivy League. The relationship between the writer and the politician became as close as father and son.

Nixon took Price with him on an Asian tour after the 1966 election. Price wrote the first draft of an article in the prestigious journal *Foreign Affairs* titled "Asia After Vietnam." Price, who heard Nixon's insightful comments on each country they together visited, came to think like Nixon. Only in the rhetorical flourishes could you spot Price's hand.

In the article, Nixon was the first to see the rise of Asian economic power outside of Japan. Nixon pointed out that Taiwan, Hong Kong, Singapore, South Korea, Thailand, and Malaysia were not far behind the Japanese. In fact, one major rationale for involvement in Vietnam was to buy time for the fragile free economies of those nations to develop. All of those nations supported the United States in Vietnam.

Nixon also called on Japan to assume its burden of military defense, which its constitution disallowed. (In 1953, Vice President Nixon had been the first to call for Japanese rearmament in a press conference in Tokyo.)

The most interesting part of the article was what Nixon himself added at the end of the draft Price had written for him.

> Any American policy toward Asia must come urgently to grips with the reality of China. We cannot simply afford to have China forever outside the family of nations, there to nurture its fantasies, cherish its hates and threaten its neighbors.

For most politicians a "vision" is an agenda for yesterday's headlines. Nixon had Churchill's ability to project into the future. In the midst of World War II, Churchill foresaw the problems of the Soviets after the war. Nixon saw that once the Vietnam War ended, America, as a Pacific power, would have to confront China.

On the home front, the Vietnam War was the searing issue in the late 1960s. Although he had contempt for the student radical movement that applauded Viet Cong victories, he sensed a growing weariness of the war in the public at large. Yet the Goldwater right wing he had to court wanted to increase the bombing and so speed up the war's ending. Accordingly, Nixon carefully plotted his strategy, promising "to end the war and win an honorable peace." This general pledge played both to those who wanted to escalate and to those who wanted to withdraw.

The nomination was now Nixon's if he could prove to the Republican leaders he could win. He proceeded to clobber former Governor George Romney in the primaries, beginning with New Hampshire.

In New Hampshire Nixon devised a new approach in political campaigning—"the man in the arena" format. Citizens with varying views were invited to question Nixon. Without a lectern or notes, Nixon dazzled audiences with his knowledge of government, reeling off statistics of local industries as well as of those in world trade. He regaled his audiences by spicing his commentaries with words from DeGaulle, Nehru, Adenauer, and Churchill, all of whom he had met on his travels. While Romney pressed the flesh like a campaigning congressman, Nixon played the role of world statesman.

Two events jolted Nixon's political calculations: first the withdrawal of President Johnson in March and then the assassination of Senator Robert Kennedy in June. Vice President Humphrey, with Johnson's backing, emerged as the Democratic nominee, but only after the most bitter intra-party strife on the war since the Democrat "wets" fought the "drys" in the 1924 Democratic Convention.

Three obstacles then stood in the way of the Nixon presidency. The Republican obstacle was Governor Reagan of California. If Nixon failed to win on the first or second ballot, the delegates, the overwhelming majority of whom were conservative, would turn to their true love, Ronald Reagan. Reagan had made a belated entry into the race in June. But Nixon had already won the endorsement of right-wing senators Barry Goldwater and Strom Thurmond. Goldwater represented the conservative seal of approval, and Thurmond led the fight to keep the South from defecting to Reagan. To take away southern support from Reagan, Nixon played on the fear of Governor Rockefeller, who had also made a late entry into the race after the collapse of Romney. Rockefeller was the demon to the political right as Nixon had been to the political left. Nixon won on the first ballot. Contrary to press predictions, however, Nixon did not pick Senator Hatfield or another moderate as his running mate but Spiro Agnew, a border state governor acceptable to Thurmond and the South for his handling of the Baltimore riots.

Nixon picked Agnew because of George Wallace's threat. Wallace was the second obstacle—the key threat to Nixon's election. Wallace's independent candidacy could draw voters away from Nixon in a race with Humphrey and throw the election to the Democratic-controlled House of Representatives if Nixon failed to win a majority of electoral votes.

Governor Wallace was exploiting the fears of the white working class, who were seeing their cities explode in crime and violence. Nixon countered Wallace by making "law and order" a major theme of his campaign. Nixon centered his attacks on Supreme Court rulings that he said had shifted its priorities away from the victim to the criminal. At the same time, Nixon reached out to blacks with speeches calling for "black capitalism."

The irony in Nixon's campaign is that for one whose expertise was foreign affairs, his campaign themes in 1968 were domestic. The Vietnam War, which had ripped the country apart, was little mentioned by Nixon. He limited himself to the promise that he had a plan to end the war, but he would not reveal what the plan was. Like Eisenhower with Korea in 1952, Nixon would not spell out the specifics that would prematurely endanger his plan's success. Only to family and close friends did Nixon reveal his plan: the "Vietnamization" of the war.

What destroyed Nixon's narrowing lead over Hubert Humphrey in the fall was President Johnson's effort to bring South and North Vietnam to the peace table in Paris. That was the third election obstacle. Just the faint possibility of peace emerging from those talks could shift the election to President Johnson's vice president. The peace bid, however, never materialized, and Nixon won a narrow victory over Humphrey, winning just 43 percent of the vote but 370 electoral votes.

Nixon had developed his conception of the presidency in his eight years as vice president. The president could delegate domestic problems to his cabinet officers. His primary responsibility was that of commander-in-chief, protector of national security and formulator of foreign policy.

To run foreign policy out of the White House, he chose a Rockefeller protégé, Dr. Henry Kissinger, a Harvard academic to head the National Security Council. The combination of this German immigrant Jew and Quaker son of a California grocer made an odd couple. Yet, like the Chou En-lai whom they both came to admire, Nixon and Kissinger both possessed a brilliance matched only by their subtlety. If Kissinger was the scholar, Nixon was the innovator—the risk taker.

In other words, Nixon was the architect and Kissinger the engineer. Like a modern architect whose modern designs for new college buildings seem jarring on an Ivy League gothic campus, Nixon was ready to challenge the status quo position of the State Department and foreign policy establishment. To throttle unneeded State Department interference in his primary objectives, Nixon appointed his old friend Bill Rogers, who had been attorney general for Eisenhower, as secretary of state. But although Rogers would have the glory of being the nation's ranking diplomat, he had little influence in shaping policy.

Although the State Department was mired in the mind-set of George Kennan's "containment policy of 1947," Nixon sensed that the geopolitics of the 1970s was now far different from the Europe he had inspected with the Herter Committee right after the war or the Asia he visited as vice president in 1953.

Nixon had forwarded his views to the Republican National Committee in July to be read in the party's platform. Like most platform positions, it was little noticed by the press. Nixon called for a move from "the era of confrontation to the era of negotiation." He realized that America, unlike Shakespeare's Julius Caesar, did not anymore "bestride the narrow world like a colossus."

In his book *Leaders* Nixon rates Churchill and DeGaulle as the two statesmen he admired the most. Churchill had said that he "did not become the King's first minister to preside over the liquidation of the British Empire." But Churchill, like DeGaulle in Algeria, recognized realities. Given the diminishment of American hegemony in the world, Nixon turned his strategic mind to reshaping a world to serve American interest and better secure world peace.

The greatest threat was the Soviet Union, the other world nuclear power, whose aggressive imperialism under the cloak of Marxism had achieved a dominion in Eastern Europe to which its czarist antecedents had only aspired. Through its subversive agenda, it offered aid and assistance to any military dictator or totalitarian clique in the Third World who would seek power cloaked in Marxist trappings.

Visiting Moscow in 1959, Nixon had looked beneath the Kremlin May Day display of military and found the merchandise shoddiness of a Third World nation. A government diverting most of its gross national product into costly missile weaponry might find the limitation of the arms race in their national interest.

Although the Soviets were eager for a summit, Nixon rejected the early feelers. To Nixon, a "summit" without substance only legitimized the U.S.S.R. as a respectable peace-loving nation, and the ephemeral euphoria such a conference aroused only eroded the free world's resolution and will.

As an old poker player in his Navy years, Nixon wanted a face card showing before entering the stakes. That ace was an ABM defense missile system. Critics argued that such a costly system would prove ineffectual. To Nixon, the presence of such a system was more important than the doubts of its practicability. Its potential capability would draw the Soviets in earnest to the bargaining table.

The ABM appropriation was Nixon's first priority as president, and he cracked the whip on such liberal Republicans as Margaret Chase Smith. ("I don't want any Republicans sick or in the bathroom . . . ")

Nixon would have another card to play before meeting with the Soviets: "the China card." He knew from his official visit in 1959 and his unofficial one in 1965 that the Soviets were paranoid about the billion-member "yellow" nation on their southern border.

Yet foreign policy experts on Asia advised Nixon that China would be hostile to any approach as long as the Vietnam War continued and Chiang Kai-shek ruled Taiwan. Nixon's instinct told him otherwise. Despite the fact that the People's Republic was a sister Communist nation, Nixon through his studies and travels knew that historically the Chinese distrusted Russia. Nixon suspected that Chinese feelings were equally ambivalent toward the Vietnamese. China would not be jubilant if a victorious North Vietnam extended their military domination to Laos and Cambodia. Only Taiwan would be a problem with the Red Chinese.

The Vietnam War was, however, a problem to Nixon's presidency. It had destroyed Johnson, and it could defeat him. His elegant inaugural, whose first draft was crafted by Ray Price, asked the nation "to lower its voices." The students answered by massive demonstrations in Washington in the fall of 1969. Nixon's hope was to arrange a solution, as Eisenhower did in Korea in 1953. The North Vietnamese were not ready to accept anything but a sell-out in South Vietnam. Time was on their side.

Nixon also knew that American patience with the bloody war that was killing their sons was running out. He tried to buy time with "the Vietnamization" of the war and instituted the gradual pulling-out of American troops. Such a withdrawal, though, would depend on a much larger congressional appropriation for an unpopular war. A total and complete return of all troops would spell victory for the Viet Cong and make allies such as South Korea and Israel question the credibility of U.S. commitment.

In May 1974, Nixon made the unprecedented presidential trip to a Communist country, Romania. Nixon had established a relationship with its president in 1966. In one sense, Nixon was showing his gratitude to a leader who had hosted him when he was out of office. But more importantly, Ceausescu had distanced himself from the Soviet Union and had cemented a relationship with China. At their meeting, Nixon asked Ceausescu to use his influence to approach China on his behalf.

Nixon sent his first signal to China in February 1970 in the long Foreign Policy Report to Congress. In it was this statement: "It is certainly in our interest and in the interest of peace that we take what steps we can toward improved practical relations with Beijing."

The Chinese responded by hinting to the U.S. ambassador in Warsaw that they might be receptive to talks at a higher level. Nixon's bombing of Cambodia at first stalled the idea, but in July the Chinese released the imprisoned Catholic Bishop James Walsh.

In an October interview with *Time* magazine, Nixon said, "If there is anything I want to do before I die, it is to go to China. If I don't, I want my children to."

It is clear that the approach to China was first and foremost Nixon's idea. Nixon was a "Pacific Ocean person" whose early memories were walking on the beaches that faced China across the ocean expanse. Kissinger was, on the other hand, a "Europeanist" who still looked at world politics through the eyes of a Metternich or Bismarck. Kissinger had been about as interested in China as he was in Antarctica. Although both were geo-politicians, Nixon's world had always included Asia.

The next step in Nixon's carefully orchestrated escalation of signals was to toast President Ceausescu on his return state visit to the United States in late 1970. Nixon deliberately referred to China as "the People's Republic of China." It was the first time a U.S. president had done so.

Along with Ceausescu, Nixon had invited to Washington President Khan of Pakistan. Pakistan had always enjoyed close relations with China, just as its border adversary India turned to the Soviet Union. At Nixon's suggestion, Pakistan sent word to Beijing, and Chou En-lai relayed the message back through Khan that a U.S. representative would be welcome in Beijing to discuss Taiwan.

For Nixon, approaching Red China was like wooing a nun—delicate and tentative. But although Chairman Mao lived almost an ascetic rustic life in his cell-like quarters, his premier, Chou En-lai, was a worldly sophisticate. His years in Paris had given him a keen appreciation of Western ways.

With Mao's authority, the premier answered Nixon's signals with a subtlety that justified Nixon's nuanced moves.

Chou relayed to Nixon through the president of Pakistan that the invitation for a meeting came from Chairman Mao. He concluded with a play on words: "We have had messages from the United States in the past, but this is the first time that the proposal has come from a Head, through a Head to a Head."

The two back channels through Pakistan and Romania were busy. From Romania came the word that Nixon would be welcome in Beijing to discuss Taiwan.

When Nixon lifted the restrictions on passports to visit mainland China in March 1971, China answered by inviting a U.S. table tennis team, then touring Japan, to visit Beijing. Ping-Pong seemed an appropriate sport to symbolize the reciprocal moves between the two nations.

When asked a few days later in a press conference about honeymoon plans for his daughter Tricia and Ed Cox, the president replied that he hoped one day soon they would "be able to go to China, see the great cities and the people." Nixon was heating up his courtship of the "People's Republic," and soon it was time to make a definite proposal.

Indirectly, through Pakistan, a bid for a secret meeting with Chou En-lai by a high U.S. official was broached. A week later a flushed Kissinger raced into the Oval Office with the news. The Chinese had agreed to a visit by Kissinger. Nixon and Kissinger toasted the acceptance with a bottle of old brandy.

The plan called for Kissinger to visit Vietnam for discussions and then stop off in Pakistan on the way back. From Pakistan, he would, while supposedly "sick," secretly fly to meet Chou.

While Kissinger was off on the *Polo II* plane to China, Nixon in Washington told his U.N. ambassador George Bush to end opposition to the consideration of the admittance of the People's Republic of China to membership in the U.N.

In Beijing, Kissinger hammered out the details preparing a visit by the U.S. president the next year. On July 15, Nixon announced from his vacation home in San Clemente the secret mission by Kissinger and the results: the Chinese invitation and his acceptance. "The meeting," said Nixon "is to seek the normalization of relations between the two countries."

In general the announcement was welcomed—except by those of the hard right, who felt Nixon had betrayed their trust. This disaffection of conservatives like Goldwater later cost Nixon in his Watergate ordeal.

On the wintry morning of February 17, 1972, the president was given a send-off at Andrews Air Force base for his flight to Beijing. Nixon said that the trip to China was more difficult than that of reaching the moon, which had been accomplished two and half years earlier. But the purpose was the same: He quoted the plaque left on the moon, "We came in peace for all mankind."

On the plane, Nixon stressed to Secretary of State Rogers and Kissinger that he must be allowed to descend from the plane alone.

On Monday morning at 11:30 A.M., Beijing time, and Sunday night at 10:30 P.M., Washington time, Nixon stepped off of the bottom step of the gangplank. He sighted Prime Minister Chou En-lai, dressed in a blue tunic and gray trousers, at the foot of the ramp. Chou, shivering in the cold wind, extended his hand. Nixon knew that Secretary of State John Foster Dulles had spurned Chou's proffered hand in 1954 in Geneva. As Nixon later wrote in his diary, "One era ended and another era began."

Down the wide, empty boulevard, Nixon rode in a curtained car. Chou told Nixon, "Your handshake came over the vastest oceans in the world—twenty five years no contact." He then added that Chairman Mao would receive him after lunch.

The frail, aging Chinese party leader bantered with Nixon about his preferring to deal with "Republicans and rightists rather than those from the left." At the end of the hour, Nixon quoted one of Mao's sayings, which he had read in Price's draft for a banquet toast the next day: "Seize the hour."

Mao clasped Nixon's hand, and in a self-deprecatory aside allowed that his short, pithy sayings "sometimes sound like a cannon." Then Mao raised his frail voice a notch: "SEIZE THE HOUR, SEIZE THE DAY!"

Privately, away from the press, Nixon stressed to Chou En-lai that his mission to renew relations with China was based not on sentimentality but realism. "What brings us together . . . is not friendship—although I believe that is important—but because of mutual security." Chou was impassive, but both he and Nixon knew it was the Soviet Union that was bringing them together.

That evening at the massive Great Hall of the People, built by Mao after his victory over Chiang Kai-shek's forces in 1949, a formal seven-course banquet was served up as only the Chinese can do.

Before leaving the White House, Nixon had talked with Ray Price about the language for a toast. From his studies and conversation with Chinese in Taiwan, Hong Kong, and Singapore, he had noted the Chinese love of metaphor. Theirs is a word–picture language whose poetry rings rich with vivid images. Still, he cautioned Price, whose own poetic lines he had come to appreciate, not to let the geopolitical reality of the occasion be drowned in rhetorical sentiment.

After his opening comments, Nixon, dressed in formal clothes, sounded his dominant note of political realism:

> In the spirit of frankness, let us recognize . . . these points. We have at times in the past been enemies. We have great differences today. What brings us together is that we have common interests which transcend these differences. As we discuss our differences neither of us will compromise over principles.

Price's draft consolidated but added only slightly to the thrust of Nixon's words to Price in the Oval Office. Price's flair for poetic imagery followed:

While we cannot close the gulf between us, we can try to bridge it so that
we may be able to talk across it."

Then, in an allusion to the famous People's March by Mao in 1935,
Nixon said,

And so let us in these next five days, start a long march together. Not in
lockstep, but on different roads leading to the same goal; the building of a
world structure of peace and justice in which all may stand together with
equal dignity.

In the White House the planners knew that the first state dinner would
be held on February 21, a day before Washington's birthday. Nixon had
asked Ray Price and his speechwriting shop to dig up some apt quotations
from the first American president. One on peace was provided from Washington's Farewell Address.

But Nixon in his first toast instead referred to a birthday in his own
family—his daughter Tricia, whom he had called from Beijing on her
twenty-sixth birthday.

The world watches, the world listens, the world waits to see what we will
do. What is the world? I think of my eldest daughter whose birthday is today.
And as I think of her, I think of all the children in the world in Asia, Africa,
in Europe, in the Americas, most of whom were born since the date of the
foundation of the People's Republic of China.

Then, in a rhetorical question, Nixon returned to the themes he had
stressed with Price.

What legacy shall we leave our children? Are they destined to die for the
hatreds which have plagued the old world? Or are they destined to live because
they have the vision to build a new world?

For his conclusion, the actual toast to Mao, Nixon had asked the Price
speech-shop researchers to comb the sayings of Mao. Accordingly, he
ended,

Chairman Mao has written: "So many deeds cry out to be done and always
urgently. The world rolls on. Time passes. Ten thousand days are too long.
Seize the day. Seize the hour. This is the hour . . . "
     And in that spirit I ask you to join to raise your glass to Chairman Mao,
to Prime Minister Chou and to the friendship of the Chinese and American
people.

The banquet at the Great Hall of the People was the culmination of the
long-nourished Nixon objective to establish relations with mainland China.

The restoration of relations was the centerpiece in his strategy for pressuring the Soviets to come to the negotiating table.

Nixon spent the next day of his visit to Beijing visiting the Great Wall north of the Chinese capital, where he said, contrary to the abbreviated press version:

> It is a Great Wall—and it had to be built by a great people.

While Mrs. Nixon visited the pandas at Peking Zoo and other tourist attractions, Nixon and Chou worked out the joint communique.[6] The sticking point was Taiwan. It was resolved by the United States by saying: "There is but one China and Taiwan is part of China." The precise wording would not be unacceptable to the Chinese Nationalists in Taipei.

At the state dinner the next night, Nixon made another talk in the form of a toast. On that occasion he used the Great Wall as his pictorial symbol as he had the bridge in the first toast. He described his awe upon visiting "one of the Great Wonders of the World" and thus added,

> The Great Wall is no longer a wall dividing China from the world, but it is a reminder of the fact there are many walls existing in the world which divide nations and peoples.

He then referred to the Washington quotation that was included in the drafted remarks for the Beijing Banquet.

> Mr. Prime Minister, you have noted that the plane which brought us here is named "The Spirit of '76." Just this week we have celebrated in America the birth of George Washington, who led America to independence in our Revolution and became our First President.
>
> He bade farewell at the close of his term with these words to his country: "Observe good faith and justice toward all nations. Cultivate peace and harmony with all."

Price had thought that Washington's words, particularly the last sentence, might have been written by Confucius himself.

Nixon gave one more toast, which turned out to be the most quoted words of his mission. It was in Shanghai, where the Nixon party flew before heading home. Ray Price had phoned in the suggestion from Washington.

At the dinner in the Municipal Hall in Shanghai on February 26, Nixon said of the historical accomplishment of the last five days: "This was the week that changed the world." It was Price's rewrite of what American revolutionary, John Reed, said of the 1917 Russian Revolution: "This was the week that shook the world."

Nixon's visit to China in February would be rivaled by his meeting in

Moscow in May. Nixon, it must be remembered, was the first U.S. president ever to visit Moscow. The Strategic Arms Limitation Treaty (SALT) was the first superpower agreement to halt the missile race. Nixon now had succeeded in beginning to move the world as he predicted, from "the era of confrontation, to the era of negotiation."

Nixon had carefully fit the building blocks in place: first the ABM deployment system, then the rapprochement with mainland China. The final one, an arms agreement, could then be firmly set in place. The first two made possible the third. The Soviets had to be made to see that it was in their interest to scale down their military spending. Nixon's strategy had forced them to the negotiating table.

A November reelection victory of record landslide proportions followed President Nixon's foreign policy triumphs in Beijing in February and Moscow in May. As the voters went to the polls in November, an end to the Vietnam War was being negotiated in Paris.

Yet both the peace and the presidency disintegrated in the welter of Watergate. A White House cover-up of an office break-in by a campaign operative led to the first presidential resignation in history.

Nixon was not the first to abuse the powers of the chief executive. Franklin Roosevelt and Lyndon Johnson had wire taps placed, and even Abraham Lincoln suspended habeas corpus. During times of war, presidents tend to amass the most power and the most potential for abuse. Such overreaching and misconduct in the executive branch stir deep resentment in the legislative branch (whose own excesses are never investigated by televised hearings).

In the wake of every conflict from the Civil War to Vietnam, congressional investigating committees have surfaced.[7] The media spotlight on the Watergate hearings unleashed a fury of attacks. Later Nixon told David Frost that he had given the Democrats the sword to kill him. But he also had thrown away his shield of the Republican right wing, which he had alienated through his China policy, wage price control, and family assistance program. As Nixon's presidency collapsed, so did congressional support for South Vietnamese military forces. Nixon's successor, Gerald Ford, would witness the Viet Cong victory.

When President Nixon was forced to resign in August of 1974, the Gallop Poll rated his approval at 20 percent. Only President Truman, in this century, when he left office in January 1953, had lesser support recorded.[8]

Like Truman, Nixon's foreign policy accomplishments will win the respect of historians. The salient difference is that Truman's moves were an immediate reaction to Soviet aggression in Eastern Europe right after the War. Nixon, by contrast, did not have his hand forced. He had the statesman's vision to foresee the future and map a strategy to shape a more stable world order. Sensing a shift in geopolitical realities, Nixon strove to open relations with mainland China as a prelude for détente with the Soviet Union. His Beijing breakthrough was the diplomatic coup of the age.

NOTES

1. Former President Ford told me, "Nixon figured in my first campaign and my last." He was referring to the Hiss case in his congressional campaign of 1948 and to the Nixon pardon in his presidential campaign of 1976.

2. In 1963, Nixon, who had not practiced law in almost twenty years, took the Bar Exams in New York and scored one of the highest marks in that state's history. His essay on the Constitution was lauded by the New York Board as brilliant.

3. Democratic congressman John Kennedy delivered to Republican colleague Nixon a check for $1,000 in Nixon's campaign to defeat another colleague, Helen Douglas, in the California Senate race.

4. At a Christmas party at his house in 1958, Nixon predicted to me that only a combination of Kennedy and Johnson could beat him. He said, "Although the press doesn't believe it, I attract more Democrats and Independents than Rockefeller. But, those Democrats are Northern Catholics and Southern Democrats." A joining of the two, which all but Nixon thought unlikely, would erode that support.

5. I have had occasion to observe all the Republicans who have been president, from Eisenhower to Bush, and have found Nixon the warmest as well as the most involved in speech presentation.

6. Julie Nixon Eisenhower told me that Premier Chou offered Mrs. Nixon cigarettes. In China, cigarettes carry a picture of two panda bears. Accordingly, cigarettes are often called "pandas" the way we might say "camels." When Mrs. Nixon was offered "pandas," she answered that the Washington Zoo would love to have them. The result of the misinterpretation was China's gift of two pandas to the National Zoo.

7. On Inauguration Day 1969, Robert Bland Smith, who was to become chief counsel of the Government Operations Committee, bet me that Nixon would be impeached. He based his forecast on the Judiciary Committee's rough handling of the Fortas nomination to the Supreme Court. Smith said, "Nixon, unlike Johnson or Truman, doesn't have his own party in control of Congress."

8. The congressional committee by a Republican-controlled Senate into the corruption of the Truman administration is little remembered today. In a scandal that reached the White House staff, some were convicted and went to jail. The attorney general was indicted, and a bill of impeachment was introduced in the House. Despite his accomplishment in foreign affairs, Truman's reputation was in tatters when he left the White House. The scenario invites comparison with that of Nixon.

16 _____

The Reagan Address at the Palace of Westminster: A Prophecy for a Free World

The march of freedom and democracy...will leave Marxism and Leninism in the ash-heap of history.

The Reagan Revolution is not a myth. Not since Roosevelt's New Deal has an administration registered such an impact on Washington. The Reagan tax cut immobilized the left. Democratic chairmen of congressional committees and their bureaucratic allies found their power to appropriate and propose new programs shorn. For the first time in a generation, the federal government was no longer automatically viewed as the agency of first resort to redress health, education, and welfare needs. And in that changing perception, those who labeled themselves "liberals" waned while those calling themselves "conservatives" doubled in strength. Republicans, who had been a minority party, began in 1988 to rival the Democrats in voting numbers. Political scientists, such as James MacGregor Burns of Williams College, concede that Reagan has been the most successful chief executive since Roosevelt in translating political principles into programs (even if many of them opposed "Reaganomics").

The comparison of Franklin Roosevelt to Reagan is strangely apt. The scenario in which an incumbent president—a decent and religious engineer—is defeated by a handsome and eloquent challenger who had earlier served as governor of the largest state is one that could refer to either Roosevelt or Reagan.

The political philosopher Walter Lippman described Franklin Roosevelt in 1932 as "shallow" in the pages of the *New Republic*; he was using language that would be applied to Reagan a half century later. As Roosevelt mastered the new medium of radio with his "Fireside Chats," so Reagan exploited his command of television. Both presidents radiated an optimism that generated hope. Each had a buoyancy and an assured presence that transcended his respective physical liability of lameness or age.

To an unemployed working class, Roosevelt offered benefits (for example, social security, WPA) financed by deficit spending. To the grandchildren of those Roosevelt voters, Reagan also delivered inducements (for example, tax cuts) that also were paid for by an increase in the federal debt. The difference was that the descendants of those Depression voters were now job-holding, tax-burdened home owners who would vote to have Reagan cut taxes, create jobs, and reduce inflation.

Yet in political beliefs as well as background, Reagan was the antithesis of Roosevelt. Republican Reagan, who came from a working-class home, was reviled by welfare groups and leaders of the black community. Democrat Roosevelt, on the other hand, was a patrician despised by business as a traitor to his class and beloved by the poor and minorities.

Unlike Roosevelt, however, Reagan came to the White House with a defined political philosophy. More than just a set of opinions, Reagan had a credo—a political religion. Other "true believers" such as William Jennings Bryan, Barry Goldwater, and George McGovern, had received presidential nominations, but Reagan, with the arguable exceptions of Thomas Jefferson and Andrew Jackson, was the first to be elected.

That in itself was a political shock to Washington, which is generally suspicious of any ideologue but particularly one with right-wing stripes. What heightened those Potomac fears about the new chief executive was Reagan's unfamiliarity with the federal government and the national scene.

Some might contend that Reagan knew less about foreign policy after eight years as president than Nixon did before he entered the White House. Certainly Reagan had less knowledge of Congress than senators Bob Dole and Howard Baker. Moreover, Reagan's experience in national or international affairs in 1980 was dwarfed by that of George Bush, a former congressman who had headed the CIA and represented our nation in the U.N. and China. Yet Reagan was the first president in a generation to serve eight years, and he left office even more popular than he was when first elected.

In some ways, Reagan's economic achievement is greater than Roosevelt's. Historians now believe that only the mobilization of World War II lifted the United States from the Depression doldrums. Reagan, however, presided over the greatest and longest peacetime expansion of the economy, and he did it while bringing down the inflation rate as well as interest rates.

Reagan's critics explain away the phenomenon of his popularity as theatrical legerdemain. The role of chief of state is a "monarchial" role, and former actor Reagan reigned with regal grace. Nevertheless, an administration is measured by the president's leadership as chief executive. The core of that leadership is the communication of ideals and objectives. No president, not even Lincoln, matched Reagan in that regard. Reagan, of course, had the use of television and the actor's gifts of poise, projection, and presence to exploit that medium brilliantly.

Reagan's Hollywood background has led to his being underestimated. His foes learned to their regret that he was more than a man with a handsome appearance who could read lines well. In his Illinois high school, he did act, but he also was a leader in the student government and wrote for the college yearbook. His high school drama teacher, who also taught English, called him "an above-average student who was curious and creative."

As in the biographies of other presidents, Reagan's mother was the dominant force in the household. Reagan may have inherited his talent for spinning a tale from his fun-loving, hard-drinking Irish father, but his drive and determination was shaped by his mother's sterner Calvinism.

Reagan's family was poor. His parents could neither buy a Scout uniform for him nor pay for his swimming lessons at the YMCA. Yet in a high school where few went to college, Reagan was determined to make it. He helped defray college expenses by working both in the kitchens of his fraternity and in the girls' dormitory.

At Eureka College, Reagan did everything but study! He was president of the student council, member of the debating team, writer for the yearbook, captain of the swim team, and a lead actor for the drama club. As one of the most active figures on campus, he registered only a "C" average. We are reminded of Justice Oliver Wendell Holmes' description of FDR as a leader with a "first class temperament and a second class mind."

But if he was intellectually lazy, Reagan had a quick mind almost photographic in its capacity to cram facts at the last minute for an exam. That ability made acting easy. He starred in a one-act Edna St. Vincent Millay play about the foolishness of war, for which he won an acting award.

The Depression year of 1932 was not the best time for a graduating student to find an acting job. But Reagan's resonant baritone lead him to radio, where opportunities were burgeoning in the biggest growth industry of that day. In Des Moines, he landed a job at WHD, an affiliate of NBC. In later years, Reagan used to regale his friends about his days when he relayed through teletype the broadcast of the Chicago Cubs baseball games. One day when the teletype transmission failed, the nonplussed Reagan called on his imagination to devise a play-by-play for an hour until service was restored.

His subsequent success as a radio announcer tends to eclipse his initial failure. Actually, he was once fired for his inability to read radio script with credibility. Reagan got himself rehired by learning to master the seemingly easy but actually difficult art of reading script convincingly. Reagan overcame his woodenness by applying his skill for memorizing lines. Reagan would look down and "eye-photograph" a line or two, then look up and away from the script and recreate the line from memory for a conversational delivery into the microphone. The momentary pause between his "eye-photograph" of a phrase or two and then the voiced rendition of that phrase simulated the natural pause of actual conversation.

Rare is the politician who can read a speech convincingly.[1] Even actors who become politicians, such as Senator George Murphy or Ambassador Shirley Temple Black, often seem stiff in their delivery when following a text. Although teleprompters, which presidents now employ, enable one to read a speech without looking down and away from the audience, still the tendency is for a reader of such a speech to adopt a more-hurried pace that is less congenial to the ear.

In 1937 when the twenty-six-year-old Reagan traveled to southern California as the Des Moines announcer for the Cubs for their spring training games, a friend arranged for Reagan to read for a Hollywood casting director. He did so well that he qualified for a screen test. His agent promoted him as "another Robert Taylor."[2]

Reagan never enjoyed such stardom. Yet, his professionalism and lack of artistic temperament made him popular with directors and fellow actors. Directors knew that Ronald Reagan would arrive at the set on time with his lines memorized.

If Reagan was light years away from the emotional range of a Richard Burton, neither did he have the emotional instability of a Burton. Reagan's winning personality advanced him from "B" pictures to some meaty roles before the war. As "the Gipper" in *Knute Rockne, All American*, he won recognition; then, as Drake McHugh in *King's Row* in 1941, he won praise from critics. The *New Yorker* said that he imparted a "rare glow."

The coming of World War II aborted any rise to leading-man stardom. Reagan spent the war years doing films for the U.S. Air Force in Culver City. After the war, despite a few strong films such as *The Voice of the Turtle* and *The Hasty Heart*, the thirty-six-year-old Reagan found himself being displaced by younger actors for romantic leads.

A frustrated Reagan turned his energies into work for the Screen Actors' Guild, the actors' union. In a profession dominated by strong egos, Reagan's affability and lack of affectation paved his way to union leadership.

Right after the war the Hollywood community was a hotbed of leftist sentiment. Certain members, particularly some of the screenwriters, were promoting pet causes of the Soviet Union. Such pro-Stalinist activities deeply divided the Hollywood community and drew the attention of the House Un-American Activities Committee.

Reagan, though a Democrat, was alarmed by the radical element in the Hollywood union. With encouragement by Jimmy Roosevelt, son of the late president, Reagan resolved to root out the pro-Soviets in the movie industry just as Mayor Hubert Humphrey was doing at the same time at the national levels of the Democratic Party.

Despite threats to his life, Reagan, as president of the Screen Actors' Guild, mounted a campaign to target and defeat the pro-Communist leftists in local union elections. His success led him to be invited to Washington to testify before the House Un-American Activities Committee.

Reagan, when asked, would not designate by name those, who, in his belief, had Communist ties. Instead he lectured Committee Chief Counsel Robert Stripling on Thomas Jefferson:

> So that fundamentally, I would say in opposing these people that the best thing to do is to make democracy work. In the Screen Actors' Guild we made it work by insuring everyone a vote and by keeping everybody informed. I believe, as Thomas Jefferson put it, if all the people know all the facts, they will never make a mistake.

When Stripling challenged Reagan's opinion that outlawing the Communist Party was unnecessary, Reagan answered:

> I never as a citizen want to see our country urged by either fear or resentment at this group, that we even compromise with any of our democratic principles.

The *New York Times* praised his stand.

In later years, Reagan, as a former actor, was criticized for his lack of political credentials. Actually, Reagan had already proved his political skills in turning around the Screen Actors' Guild. In one of the most competitive unions, he had risen to the top. Years later, Reagan, in an overstatement, described his political thinking in those post-war years as that of "a dewy-eyed liberal." Actually, Reagan did not have much of a thought-out political philosophy at that time. He became a Democrat because that was the party of his hero, Franklin Roosevelt. In 1936, Reagan was on hand to cheer the Democratic president when he came to campaign in Des Moines. In his radio days, Reagan even tried to imitate Roosevelt's radio style of relaxed but measured cadence.

As a Roosevelt Democrat, Reagan supported President Harry Truman in 1948. Although Reagan made speeches, the only issues he discussed in detail were local union matters. When Reagan spoke in the 1948 presidential campaign, he confined his remarks to attacks on big business and support for Roosevelt's successor Truman. What attracted Reagan to politics was the real-life theater of history in the making.

Nevertheless, his interest in politics, and particularly in the issues of the Screen Actors' Guild, was the root cause of his divorce by actress Jane Wyman. Reagan's political talk bored her. "Most of their discussions," she said "were above me."

For an optimist like Reagan, the post-war 1940s was a time of despair. He had lost his wife, and now he was losing his livelihood. The future was bleak. If he had voiced his feelings, he might have echoed the character

Drake McHugh, whom he played in *King's Row*. McHugh, who lost both his legs after an operation, said: "Where's the rest of me?" Reagan, like Franklin Roosevelt after World War I, must have pondered the rest of his life.

In the next decade Reagan found a new wife and a new career. Nancy Davis was a starlet whom he met in discharging his duties as head of the Screen Actors' Guild. The job came from the new medium of television. Reagan became host of a new television series sponsored by General Electric. Reagan introduced the weekly drama, taking roles in a few of them. He also toured the country for ten weeks a year plugging G.E. products while visiting the 138 G.E. plants with over a quarter-of-a-million employees.

His trips to the various cities where G.E. had plants prompted speech invitations by business groups wanting to take advantage of the Hollywood celebrity's appearance in their city. Even the heartiest speakers grow weary of the banquet life, but Reagan relished what he called the "peas and potato" circuit.

At first his talks approximated Churchill's "pudding"—"no theme." He interwove his pitch for General Electric with a raft of anecdotes collected from his Hollywood days.

But Reagan soon realized that a successful speech must do more than just titillate his audience—he had to leave them with the meat of a message. At G.E. headquarters, the chairman, Ralph Cordiner, told Reagan what he himself had been thinking: "Ron, you must get yourself a philosophy."

Although he was still a Democrat, Reagan had drifted away from that party. He had supported Eisenhower in 1952. Like many other Democrats, he felt that twenty years of rule by one party had spawned a wasteful government with a bloated bureaucracy. He spent nearly his entire adult life in Los Angeles, but his bearings were still rooted in the small-town Midwest. For a romantic like Reagan, the homespun virtues of thrift, hard work, and self-reliance that he remembered in Dixon, Illinois, glowed more brightly than the tinsel of Hollywood.

Banquet-speaker Reagan sounded those conservative notes that his middle-class audiences wanted to hear, and those were the chords in any symphony to private enterprise. As a representative of a major corporation speaking to business groups, Reagan was converting himself to Republicanism. The former Democrat who once had railed against "big business" was now reviling "big government."

What Reagan wrote out for his speaking appearances did not at first resemble a speech. The five-by-seven cards he used to jot down his various jokes now began to include statistics about government waste or anecdotes about welfare fraud. Soon these were joined by quotations by Thomas Jefferson, Alexis de Toqueville, and Edward Gibbon on the evils of big government and big spending. He collected those sayings of statesmen and historians not by reading their works but by clipping out quotations from editorials and columns in the many newspapers he read each day. Because he knew he had to entertain his audience while educating them, he would latch onto a historical anecdote about inflation in ancient Rome or copy down a remark by Lenin that mocked democracy.

Always a foe of communism, he became increasingly a defender of capitalism. To Reagan, Marxism and the totalitarian tyranny it spawned represented a godless anti-Christ, an evil threat to the virtues he saw embodied in "the Norman Rockwell" America of his youth. Like the nominal Christian who becomes "born-again" in mid-life, Reagan now spoke with the newly arrived faith of a convert.

Ironically, the language with which he stitched together his anecdotes and quotations to proclaim his capitalist credo often echoed Franklin Roosevelt. Reagan had listened to and even memorized radio addresses by the New Deal president to practice his radio delivery. In other words, Reagan was a Republican who didn't speak in the economic abstractions of Robert Taft or with the stridency of the just-emerging Barry Goldwater. Like Roosevelt, he radiated hope for the common man—that "the little guy" could be liberated from the burden of government at home and from the tyranny of communism abroad.

What made Reagan a phenomenon in his communicating ability was not so much his years as an actor in the 1940s but his hundreds of speaking engagements in the 1950s. As a Shakespearean actor masters his craft by playing Hamlet every day on the stage, Reagan honed his basic speech. Without conscious effort, he learned the power of a pause and the impact of a shift in modulation. Reagan, with the audience reaction as his director, could polish his delivery as well as test his material a thousand times.

As his own writer, Reagan developed the commitment of a "true believer." The politician of today who depends on a speechwriter can change one's views as one would change clothes. Reagan labored over his set talk, adding new lines and deleting others; and in the process he forged an unshakable attachment to the message he was propounding in the way an author becomes one with his book.

The middle-class businessmen applauding Reagan's homilies in the early 1960s were reading and talking about Senator Barry Goldwater's *Conscience of a Conservative*. The book, ghosted by *National Review* publisher William F. Buckley, was a jeremiad against the sins of statism and the menace of Marxism.

In the key California primary that had seen Senator Goldwater prevail against Governor Nelson Rockefeller, Ronald Reagan was a frequent political rally speaker. Those Californians bankrolling the Goldwater campaign came to believe that Reagan could sell the conservative message better than Goldwater. At their suggestion, Reagan was asked to deliver a nationwide television address in behalf of Goldwater. Goldwater aides demurred, believing that Reagan evangelism would only accentuate the "extremist" label that the Johnson campaign operatives were successfully hanging around the neck of the Republican presidential candidate.[3]

The Goldwater campaign begrudgingly approved the speech in the closing days of the national campaign, and Reagan delivered his television address on October 27 for a candidate who had no chance of being elected. To most of the nation who heard him for the first time, Reagan was a washed-up old movie actor whom they had recently seen hosting westerns on television.

In political history, Reagan's "Time for Choosing" was the most successful political address on television since Richard Nixon's "Checkers" talk a decade earlier. If Nixon was a defense counsel addressing a jury, Reagan was a preacher propounding the gospel. Like a televangelist, Reagan stirred thousands to send in their dollars. Columnist David Broder, writing for the *Washington Star*, called it "the most successful political address since William Jennings Bryan electrified the 1896 Democratic Convention with his 'Cross of Gold' speech."

Reagan's address represented the distillation of what he had refined and polished in a thousand talks. He cited his favorite statistics, showing that the "cost of the federal government [had] increased 234 times while [the] gross national product had risen only 33 times." To buttress his case against collectivism, Reagan contrasted present-day liberal Democratic senators William Fulbright and Joseph Clark, who respectively said that the Constitution was outmoded and that massive centralized government was needed, to Founding Father Alexander Hamilton, who warned that big government could tyrannize the individual.

Reagan also recounted the best of the "welfare stories" he had been telling countless Rotary Clubs and Chambers of Commerce.

> Recently a judge told me of an incident in court. A fairly young woman with six children, pregnant with her seventh, came to him for a divorce. Under his questioning it became evident that the husband did not share this desire. When the whole story came out, her husband was a laborer earning $250 a month. By divorcing him she could get an $80 raise. She was eligible for $330 a month from the Aid to Dependent Children Program. She had been talked into the divorce by two friends who had already done this very thing.

He ended the story with a practiced shake of his head. The welfare case was a "morality tale" against big government. Such a note of sad resignation was far more persuasive than Goldwater's shrillness. If the import of Reagan's words was almost radical, the tone was reassuring. If the philosophy was Goldwater, the performance was Roosevelt.

For his closing, Reagan borrowed from one of Roosevelt's most quoted lines and joined it to one by Lincoln. Looking directly into the camera, Reagan in a voice slightly more than a whisper, said:

You and I have a rendezvous with destiny. We can preserve for our children this, the last hope of man on earth or we can sentence them to take the first step into a thousand years of darkness. If we fail, at least let our children and our children's children say of us we justified our brief moment here. We did all that could be done.

The speech did not alter the course of the election, but it did change the course of Reagan's career. As Reagan himself later noted, "It raised eight million dollars and soon changed my entire life." In the wreckage of Goldwater's catastrophic defeat in California, a few Los Angeles business leaders began to push Reagan as the candidate against Democrat Governor Pat Brown, who had defeated Richard Nixon two years before.

Governor Pat Brown and the Democrats were jubilant at the prospect of facing a candidate from the ideological right such as Reagan. In the California Republican primary, where conservatives predominate, particularly in populous southern California, Reagan was an easy victor. In the general election, Governor Brown made Reagan's lack of administrative experience the issue. Reagan replied, "The man who has the job has more experience than anybody. That's why I'm running!"

Brown countered that Reagan's running for governor was like a "man saying he always had a great interest in aviation and now he wanted to fly the plane."

"Citizen" Reagan turned his liability into an asset. In a society where politicians are ranked only somewhat above an aluminum-siding salesman, the clean and strong planes of the Reagan face came across the TV screen as something fresh and new. In contrast, the pudgy Brown looked like a political "Willy Loman." When Brown talked about being a "professional" in government, the voters interpreted that to mean "professional politician." As the polls showed a shift toward Reagan, the bumbling Brown said in an unfortunate aside, "You know, it was an actor who killed Lincoln!" In a state where the movie industry plays a leading role in the economy, Californians resented the remark. Reagan's margin of victory was huge—nearly a million votes.

When Ronald Reagan arrived in Sacramento in January 1967, he had principles but no programs. In his announcement speech for governor almost a year before, he had talked of "a future as bright and as gold as California." But the prospects for the state looked black, and the state of its treasury was red.

The conservative rhetoric of the Reagan campaign crashed into fiscal reality. Even if Reagan proposed no new programs and approved no departmental increases in spending, he was looking at a deficit. Reagan the purist yielded to Reagan the pragmatist. Faced with a draconian slash in services or a new tax increase, he chose the latter.

Reagan cut a deal with the Democratic leader of the House, Jesse Unruh.

Unruh supplied the necessary Democratic votes in return for a tax increase
bill that Unruh himself shaped—one that increased the taxes on corporations, banks, and the very rich.

Although the extreme right wing of his own party denounced him, Reagan escaped with his popularity largely undented. For one thing, on the
public relations front, Reagan painted himself as a budget-cutter. He collected an assortment of economy proposals in one document and brandished
it to the public with the comment, "The symbol of our flag is the Golden
Bear; it is not a cow to be milked."

If the rhetoric of Governor Reagan was right-wing, the actual record was
closer to the center. Reagan, for example, signed a liberalized abortion bill,
and the far right screamed.

Yet what Californians mostly heard from Governor Reagan were his
attacks against the student demonstrations and riots in the state universities.
In the 1960s, middle-class Americans were troubled by the rise of crime,
the emerging Black militancy, and the student anti-draft protests spurred
by the Vietnam War. Most parents who had strived to put their children
in college particularly did not like what they thought was happening at
Berkeley, the University of California's best known campus.

Like Roosevelt, Reagan knew how to choose his enemies. For Roosevelt
in the Depression it was "the economic royalists" of big business. In a time
of increasing violence of protests and demonstrations, Reagan attacked "the
criminal anarchists" and "off campus revolutionaries." With those words
Reagan voiced the feelings of middle- and working-class voters who were
seeing the education dreams for their children turning into nightmares.

Governor Reagan, like President Kennedy a few years later, won legions
of political admirers not so much by the few bills he signed as chief executive
but rather by the reiteration of beliefs he enshrined in his speeches. Like
the liberal Kennedy in his presidential years, the conservative Reagan's
legislative record in his first term was not only thin but much closer to the
center than the thrust of his speeches.

Reagan did battle the academic liberals with mixed success. He succeeded
in forcing Clark Kerr, the president of the University of California, to
resign. He also managed to impose tuition fees on the state university
system, a plan former Governor Brown's director of finance had called for.
Reagan's enemies on the intellectual left saw it as a Reagan attempt to punish
free speech.

If the exhilarating part of being governor was the role of "communica-
tor," the dreary business for Reagan was that of being an "administrator."
To put it another way, if Reagan in the state was governor of California,
he was in the nation the champion of a growing conservative movement
and heir to the fallen Goldwater.

Yet despite urgings from political strategists on the ideological right such
as Clifton White, Reagan was hesitant about running for president in 1968.

Eventually the governor was persuaded to be "a favorite son" presidential candidate to hold the California delegates. The rationale, with which his advisers convinced Reagan, was that conservatives should have a fall-back position if Nixon stumbled in the primaries against Rockefeller.

Yet even after Nixon's election, Reagan continued as a national spokesman for the ideological conservatives whose suspicions about Nixon were reflected in William Buckley's *National Review* and Stanton Evans's *Human Events*.

In 1976, when Nixon would have served two terms, Reagan could then obtain the presidential nomination he had lost in 1968. For that reason Reagan was anxious to broaden his base. He was delighted when he received an invitation to speak at the cornerstone laying of Eisenhower College in New York State in 1969.

Reagan's topic was the civil unrest caused by the rise of crime and the Vietnam protests.

> We've known rioting in our streets. The abuse of drugs and narcotics soars . . . We have campus demonstrations to force the college to divorce itself from participating in the defense of the nation. We no longer walk in the countryside and on our city streets after dark without fear. The jungle seems to be closing in on this little plot we've been trying to civilize for 6000 years.

To the audience of Eastern moderates, Reagan had been viewed as another Goldwater, but his low-key conversational style that addressed their middle-class fears won converts and proved the potentiality of a Reagan appeal.

Reagan told of speaking at a huge Midwestern university where a parent asked why students were rebelling.

> I almost answered the question with a question, because frankly I wasn't sure I had the answer. But then I suggested that perhaps young people aren't rebelling against our standards, they are rebelling because they don't think we *ourselves* are living the standards we tried to teach them.

The audience roared their applause to a kind of spiritual warning General Eisenhower himself had so often delivered.

Reagan's staff began to limit the governor's out of state appearances in 1970. Any timetable for a run for the presidency in 1976 required his re-election as governor. By the time Reagan would leave office completing his second term in 1975, he would be able to devote full time to a national campaign.

Reagan chose welfare reform as his campaign issue. The exploitation of such a burning issue with the middle and working classes would force attention away from his scant record and put the Democrats on the defensive.

Jesse Unruh, the former California speaker of the house, was Reagan's Democratic opponent. In a sense, it was a re-run of 1966. "Citizen Reagan" was pitted against "politician Unruh." Unruh, who was nicknamed "Big Daddy," despite his slim-down in weight for the campaign, was a caricature of the cigar-smoking political wheeler-dealer. Reagan won by more than half a million votes.

Reagan was justifiably proud of his second term accomplishments: property tax relief, an improvement in school financing, and, most importantly, a California Welfare Reform Act that Reagan hailed as a model for the nation. The plan increased assistance while tightening eligibility. The act was the centerpiece in Reagan's conservative programs that he billed as "the Creative Society."

Such a record as chief executive of what was becoming the biggest state in the union would have solidified Reagan's credentials as the presidential successor to Nixon—but for one thing: Watergate. The congressional hearings on the cover-up of the burglary toppled Nixon and made Gerald Ford president.

Under the 22nd amendment to the Constitution, Nixon would have been barred from running for a third term, but Ford as the incumbent president would run in 1976 for a full term. On an even playing field, Reagan would have been favored to defeat any Republican candidate in 1976. But the powers of incumbency made the wresting of the Republican presidential nomination from Ford an uphill race.

"Movement conservatives" believed that the succession of Ford to the presidency cheated them out of their political legacy. They also were angered by Ford's selection of Governor Rockefeller as his vice president. To conservatives, it was not only a move to mobilize campaign resources for a 1976 presidential run by Ford but also a deliberate affront to the right-wing philosophy of most party workers.

When Reagan left Sacramento in 1975, his former aide, the advertising executive Peter Hannaford, set up for the former governor a livelihood that exploited his skills as a spokesman on public affairs. Reagan taped a syndicated radio column and collaborated with Hannaford on a weekly column for newspapers. In addition, Hannaford served as an agent promoting Reagan's availability for the banquet circuit.

As Reagan left the pragmatic politics of the state capitol for the ideological purity of the ivory tower, his opinions veered to the right. As a commentator and columnist, he knew what he had to say to please his right-wing market.

No more was he as governor reading the daily mini-memos by Edwin Meese offering pro and con recommendations on state problems. Freed from the restraints of office, Reagan could offer the certitude of the ideologue. Letters from his fans and response by his audiences hardened his opposition to Ford's presidency.

From his old press secretary, Lyn Nofziger, and his new political adviser, John Sears, he was hearing the counsel that President Ford could be beaten in the Republican primaries. Operatives on Reagan's behalf began organizing in the South and West.

Reagan should have won the first primary in New Hampshire. If he had won, he probably would have gone on to defeat the deflated "accidental president" at the convention in Kansas City. Ironically and improbably, a speech turned out to be Reagan's downfall. Jeff Bell, a conservative economist, drafted a major address in which Reagan urged a massive transfer of federal programs—such as welfare and housing—back to the states. "Movement conservatives" had been tiring of Reagan's boilerplate talk—the updated "Time for Choosing" speech—which now included mention of Reagan's welfare reform as governor of California. Reagan's lack of political depth on national issues betrayed him. If he had followed his own gut instincts and continued to serve up the latest version of the "Time for Choosing" talk, he would have beaten Ford.

Although the press initially ignored the implications of such a radical proposal, Ford strategists did not. They labelled it "the Ninety Billion Give-Away." Reagan's defensiveness on the issue turned what would have been a romp into a race. In a bigger than expected turnout, Ford squeaked by Reagan. The "accidental president" was now a winner.

Just as most pundits were writing off the challenger's chances, Reagan mounted a late spring comeback. Television again provided the means for political rebirth. In Florida where anti-Communist sentiment ran strong, Reagan attacked Ford's secretary of state (and Rockefeller protégé), Henry Kissinger, for his support of a treaty with Panama ceding back the Canal to the Panamanians. Reagan, with Teddy Roosevelt rhetoric, said, "We bought it, we paid for it—it's ours and we're going to keep it." The speech struck a nerve with Southern Republicans. The unexpected result was an upset victory by Reagan in North Carolina, followed by more Reagan victories in the South and West.

Yet in the end Reagan could not prevail against the powers of an incumbent president. To his dispirited campaign workers, Reagan, from his Kansas City Hotel, delivered an emotional address ending with his favorite historical quotation—by Massachusetts Bay governor John Winthrop in 1640.

"We shall be as a city upon a hill. The eyes of all people are upon us so that if we deal falsely with our God in this work we have undertaken and so cause Him to withdraw His present help, we shall be made a story and a byword through all the world."

Then Reagan added:

Don't get cynical because if you look at yourselves, and what you were willing
to do and recognize that there are millions out there that want what you
want, they want it that way—they want it to be a shining city on the hill.

Most of Reagan's listeners, including his wife Nancy, wept at the words.
Interestingly, John Kennedy used the Winthrop "city on the hill" quotation
frequently in his 1960 campaign. Kennedy, Roosevelt, and Reagan were
arguably the three best presidential speakers of this century. Each chose
their speechwriters carefully and put a priority on presidential speechmaking. Yet there were differences. Roosevelt delivered the elegant lines by
Archibald MacLeish or Robert Sherwood "conversationally."

Reagan disdained the speechwriter's polished phrases as too rhetorical
and artificial. He liked the muscular workaday prose that sounded more
spontaneous and thus more sincere. Reagan, like Roosevelt, adopted a conversational manner.

Of the three presidents, Kennedy was the least conversational and the
most rhetorical. Reagan was like Kennedy, however, in his fondness of
citing a statesman's quotation or recounting some patriotic vignette as the
emotional cap to a speech.

Reagan lost in Kansas City, but he solidified his role as leader of the
conservatives.

In the summer of 1978, Reagan at his California ranch gave the go-ahead
to political operative John Sears to begin organizing for 1980. Reagan had
two major enemies, and they were not George Bush or John Connally, the
two principal contenders; they were his age and his penchant for off-the-
cuff comments.

Reagan, ever the optimist, discounted age—despite concern by his pollster
Wirthlin. To Reagan, age, like Roosevelt's disability, would not be a decisive issue. Reagan knew he looked vigorous on television.

Reagan handlers were more fearful of some off-hand answers blurted out
by their candidate on such sensitive subjects as civil rights or foreign policy.
A gaffe by Reagan in the hands of the press could make him seem like a
bigot, "bomber," or "bumbler" unworthy to entrust with the highest office
of the land.[4]

His front-runner position was toppled in the Iowa caucuses in the fall of
1979, when George Bush, a favorite of the Republican establishment, "stole
a march" by out-organizing the Reagan forces in the district caucuses.

As it had been four years earlier, New Hampshire in 1980 was "a make
or break" for Reagan. His poise before the cameras once again was the
deciding difference. George Bush insisted that a televised debate between
him and Reagan should not include the other candidates, such as senators
Bob Dole and Howard Baker and congressmen John Anderson and Phil
Crane. A brouhaha developed with the four Republican presidential candidates clambering onstage to be heard. The Bush partisans shut off the

podium microphone. A deliberately angry Ronald Reagan, without telling his staff, strode to the podium in the Nashua High School gymnasium. "Gentlemen, I paid for this microphone." A flustered Bush could not regain his composure, and an emboldened Reagan went on to score heavily in the debate.

Reagan won easily in New Hampshire. The Bush momentum (Bush called it "the big Mo") collapsed and along with it Bush's hopes for a victory.

At the convention, a quixotic exploration of former President Ford as a possible running mate was launched by Reagan, who had been impressed by Ford's convention address. The Ford vice presidential balloon—after examining the implications of a former president being vice president—was eventually punctured as unworkable, and Reagan's pollsters and advisers persuaded him that Bush, with his more moderate image, was the only one who might help him win.

President Carter, to be sure, had his own liabilities. He was dogged by the captivity of the hostages in Iran he could not free and by an economy he could not improve. Like Nixon, he did not have a popular personality. Yet still Carter commanded a residual respect as a decent, honorable man of religious principles. The downside of such moral piety was a certain streak of meanness. He had said of Ted Kennedy's challenge the year before, "I'll whip his ass."

Someone who believes he or she is on God's side often indulges in apocalyptic hyperbole. President Carter, speaking in the late Martin Luther King's church in Atlanta in September, described Reagan as "one who seeks the Presidency with the endorsement of the Ku Klux Klan." Later that month at an AFL-CIO convention in California, Carter said that the November election would decide "whether we have peace or war." At a dinner in Chicago in October, Carter warned "If I lose . . . Americans might be separated, black from white, Jew from Christian, North from South, rural from urban."

Carter intended to exploit the doubts about a Reagan presidency, but he succeeded only in raising doubts about himself. The debate between Carter and Reagan on October 27 was the last chance the president had to crack the electoral lock Reagan was assembling with his base in the states west of the Mississippi.

Reagan was eager to debate the president even if some of his advisers were not. He had witnessed how challengers Kennedy in 1960 and Carter in 1976 had destroyed the aura of presidential incumbency. Through the forum of a debate, both Kennedy and Carter had blown away the issue of inexperience.

Yet many of Reagan's oldest advisers, including his wife, had reservations. One blunder like Ford's reference to Poland as "free" could shatter Reagan's shaky lead in the polls.

Reagan, however, did not fear the medium that had always been his friend. Once the American public saw him in their living rooms he could dispel "the right-wing bogeyman" caricature. Furthermore, Reagan reasoned that he had to debate Carter. It had been Carter who had earlier rejected a three-way debate that included third-party candidate John Anderson. In the resulting two-man debate, Reagan had emerged unscathed from his face-off with Anderson. Although Reagan had seemed unsure on the issues, the politically moderate Anderson argued stridently as the right-wing Reagan conversed moderately. Carter, who had been hurt by his early refusal to debate, now challenged Reagan, whose lead in the polls was increasing.

Carter bested Reagan in his command of statistics. Yet if a viewer had turned down the sound to a drone and concentrated on the style instead of the statistics, it was the president who was nervous while the challenger was poised. At one point Carter recited with detail Reagan's opposition to Medicare. Reagan jumped on the statement with a wistful shake of his head: "There you go again."[5] It was the tone of an uncle mildly rebuking a nephew given to tall tales. Although Carter had his facts right on Reagan's health record, he later stretched credibility when he recounted that his eleven-year-old daughter Amy had told him that the most important issue "was nuclear weaponry and the control of nuclear arms."

In such a rhetorical overkill, Carter allowed his best issue—that of peace—to be parodied by television comedians. Although commentators right after the debate generally rated the respective performances as a draw, Carter came off the loser in the media aftermath, where any mistake, such as the Amy reference, is egregiously magnified. Reagan, despite his unsteadiness with facts, was reassuring in presence. He also succeeded in defining his candidacy in a simple understandable message. Kennedy in 1960 kept reciting, "We must get this country moving again." Carter in 1976 had as his theme, "We want a government as good as its people." Reagan in the closing statement of his television appearance, said, "If you feel you are better off in 1980 than you were in 1976, then vote for Mr. Carter . . . but if you don't then vote for Reagan–Bush."

That simple line, crafted by Ken Khachigian, a former Nixon speech-writer, epitomized the hope that Reagan offered to a nation that had become unsure of its greatness.

Eight years before a Democratic governor in a Sunday *New York Times* article had warned Democratic candidates such as McGovern not to let a Democratic attack on the administration record be interpreted as an attack on America and the American people. The writer was Jimmy Carter, and he later failed to follow his own advice.

On July 15, 1979, President Carter after an "economic summit" at Camp David with his cabinet and top advisers, delivered what the White House staff said would be the most important speech of his presidency. Carter and his speechwriter, Rick Hertzberg, had Churchillian "blood, sweat and tears" ambitions for the nationally televised address—a speech that would jolt America with stark reality of the economic facts of life. Carter asserted that future generations could not expect the standard of living their parents had enjoyed.

The press called his address "the malaise speech" although the president actually never used the word.[6] What Carter did say in the manner of a Sunday school teacher admonishing his students was that Americans were suffering from "a crisis of confidence . . . that strikes at the heart and soul and spirit of our national will."

Like a Biblical prophet, Carter was finding his people "wanting in spirit." Yet the unintentional consequence turned the focus on his own leadership ability. A week later Senator Kennedy announced his candidacy. One of the reasons he gave was his deep dismay in a president who would offer despair instead of hope.

Reagan closed his 1980 campaign with a televised address he called his vision for America. The speech, written again by Ken Khachigian, was a vision inspired by the past—the pilgrims landing in New England, American prisoners of war returning from Vietnam, and astronauts landing on the moon.

Does history still have a place for America, for her people, for her great ideals? There are some who answer "no" [who say] our energy is spent, our days of greatness at an end, that a great national malaise is upon us.

Toward the end of the talk, Reagan gave his answer:

I find no malaise. I find nothing wrong with the American people.

He then asked whether President Carter "instills in you pride for your country and a sense of optimism about our future." As in his debate, Reagan closed with this question:

Are you personally more secure in your life? Is your family more secure? Is America safer in the world?

And most importantly—quite simply—the basic question of our life. Are you happier today than when Mr. Carter became President of the United States?

Like Roosevelt over half a century before, Reagan embodied a message of hope, and Americans overwhelmingly responded. Reagan won by a plurality of 8,417,492 votes, carrying 44 states. More significantly, the Reagan landslide brought in with him a Republican Senate, the first in 35 years.

The inaugural address of the fortieth president was a hymn to heroism.

Reagan's tribute to the average American working man and woman was his answer to his predecessor, who sat stiff and expressionless in a seat behind the podium.

Reagan extolled "the men and women who raise our food, patrol our streets, man our mines and factories, teach our children, keep our homes . . . "

> We have every right to dream heroic dreams. Those who say that we're in a time when there are no heroes, they just don't know where to look. You can see heroes every day going in and out of factory gates.

Speechwriter Ken Khachigian caught the style of Reagan that disdained the alliteration and internal rhyme of a Ted Sorensen. ("We are a nation that has a government—not the other way around." "It's not my intention to do away with government. It is rather to make it work. . . . ")

Khachigian joined to his own contributions some favorite lines from Reagan's old card file ("government is not the solution to our problem; government is the problem" and "the federal government did not create the states; the states created the federal government").

It is curious that Reagan phrases have not become immortalized in the pages of a *Bartlett's Quotations*.[7] One reason is that Reagan resisted setting up potentially quotable lines by rhetorical devices.

Roosevelt, to underline his famous first inaugural line, said, "*Let me again assert my firm belief* that the only thing we have to fear is fear itself" (emphasis added).

In his inaugural, Kennedy said, "*And so my fellow Americans,* ask not what your country can do for you; ask what you can do for your country" (emphasis added). Lines like "I say to you" and "Fellow Citizens" are rhetorical gambits by which orators can apply magic markers to lines they want to become "catch phrases."

It was recommended to Reagan that he "set up" one potentially quotable line in his address: "So my fellow Americans, if we can love our country why can't we love our countrymen?" By conversationalizing the line, Reagan smothered the poetry of it to read "How can we love our country and not love our countrymen and loving them reach out a hand."

Here was an "echo" line, but Reagan disdained such devices as "My fellow Americans" or "I say to you" as the hackneyed hallmark of a state senator at a courthouse rally. He tried to sound less like an orator and more like a neighbor talking in the living room, over a backyard fence, or even on a barroom stool.

Although Reagan was wary of rhetorical elegance, he did like using the poignant anecdote or poet's verse to appeal to the emotions of his audience. Some of his "tear-jerker" tales might have sounded mawkish from Carter or Dukakis, but Reagan got swallowed up by his emotions. He was not acting when his feelings welled up talking about the courage of a citizen rescuer or the tragedy of the doomed astronauts. He is, in the words of Reagan speechwriter Joshua Gilder, "a very emotional guy."

In his inaugural, Reagan capped his patriotic paean by reading a letter from a barber who had been killed in World War I.

> We're told that on his body was found a diary. On the flyleaf under the heading "My pledge" he had written these words: "America must win this war. Therefore I will work. I will save. I will sacrifice. I will endure. I will fight—cheerfully—and do my utmost as if the issue of the whole struggle depended on me alone."

With the new captain at the helm, the ship of state turned sharply to the starboard. Not since Roosevelt had Washington experienced such a sea change. Conservative "supply-siders" saw their theories implemented with the passage of a major personal income tax cut. Conservative "hawks" saw a debilitated Carter defense budget fortified by massive appropriation increases. The business community applauded when Reagan's transportation secretary Drew Lewis cut the striking air traffic controllers off at the knees. The Gramm–Rudman–Hollings Act put a cap on spending. And strict constructionists welcomed Reagan's first appointee to the Supreme Court, a conservative, Sandra Day O'Connor, who was the first woman to be a justice. What caused an even greater shift in the judicial philosophy of the nation were scores of federal judges Reagan appointed with the approval of a Republican Senate.

The eloquent presence and decisive initiatives of the new president began to generate a lift in American spirits and renew faith in government. Yet by the next year his approval ratings dipped as the economy soured.

Reaganites blamed the monetary policies of the four Carter years, but Democrats called the cause of the recession "Reaganomics," a shorthand description of the administration's cut in the domestic budget.

Just as Reagan's personal popularity began to slide, it soared again in the wake of a near tragedy—the shooting of the president at the Washington Hilton Hotel. The wit of the severely wounded president captured American hearts. In George Washington University Hospital, where he was rushed for emergency surgery, he said "You know what Churchill said 'There is nothing more exhilarating than to be shot at without result.' "[8]

By the summer of 1982, the recuperating seventy-one-year-old president was beginning to regain some of his former energy. At the same time, the flagging economy started to feel the effect of the tax cut. The administration, which had directed most of its attention toward domestic concerns, now focused its sights internationally.

In June the president was to speak at the Palace of Westminster in London. British Prime Minister Margaret Thatcher, who had visited Washington in

February, had conveyed the invitation. Such a singular honor, which had been extended to no previous president, was arranged by Thatcher, who admired Reagan's championship of conservative principles.

Tony Dolan, one of Reagan's speechwriters, saw in the upcoming London address the history-making parallel of Churchill's "Iron Curtain" speech in America in 1946: a leader of the free world speaking in a fellow Anglo-American democracy at the invitation of the head of government.

Yet if Churchill called for the containment of communism, Dolan thought Reagan should stress a crusade for freedom. After thirty-six years, it was time to turn from the military defensive to the psychological offensive. A former Connecticut reporter, Dolan was a "movement conservative" out of the Pat Buchanan school of hardball politics.[9]

In writing his draft for Reagan's London address, Dolan took as his text Churchill's 1946 speech in Missouri. Dolan's efforts in behalf of Reagan called to mind Alexander Hamilton, who had referred to the essays of Prussian leader Frederick the Great before drafting Washington's Farewell Address. Both aides idolized their chief for inspirational qualities other than intellectual brilliance. Each writer had read thoroughly an earlier statesman for speech guidance.

In May, Dolan submitted his draft to his superior, Dave Gergen, the head of the communications "shop." Gergen, a moderate who had written speeches for both Nixon and Ford, thought the hard-edged Dolan was the wrong writer for a European audience who imagined Reagan as a kind of John Wayne—an actor–cowboy known to be a little too fast on the draw. Gergen pigeonholed Dolan's draft and asked other writers to offer contributions, but Dolan, anticipating such a reaction, had backchanneled his draft to Reagan. Reagan read it and saw in it something he had been wanting to say in his role as leader of the free world—that the idea of freedom would triumph. Reagan, who could be passively deferential to his aides' advice, occasionally could rear up like a mule when the counsel challenged a deeply-felt conviction. He insisted on going with Dolan's draft.

Curiously, although Reagan viewed his speeches as a prime requisite of leadership, he did not enjoy a close relationship with his major speechwriters. Kennedy with Sorensen and Goodwin, and Nixon with Price, Buchanan, and Safire enjoyed an intimacy the remote Reagan never did.

In his upstairs study at the White House, Reagan read over the drafts of a speech carefully. Unlike Nixon or Kennedy, he practiced them aloud. If Nixon edited every nuance for substance, Reagan rewrote for reasons of style. He broke up long sentences and rewrote lines to fit his conversational delivery. Reagan reshaped some of Dolan's ornate lines and added a joke from his own repertory of anecdotes. On the Air Force One flight to Europe, Reagan rehearsed his delivery.

In London on June 8, 1982, President Reagan sat edgily in the Robing Room—which is reserved for the queen when she addresses Parliament.

Reagan had an uncharacteristic case of the jitters. Usually a study in informality, Reagan, and his wife even more so, were awed by the ceremonial majesty of the British crown.[10] Even though speaking became Reagan's vocation, the aura of the Palace of Westminster together with an audience of skeptical British parliamentarians was the supreme challenge in his performing career.

Originally, Reagan was to speak in Westminster Hall, but the objections of the Labour Party had forced a switch to the Great Gallery, which was just off the House of Lords. At eleven o'clock, Reagan was ushered from the Robing Room into the Gallery. There, attended by Beefeater Guards behind him and flanked by the lord chancellor on his right and the speaker of the house on his left, Reagan began his address.

After some preliminary observations on his just concluded visits to Italy and France, Reagan opened:

> Speaking for all Americans I want to say how very much at home we feel in your house. Every American would, because this is, as we have been so eloquently told, one of democracy's shrines.

Then Reagan quoted what Prime Minister Thatcher told him when he had found himself staring at a portrait of King George III at an embassy dinner a year-and-a-half before. "Most Englishmen," said Mrs. Thatcher, "would agree with Thomas Jefferson that 'a little rebellion now and then is a very good thing.' "

The British embassy anecdote was one that Reagan himself added to the text. The light note, that is a patented Reagan touch, brought laughter from the audience.

Reagan then came right to the theme of the address by citing the British statesman William Gladstone on the developing Solidarity movement in Poland:

> Gladstone, defending the Reform Bill in 1866, declared "You cannot fight against the future. Time is on our side."

"Optimism is in order," added Reagan, "because day-by-day democracy is proving itself to be a not-at-all fragile flower."

The next line was a deliberate attempt by speechwriter Dolan to echo the Iron Curtain words of Churchill:

> From Stettin on the Baltic to Varna in the Black Sea, the regimes planted by totalitarianism have had more than thirty years to establish their legitimacy. But none—not one regime—has yet been able to reach free elections.

Reagan summarized with an alliterative aphorism. "Regimes planted by bayonets do not take root." The maxim was buttressed by an underground Polish joke.

It is that the Soviet Union would remain a one-party nation even if an opposition party were permitted because everyone would join the opposition
party.

Just as the chuckles of the audience were quieting, Reagan recharged the
laughter by unleashing a Churchill bon mot about John Foster Dulles. It
alluded to the often heavy-hand of American diplomacy.

Winston Churchill said in exasperation about one of our most distinguished
diplomats: "He is the only case I know of a bull who carries his china shop
with him."

Reagan's audience roared with delight. The self-deprecation that is a
trademark of British as well as Reagan humor won the hearts of even those
on the Labour side who regarded Reagan's right-wing philosophy even
more unpalatable than Thatcher's. They found themselves beginning to like
the genial Reagan, even if they might not like his views.
The light tenor turned somber as Reagan noted,

It was not the democracies that invaded Afghanistan or suppressed Polish
Solidarity or used chemical and toxic warfare in Afghanistan and Southeast
Asia.

Reagan's reaction to Soviet aggression bore the stately cadence of a
Churchill:

If history teaches anything it teaches self-delusion in the face of unpleasant
facts is folly.

Reagan then asked rhetorically:

What then is our course? Must civilization perish in a hail of fiery atoms?
Must freedom wither in a quiet deadening accommodation with totalitarian
evil?

For his answer Reagan quoted directly from Churchill's Iron Curtain
speech:

"I do not believe the Soviet Union desires war. What they desire is the fruits
of war and the indefinite expansion of their power and doctrines. But what
we have to consider today while time remains is the permanent prevention
of war and the establishment of conditions of freedom and democracy as
rapidly as possible in all countries."

Churchill's statement, said Reagan, "is our mission today: to preserve freedom as well as peace. It may not be easy to see, but I believe we live at a turning point."

Reagan, a prophet of capitalism, now turned to the prophet of communism to make his point:

> In an ironic sense Karl Marx was right. We are witnessing today a great revolutionary crisis, a crisis where the demands of the economic order are conflicting with those of the political order. But the crisis is happening not in the free non-Marxist West but in the home of Marxism-Leninism, the Soviet Union. It is the Soviet Union that runs against the tide of history. . . .

As proof Reagan cited the shattered economy of the "over-centralized" Soviet Union that is "on the brink of famine."

Then Reagan invited his audience to compare those nations where free market democracies operate next to socialist dictatorships "the free and closed societies—West Germany and East Germany, Austria and Czechoslovakia, Malaysia and Vietnam."

The yearning for freedom, Reagan said, is evidenced by the millions of San Salvadoreans in Central America who risked guerilla gunfire to vote. He cited a grandmother who said, "You can kill me, you can kill my family, but you can't kill us all."

Then Reagan directed the audience's attention much farther south in that hemisphere:

> On distant islands in the South Atlantic young men are fighting for Britain. And yes, voices have been raised protesting their sacrifice for lumps of rocks and earth so far away. But those young men aren't fighting for real estate. They fight for a cause—for the belief that armed aggression must not be allowed to succeed and the people must participate in the decision of government . . .

Tumultuous applause for the British soldiers in the Falklands interrupted before he could continue:

> . . . the decisions of government under the rule of law.

The world, said Reagan, is now turning from dictatorship to democracy. He then noted that "sixteen of the twenty-four countries in the Caribbean and Central America have free elected governments" and that "eight of the new nations in the United Nations are democracies."

Reagan then issued his challenge to the Soviets:

> We ask only that these [Soviet] systems begin by living up to their own constitutions, abiding by their own laws. . . .

   Next Reagan checked off four institutions that constitute "the infra-
structure of democracy." These, he said, are: "free press," "unions," "political parties," and "universities." The repression of those institutions,
Reagan continued, challenges the sincerity of Chairman Brezhnev's contention that he welcomes the competition of ideas and systems.
   Reagan's belief in the inevitability of freedom was almost palpable to his
audience of the British parliament. His ruddy face beamed as he shook his
head and in his husky tone voiced his prediction:

> Now I don't wish to sound overly optimistic, yet the Soviet Union is not
> immune from the reality of what is going on in the world. It has happened
> in the past—a small ruling elite either mistakenly attempts to ease domestic
> unrest through greater repression and foreign adventure or it chooses a wiser
> course. It begins to allow its people a voice in their own destiny.

Reagan's faith in the eventual triumph of freedom rang with the conviction
of a "true believer":

> Even if the latter process is not realized soon, I believe the renewed strength
> of the democratic movement, implemented by a global campaign for freedom
> will strengthen the prospects. . . .

Reagan then called for a plan that was a prophecy:

> What I am describing now is a plan and hope for the long term—the march
> of freedom and democracy which will leave Marxism–Leninism on the ash
> heap of history. . . .

   With these words, Reagan hurled the Communist's own dialectic predictions back in the Kremlin's face.
   This "crusade for freedom," said Reagan, will not be fought "by bombs
and rockets but by a test of wills and ideas, a trial of spiritual resolve, the
values we hold, the beliefs we cherish." The voice was Reagan's but the
words sounded Churchillian.
   "The British people know," continued Reagan, that "the forces of good
ultimately rally and triumph over evil."

> Here among you is the cradle of self-government, the mother of parliaments,
> here is the enduring greatness of the British contribution to mankind, the
> great civilized ideas: individual liberty, representative government and the
> rule of law under God.

   Reagan again interjected into Dolan's redraft of Churchillian rhetoric a
World War II anecdote:

I've often wondered about the shyness of some of us in the West about standing for these ideals. . . . This reluctance . . . reminds me of the elderly lady whose home was bombed in the blitz. As the rescuers moved about, they found a bottle of brandy she stored behind the staircase which was all that was left standing. And since she was barely conscious, one of the workers pulled the cork to give her a taste of it. She came around immediately and said "here now, put that back. That's for emergencies."

There has not been a president or prime minister who was a better raconteur than Ronald Reagan. By the alchemy of his timing and delivery he could turn the most prosaic of anecdotes into uproarious laughter, and this was no exception. Reagan's story had a moral:

Well, the emergency is upon us. Let us be shy no longer. Let us offer hope. Let us tell the world that a new age is not only possible but probable.

Reagan closed by elaborating on two Churchill quotations. The first came from Churchill's address to the Joint Session of Congress in December 1941:

During the dark days of World War II, when this island was incandescent with courage, Winston Churchill exclaimed about Britain's adversaries "What kind of people do they think we are?"

After repeating Churchill's rhetorical question Reagan replied:

And let us answer: Free people worthy of freedom and determined not only to remain so but to help others gain their freedom as well.

He then added Churchill's remarks when he had left the prime ministership and assumed the role of leader of the opposition:

"When we look back on the perils through which we passed and at the mighty foes that we have laid low and all the dark and deadly designs that we have frustrated, why should we fear for our future? We have come safely through the worst."

Reagan closed with this peroration:

Let us now begin a major effort to secure the best—a crusade for freedom that will engage the faith and fortitude of the next generation.

To a British audience that had too glibly accepted a caricature of the Hollywood president, Reagan had proved himself as leader of the free world. With the language of Churchill, he had turned the Marxist predictions upside down. He had delivered a prescription as well as a prophecy that would have done credit to the statesman he was emulating.

In November 1988, right after the election of George Bush, a conference in Texas of foreign policy experts, drawn from the ranks of diplomacy and universities, foresaw no suggestion of the emerging cataclysm in Eastern Europe months later that was symbolized by the tearing down of the Berlin Wall. Except for Poland, no change in the one-party Communist rule was predicted in the decades ahead. No one had come close to the prophecy Ronald Reagan had delivered six years earlier.

Reagan's speeches carried not the historical judgment of Churchill or the poetry of Lincoln, but he did give shape and texture to the abstraction of capitalist principles. He made "free market" an integral part of "freedom." As leader of the free world, Reagan embodied the hope that free societies have to offer to repressed peoples in totalitarian economies.

Ronald Reagan left office almost exactly two-hundred years after George Washington was sworn in. The first president, in his *Farewell Address*, saw in the fledgling republic a political ideal that contrasted the autocratic regimes of Europe. To safeguard our free government, the first president counseled us to turn inward, away from the intrigues of Europe.

Two centuries later, when the free society of America had ripened into the greatest nation in the world, the fortieth president also made foreign policy the theme of his address. Reagan, however, asked his listeners to take up the gospel of democracy and carry it to that part of Europe still in thrall to tyranny. Ronald Reagan has been the free world's most fervent advocate of freedom since Churchill, and he has lived to see his prophecies come true.

NOTES

1. Some exceptions include Winston Churchill, Franklin Roosevelt, Douglas MacArthur, and Martin Luther King, all of whom read their speeches. Jesse Jackson, one of the best current speakers, is not so effective when he reads from a text. On the other hand, Edward Kennedy's skill in this art surpasses that of his brother, John Kennedy.

2. In 1969 Reagan delivered an eloquent eulogy for Robert Taylor. The matinee idol of the 1940s gained the hatred of the left when he identified several in the Hollywood community in 1947 as toeing to the Stalinist line. Ironically, in 1989 while the tyrannical Communist regimes in Eastern Europe that Taylor attacked were crumbling, an entertainment building in Hollywood named in honor of Taylor was given another name as punishment for his so-called "witch-hunting" decades before.

3. Goldwater wanted to use the money raised for the Reagan address to finance a national spot showing the Republican candidate with General Eisenhower at Gettysburg. Reagan refused, saying that the contributions were raised specifically for his speech to pay for the televising of the address.

4. In March 1975, Reagan gave a speech to the World Affairs Council of Philadelphia, a major forum for presidential contenders. The address centered on Africa and Asia and contained the phrase "Third World" on several pages of the text. To the discomfiture of this writer, who had contributed to the speech, Reagan read the phrase as "Third World War." The press played it up as a Freudian slip.

5. Reagan came up with the phrase at the end of a mock debate session in which the statistic-laden David Stockman had played President Carter.

6. Similarly, in 1976 Ford was attacked for saying "New York City drop dead." The quotation was from a *New York Daily News* headlines in 1975 on a story about President Ford's rejection of a plea to bail out the financially troubled city. The words were never spoken by Ford.

7. One exception may be "the evil empire," which Reagan used in a Dolan-drafted speech to describe the government of the Soviet Union in 1983. At the time, *Time* magazine attacked the phrase, but in their year cover story in January 1990, the magazine described the structure of the soviet government as "inherently evil." In 1991 Boris Yeltsin acknowledged the correctness of the phrase.

8. Actually, the president had first used this quotation in a White House State Dinner toast to visiting Prime Minister Margaret Thatcher. For that occasion, I had sent in selected quotations from his book, *Churchill, Speaker of the Century*.

9. Tony Dolan was a brother of Terry, the right-wing organizer whose savage campaign ad had helped unseat Democrat senators McGovern, Culver, and Church in 1980. Dolan later died of AIDS.

10. In her office in the East Wing of the White House, Nancy Reagan had only two pictures prominently displayed. One was her husband and the other a signed photograph of Prince Charles.

Bibliography

CHAPTER 1

Flexner, James Thomas. *George Washington in the American Revolution*. Boston: Little, Brown, 1967.
———. *George Washington, Anguish and Farewell*. Boston: Little, Brown, 1969.
———. *George Washington, Forge of Experience*. Boston: Little, Brown, 1969.
———. *George Washington, the New Nation*. Boston: Little, Brown, 1964.
Hoskins, Joseph A., ed. *President Washington's Diaries 1791–1799*. Summerfield, N.C.: n.p., 1921.
McDonald, Forrest. *George Washington, President*. Lawrence: University Press of Kansas, 1974.
Palart, V. H., ed. *Washington's Farewell Address*, with transliterations in facsimile of all the drafts of Washington, Madison and Hamilton. New York Public Library.
Schwartz, Barry. *George Washington: The Making of an American Symbol*. New York: The Free Press, 1987.

CHAPTER 2

Cunningham, Noble E., Jr. *In Pursuit of Reason: Life of Thomas Jefferson*. Baton Rouge: Louisiana State University Press, 1987.
Koch, Adrienne, ed. *Life and Selected Writings—Jefferson*. New York: Modern Library, 1984.
Malone, Dumas. *Sage of Monticello*. Boston: Little, Brown, 1981.
———, ed. *Jefferson, Autobiography*. New York: Capricorn, 1959.
Padover, Saul, ed. *The Complete Jefferson*. New York: Duell, Sloan, and Piercer, 1943.
Smith, Page. *John Adams*, vol. 2. New York: Doubleday, 1962.
Wills, Garry. *Inventing America*. New York: Doubleday, 1978.

CHAPTER 3

Adams, John Quincy. *Memoirs of John Quincy Adams*. Philadelphia: J. B. Lippincott, 1852.
Ammon, Harry. *James Monroe*. New York: McGraw Hill, 1971.
Bemis, Samuel Flagg. *John Quincy Adams and the Union*. New York: Alfred A. Knopf, 1956.
Brown, S. G., ed. *James Monroe Autobiography*. Syracuse, N.Y.: Syracuse University Press, 1959.
Cresson, James. *James Monroe*. Durham: North Carolina Press, 1946.
Dangerfield, G. *Monroe Doctrine*. New York: Harcourt, Brace, 1952.
Ford, W. C., ed. *Papers of James Monroe*. Washington, D.C.: U.S. Library of Congress, Department of Manuscripts, 1904.
May, Ernest R. *Making of the Monroe Doctrine*. Cambridge, Mass.: Harvard University Press, 1975.
Merck, Frederick. *The Monroe Doctrine and American Expansionism 1843–1849*. New York: Knopf, 1966.
Morgan, George. *Life of James Monroe*. Small, Maynard & Co., 1921.
Smith, Page. *The Shaping of America*, vol. 3. New York: McGraw-Hill, 1980.
Wilson, Charles Morrow. *The Monroe Doctrine*. Princeton, N.J.: Auerbach, 1971.

CHAPTER 4

Bassett, J. S., ed. *Jackson Correspondence*. New York: Carnegie Institution, 1934.
Chambers, William Nesbit. *Old Billion Benton*. Boston: Little, Brown, 1956.
Davis, Burke. *Old Hickory*. New York: Dial Press, 1977.
Holbrook, Richard. *Andrew Jackson*. New York: MacMillan, 1964.
———. *Hero and the People*. New York: Brown, MacMillan, 1964.
James, Marquis. *Andrew Jackson*. New York: Dobbs-Merrill, 1937.
Lewis, Walker. *Without Fear or Favor*. Boston: Houghton Mifflin, 1965.
Remini, Robert V. *Life of Andrew Jackson*. New York: Harper & Row, 1988.
Schlesinger, Arthur. *Age of Jackson*. Boston: Little, Brown, 1946.
Smith, Page. *Nation Comes of Age*. New York: McGraw-Hill, 1981.

CHAPTER 5

Baily, Thomas Andrew. *The Pugnacious Presidents: White House Warriors on Parade*. New York: Free Press; London: Collier MacMillan Publishers, 1980.
McCoy, C. A. *Polk and the Presidency*. Austin: University of Texas, 1960.
McCurmec, Eugene Irvine. *Polk*. Russell & Russell, 1922.
Morrell, Martha McBride. *Young Hickory*. New York: E. P. Dutton, 1949.
Polk, James K. *Documents and Bibliography Aids*. 1795–1849: Chronology, John J. Farrell, ed. Dobbs Ferry, N.Y.: Oceana Publications, 1970.
Sellcus, C. S. *James Polk Continentalist*. Princeton: Princeton Press, 1960.

CHAPTER 6

Beveridge, Albert. *Abraham Lincoln*. Cambridge, Mass.: Riverside Press, 1928.
Carr, Clark Ezra. *Lincoln at Gettysburg*. Chicago: Q. C. McClurg, 1906.

Charnwood, Lord Godfrey Rathbone Benson. *Abraham Lincoln*. New York: Henry Holt and Co., 1917.
Current, Richard N. *Lincoln 1809–1865 Addresses, Essays, Lectures*. Urbana: University of Illinois Press, 1970.
Fehrenbacher, Don E. *Lincoln in Text and Context*. Stanford: Stanford University Press, 1987.
Kunhardt, Philip. *A New Birth of Freedom*. Boston: Little, Brown, 1983.
Neely, Mark E. *Abraham Lincoln Encyclopaedia*. New York: McGraw-Hill, 1902.
Sandburg, Carl. *Abraham Lincoln*. New York: Harcourt, Brace, Jovanovich, 1938.

CHAPTER 7

Cleveland, Grover. *Grover Cleveland Manuscripts*. Washington, D.C.: U.S. Government Printing Office, 1965.
Hollingworth, J. Rogers. *Whirligig of Politics*, vol. 12. Chicago: University of Chicago Press, 1963.
Kintz, Henry J. *Inauguration of Grover Cleveland, The President-Elect*. Philadelphia: W. F. Fell and Co., 1885.
Merrill, Samuel H. *Grover Cleveland*. Boston: Little, Brown, 1957.
Nevins, Allan. *Grover Cleveland*. New York: Dodd, Mead, 1932.
Parker, George Frederick, ed. *Recollections of Grover Cleveland*. New York: The Century Co., 1909.
Tugwell, R. G. *Grover Cleveland*. New York: Macmillan, 1964.

CHAPTER 8

Abbot, Lawrence, ed. *Letters of Archie Butt*. Garden City, N.Y.: Doubleday, Page & Co., 1927.
Beale, H. K. *Theodore Roosevelt, Rise of America to World Power*. Baltimore: Johns Hopkins University Press, 1956.
Blum, J. M., ed. *The Letters of Theodore Roosevelt*, 6 volumes. Cambridge: Harvard University Press, 1952.
———. *The Republican Roosevelt*. Cambridge, Mass.: Harvard University Press, 1954.
Hagedorn, Hermann. *The Roosevelt Family of Sagamore Hill*. New York: Macmillan, 1954.
———, ed. *The Free Citizen, selections from his writings*. New York: Macmillan, 1986.
McCullough, David. *Morning on Horseback*. New York: Simon & Schuster, 1981.
Morris, Edmund. *Rise of Theodore Roosevelt*. New York: Coward, McCann, 1974.
Pringle, H. F. *Theodore Roosevelt*. New York: Harcourt Brace, 1956.
Smith, Page. *America Enters the War*. New York: McGraw-Hill, 1985.

CHAPTER 9

Baker, Ray Stannard. *Woodrow Wilson, Life and Letters*, 4 volumes. New York: Doubleday, 1937.
Blum, J. *Woodrow Wilson and the Politics of Morality*. Boston: Little, Brown, 1956.

Cooper, John Milton, Jr. *The Warrior and the Priest*. Cambridge, Mass.: Belknap Press, 1983.

Dodd, William Edward. *Woodrow Wilson and His Work*. New York: P. Smith, 1932.

Ferrell, Robert H. *Woodrow Wilson and World War I*. New York: Harper & Row, 1985.

Gardner, Lloyd C. *Woodrow Wilson*. New York: Oxford University Press, 1984.

Hecksher, August, ed. *The Politics of Woodrow Wilson, Selections from his Speeches and Writings*. New York: Harper, 1956.

Link, Arthur S. *Woodrow Wilson*, 5 volumes. Princeton: Princeton University Press, 1965.

Peare, Catherine Owen. *The Woodrow Wilson Story*. New York: Crowell, 1963.

CHAPTER 10

Abels, Jules. *In the Time of Silent Cal*. New York: Putnam, 1969.

Coolidge, Calvin. *The Autobiography of Calvin Coolidge*. 1929. Reprint. Rutland, Vt.: Academy Books, 1984.

Latham, Edward Connery. *Meet Calvin Coolidge: The Man Behind the Myth*. Brattleboro, Vt.: Stephen Greene Press, 1960.

Silver, Thomas B. *Coolidge and the Historians*. Chapel Hill: University of North Carolina Press, 1982.

Slemp, C. Bascom, ed. *Calvin Coolidge: The Mind of the President*. New York: Doubleday, 1926.

CHAPTER 11

Burns, James M. *Roosevelt, the Lion and the Fox*. New York: Harcourt Brace, 1956.

Davis, Kenneth. *FDR, New Deal Years*. New York: Random House, 1986.

Hately, Alda. *Franklin Roosevelt*. New York: Dobbs, 1947.

Morgan, Ted. *FDR*. New York: Simon & Schuster, 1985.

Oulahan, Richard. *The Man Who—Story of Democratic National Convention*. New York: Dial, 1971.

Rollins, Alfred Brooks. *Roosevelt and Howe*. New York: Knopf, 1962.

Roosevelt, Elliott, ed. *FDR, Private Letters*. New York: Duell, Sloane & Pierce, 1950.

Rosenman, Samuel Irving. *Working with Roosevelt*. New York: Harper, 1952.

Schlesinger, Arthur. *Age of Roosevelt*, 3 volumes. New York: Houghton Mifflin, 1957–66.

Sherwood, Robert. *Roosevelt & Hopkins*. New York: Harper, 1936.

Ward, Geoffrey C. *Before the Trumpet, Young Franklin Roosevelt*. New York: Harper & Row, 1985.

CHAPTER 12

Acheson, Dean. *Present at the Creation*. New York: W. W. Norton, 1969.

Cochran, Bert. *Harry Truman and the Crisis Presidency*. New York: Funk & Wagnalls, 1973.

Gosnell, H. F. *Truman.* Westport, Conn.: Greenwood Press, 1980.

Hechler, Ken. *Working with Truman.* New York: Putnam, 1982.

Miller, Merle. *Plain Speaking* (Oral biography). New York: Putnam, 1974.

Ross, Irwin. *The Loneliest Campaign.* New York: New American Library, 1968.

Truman, Harry S. *The Memoirs of Harry S Truman,* 2 volumes. New York: Doubleday, 1955, 1956.

———. *The Autobiography of Harry S Truman.* Robert Ferrell, ed. Boulder: University of Colorado Press, 1960.

———. *Letters.* Monte M. Poen, ed. Boston: Little, Brown, 1982.

CHAPTER 13

Ambrose, Stephen E. *Eisenhower, Soldier General.* New York: Simon & Schuster, 1983.

———. *Eisenhower, President.* New York: Simon & Schuster, 1984.

Eisenhower, David. *Eisenhower at War.* New York: Random House, 1986.

Eisenhower, Dwight. *Crusade in Europe.* New York: Doubleday, 1948.

Ewald, W. C., Jr. *Eisenhower, the President.* Englewood Cliffs, N.J.: Prentice Hall, 1981.

Ferrell, Robert H., ed. *Eisenhower Diaries.* New York: Norton, 1981.

———. *Eisenhower Diaries.* New York: Norton, 1981.

Greenstein, Fred I. *The Hidden Hand Presidency.* New York: Basil Books, 1982.

Parmet, Herbert. *Eisenhower.* New York: Macmillan, 1972.

CHAPTER 14

Burns, James McGregor. *Kennedy.* New York: Harcourt Brace, 1960.

Marmuto, Herbert S. *Jack.* New York: Dial, 1980.

Parmet, Herbert. *JFK, the Presidency.* New York: Dial, 1983.

Salinger, Pierre. *With Kennedy.* New York: Doubleday, 1966.

Schlesinger, Arthur. *A Thousand Days.* New York: Houghton Mifflin, 1965.

Sorensen, Theodore C. *Kennedy.* New York: Harper & Row, 1965.

Wills, Garry. *The Kennedy Imprisonment.* Boston: Little, Brown, 1981.

Wofford, H. *Kennedy & Kings.* New York: Farrar, Straus, Giroux, 1980.

CHAPTER 15

Ambrose, Stephen E. *Nixon, Education of a Politician.* New York: Simon & Schuster, 1987.

Kissinger, Henry. *White House Years.* Boston: Little, Brown, 1974.

Mazo, Earl. *Richard Nixon.* New York: Harper, 1954.

Nixon, Richard. *R.N.* New York: Simon & Schuster, 1990.

Price, Raymond. *With Nixon.* New York: Viking Press, 1977.

Safire, William. *Before the Fall.* Garden City, N.Y.: Doubleday, 1975.

de Toledano, Ralph. *One Man Alone: Richard Nixon.* New York: Funk & Wagnalls, 1969.

CHAPTER 16

Boyarsky, Bill. *The Rise of Ronald Reagan*. New York: Random House, 1968.

Cannon, Lou. *Reagan*. New York: G. P. Putnam's, 1982.

Kucharsky, David. *The Man from Plains*. New York: Harper & Row, 1976.

Reagan, Ronald W. *Speaking My Mind: Selected Speeches*. New York: Simon & Schuster, 1989.

Wills, Garry. *Reagan's America*. New York: Doubleday, 1987.

Index

About the Author

JAMES C. HUMES, an adjunct professor at the University of Pennsylvania, is a former presidential speechwriter for Eisenhower, Nixon, Ford, Reagan, and Bush. In addition, he is a former Woodrow Wilson Fellow at the Center for International Scholars at the Smithsonian, and he has lectured across the country and abroad on the theme of presidential history. Humes is also the author of seven books on speech making and preparation, a biography of Winston Churchill, and was the editorial advisor for former President Ford's memoirs *Time to Heal*.